Accumulating Insecurity

Accumulating Insecurity

VIOLENCE AND DISPOSSESSION
IN THE MAKING OF EVERYDAY LIFE

Edited by **SHELLEY FELDMAN**
CHARLES GEISLER and
GAYATRI A. MENON

THE UNIVERSITY OF GEORGIA PRESS
Athens & London

© 2011 by the University of Georgia Press
Athens, Georgia 30602
www.ugapress.org
All rights reserved
Based on design by Walton Harris
Set in 10/13 Minion Pro by Graphic Composition, Inc.

Printed digitally in the United States of America

Library of Congress Cataloging-in-Publication Data

Accumulating insecurity : violence and dispossession in the making of
everyday life / edited by Shelley Feldman, Charles Geisler, and
Gayatri A. Menon.
      p.   cm. — (Geographies of justice and social transformation ; 9)
Includes bibliographical references and index.
ISBN-13: 978-0-8203-3872-9 (hardcover : alk. paper)
ISBN-10: 0-8203-3872-9 (hardcover : alk. paper)
ISBN-13: 978-0-8203-3873-6 (pbk: alk. paper)
ISBN-10: 0-8203-3873-7 (pbk : alk. paper)
1. Social change—Psychological aspects.
2. Violence—Social aspects.
3. Violence—Psychological aspects.
4. Internal security—Psychological aspects.
5. National security—Psychological aspects.
I. Feldman, Shelley. II. Geisler, Charles C. III. Menon, Gayatri A.
HM831.A28 2011
303.45'09051—dc22   2010039655

British Library Cataloging-in-Publication Data available

.

For Mollie Cohen Feldman (1922–2008) whose intellectual curiosity, commitment to progressive goals, and encouragement to be all you can be, regardless of class, gender, race, or sexual preference serves as a constant guide to sustaining the integrity of research and teaching.

CONTENTS

PREFACE

This collection of essays is the culmination of a collective process of inquiry that took place over a series of workshops and a conference. As with many exciting intellectual projects, our efforts to bring together cutting-edge scholars around the theme of accumulating insecurity and securing accumulation were realized through the generous contributions of the participants and the financial support of numerous others. We are deeply appreciative of the support extended to us by a host of Cornell institutes and special programs that recognized the unusual interdisciplinary character of the project and embraced the risk of supporting it. Our sponsors included Cornell's Africana Studies and Research Center; College of Arts and Sciences; Dorothea S. Clarke Program in Feminist Jurisprudence, Cornell Law School; Institute for European Studies; Mario Einaudi Center for International Studies; Office of the Provost; Peace Studies Program; Polson Institute for Global Development; Rose Goldsen Lecture Series; Society for the Humanities; University Lectures Committee; and the Departments of Anthropology, Comparative Literature, Development Sociology, History, and History of Art. They each deserve a special thank you. We are particularly grateful to Brett deBary and Tim Murray for appreciating the connections we sought to make between the humanities and social sciences.

The workshops and conference benefited from the participation of Rebecca McLennan and Bulent Diken, and from public lectures by Marita Sturken, Allen Feldman, and Michael Geyer. To each we extend our appreciation for joining and enriching our conversation. Students from Binghamton and Cornell Universities also raised a host of interesting questions during the conference that enhanced discussion and contributed to the vibrancy of these discussions.

During our meetings we benefited as well from the artistic contributions of An-My Lê's *Small Wars: Explosion* (1999–2002, Gelatin silver print courtesy of Murray Guy Gallery, New York). She allowed us to use her print on a poster announcing our first workshop. We thank Cathy Klimaszewski, Associate Director, Johnson Museum of Art, Cornell University, for facilitating this use and for opening the museum to us for a private tour of An-My Lê's exhibit. We also thank Renate Ferro who shared her provocative video installation, *Facing Panic*, during our second workshop.

Unusual about this project was the additional contribution garnered from ongoing campus discussions among a group of scholars who not only met regularly during the year, but also contributed to critical exchanges at the workshops and conference. We extend our special thanks to Anindita Banerjee, Cynthia Bowman, Eric Cheyfitz, Matt Evangelista, Maria Fernandez, Renate Ferro, Tyrell Haberkorn, Jane Juffer, Sherry Martin, Barry Maxwell, Tim Murray, Judith Reppy, and especially Dag Woubshet who coauthored with Shelley Feldman the proposal that supported this latter endeavor.

No undertaking of this magnitude can be accomplished without the assistance of dedicated staff. These are the people essential to carrying out the feat at hand—that tide of details and difficult issues accompanying any complex, multistage, intellectual project. We owe gratitude and appreciation to Hope Mandeville for her abiding attention to detail, her care, and her tireless concern for the particular needs of workshop/conference/reading group participants during the course of our colloquia. Amy Sindone and the staff of the Feminist, Gender, and Sexuality Studies Program were central to having this year of activities run smoothly. We are also delighted to be working with Derek Kristoff and professional staff at the University of Georgia Press who have moved the volume forward with great enthusiasm.

Accumulating Insecurity

A New Politics of Containment

SHELLEY FELDMAN, GAYATRI A. MENON,
and CHARLES GEISLER

Over half a century ago, Hannah Arendt, reflecting on the human condition in the wake of the horrors of the Holocaust, insisted that explanations for it were not to be found by fixating on the extraordinariness of political evil. Instead, she urged us to consider the banality of evil, the everyday practices and normal people who perpetrate the mass destruction of humanity.[1] For Arendt, political evil was located in alienation, the historical dynamic of capitalist modernity, and the substance of its moral economy. This emphasis directs our attention to the myriad ways in which accumulation practices order life, as well as to the insidious conditions of their reproducibility. Yet today, analyses of what is considered "political evil," the large-scale annihilation of human beings, seems remarkably narrow when the body counts of martial combat appear to be the only bodies that actually count in what is recognized as political evil (Hayden 2007).[2] This narrow conceptualization of acts that deprive humans of life seems remarkable precisely because it is taking place at a moment when we witness the world careening toward a crisis of social reproduction; a crisis, we argue, that takes more lives than do acts of direct violence, and is no less an act of violent politics.

There is growing consensus that the world today is in dire social and economic crisis that extends to housing, personal financial debt, and the absence of adequate health care and education, a crisis that finds increasing numbers of people vulnerable to dearth and death as the ability to secure daily life is eroded. Despite this acknowledgment, human security, and indeed homeland security, is increasingly framed by a concern with war and the protection of corporate finance. Moreover, even as more people face morbidity and mortality through deprivation than from battlefield encounters, public concern for security continues to rivet solely on the body counts and body bags from military conflicts, and state leaders seem oblivious to the ongoing processes of dispossession and alienation that renders vast populations materially and politically insecure.

Provoked by this acute state of dispossession and alienation, in a colloquium that brought together a range of disciplinary perspectives for a year-long conversation, we examined the relationship between security and insecurity in the contemporary moment. We challenged thinking that conflates security with stockpiled arms, military engagements, and Homeland Security budgets; in its place, we brought into focus the daily lives and human bodies that these martial practices purport to secure.[3] The outcome of our efforts was to re-embed constructions of security and experiences of insecurity within the realm of social reproduction. By social reproduction we reference the historically contingent processes by which we reproduce the conditions and relations of economic and social security. These include not only the technical means of reproducing the physical integrity of our bodies, but also the methods by which we reproduce ourselves as political subjects—that is, the relations of rule that we legitimate. Our aim is to draw attention to the violent conditions of social reproduction in the current moment, a moment marked by dispossession, revanchism, and the penalization and privatization of poverty (Araghi 1995; Smith 2002; Harvey 2003; Mitchell 2003; Passavant 2005; Gilmore 2007; Hayden 2007; Wacquant 2008a).

The skewed calculus of violence that now prevails prompted us to ask the following set of questions: What is the relationship between different orders of violence—direct conflict and indirect structural violence? How are certain forms of human degradation normalized, made "banal," and at what price? How does human welfare come to be equated with the diminution of rights rather than the strengthening and extension of rights? What might we discover about the character of political exclusion and alienation in the contemporary social order if we were to connect an internment camp for farmers deemed antinational by the Thai state, the retraining of prison populations as soldiers in the U.S. Army, a migrant detention facility in Iowa, the surveillance of taxi drivers in New York City, and an export-processing zone in Tijuana? What might these diverse expressions of political exclusion and alienation reveal to us about the contemporary human condition, about the terms through which we recognize another's status as that of a human being, and about the organization and administration of everyday violence?

By rejecting the equation of security with the stockpiling of armaments and embracing instead a notion of social reproduction as the crux of human security, our project breaks new ground for inquiring into the everyday practices that make life expendable. Such a framing illuminates the banal ways in which the administration of violence—and a calculus of risk that we typically associate with the battlefield—configures civilian space. This enables us to apprehend the multiple ways in which state-society relations, the rights of citizenship, and the meanings of civil/civilian society are being reconfigured to produce new terms for securing human subjectivity.

SUBJECTS OF DISPOSSESSION

The precarity of current material and political conditions also signals new relations of rule that confront growing numbers of people worldwide. In the post–World War II era, the era of mass production, normative political subjectivity derived from people's relationship to production, where nations assessed their power and progress on the basis of their worker-citizens' abilities and prowess in the manufacture of industrial and agricultural products. This national organization of material and political relations, common to the West and the recently independent nations of the "developing" world, gave way, in the 1970s and 1980s, to the ascendance of the global organization of production.

Politically, this new configuration of economic relations and accumulation processes precipitated a shift in the terms of political recognition from producer to consumer. As the global competition for investment became the context within which national governments derived their legitimacy, there was the innovation of export processing zones, an increased casualization of labor, and a dismantling of hard-won labor protections. Thus, whereas the welfare of worker-citizens provided the moral economy of the postwar nation-state, the erosion of state accountability and an emphasis on individual entrepreneurship and personal responsibility to secure human well-being have become hallmarks of contemporary relations. Whereas welfare and development held out a promise of inclusion into the realm where subjects are to be recognized as citizens, today exclusion, marginalization, and a decline in support for welfare alter the subject of political recognition and reveal the expendability of an increasing number of the world's population. In this era of globalization, in other words, it is the citizen-consumer rather than the citizen-worker who is the normative political subject (cf. Passavant 2005; Neilson and Rossiter 2008).

The shift from worker to consumer as the basis of political recognition is suggested by the changing global labor market and is confirmed in International Labour Organization (ILO) findings. As the ILO (2009, 13) reports, examining data from 1991 onward (as the approximate starting point of a more integrated global economy), "The global labor force in recent years has expanded at an average rate of around 1.6 percent or 45 million . . . [to suggest] a severe potential shortage of new employment opportunities." Noting that 2009 represented the worst global performance on record in terms of employment creation, the ILO cautions that "some regions are actually expected to show a contraction in employment . . . reflecting the severe effects of the crisis in terms of job destruction" (ILO 2009, 13). This potential redundancy, represented by the sudden drop in the availability of job opportunities, signals other deteriorating circumstances for the "more than 1.2 billion workers around the world [who] were living with their families in poverty prior to the onset of the crisis, with more than 620 million living in extreme poverty of less than USD 1.25 per day" (ILO 2009, 5). As a consequence, many youth who would otherwise be expected to join the labor force are now likely to go directly into the ranks of the unemployed. What is damning about these findings is not the prevalence of precarious employment, for informal labor has always been a part of the history of capital, but rather that labor market insecurity and informality now constitute the future of work and workers; they are no longer a residue of capital but its principal character.

This increasingly generalized crisis of social reproduction is confirmed by two prominent U.S. economists, Daniel Sullivan of the Federal Reserve Bank of Chicago and Till von Wachter of Columbia University, who "were convincingly able to show that if you lose your job, you die earlier" (Jacobs 2009, 1). And, as Jacobs goes on to suggest, "[t]he risk of premature death isn't limited to those who have actually been let go [but rather] . . . that a nagging, persistent fear of losing one's job is also detrimental to one's health." This is based on the assumption that if long-term job security is largely a thing of the past, the public health consequences could be enormous. Exploring the relationship between employment and health indicates that even "among people who are currently employed, those who . . . persistently worried about losing their jobs have significantly worse self-rated overall health than those who haven't been consistently worried" (Burgard et al. in Jacobs 2009, 2). Strikingly, these health effects seem to be associated more with fear and a preoccupation with a sense of insecurity than with actual changes in employment.

For us, then, the tension provoked by the difficulty of securing everyday life confirms our recognition of the need to focus on social reproduction as a central site for explaining the current crisis of capitalism. Some may view the generalizability of these shared circumstances as positive (Cohen in Jacobs 2009, 3): "[T]here is some good news: The fact that job anxiety is so widespread could actually dampen its destructive impact." We find this sensibility limited, if not outrageous, and instead posit that the crisis of social reproduction can lead to forms of redundancy and superfluous populations that leave people without rights or recourse to be able to secure their survival and reproducibility, especially given the context of soaring public and private debt.

Our finding is echoed in other changes in the accumulation of insecurity. As Scheper-Hughes and Bourgois (2004, 20) ask in their discussion of prevailing incarceration trends in the United States, "What can it *possibly* mean when incarceration becomes the 'normative' socializing experience for ethnic minority youth in a society, i.e., over 33 percent of young African American men?" (italics in the original). We also need to question the terms by which social service workers undertake searches of the homes of needy families (who are presumed to bear the guilt of fraud) before welfare benefits are deemed legitimate (Swan and Shaw 2008; Nice, chapter 2, this volume). How do we justify the growing population of underemployed racialized men who provide labor for a growing security industry in North America, or export processing zones workers who lose rights even as they improve their status (Cowen and Siciliano, chapter 4, this volume; Cheah, chapter 13, this volume)? The recasting of state responsibility, the alienation of rights, and the criminalization of citizens point to current crises that alter relations between citizens and states, reduce social accountability, and place increasing responsibility and cost for social reproduction on the backs of individuals.

As the precariousness of social reproduction becomes the context within and through which political subjectivity is configured, there are consequences for how we understand state responsibility, citizenship, and rights. While the death of the nation-state may be much exaggerated, what is clear is that the constitution of this political entity is changing dramatically, as global economic processes penetrate and reconfigure not just national borders but also laws, regulations, crop cycles, public space, health-care systems, and industry—that is, the relations through which populations are made subject and the constitution of their reproduction. Today, as new forms of mobility transform everyday life, Michael Kearney reflects on what this means for social reproduction:

> Capitalism in general effects the alienation of labor from its owner, but immigration policy can be seen as a means to achieve a form of this alienation that increases greatly in the age of transnationalism, namely the spatial separation of the site of the purchase and expenditure of labor from the sites of its reproduction, such that the locus of production and [social] reproduction lie in two different national spaces. (in Mitchell, Marston, and Katz 2004, 17–18)

As Foucault, among others, also points out, social reproduction itself has become a matter of politics and governance (Cheah, chapter 13, this volume). The precipitous conditions in which many struggle to secure their reproduction, particularly when juxtaposed with the preoccupation of governments to secure capital, provide a clear indication that what constitutes the state, the nation, and the national interest has been transformed. Citizenship, while always an exclusive entitlement, has become even more exclusive, although not necessarily through an intensification of existing terms of political recognition, as debates on immigration reform reveal (de Genova, chapter 6, this volume). Here, too, we see a shift in the bases of political recognition from its postwar frame in the idiom of work and workers being replaced by consumption and the consumer as the staging ground of citizenship.

A POLITICS OF CONTAINMENT

The globalization of economic processes has precipitated a free fall in wages, as national and corporate prospects of economic growth derive from "a race to the bottom." This "race" is evidenced in the removal of hard-won worker protections, the rise of export processing zones, the persistent state-cum-private sector opposition to organized labor, and the erosion of supports for programs that ensure social protections. These changes are made possible by perceiving populations as superfluous and by normalizing redundancy (cf. Hayden 2007). The evidence of humanity rendered superfluous is everywhere, even if it is largely unrecognized as such: minimum wage jobs that do not provide the minimum income necessary for people to live, soaring rates of violence within impoverished communities, growing under- and unemployment, the criminalization of poverty, the widespread prevalence of incarceration, and a cultural hollowing-out as populations anxiously face their uncertain future.

Our project, as the title *Accumulating Insecurity: Violence and Dispossession in the Making of Everyday Life* suggests, seeks to understand the production and management of the conditions and consequences of the widespread experiences of alienation wrought by processes of capital accumulation in the contemporary world. As the rights of citizens and, indeed, human rights more generally are diminished and the securing of individual lives is increasingly seen as an individual rather than a social responsibility, the substance and subject of politics changes qualitatively. In the chapters that follow, we interrogate these changes in everyday lives and livelihoods as widely experienced in the ongoing attenuation of the body politic.

In so doing, we offer an interpretation of the current economic and social crisis focusing on the ways in which it instantiates new relations of social reproduction. This focus exposes a growing uncertainty and insecurity in the material and political conditions of everyday life, which represent, in a nutshell, a crisis of contemporary capitalism—of accumulation, the social wage, and the social contract. These crises prompt our investigation of the material processes that Harvey captures in the term "accumulation by dispossession," where populations are progressively stripped bare—that is, dispossessed of the means of social reproduction so that accumulation can be secured and capital can be reproduced (Harvey 2003).

The security of capital, while always of paramount concern to states is, today, legitimized through discourses of global competitiveness that compel a downward spiral of wages and the removal of protections necessary for the social reproduction of laboring bodies.[4] It is currently reinforced through discourses of terror that enable invasions of surveillance technologies into our lives, the curtailment of civil and social rights and the consequent growth of a space of impunity, the unwillingness to perceive dissent as a normal aspect of, rather than an extraordinary and even dangerous rendition of, political subjectivity, and the exclusion of public safety as central to the meaning of national security (Zalik, chapter 11, this volume; Wright, chapter 12, this volume; Haberkorn, chapter 5, this volume). Galvanized by a concern for the treacherous conditions in which individuals reproduce themselves as corporeal subjects, we investigate the practices—and the magnitude thereof—by which citizens and civilian life are being dissociated from processes of public accountability and redress as governments direct their efforts to ensuring the security of capital, with growing disregard for the securing of labor. "Abatement," the term T. H. Marshall used to describe the mediating role of the state in the postwar period—as one that sought to mitigate the deleterious effects of unchecked capital on its citizens—is no longer an appropriate way to understand the relationship between states, capital, and citizens, especially in light of the decreasing dependence on labor power to ensure productivity and economic growth (Marshall 1950).

The paradox, as many scholars of neoliberal policy note, is that as efforts to secure accumulation succeed, the dispossessions through which this security is realized necessarily increase the magnitude of the losses incurred by marginalized populations and compounds their insecurity (Mitchell 2003; Wacquant 2008b). This deepening process of alienation prompts renewed efforts to secure the reproduction of capital, efforts that perpetuate rather than mediate this process of alienation. While alienation is a constitutive element of capitalist modernity and, as such, is not new, what is distinctive about alienation in the era of neoliberalism is its form, magnitude, and management. Today, just as production gives way to consumption as the economic motor, the worker is superseded by the consumer as the normative political subject.

What this means in practice is that populations alienated through processes of capitalist accumulation are no longer perceived as potential reserves for incorporation as producing citizens but instead are viewed as both superfluous and possibly even threatening to the material and political order. Mobilizations of precariously placed populations against the conditions of their reproduction bring to light the ways in which they become a security concern rather than the processes by which their bodily security is threatened (Zalik, chapter 11, and Wright, chapter 12, this volume). As such, citizens become subject to new forms of governance insofar as they are now imagined to require efficient, ubiquitous control in order to prevent their disrupting processes of capital accumulation (Feldman, chapter 8, this volume). It also is a moment when accumulative processes require fewer and fewer workers to secure their reproduction, thereby creating new relations and forms of labor deployment: the informalization and casualization of work, employment where labor mobilization is restricted if not illegal, such as in export processing zones, private military companies, the security sector, and the armed forces (Cowen and Siciliano, chapter 4, this volume), and the proliferation of trade in illegal goods such as trade in drugs, bodies, and body parts.[5] Together, these changes transform processes of social reproduction.

These relations are secured through new, neoliberal configurations of relations between the state and the market, where markets "surveil the state," rather than the other way around [and where,] . . . consequently, the full force of the state's surveillance powers are trained on populations compelled to be on-the-move (Wade 2009, 41). As this configuration of the object of surveillance suggests, security derives from the creation of safe conditions for the reproduction of capital, a formulation that typically entails restricting movement, but today need not do so, and thereby alters how people secure their own reproduction (Mitchell 2003; Feldman, Geisler, and Silberling 2003; Feldman, chapter 8, and Zalik, chapter 11, this volume).

Portraying as threatening those who are compelled to live in conditions of material deprivation and insecurity is certainly not new, as is attested to by the post–World War II policies of cold war warriors to contain the red menace from making inroads into the third world and domestic pacification of the poor via social welfare (Piven and Cloward 1971, 1982, 1997). Here we reference a marked difference between containment as advanced through *consensus building* measures embedded in modernization and welfare policies and those implemented today through increasingly *coercive* means (Swan and Shaw 2008;

McCluskey, chapter 1; Nice, chapter 2; Haberkorn, chapter 5; and Salime, chapter 9, this volume). Consensus building measures sought to extend, even if only nominally, social welfare to disadvantaged populations and to code individuals as they entered the taxonomy of the nation-state via electoral lists, welfare rolls, social security numbers, and the census round. In contrast, today containment assumes a physical presence: the raising of fences and walls, the policing of movements using checkpoints and bollards and the wide arc of surveillance cameras, the patrolling of borders, and the issuance of and demand for new forms of identification (identity cards, chips inserted into the body and sold to ensure personal health data, and new modes of prescribing and monitoring movement) (Wright, chapter 12; de Genova, chapter 6; and Feldman, chapter 8, this volume). These varied forms of coding, monitoring, and detection indicate how both polities and the space and subjects of the political are invigilated.

Evidence of the increasing use of coercive means to govern populations is provided not only in escalating rates of incarceration but also, paradoxically, in the return to bootstrap citizenship demanded by neoliberal ideology where, even in conditions of increasing inequality and growing marginalization, the survival of individual citizens is tied to their *individual* ability and proclivity to "pull themselves up by their bootstraps" (Walmsley 2008). This contrasts with the *social* responsibility to "abate" the inequalities that ensue from an unfettered capitalism (Marshall 2006). What we see unfolding are the transformations wrought by neoliberalism—whereby the welfare of disadvantaged populations is recused from the space of the social wherein individual welfare as a right is attenuated since the right to have one's basic needs met now becomes "public charity for the needy . . . [where] government social expenditures are decided without any real participation of civil society" (Oliviera 1996 in Dagnino 1998).[6] Framed thusly, we witness the emergence of a substantially new moral economy, one where the social obligation of the liberal state shifts to the neoliberal market that is not held accountable by norms of social responsibility or presumptions of the collective good.

Passavant's analysis of the partnership between public and private surveillance agencies, precipitated by consumerism, is critical for understanding this shift. He reveals how the construction of secure spaces for the normative political subject, the consumer, both extends the reach of surveillance into our lives and circumvents public protections of the privacy of citizens: "Consumer capitalism has made extensive and intensive systems of surveillance, which, through a process of articulation, have vastly extended state surveillance powers" (Passavant 2005, 49). Significantly, too, the expansion, as well as the dependence, of the security industry on government contracts reveals the growing power of those who hold a financial stake in this state form (Passavant 2005). With this institutional shift, the rights of citizens and the power of collective action are displaced by new forms of containment where surveillance is creatively packaged in the idiom of protection and/or play, rather than as a form of social control (Giddens 1990). Child and pet monitoring devices, toy spy kits, surveillance cameras, reality television shows, Webcams, wire tapping, Internet analyzers (packet sniffers), and medical imaging technologies are aspects of a deepening and increasingly complex set of practices in which surveillance, voyeurism, defense, and recreation overlap and morph to construct unwittingly complicit subjects.

A POLITICS OF DISPLACEMENT

The genesis of this project lies in our earlier work on displacement in which we sought to explore the significant growth in the number of people experiencing a loss of place (Feldman, Geisler, and Silberling 2003). We appreciated that these mobilities offered creative opportunities for those choosing to move but also coercive dislocations for those forced to do so. Like others, we recognized the vital importance of understanding the "power geometry" (Massey 1993) that differentiated mobile populations and their conditions of social reproduction and were especially attentive to the importance of distinguishing, for example, global power brokers in pursuit of their next lucrative investment opportunity from low-wage migrants who embarked on an often dangerous livelihood search for subsistence. Further, we argued that any attempt to capture the contemporary experience of loss of place must include not only the production of refugees and migrants, but also those growing populations whose displacement was manifest in their declining sense of economic and social security as labor, like capital, was compelled by a global "race to the bottom" (see Johnson, chapter 3, this volume). Following the lead of anthropologists and geographers, we understood place as a complex of historical conditions that enables individuals and communities to engage their worlds creatively as subjects (cf. Appadurai 1996).

Engaging this enriched understanding of displacement, we acknowledged that its traditional subjects—those produced as a consequence of fairly distinct public and privately financed investment projects—need to be juxtaposed to the more banal everyday experiences of subjects, such as those caught in the wake of the globalization of industry and finance and who face an attrition of wages, home ownership, and the hard-won public guarantees of individual human welfare. Overall, our intervention articulated these various forms and sites of displacement and revealed them to be endemic to a singular historical process that is capitalist modernity. Our analysis laid the ground for investigating the political consequences of widespread displacement and interpreted the current magnitude of the population experiencing "loss of place" to signal a crisis that marked the nation-building project of the post–World War II world. Here, a loss of place references not only movement from one environment to another but also a shift in economic, social, and political security while remaining in place. These investigations prompted us toward our current exploration of the state of insecurity as we began to ask: What does the loss of place "in place" mean for the ways in which populations are now governed and rights exercised? In other words, under changing conditions of social and cultural reproduction, what forms might subjectivity assume? How might the frame of social reproduction offer us a window on the price to be paid by new forms and relations of insecurity?

While David Harvey has captured many aspects of this conjuncture through his evocative formulation "accumulation by dispossession," his focus tends to be on the expropriation of hard-won public guarantees of human welfare through the privatization of public resources and the liberalization of markets, including the labor market (Harvey 2003). Less elaborated by Harvey are the ways in which these populations—and their loss of place through policies of material dispossession as experienced particularly under neoliberal economic policy—relate to populations typically seen to be in excess. The latter include refugees, people ousted from sites of development projects through the state's exercise of eminent domain, and migrant workers, all of whom have typically only had a tenuous, if any, sense of belonging to the body politic. The perspective offered by our formulation of displacement allows us to apprehend the dispossession of private property rights by the public sector in the name of state security and various forms of loss of place as distinct but related expressions of the unfolding crisis of the nation-state (Agamben 2005; Geisler, chapter 10, this volume).[7] Today, if refugees and migrants are obviously populations that are superfluous to the nation, the industrial worker—once fulfilling the normative subjectivity of citizenship—also is a residue of a particular historical moment, one where citizenship was defined primarily through acts of production. With the disappearance of work, the worker, too, joins the ranks of the refugee and migrant to become one who is no longer accommodated in the place-making project that is the nation (Arendt 1951).

As we examine the political conditions under which social reproduction currently takes place, we see now, more than ever before, that displacement is the predominant sociopolitical dynamic with which governance structures wrestle as they formulate decisions regarding their polities and position themselves as secure investment environments for global finance (Zalik, chapter 11, this volume). As Wade recently confirmed, in the United States "more than 3 million houses were foreclosed in 2008, meaning that about 10 million people shifted into rented accommodation, vans or shelters" (Wade 2009, 40). Similar processes of mass displacement take place throughout the world. Indonesia, for example, "the fourth most populous country in the world, is experiencing surging unemployment at the same time as tens of thousands of migrant Indonesian workers are coming home after being laid off in neighboring countries like Malaysia and Singapore" (Bradsher 2009 in Wade 2009, 40).

What is to be done with the vast number of people no longer able to secure their own subsistence? What new relations emerge between states and their citizen subjects under conditions that now depend on the privatization of social reproduction? What is the meaning of social reproduction under conditions that are recognized as fragile and tenuous for a growing majority? Whether packaged as microcredit, microfinance, or the "other path," each new relation of individual debt reveals forms of insecurity about which we still know far too little (de Soto 1989). What is evident, however, is that the choice that increasing numbers of governments have elected to pursue is to surveil the movements of people, rather than scrutinize and regulate the highly volatile movements of capital. This is accomplished through practices that precipitate, exacerbate, and condone dispossession and displacement in the name of economic and political security, privilege individual over collective solutions to insecurity, and recast relations of rule.

STATES OF INSECURITY

Rights in Suspension

The emergence of global forms of governance has reconstituted economic and political processes in ways that diminish the sovereignties of the nation-state and the rights they accord their citizens. While acknowledging that rights always have been merely nominal for the majority of the world's population, even in the heyday of the welfare and developmentalist state, what is increasingly apparent today is that the potential such rights once held as vectors of progressive politics has diminished. Moreover, with the absence of new ways to exercise popular sovereignty, there has been a simultaneous recasting of human subjectivity (Arendt 1951). Such is the current state of insecurity, one that is not marked by a single event, but rather, as we have suggested, a condition constituted by new relations of rule and new articulations of alienation.[8]

In this section we highlight these critical themes in the idiom of social and human rights. Martha McCluskey examines inegalitarian welfare policies that enforce *losing choices* for many welfare recipients, even as they are rationalized on the ground that these new "market" policies promote "freedom of choice." In her view, welfare state policies are identified with *market losers* whose security threatens others' winnings and thus are "losers" who need *securing* as much, or perhaps more, than they need secur*ity.* The instantiations of these new security relations include, at their core, a moral and market fundamentalism that undermines the liberal democratic welfare state of the postwar period.

Julie Nice elaborates this theme, arguing that the very conception of economic justice under the neoliberal project remains unintelligible within U.S. law. Honing in on the political economy of welfare policy, her chapter tracks the legal abandonment of those most economically vulnerable, uncovering the doctrinal methods of deconstitutionalization that result in dual rules of law based on economic status. She concludes that there is an official "war on welfare" and notes that the state no longer is concerned with disciplining and regulating the poor through mechanisms of inclusion. Instead, the poor, like other marginalized groups, are excluded from state responsibility and forced to fend for themselves in a marketplace that offers only limited opportunities for their ability to secure adequate sustenance.

Welfare is but one arena in which the actions and decisions of state and private institutions and actors converge to produce and deepen insecurity among primarily poor and working-class people of color. Paula Johnson turns our attention to these practices in her analysis of the violence of gentrification. Exploring the physical and psychological effects of gentrification and the loss of political voice among residents, Johnson examines the massive dislocation of black residents from Harlem, New York, and New Orleans, Louisiana. In both locations, public officials have "legally" sanctioned evictions, eliminated rent control, and redefined zoning, urban renewal, eminent domain, and financial policies in ways that make area residents invisible, disappearing in voice as well as in body. As a consequence, forty-six thousand fewer African Americans voted in New Orleans in the gubernatorial election held in 2007 than voted in 2003 due perhaps, in large measure, to the failure of FEMA to inform displaced New Orleans residents that they could cast absentee ballots in critical elections after Katrina. As Johnson shows, vigorous resistance movements shape the response of residents as they struggle to hold onto their homes, cultures, voices, and freedom.

Deborah Cowen and Amy Siciliano maintain the focus on marginalized communities and state practices that constitute their contemporary economic opportunities and political subjectivities in their investigation of the geographies of military recruitment and urban policing. In tracing the changing configurations of criminality, they reveal how populations made redundant by deindustrialization, patterns of uneven development, and the growth of high tech and professional industries are targeted for military service and policing. Prisons, not welfare supports, are expanded and privatized to warehouse this reserve army of predominantly racialized young males who then provide labor for a growing securities sector.

This spotlight on the criminalization of North American poverty is complemented by the contribution of Tyrell Haberkorn, whose empirical focus is the arbitrary arrests of Thai citizens suspected of being terrorists. Analyzing the abrogation and violation of rights in the so-called service of democracy and the nation, Haberkorn illustrates how Thai state actors help to constitute their nation as they interpret the Islamic insurgency in the country's three southern provinces. Their construction, instantiated in the arrest and "occupational training" of particular citizens, normalizes the violation of human rights rather than presumes its exceptionality. Importantly, Haberkorn also illustrates how the arbitrary application of illegal laws produces a generalized fear across southern Thailand that leads her to propose that the arbitrariness of rule and dispossession of particular segments of the population are at the core of belonging in Thailand.

Fugitive Corporeality

As we have suggested, the accumulation of insecurity is, at base, a crisis of social reproduction by which we reference not only the reproduction of the capitalist system or the physical existence of individuals but also the relations, conditions, and activities that express and sustain people's lives and livelihoods. As Marx reminded us, "As individuals express their life, so they are. What they are, therefore, coincides . . . both with *what* they produce and with *how* they produce" (Marx and Engels 1998, 37). In our framing, we do not adhere to a strict separation between production and reproduction, as many Marxists are inclined to promote, but instead recognize the constitutive character of reproduction—of life, diverse livelihoods, and of the nation-state as a social form. As noted earlier, the current neoliberal project has forced increasing numbers of people into individuated forms of reproduction and various forms of vagabondage as they struggle to secure the material goods and social practices that enable them to meet their subsistence needs. Following Katz (2001), we concur that the lens of social reproduction provides a relatively undertheorized but critical arena for understanding the current crisis of social, economic, and political insecurity that occurs as increasing numbers of people are compelled to labor in highly surveilled environments or turn fugitive from the law in order to make ends meet. In the words of the current secretary-treasurer of the American Federation of State, County and Municipal Employees AFSCME (Lucy 2008), we are now living in a predatory economy where economic security is gone for poor and marginal citizens, but also, and increasingly, for the middle classes.

In this predatory economy the consumer is the central figure, one whose trained consumption parallels Haberkorn's rich understanding of reeducation: the construction of "a certain type of active subject—the consumer—that is useful for not only the present mode of capitalism but also for reproducing state power" (Passavant 2005, 47). By mobilizing nation populations to become good consumers and purchasing commodities that enact both U.S. military might, war, and hatred in the form of computer simulations of real events, we come to inhabit, and to normalize, the present state of being, the neoliberal subject. By imagining ourselves as consumers, and witnessing "their presence on our bodies, in our living spaces, in the stores, and in our everyday lives, consumers . . . create a visual culture that manifests support for the present state of affairs and its projects" (Passavant 2005, 47). In a context that challenges our material sustenance and our social being, our subjecthood, the quotidian act of social reproduction, can be recognized as one of ongoing struggle.

Nicholas De Genova's focus on the illegal alien reveals that the spectacle of terror is inseparable from a spectacle of security and the security state as savior and redeemer. In his account, the "illegal alien" is the embodiment of the nebulous "foreign" menace and the icon of borders perceived to be woefully violable. This icon also signals the putative border crisis that has become synonymous with a nation-state in the throes of a veritable "invasion." In this post–September 11, 2001, and Homeland Security State explanation, the migrant stands in for the figure of "terrorism" as the purportedly antiterrorist security state stages transnational mobility as a menacing figure of transgression.[9] In recasting both the nation-state form and the rights of citizen-subjects, De Genova aids us in recognizing a critical site where the ostensible "war on terror" is practically and physically enacted.

Claudia Aradau moves this enactment to a terrain that is ostensibly distinct from Homeland Security concerns to trace the dividing line commonly drawn between lives worthy of securing and those open to being punished. Through her examination of the treatment of victims of human trafficking, Aradau shows how trafficked women are increasingly represented as the embodiment of lives deserving compassion rather than as undesirable subjects who are potentially risky noncitizens to be deported or detained. She illuminates how narratives and imageries of suffering are mobilized to inform a politics of life whereby trafficked women are no longer treated as abject and "infamous" but are tentatively extracted from categories of illegal migrants, prostitutes, and criminals and represented instead as suffering victims. In addressing the concept of sovereign pardon as a politics of life, Aradau confirms a politics that punishes disorganized families and unscrupulous individuals and normalizes family integration, work, and moral rehabilitation.

Shelley Feldman elaborates the focus on social reproduction and its elision from popular discourse, an elision, she suggests, that blinds us to the everyday and increasingly creative practices of inclusion that hide the ways in which social control is being made both invisible and normal. Focusing on the widespread prevalence and acceptance of surveillance technologies, she unpacks fear as a social relation of rule to show how surveillance technologies have emerged and are sustained, less because they protect, than because they contribute to dominating and managing, particularly those economically marginal and redundant populations who are no longer perceived as a reserve army of labor. Her discussion of the New York City taxi drivers' struggle against the use of the Global Positioning System (GPS) reveals how their claims for autonomy assert the very values that supposedly the war on terror seeks to protect—choice, competition, and imagination—yet their claims become the subject of increasing control in the interests of securing the conditions of accumulation. Feldman also draws attention to the acceptance of new regulatory practices as forms of personal control to show a decline in the expectation of citizens for public sector accountability in the provision of everyday safety. She concludes that contemporary tensions over the meaning and use of surveillance technologies are increasingly likely to be less about invasions of privacy than they are about the control of the conditions of social reproduction.

Displacement of Politics

In this section we suggest that politics is rendered sterile when dissent is considered to be an extraordinary rather than ordinary rendition of politics. This differentiates our analysis from those that engage a trope of "the war at home" or the domestic costs of war (cf. Piven 2004) and brings us closer to one that is perhaps better approximated by the *domestication of war,* and *bloodshed made banal* (Duffield 2007). To be sure, this shift builds on the important contributions of those who have offered us critical assessments of war and how its discursive construction (it happens elsewhere) and its costs at home (challenging domestic budgets and securing the capacity to support health, education, and welfare investments) are an elision of both its actual costs and, importantly, its rituals and practices. Here we refer to a world economy that is characterized by sustained, if declining, accumulation at the cost of human superfluousness, where the conditions by which people secure their reproduction are increasingly made insecure.

The work of Zakia Salime on the construction of a "Green Zone" addresses how trade and defense, war and economy, are intertwined projects. Focusing on the "Middle East Partnership Initiative" (MEPI) as a program to reform the political, economic, and educational systems in the Middle East, she shows that these "soft reforms" to enhance citizen-entrepreneurship, women's leadership, and civil society organizations, represent a political rationality to uproot terrorism and spread democracy. Evident from the range of players and their neoliberal discourse, this development initiative is animated by the synergy that is formed by how civil society, the state, and private investment work together to secure democracy, more appropriately read as securing accumulation. As posed by Salime, the normative meanings of civil society in the MEPI, and the reshaping of subjects and subjectivities, opens the important question of the connection between social engineering and political intervention.

The disposability of workers is accompanied by subtle but significant alterations in property rights. Charles Geisler explores the insecurities of the immigrant workforce, noting the range of personal and real estate interests they hold and the perils they encounter when dispossessed of these holdings. Their involuntary property loss, in some ways a continuation of past immigrant experience is, in other ways, unique and reflects a recent juggernaut of immigrant criminalization. Geisler argues that the U.S. wars on drugs and terror, agitated by overpopulation fears and the evermore aggressive use of forfeiture law, are combining to disable the property of illegal immigrants and set the stage for more far-reaching property seizures.

Anna Zalik, too, queries the constitution of legitimate forms of political expression by examining another aspect of property rights, transformations in civil society. Engaging examples from southern Nigeria and northwestern Canada, she examines how formal state and corporate-industrial approaches to pacification—whether via the means of force and state violence or its official legal counterpart—inform and shape protest in the spatial setting of the oil field. Highlighting the harnessing of legality as a means to suppress popular protest against fossil capitalism, Zalik first examines the juridical and discursive means that secure control of the licit and illicit claims on oil extractive where any obstruction to its extraction is viewed as violence. In the second case, Zalik explores a strategy of resistance that employs political violence in full knowledge that it will be outlawed by the state. She concludes by showing how dispossessed residents, whether through formal legal challenges or the discursive labeling of legitimate extraction, respond to claims on strategic, heavily policed petroleum assets and how in these circumstances protest is criminalized.

The constitution of legitimate protest also is the focus of Melissa Wright's chapter on gendered violence along the U.S.-Mexico border. As Wright argues, the murders of women and girls in the cities of Ciudad Juárez, Chihuahua City, and Tijuana ushered in an era of violent infamy—femicide—that has been followed today by the violence of the drug cartels. Together, these conditions of extreme insecurity and fear make Mexican border cities some of the most dangerous in the western hemisphere. Focusing on Ciudad Juárez and the Coalition of Non-Profit Organizations for Women, Wright relates this violence to the political economy of export processing zones in order to challenge practices that marginalize "public women" workers. In contrast, during the current drug wars, the state allows drug violence to impede with impunity. The complicity of the state in creating this space of impunity, where few are held to account for femicide or for the murders that take place as the drug cartels and the state joust for sovereignty, demonstrates the marked separation of national security and a commitment to public safety.

In our concluding chapter, Pheng Cheah's exploration of particular forms of labor contributes to our reworking of the meanings attendant to practices of inclusion and exclusion. He does so by complicating and challenging contemporary deployments of the Foucauldian notion of bio-power to account for the obviously repressive conditions of social reproduction. Cheah insists that bio-power is more accurately conceived as an inclusionary rather than exclusionary force that animates practices of capital accumulation. He supports this claim by examining practices of accumulation involving two different modalities of female labor, foreign domestic workers and sex workers, to argue that these forms of labor should not be understood in terms of exclusionary forms of power that lead to slavery but rather in terms of the inclusionary processes of modern governmentality and the concept of human capital that underwrites these processes.

Fundamental to this project is an investigation of the ways in which the conditions of social reproduction have, for increasing numbers of people, been rendered insecure. Collectively, the contributors offer an understanding of the production and management of the consequences of widespread experiences of alienation, both material and discursive, wrought by processes of "accumulation by dispossession." We have sought to do so by querying processes and policies by which questions regarding the security of human life and the conditions of social reproduction are progressively being removed from civilian spaces. With a focus on the everyday we make visible the insidious, often unacknowledged, and seemingly innocuous ways the political order and our lives and prospects are being transformed. The various contributions expose the choices that produce inequality and the moral economies within which these choices are perceived as legitimate and rendered ordinary rather than exceptional. In this way, we take a cue provided by Arendt's argument on the banality of evil and draw attention to the normalization of human destruction even as the reproduction of capital is secured.

Together, the authors bring to the fore the particular forms of violence that are attendant to contemporary processes of accumulation and manifest in the increasingly strained, often terrifying circumstances in which people struggle to socially reproduce themselves. With security often identified primarily in terms of armaments and containment, an identity that has led to the impoverishment rather than the nourishment of laboring bodies, the authors allow us to see how the very act of social reproduction becomes suspect and subject to invigilation. As populations become redundant, interest moves from whether populations are able to socially reproduce themselves to monitoring how they (attempt to) do so. What is now evident through the instances showcased in this volume, is that for increasing numbers of people social reproducibility transgresses the terms of normative liberal-democratic political subjectivity in ways that invite punitive action upon their already beleaguered selves. This means that people's ability to reproduce corporeal being can only be realized, and increasingly so, through fugitive means.

The substance and subject of politics is qualitatively altered when rights are diminished and the prospects of individual lives are increasingly understood as an individual rather than social responsibility. Collectively the authors address the place of dissent and the struggle for social reproduction in a politics that is propelled by fear. Examining the narrowing terms of protest, the authors enable us to trace a concomitant narrowing of the public that is expressed when deliberation and holding power to account are increasingly considered to be illegitimate and dissent is deemed to be pathological. These political transformations are the counterpart of the economic practices of neoliberalism that eschew the liberal democratic conception of public and social accountability and rely instead on a view of individual responsibility in the construction of its moral economy. In short, the chapters in this volume have interrogated the ongoing attenuation of the body politic through a focus on the insecure conditions of social reproduction. In so doing, they challenge understanding security almost exclusively conceived in terms of armaments and surveillance better able to protect the conditions of accumulation, to offer instead an appreciation, appropriation, and reinscription of the notion of security in ways that expose how accumulative practices are complicit in perpetuating and extending the material insecurity of civilians and the political insecurity of civil society.

NOTES

1. For Arendt (1951), these conditions were amplified, but not created, by totalitarianism.

2. Also crucial in this understanding is reference to Arendt (1970), *On Violence*, and the distinction she draws between power and violence. See also Young (2002).

3. Indeed, when we consider the impetus, administration, and experience of economic sanctions it is clear that distinctions between the event of martial conflict and the banality of social reproduction are blurred.

4. There are excellent studies that explore contemporary forms and relations of accumulation, and while the debates that differentiate them are suggestive, this is not the focus of our current intervention. See, for example, Bakker and Gill 2003; Bezanson and Luxton 2006; Gill 1995, 2002, 2003; Harvey 2003, 2005; and Smith 2002. Instead, our contribution recognizes the particularity of the political economy of the current conjuncture and interrogates the politics of alienation and the practices of dispossession that cohere in its expression/formation.

5. As Pravinchandra's (2008) discussion of the international trade in human organs reveals, this market constitutes a shift that signals the transformation of the laboring body to the body as thing, composed of parts with different market values that, as a last resort, can be sold to secure subsistence through a radically transformed understanding of social reproduction.

6. Witness, too, the extraordinary debates and decisions of the California senate, summer of 2009, which include furloughs for state employees and massive reductions in support of primary, secondary, and higher education, social services, and access to health care.

7. Nation-building in this context emerged as a predominant political matrix in the mid-twentieth century; in the war-ravaged West it came in the guise of the extension of universal franchise, welfare, and substantive citizenship rights (Marshall 1950/2006), while in the global South, emerging from under the shadow of colonialism, it took the guise of development. The economy was seen primarily in national terms, and the industrial worker was held out as the normative political citizen-subject who, through acts of production, enhanced the strength of the nation, the body politic. Geopolitically, in the context of the cold war, the abatement (to return to T. H. Marshall's term) of the alienating tendencies of capitalism, through welfare in the West and development interventions in the South, governments strived to contain potentially restive, alienated

populations and bring them into the fold of the nation. This was quintessentially a moment marked by processes of inclusion.

8. Here we appreciate Neil Smith's contention that the contemporary moment "does not constitute a 'war on terrorism,'" but rather a "continuation of globalization by military means" that can be traced back to and are integral elements of liberalism (2005, ix).

9. In this volume we follow Dana Heller (2005) and use September 11, 2001, rather than the more common 9/11 to distinguish ourselves from the commodification of the event and its subsequent fetishization.

REFERENCES

Agamben, Giorgio. 2005. *State of exception*. Chicago: University of Chicago Press.

Appadurai, Arjun. 1996. *Modernity at large: Cultural dimensions of globalization*. Minneapolis: University of Minnesota Press.

Appadurai, Arjun, and Carol Breckenridge. 1989. On moving targets. *Public Culture* 2 (1): i–iv.

Araghi, Farshad A. 1995. Global depeazantisation, 1945–1990. *The Sociological Quarterly* 36 (2): 337–68.

Arendt, Hannah. 1951. *The origins of totalitarianism*. New York: Harcourt, Brace and Company.

———. 1963. *Eichmann in Jerusalem*. New York: Vintage.

———. 1970. *On violence*. New York: Harcourt Brace Jovanovich.

Bakker, Isabella, and Stephen Gill, eds. 2003. *Power, production, and social reproduction: Human in/security in the global political economy*. London: Macmillan-Palgrave.

Bezanson, Kate, and Meg Luxton, eds. 2006. *Social reproduction: Feminist political economy challenges neo-liberalism*. Montreal: McGill-Queen's University Press.

Dagnino, Evelina. 1998. Culture, citizenship, and democracy: Changing discourses and practices of the Latin American Left. In *Culture of politics, politics of cultures: Revisioning Latin American social movements*, ed. Sonia E. Alvarez, Evelina Dagnino, and Arturo Escobar, 33–63. Boulder, Colo.: Westview.

de Soto, Hernando. 1989. *The other path: The invisible revolution in the Third World*. New York: Harper & Row.

Duffield, Mark R. 2007. *Development, security and unending war: Governing the world of peoples*. Cambridge: Polity.

Feldman, Shelley, Charles Geisler, and Louise Silberling. 2003. *Moving targets: Displacement, impoverishment, and development: An introduction*. International Social Science Journal 175:7–13.

Giddens, Anthony. 1990. *The consequences of modernity*. Stanford, Calif.: Stanford University Press.

Gill, Stephen. 2003. *Power and resistance in the new world order*. New York: Palgrave Macmillan.

———. 2002. Constitutionalizing inequality and the clash of globalizations. *International Studies Review* 4 (2): 47–65.

———. 1995. Globalisation, market civilisation, and disciplinary neoliberalism. *Millennium: Journal of International Studies* 24:399–423.

Gilmore, Ruth Wilson. 2007. *Golden gulag: Prisons, surplus, crisis and opposition in globalizing California.* Berkeley: University of California Press.

Gregory, Derek, and Allan Pred, eds. 2007. *Violent geographies: Fear, terror, and political violence.* New York: Routledge.

Harvey, David. 2003. *The new imperialism.* Oxford: Oxford University Press.

———. 2005. *A brief history of neoliberalism.* New York: Oxford University Press.

Hayden, Patrick. 2007. Superfluous humanity: An Arendtian perspective on the political evil of global poverty. *Millennium: Journal of International Studies* 35 (2): 279–300.

Heller, Dana. 2005. "Introduction: Consuming 9/11." In *The selling of 9/11: How a national tragedy became a commodity,* ed. Dana Heller, 1–26. New York: Palgrave Macmillan.

International Labour Organization. 2009. *Global employment trends update.* Geneva: International Labour Organization, May.

Jacobs, Tom. 2009. Pink slips and poor health: The toxicity of job insecurity. *Miller-McCune Magazine* (June 29). Accessed 28 June 2009. http://www.miller-mccune.com/health/the-toxicity-of-job-insecurity-1315.

Katz, Cindi. 2001. Vagabond capitalism and the necessity of social reproduction. *Antipode* 33 (4): 709–28.

Kearney, Michael. 1991. Borders and boundaries of state and self at the end of empire. *Journal of Historical Sociology* 1 (4): 52–74.

Lucy, William. 2008. The predatory economy. *AFSCME Works Issues* (January/February). Accessed 19 June 2009. http://www.afscme.org/publications/17231.cfm.

Marshall, T. H. 1950/2006. Citizenship and social class. In *The welfare state reader,* ed. Christopher Pierson and Francis G. Castles, 30–39. Cambridge, Mass.: Polity Press.

Marx, Karl, and Friedrich Engels. 1998. *The German ideology.* Amherst, New York: Prometheus Books.

Massey, Doreen. 1993. Power-geometry and a progressive sense of place. In *Mapping the futures: Local cultures, global change,* ed. J. Bird, B. Curtis, T. Putnam, G. Robertson, and L. Tickner, 59–69. London: Routledge.

Mitchell, Don. 2003. *The right to the city: Social justice and the fight for public space.* New York: Guilford.

Mitchell, Katharyne, Sallie A. Marston, and Cindi Katz. 2004. Life's work: An introduction, review and critique. In *Life's work: Geographies of social reproduction,* ed. Katharyne Mitchell, Sallie A. Marston, and Cindi Katz, 59–69. Malden, Mass.: Blackwell.

Nielson, Brett, and Ned Rossiter. 2008. Precarity as a political concept, or Fordism as exception. *Theory, Culture & Society* 25 (7–8): 51–72.

Oliveira, Francisco de. 1996. "O 'Reino' de 20 Anos." *Folha de São Paulo* (October 13).

Passavant, Paul A. 2005. The strong neo-liberal state: Crime, consumption, and governance. *Theory & Event* 8(3). Accessed 20 September 2010. http://muse.jhu.edu/journals/theory_and_event/voo8/8.3passavant.html.

———. 2004. The governmentality of consumption. *Interventions: The International Journal of Postcolonial Studies* 6 (3): 381–400.

Piven, Frances Fox. 2004. *The war at home: The domestic costs of Bush's militarism*. New York: New Press.

Piven, Frances Fox, and Richard A. Cloward. 1971. *Regulating the poor: The functions of public welfare*. New York: Pantheon Books.

———. 1982. *The new class war: Reagan's attack on the welfare state and its consequences*. New York: Pantheon Books.

———. 1997. *The breaking of the American social compact*. New York: New Press, distributed by Norton.

Pravinchandra, Shital Laxmidas. 2008. *Inhuman transactions? Representing the commodification of human body parts*. Ph.D. diss. Cornell University, Ithaca, New York.

Scheper-Hughes, Nancy, and Philippe Bourgois. 2006. Introduction: Making sense of violence. In *Violence in war and peace: An anthology*, ed. Nancy Scheper-Hughes and Philippe Bourgois, 1–31. Malden, Mass.: Blackwell.

Smith, Neil. 2002. *The new urban frontier: Gentrification and the revanchist city*. London: Routledge.

———. 2003. *American empire: Roosevelt's geographer and the prelude to globalization*. Berkeley: University of California Press.

———. 2005. *The endgame of globalization*. New York and London: Routledge.

Swan, Richelle S., and Linda L. Shaw. 2008. The untold story of welfare fraud. *Journal of Sociology and Social Welfare* 35 (September): 133–51.

Wacquant, Loic. 2008a. The militarization of urban marginality: Lessons from the Brazilian metropolis. *International Political Sociology* 2 (1): 56–74.

———. 2008b. The penalisation of poverty and the rise of neo-liberalism. *European Journal on Criminal Policy and Research* 9:401–412.

Wade, Robert. 2009. Steering out of the crisis. *Economic and Political Weekly* 44 (13): 39–46.

Walmsley, Roy. 2008. *World prison population list* (8th edition). London: International Centre for Prison Studies, King's College.

Wright, Melissa W. 2006. *Disposable women and other myths of global capitalism*. New York: Routledge.

Young, Iris Marion. 2002. Power, violence, and legitimacy: A reading of Hannah Arendt in an age of police brutality and humanitarian intervention. In *Breaking the cycles of hatred: Memory, law, and repair*, ed. Martha Minow and Nancy L. Rosenblum, 260–87. Princeton, N.J.: Princeton University Press.

PART ONE

Rights in Suspension

CHAPTER ONE

From the Welfare State to the Militarized Market

Losing Choices, Controlling Losers

MARTHA T. MCCLUSKEY

By the end of the twentieth century, the ideology of the free market was a powerful force pushing back against the growth of the welfare state both in the United States and around the globe. According to that ideology, welfare state policies spread neither prosperity nor security, but instead sacrificed individual freedom for government control. That story contrasts the welfare state with a free market where individuals rule by exercising the power to choose. In that storied market, decentralized voluntary exchanges based on competitive calculations of individual gain add up to maximize overall resources, so that individual self-interest benefits society as a whole. This idea helped justify a triumphant wave of neoliberal policies claiming to unleash market risk and reward from egalitarian government regulation and spending (Yergin and Stanislaw 2002).

This chapter aims to help clarify the ideas challenging economic equality and the possibilities for resisting those ideas by analyzing how the free market story connects freedom of choice with unequal government control. The story of market freedom has helped present neoliberalism's increased insecurity and upward distribution of economic gains as temporary bumps on a new road toward broad peace and prosperity rather than a sign of timeworn class politics. Even as those bumps have grown to full-fledged economic crisis, following on the heels of new waves of global political violence, the free market story retains substantial power to resist new commitments to welfare state policies.

Alongside this neoliberal ideology and policy, a growing neoconservative movement in the United States has also challenged the late twentieth-century welfare state through policies emphasizing forceful government moral control, not public economic support, as the key to security and long-term political freedom (Steinfels 1979). That moralistic authoritarianism was often presented in opposition to market freedom, attributed in part to divisions between libertarian economics and communitarian morality within U.S. conservativism, or between modernism and parochialism abroad.

But to the contrary, the prevailing free market ideology is itself grounded in an embrace of expansive collective coercion and control that dovetails with the more overtly authoritarian critique of welfare state policies. Market and moral fundamentalism together support and legitimate a new vision where both political liberty and economic security are denied to most people. Free market ideology works to transform the idea of the democratic rule of law for the benefit of the people to the rule of force for enhancing the wealth of a few.

Two rhetorical steps have grounded the ideological formula justifying the move from democratic governance to the rule of a militarized market. First, inegalitarian policies that enforce *losing choices* for most are rationalized on the grounds that these market policies promote freedom of choice. Second, welfare state policies are identified with *market losers* whose security threatens others' winnings, so that these losers need secur*ing* as much as secur*ity*.

To some extent, the global financial crisis that erupted in 2008 burst the popular and political illusion of individual choice bringing social abundance, instead revealing a reality of immense and indiscriminate loss bearing down from the mysterious and interdependent actions of an elite minority. The crisis has also increased attention to the threat of market "winners" and their disproportionate and destructive government power, potentially replacing or deflecting efforts to scapegoat and police the growing number of market "losers."

Yet this period of crisis and change also has brought enhanced opportunities for wealthy elites to consolidate antidemocratic government power over others as the way to restore market freedom and political security. Even in the face of spectacular failures, the militarized market ideal retains substantial ideological and institutional power to make increased economic security and democratic freedom appear to be too costly. In a well-honed rhetorical formula, proponents of the militarized market construct the bad choices they have bequeathed as the best of all possible worlds, explaining newly constrained choices and horrific losses as the price of natural scarcity that must be paid to avoid further destruction. As legal structures continue to provide unequal security against loss, growing popular fear, despair, and distrust may produce pressure for concentrated authority backed by force in place of broad participation in shared economic and political power.

As the global financial crisis unravels the proclaimed "freedom" of the fundamentalist market, uncovering its dependence on lavish government support and extensive private fraud, the rule of law needs to be revised as well as the rule of markets. A crucial step toward undoing the militarized market will be to restructure its rules to turn around the power to control economic choices so that more people will be winners. In addition, replacing market fundamentalism requires a shift from authoritarian control over market losers to democratic control over the current market "choosers," whose gains depend on imposing staggering losses on others.

LEGALIZING THE WELFARE STATE

The United States' move toward a welfare state in the first half of the twentieth century grew out of a similar ideological and legal struggle over the question of whether democratic controls on unequal economic power foster or hinder a free society. Prior to 1937, Supreme Court decisions during what has come to be called the Lochner era used the two-pronged rhetoric about choice and control to block many legislative efforts to promote economic security for the nonwealthy.

First, the Lochner era opinions defined democratic efforts to change economic rights and policies as a move from individual freedom to government intervention. Judges claimed that by striking down labor or consumer protections, such as minimum wage and maximum hour legislation, they were enforcing a constitutional right to freedom of contract. For example, in the *Lochner* ruling, the Court decreed that constitutional freedom meant enforcing an individual baker's right to "choose" to work long hours at low wages in unhealthy conditions without government regulation (*Lochner v. New York* 1905). Through this reasoning, the courts constructed the political power of workers and other economically vulnerable groups to create *different*, and arguably *better* choices, as efforts to *take away* choice.

The key to reconstructing *constrained* choice as *free* choice was masking the pervasive and powerful role of existing law—and government coercion—in restricting workers' or consumers' choices and privileging the wealthy. Any real-world market choice does not simply reflect the chooser's individual desires, but instead depends on others' willingness and ability to satisfy that desire and on the price of that satisfaction compared to other alternatives. What particular options, at what prices, are available to a given worker, consumer, or entrepreneur will, of course, depend on the context, and in particular on how the law distributes and regulates property and power. The baker who chooses to labor long hours at low wages to increase his income makes that choice against, for example, a backdrop of law that gives the owner of the bakery rather than the bakery worker the title to the profits made from the sale of the bread, along with a backdrop of government force that gives that owner the right to call the police if the bakery worker pockets the money from that sale (Hale 1952). Regulations of wages and hours only *appear* to be coercive government intervention in a free market by obscuring the background legal systems, such as the rules of corporate finance, property, tort, and contract and criminal justice, so that these laws governing the existing market appear to represent a state of nature affording perfect free choice (Sunstein 1987).

Second, the Lochner era opinions also supported an era of substantial government control over vulnerable individuals by tending to define those seeking more egalitarian government economic protections as dependent; that is, as persons incapacitated from freedom, authority, and self-sufficiency (McCluskey 2003). This characterization could sometimes justify government protection for some of those most at risk of losing out in the market. For example, the Lochner era judiciary upheld minimum wage laws when applied to women, but not to men (*Muller v. Oregon* 1908). This reasoning tended to mark those who sought egalitarian economic protection as second-class and suspect citizens deserving of extensive government control along with only meager or even illusory protection. For example, wage and hour limits that applied only to women tended to work to enhance their economic marginality, enforcing low incomes and exclusion from mainstream employment (Kessler-Harris 2001). When workers successfully asserted their collective choice for better wages and work conditions through supposedly private market bargaining by striking against employers, federal courts often issued injunctions authorizing military intervention, thereby treating workers' potential market freedom as unjust coercion of more deserving market winners (Casebeer 1995).

As part of the New Deal's dramatic shift in ideology and policy, prevailing jurisprudence repudiated *Lochner*'s market fundamentalism and opened the door to the twentieth-century welfare and regulatory state. By the end of the 1930s, the U.S. Supreme Court had rejected the idea that fundamental freedom requires *barring* democratic policy measures aimed at advancing economic equality. In undoing *Lochner*'s jurisprudence, courts partly rejected the opposition between market choice and government coercion, instead reconstructing expanded state and federal legislative and executive power as the product of democratic political freedom (*NLRB v. Jones & Laughlin Steel Corp.* 1947). The Court affirmed that the power to choose could mean not just the individual freedom to decide whether the personal benefits of a particular job or product outweighed the costs, but also the freedom to assert collective power in state or market to change the costs and benefits of particular decisions, thereby producing a different, better array of choices for many.

Nonetheless, the United States' renunciation of *Lochner*'s market fundamentalism also served in part to reframe and legitimize many aspects of a militarized market ideal. The prevailing explanation of *Lochner*'s mistake was that it wrongly made economic policies integral to political and civil rights, not that it wrongly enforced a political economy with rules skewed to keep many from political and economic power (Sunstein 1987). As a result, U.S. law stopped short of joining the global trend to constitutionalize rights that would have gone further to define economic and political power for nonelites as fundamental to meaningful freedom (Sunstein 2006).

DELEGITIMIZING THE WELFARE STATE

Losing Choices

Although this post-*Lochner* separation of economics from basic political and civil rights enabled the growth of a (limited) U.S. welfare state, it also set the stage for its weakening in the late twentieth century. While government policies promoting economic equality usually were not directly blocked by the Constitution, neither were many policies and institutions promoting the inegalitarian and coercive concentration of economic and political power. By constructing basic democratic freedom and equality in terms of government's *abstention* from disturbing a presumptively neutral process of politics and market, the prevailing legal framework has often continued the Lochner era's naturalization of extensive unequal losses and dangerous losers in need of control. If the process of producing winners and losers in state and market is viewed as generally free, then those who win will generally be seen to have made better choices, giving them deserved authority to harness further power in market and all branches of government to protect and enhance their gains.

The ideological definition of freedom as minimized government control of economics contains a paradox. If true freedom equals unconstrained self-interest maximizing in a harsh world of zero-sum competition for scarce resources, then the most freedom will come from imposing the most constraint on others. The rational way to win an ideal competition for scarce resources will not necessarily or normally be to choose the option that maximizes one's own benefits within given resource constraints. Instead, self-interested market actors will seek to get better choices by using public and private power to constrain others. By rejecting fundamental constitutional protection for broad-based economic security and equitable economic power, the post-*Lochner* legal system set the stage for winners to build and concentrate gains by creating and controlling more market (and state) losers. In a legal system that denies the connections between economic power and political freedom, these constraints on others' choices will tend to be legitimated and protected as neutral politics, economics, and law. Manipulating the imagined line between free market and coercive politics is one of the most powerful ways of gaining market power to limit others' choices.

By the late twentieth century, wealthy elites used the rhetoric of market freedom to help mobilize a broader coalition against the welfare state vision spurred by the New Deal and expanded in new regulatory systems and government social programs in the 1960s through the early 1970s (Phillips-Fein 2009). This coalition succeeded in weakening law reforms, establishing new legal rights for corporations, controlling regulatory agencies, influencing the judiciary, and building new political, academic, and legal institutions to advance elite business interests. Indeed, this mobilization has helped to reestablish some substantive constitutional protections for concentrated wealth in the guise of basic due process and neutrality (McCluskey 2007).

This legal context has helped give material substance to the ideological claim that the bad choices facing existing market losers are the tragic result of scarce economic resources, not the unjust result of unequal political power. For example, changes in the regulation of international trade and finance in the 1970s through the 1990s helped increase the mobility and volatility of capital in relation to workers and communities. Those changes in background laws helped make collective action for better wages—either through legislation or labor organizing—a costlier choice more likely to risk capital flight (to jurisdictions with less state labor protection), and thereby jeopardize jobs and wages for those workers and communities.

Conservative activists harnessed this real (but contingent and political) increase in scarcity to further advance the free market story. That story explained that the only way to effectively resist this scarcity is to further loosen the constraints on the market winners with the power to control the limited resources on which others increasingly depend. In this view, workers, communities, and nations faced with capital flight can only retain jobs or wealthy taxpayers, for example, by further shifting taxes and market risk to those without the power to transfer assets elsewhere, or by further directing government spending and regulatory support to protect investors rather than schools, the environment, public health, general infrastructure, or social services (Enrich 1996). Although promoted by conservatives, this story has convinced many across the political spectrum in the United States since it exposes the real economic insecurity perceived by many of the middle class in the late twentieth century.

But the argument that this market scarcity is inevitable, and inevitably perpetuated by market winners, is essentially an argument about power couched in the language of impersonal, objective forces of economic incentives. If the power to control others' choices is a natural, fixed, infinitely resilient force, and if that mysterious suprahuman irresistible force is called the market, then we have little choice but to give in to the bad choices dictated by that market and even to give that market more power to control our choices. By reifying the power to control others' choices, this idea of the market ironically makes those bad and worse choices seem to be the route toward the best choices possible. If the existing distribution of power to reap gains and avoid costs is inevitable and natural, then accommodating that power will be the best option, since resisting it will bring only further costs to those who lack that power. The credibility of the free market story's promise of eventual abundance, in the face of increasing scarcity, depends on trusting that this unequal market power is nonetheless sufficiently diffuse and its concentrated gain so big that it eventually will spill over to a significant number of others.

Controlling Losers

Welfare states and their beneficiaries have often taken political and economic action to push back against neoliberalism's losing choices. Yet welfare states are under attack not just from neoliberal policies increasing global economic competition, but also from renewed global assertions of overt and covert public and private force that often have enabled a wealthy few to extract gains from the majority of others.

As the U.S. economy, and its wealthy business owners and investors, became more threatened under global competition and increased nonelite political power in the 1960s and 1970s, the prevailing policy response has been not simply to win that competition by producing more and better economic goods, but to enlist militarism and government control to change the global and domestic rules of the game in the favor of the wealthy. As Chilean dictator Pinochet explained in a 1979 speech written by his "Chicago Boys" free market economic advisors, democracy is only an expendable means to the more important end of absolute economic freedom; or, as writer Eduardo Galeano observed, Pinochet was "torturing people so prices could be free" (Grandin 2006, 175).

Historian Greg Grandin explains how free market ideology ironically helped promote a U.S. policy of heightened intervention through terror that brought mass poverty, violence, and dictatorship to much of Latin America during the late twentieth century (Grandin 2006). Many of the democratic welfare states or egalitarian political movements that grew around the globe after the fall of colonialism and World War II lost ground or failed in significant part because they appeared too powerful in that global competition, not too weak. Grandin argues that U.S. leaders inverted moral rhetoric about democratic freedom, joining moral and market fundamentalism, to justify military intervention that undermined the choice to increase economic and political equality in Latin American countries through the 1980s. In that period, the United States helped prevent El Salvador from becoming a more democratic, egalitarian, and economically successful state not simply by promoting free market ideas, but also by spending over a million dollars a day for a decade to support a military counterinsurgency operating through what a 1991 U.S. Defense Department report called "lavish brutality"—death squads willing and able to murder thousands of people (Grandin 2006, 71, 98, 105). These Latin American policies have served as a model for foreign policy in the Middle East, where lofty claims of promoting democracy and free market prosperity have been accompanied by the pillaging of resources and assets, rampant violence, and infrastructure destruction along with new systems of military rule backed by murder, torture, extra-legal detention, and long-term foreign occupation.

Within the United States, criminalization has long been used to control those whose occasional market winnings have been contrary to the moral order. The combined rise of market and moral ideology constructing poverty as the result of bad choices has helped to rationalize the growth of government control over those whose winnings threaten to undermine the gains of market elites. In the 1980s and 1990s, new policies of mass incarceration placed large numbers of poor people of color under militarized control, often for participating in the illegal drug market in the absence of better alternatives for jobs or family care. In addition, this growth of the criminal justice industry increased economic and political pressure on government to further divert government spending from social support for better choices to authoritarian control of choice. This criminalization of poverty has contributed to an escalating system of public and private violence in poor communities. Incarceration leaves many families and communities without access to support necessary for legitimate market success, thereby encouraging further dependence on violent gangs and illegal activity.

In addition to incarceration, the withdrawal of welfare support for poor mothers has subjected many poor families of color to the public control of the child welfare system, as children subject to unsafe communities and poverty are removed to the sometimes violent and often inadequately supported foster care system. Criminalization and militarization of immigration, combined with neoliberal policies driving many outside the United States to illegal migration and many employers within the United States to rely on cheaper or more vulnerable immigrant labor, has meant that work opportunities often lead to state detention and policing along with private denial of rights.

These policies of force and insecurity can nonetheless appear as beacons of freedom and opportunity through an ideological lens that dismisses and justifies this force and devastation as marginal or temporary side effects to those whose failures prove their moral and economic inferiority. In contrast, decreased policing and decriminalization of unlawful cost-shifting by powerful economic winners is excused by market and moral ideology romanticizing their gains as a sign of superior power, or rationalized as the inevitable price of encouraging entrepreneurial risk-taking and ambition that will lead to long-term prosperity.

Losing Choice and Control in Welfare Reform

One key symbol of the late twentieth-century ideological turn away from the welfare state to the free market (and to moral conservatism) was the 1996 federal legislation eliminating Aid to Families with Dependent Children (AFDC). Examining the role of choice and control in the political debate about this symbol of welfare reform sheds light on the reasoning that naturalizes government enforcement of losing choices and control over losers as enhanced market freedom.

The former AFDC program, which grew out of the New Deal's Social Security Act and was significantly expanded in the 1960s, provided an alternative to work income for impoverished single parents (mostly mothers). In its place, Congress established a new program, Temporary Assistance to Needy Families (TANF), which made access to benefits not a matter of individual right, but contingent on discretionary allocations from federal block grants to states (Personal Responsibility and Work Opportunity Reconciliation Act of 1996). This federal funding was subject to state compliance with a number of requirements designed to limit individual benefits, to move recipients into the workplace, to encourage marriage, and to discourage teenaged single parenting (Handler and Hasenfeld 1997).

In the prevailing political view, these restrictions increased individual opportunity for meaningful choice by replacing AFDC's policy of dependency on government benefits with a policy of market participation. Policy experts and popular opinion both held that government income support had, in fact, harmed impoverished single mothers and their children by distorting their choices about work, marriage, and family (Mead 2001). Indeed, AFDC tended to offer poor families losing choices. Not only were benefits often too low to sustain families in the short run, but also those benefits could hinder opportunities for long-term security because they were conditioned on low income levels that generally precluded formal work or marriage to a worker. As a result, many single mothers felt compelled to supplement this aid with informal work and family relationships that could exacerbate their economic instability, their exclusion from mainstream opportunities, and their vulnerability to violence or addiction.

But beyond the rhetoric of increased "work opportunity" (used in the title of the TANF legislation), in its design and implementation TANF has tended to produce tightened government control of single mothers in poverty, leaving many with much worse options. The change to TANF has restricted access to government income support that could sometimes provide an alternative source of income to single mothers seeking to escape harmful jobs, harmful child care, or harmful intimate relationships. By limiting that alternative (or making it more costly to access), TANF tends to give impoverished single mothers even less power than AFDC to hold out for better choices for work and family (McCluskey 2003).

By identifying formal wage work with a naturalized market and government welfare with perverse politics, free market ideology helped present that shift from bad to worse choices as a move toward legitimate freedom and opportunity for single mothers in poverty. Advocates of welfare reform characterized government income support for impoverished families as redistribution that shifts the real market costs of having and raising children onto those who do not voluntarily choose to assume those costs—that is, taxpayers, many of whom are struggling working parents themselves (McCluskey 2005). This view led to the conclusion that the high costs of work for single mothers (such as poor child care, low wages, high commuting expenses, or poor health) are a problem of irresponsible personal choices to bear and raise children without first establishing economic security (Solinger 2002).

This logic about responsible choice also rationalized TANF's increase in punitive regulation of welfare recipients' behavior. Government controls on individual choice, such as caps on benefits designed to reduce family size, marriage incentives, or workfare requirements, seem to be a way to *increase* responsible personal choice by ensuring that recipients pay what are deemed to be the real market costs of single parenting. In this view, social and legal structures that privatize much of the responsibility for raising children to gendered and un-paid work within the family are presumed to be natural and normal systems of voluntary choice. Similarly, this view presents jobs with low wages and poor working conditions as normal and necessary features of the labor market. This picture thereby obscures how low-wage work is produced by government poli-cies protecting the interests of employers and investors—such as the failure to adjust the minimum wage to keep up with inflation, or the failure to vigorously enforce antidiscrimination laws, or legal barriers to robust unionization. By obscuring the policies that help make single parenthood so costly, the use of government power to force single mothers to personally bear the high costs of combining work and family can seem not only to enhance their own free-dom, but to expand other people's choices. In the free market story, replacing government redistribution with efficient pricing maximizes overall growth, so that welfare reform could be perceived as a way of enhancing middle-class job opportunities rather than creating more low-wage competition, which is likely to depress wages.

In response to these free market arguments, advocates of more generous welfare support often portrayed welfare recipients as incapable of free choice. Instead of challenging the assumptions of the naturalized market, these argu-ments attempted to place single mothers outside of its reach by emphasizing the degree to which jobs, husbands, or meaningful birth control are unavailable, or the degree to which impoverished women or children lack the knowledge or freedom from others' control to make choices that rationally advance their interest (Graetz and Mashaw 1999). But such arguments can logically reinforce the free market attacks on welfare and its recipients. The structural barriers that often give poor mothers losing choices were frequently constructed as lying outside the market—produced by cultural constraints, individual incapacity, or exceptional market failures—rather than the product of a political economy normally structured to shift downward much of the costs of work and family (McCluskey 2003). If the barriers to choice are viewed as outside the normal market, welfare state protections from those bad choices will likewise seem de-signed to protect people from normal market choices. Free market opponents of welfare protections, in contrast, could claim that they were the ones who truly respected poor mothers by treating them as capable of making free and responsible choices to advance their family's interests in the market. By con-structing "liberal" defenders of welfare as denying recipients' power to choose, critics could portray liberal support for welfare as patronizing or even as a form of covert exploitation driven by a wasteful government bureaucracy and self-serving poverty industry.

At the same time, this liberal emphasis on welfare recipients' incapacity for good choices reinforced the conservative welfare critics' arguments for stricter government controls on poor mothers' behavior and for less generous support for their families. Popular and political opposition to welfare programs has long been fanned by accusations of widespread fraud. Portraying welfare recipients as freely rational but immoral actors, reform advocates used racial and sexual stereotypes to blame poor mothers for shirking the real costs of their own short-term, self-centered gain, indulgently choosing laziness over work and sexual profligacy or careless pregnancy over marriage while expecting taxpayers or their children to pick up the costs (Neubeck and Cazenave 2001; Gilens 1999).

In contrast, during the New Deal, advocates of the program that became AFDC explained that its purpose involved giving poor mothers *better* choices. Focusing on widowed white mothers, proponents emphasized the benefits of helping white, formerly middle class, women to stay out of wage work to increase maternal time with their children, allowing the family to go to church together, for example (Solinger 2002). The economic pressure for hasty remarriage, dangerous or exploitative work (in factories, farms, or prostitution), with children neglected or abandoned to orphanages or to their own work, was not in this view the real or necessary price of white widowhood. That is, this view of free and responsible choice did not require forcing poor widows to bear the market consequences of their irresponsible decision to enjoy the benefits of children and marriage without accumulating sufficient property wealth, life insurance, or paternal health to protect against the economic risks of a breadwinning father's premature death. Instead, welfare proponents constructed government support for white widows as a way to encourage virtuous maternal investment in their children's well-being for the benefit of society overall.

If government welfare support is understood to advance rights to better market choices, rather than to protect against bad market choices, then the recipients of that support will seem more deserving of political power as well as market gains. Of course, the question of whose winnings from market and political power are natural and normal to a good society, and whose gains are artificial and dangerous, will be answered by making moral judgments about what and who count in measuring social and personal good. What gets construed as an expansion of market-enhancing choice versus market-inhibiting coercion that cannot be a matter of technical cost-benefit calculation, scientific laws, supply and demand, or neat separation of economics from politics. As AFDC became more publicly identified with and available to unmarried mothers of color, inegalitarian race and gender ideology supported the idea that its benefits involve government coercion to protect irresponsible choice to the detriment of overall market growth and security. In short, to draw the line between choice and coercion, we need to decide who deserves the power to choose, and on what terms.

THE MILITARIZED MARKET IN CRISIS

Big Losers, Bad Choices

The 2008 financial market crisis starkly presented the two strategic steps linking market freedom with forceful control. First, it collapsed the market promise of dazzling expansion of choice into a reality of stunningly losing choices. Trillions of dollars of imagined financial and housing market gains evaporated, representing not innovative expansion of societal resources, but instead a system of speculation that shifted and concealed mounting risk with little sustainable benefit. Former federal banking regulator William K. Black explained that this crisis was produced by systemic, normalized fraud at all levels of the financial system, as high profits in financial and real estate markets increasingly depended on falsifying and hiding the high risk of loss (Moyers 2009). As the smoke and mirrors cleared, many financial institutions, businesses, governments, individuals, and organizations have been left with high debts and highly risky assets now recognized as having low value. In addition to producing these losses, the years of heavy investment in illusory, short-term, or narrowly distributed gains has siphoned off resources from what could have been more secure and widely spread economic growth.

Although the resulting heightened economic scarcity has exacerbated the losing choices for most, some of the central winners from the speculative bubble have been treated as too big to fail. Despite the overwhelming bipartisan unpopularity of financial market bailouts at the end of 2008, political and economic leaders confronted the reality that if the major Wall Street players were left to pay the bill for their ill-gotten and illusory gains, a bill large enough to destroy many existing financial institutions, then Wall Street would bring down Main Street along with it. In the current system, Main Streets around the world depend on Wall Street for capital and credit. Having and wielding market power, after all, means the power to control others' alternatives so that others will have no choice but to pay a high price for what they need. With Wall Street's gun at its head, Congressional Democrats and the new Obama administration put down their rhetoric of egalitarian economic and political change, and handed over virtually unimaginable amounts of government funds and credit to financial institutions that had been involved in producing colossal failure.

Along with bad economic choices, this crisis brought glimpses of heightened militarization and authoritarian control of the increasing numbers of devastated losers. This rule of force threatens to come at a number of levels. First, ongoing military misadventures in Iraq and Afghanistan, driven in part by political power to reap private gains from oil, arms sales, and defense contracts, present losing choices for those who might be concerned that the price of this military action is too high. Once military occupation and destruction has exacerbated socioeconomic and political insecurity, the resulting disorder threatens to spill over national borders and to fuel the further global growth of warfare and terror—becoming too big a failure to be abandoned (Scahill 2009). But continuing military control offers little hope of doing anything but increasing this threatening insecurity (Gall 2009). At the same time, efforts to address the economic crisis through increased funding for the structures that will lead to economic growth and security in the United States and beyond are hampered by the enormous, continued cost of these military quagmires (Berrigan 2009).

Second, severe economic devastation is likely to bring despair and the breakdown of security that leads both to a surge in the power of private violence to limit peoples' lives and freedom and also a surge in public force to secure against that violence (Klare 2009). A number of mass shootings and murder-suicides in the United States appear linked to loss of jobs or homes in the crisis. Around the globe, economic collapse threatens to exacerbate the decline of the power of some nations to effectively control violent drug gangs, warlords, slave traffickers, and pirates, leading again to the increased militarization of borders and to the militarization of work and business for many.

Third, as the Wall Street winners walk away from their failures with lavish bonuses, some in the United States seek to pin responsibility for massive economic failure on the usually suspected losers. Right-wing pundits have heaped blame for the underlying mortgage crisis on poor, urban people of color, on the dubious theory that liberal government antidiscrimination laws (enacted in earlier decades) forced hapless and defenseless bankers to provide irresponsible loans to those undeserving of homeownership. This new mobilization of timeworn blame may help justify or excuse further policies of punishment and control of the racialized poor.

Fourth, the economic crisis brings the risk that it will be more difficult to mobilize the government resources and power to effectively police the fraudulent risk-shifting that helped to produce the crisis. Government power to hold winners accountable to the law, and to prevent continued coercive winnings, may be jeopardized if the crisis increases the concentration of private power to control credit. In addition to increasing its political dependence on Wall Street financiers, the U.S. government may increase its efforts to seek funds from foreign governments whose economic might is partly tied to military power. That perceived dependence may exacerbate economic pressure to accommodate rather than challenge foreign policies undermining political dissent and human rights. Again, the result could be increasing unequal international and national policing of vulnerable market losers in a context where winners remain above the law.

Controlling Winners, Becoming Choosers

To solve the financial crisis, many free market advocates admit the need for new government funding and regulation, but they tend to advocate structuring that intervention to better enhance the power of market winners to withstand market cycles or "systemic" risk (Posner 2009). In the free market story, government support that strengthens the market must be sharply distinguished from government intervention that overpowers the market. Although that line between supporting and supplanting the market seems to protect individual choice from government power, it instead reserves government backing for the power to choose as an elite privilege.

To increase winning choices for those losing out in the recent crisis, market regulation would need to affirmatively create alternatives to existing market power. As long as the large banks, insurers, and other financial institutions control the supply of credit and capital, for example, then they will be able to continue to shift much of the costs of their gain to those who depend on that supply. If government financial backing simply replenishes the supply of credit and capital of existing institutions without major changes in control, it is likely that the credit supply will continue to be in need of further government replenishing. That funding is likely to be directed toward continuing to secure short-term returns for managers and investors at the expense of others.

If government is in fact a vital supplier of the credit needed to stabilize the market, then the price of that credit could be cheaper if the government supply were structured to effectively compete against, rather than cooperate with, those large failed institutions. It is logically possible, for example, that a government competitor could reduce risks through greater transparency and greater checks on illusory and fraudulent gains, and to prioritize sustainable gains to borrowers and society rather than short-term gains to managers and investors.

That public financial competitor could come in a variety of forms, such as new public financial institutions, increased government control and redirection of private institutions receiving government funds, or redirection of government funding toward smaller, specialized banks and other institutions designed to serve small business development and homeowners more than wealthy speculators.

However, the free market rhetoric celebrating choice and consumer sovereignty is not so easily turned toward policies that would meaningfully improve the choices for most borrowers and taxpayers. Despite the logic of joining public control to public funding, the free market story emphasizes that concentrated *private* power is necessary for economic growth, because democratic government can only create the *illusion* of abundance. In this theory, the market forces real and responsible choices because it is driven by natural laws of supply and demand rather than by political artifice. It warns that government control by definition avoids hard choices, giving into irrational demands of special interests to increase waste and scarcity in the long run. For example, this theory suggests that although populist outrage might push government-controlled financial institutions to cut executive compensation, if that compensation is below the presumed market price for skilled leadership, then it will lead to incompetent managers who will squander resources in the long run. Or, more plausibly, it cautions that government-controlled financial institutions will be induced to steer credit toward powerful political players and their constituents, regardless of real risk, diverting investment away from the most productive uses likely to increase and spread economic growth.

Despite dampened faith that the market naturally corrects private managers and investors who pursue short-term gains without regard for long-term costs, the free market story nonetheless presents this market failure as an aberration set apart from and against a norm of government failure. As a result, the prevailing regulatory response to the crisis has been to concentrate more control in a federal super-regulator protecting the super-financiers rather than to break up and segregate financial institutions so that they are more amenable to transparent and democratic regulation (Greider 2009, 2010).

The free market story rejects expanded and improved *private* choices, as well as expanded democratic control, on the theory that the benefits of the free market depend on controlling the bargaining power of nonelites. Another economic policy reform recently before Congress has been the Employee Free Choice Act, which would provide for unionization based on a process of signing membership cards rather than an electoral process regulated to give employers more power to contest and control union organizing efforts. Opposition to that law has gained broad political legitimacy based on arguments that increased unionization violates natural scarcity. According to legal expert Richard Epstein, this increased choice—and power—for workers will increase capital flight, thereby hurting not just politicians' campaign financing but also destroying jobs and depressing wages (Epstein 2009).

In effect, such arguments naturalize a given distribution of political and economic bargaining power as a mysterious, but ultimately beneficial, market transcending human intentions. That is, these arguments suggest that true freedom of choice for most consists of ceding power to make meaningful choices, submitting to the control of those with the most power to gain at most others' expense. This perverse conclusion follows from the theory that those elite gains naturally and normally represent the natural, normally beneficial moral, economic, and political order. That grim "choice" to lose meaningful choices retains substantial power to win popular appeal and expert approval because of a lack of faith in alternatives. In the face of concentrated and globalized market power, government promises of increased abundance often seem hollow.

This embrace of the market's losing choices out of a sense of ultimate choicelessness stems from an assumption that real power is beyond the control of democratic politics or law. The possibility that government can produce abundance—better choices—depends on the government being able to shift its power from controlling market losers to extending the rule of law over powerful economic winners. Fostering and sustaining better choices requires not just providing and controlling an alternative supply of resources, but also increasing democratic political control over the economic institutions that structure the market.

The recent financial crisis has reinforced cynicism about the possibilities for popular control, since it underscores the extent to which government, experts, debtors, and investors all can be swayed or misled into mistaking highly concentrated short-term gains to elites for broad-based security and prosperity. But the real alternative to the threat of undemocratic government power is not an imaginary free market beyond human agency, but instead a government and economy directly structured to enhance democratic ends. When political leaders assure us that public funding of private businesses such as American International Group or General Motors will not lead to public control, they evoke the Lochner era's passive idea of democracy. In that ideology, government action that sought better choices was itself a sign of dependency deserving of control and exclusion more than economic and political power.

Ironically, acquiescence in the market's bad choices has sometimes become a superficial badge of deserving citizenship status, differentiating market players who can dream of winning big from the real losers outside the game. A culture of white masculine military toughness can reinforce the idea that accepting rather than resisting losing choices is a sign of mature and rational independence. In this culture, choosing to lose rather than to change the rules in a game with others who are more powerful makes one a good sport, deserving of the approval of those with greater strength. In contrast, the prevailing culture often disparages government protection against economic insecurity as a feminized and racialized "nanny state" in which better economic choices became unrealistic or perverse nursery tales appropriate for "girlie men" not capable of heroic self-sacrifice (McCluskey 2007). For example, campaigning for Republican nominee John McCain in the 2008 presidential election, California Governor Arnold Schwarzenegger used images of feminized physical weakness—such as "skinny legs"—to mock opponent Obama's allegedly egalitarian economic policies as "unaffordable" and unsuitable for an "action hero" like McCain (Campanile 2008).

This sense of choicelessness pervaded the recent debate over health insurance, an urgently gaping hole in the U.S. welfare state that has widened as jobs providing private health insurance become more scarce in the wake of the financial crisis. Supporters of President Obama's health insurance reform initiative debated the question of creating a public option to compete with private insurance instead of simply expanding government support for the private insurers who have largely failed to provide adequate, affordable coverage. By framing public health insurance as an additional choice, proponents of the public option appropriated the market rhetoric that had helped undermine previous reform efforts.

In response, opponents of the public insurance alternative warned that departing from the free market threatens individual choice by offering choices that challenge the natural scarcity that supposedly brings real security. For example, prominent economist Gregory Mankiw criticized the idea that a public health insurance option might be able to provide better and cheaper coverage for most people (Mankiw 2009). He admitted that government health insurance, like Medicare, can produce major administrative savings, potentially increasing resources for health care. Furthermore, he emphasized that a government health insurer would be likely to reduce costs by wielding greater market bargaining power over health care providers. Nonetheless, using the standard argument of false abundance, Mankiw suggested that the "choice" to buy more health care at lower cost to patients would nonetheless be an irresponsible denial of market scarcity. Because some health care providers could lose money, and because some of those providers might have the power to protect their interests by reducing the quality or quantity of their services, he concluded that consumers would have worse choices in the end. His analysis assumed that the current prices charged by health care providers are natural, necessary, competitive, and beneficial to consumers (and providers) rather than the result of unequal public and private bargaining power by private insurance companies and specialized medical providers largely protected against competition and innovation. He raised the specter of government rationing to explain why we cannot expect much better choices from government reform of the health insurance market.

To create a political culture where government action for better choices appears more credible and more powerful, it will be necessary to challenge not only the naturalization of scarcity, but also the naturalization of economic losers as moral failures undeserving of better choices in a better economic and political game. The moral problem with *Lochner* was not simply that unelected judges imposed a normative preference for economic growth over equality—a policy choice better left to democratic process—rather, the Lochner era rulings were problematic in their moral belief that ordinary workers or consumers did not normally deserve to have equal legal power to control economic growth for their own interests. Similarly, TANF's rejection of the New Deal era's support for some single mothers reflects the moral and political idea that poor single mothers do not deserve to assert power at work and in the family (drawing on racial and sexual ideology), not a new emphasis on market choice over government protection. In the recent health insurance reform debate, "tea party" activists joined economic experts in insisting that freedom and dignity for most requires accepting the current situation of costly, scarce, and insecure health insurance protection. Finally, the losing choices presented to the general public in response to the recent financial crisis likewise depend on the construction of a public consisting of voters, workers, and consumers who are not deserving of the responsibility and power to choose—and so must have their organized power subject to the control of elite others, whether in a super-regulator or supervised union election.

In contrast, as a number of countries in Latin America have recently emerged from military control to greater democracy, their leaders have asserted political, legal, and cultural power to claim better economic choices for more of their citizens. Resisting the ideology of scarcity imposed by market and moral fundamentalism, these countries now provide a range of possible examples of democratic efforts to change the rules of law and market to seize public control of natural resources, and to organizing alternative supplies of credit and investment to increase the power to bargain for a greater share of the gains of economic development.

In conclusion, the rhetorical and ideological separation of the market from government helps legitimate constraints on meaningful individual choice by naturalizing control and coercion as the result of beneficial and liberating economic forces. Substituting overt government power and control for the illusion of natural market freedom does not, however, necessarily bring the increased freedom and security of better choices for most. Government involvement in the financial crisis, in health care, and in welfare programs is not naturally separate or separable from coercive and unequal market bargaining power any more than the market is separate from government.

To undo the two strategic steps whereby public and private structures produce losing choices and pressure for increased control of those who bear those losses, we must translate the question of choice into a question of power. The Lochner era rulings were wrong because they presented power as a matter of freedom from coercion separate from the freedom to organize, institutionalize, and regulate the rules determining the terms and boundaries of individual choices. Government regulation of the market has often failed to provide better choices—whether for workers, single mothers, or borrowers—not because that intervention has been coercive or paternalistic, and not because better choices inevitably lie outside human power. Instead, effective policies providing better choices and more capacity for freedom require structures aimed at changing the power to bargain for a greater share of resources both in state and market. Those policies of better choices require challenging a moral order in which economic vulnerability is linked to moral, legal, and political incapacity. More equal government economic security is compatible with, and indeed necessary for, more political and economic freedom. Achieving both freedom and security depends on a legal system structured to assume more equal authority to have better choices and more equal responsibility for choosing to gain in ways that minimize others' losses.

REFERENCES

Berrigan, Frida. 2009. Is the next defense budget a stimulus package? *The Nation.* March 30.

Campanile, Carl. 2008. Arnold kicks sand in "skinny" Obama's face pumps up Mac rally. *New York Post.* November 1.

Casebeer, Kenneth. 1995. Aliquippa: The company town and contested power in construction of the law. *Buffalo Law Review* 43:617–88.

Enrich, Peter D. 1996. Saving the states from themselves: Commerce clause constraints on state tax incentives for business. *Harvard Law Review* 110:377–468.

Epstein, Richard. 2009. *The case against the Employee Free Choice Act*. Stanford, Calif.: Hoover Institution Press.

Gall, Charlotte. 2009. U.S. faces resentment in Afghan region. *New York Times*. July 3.

Gilens, Martin. 1999. *Why Americans hate welfare: Race, media, and the politics of anti-poverty policy*. Chicago: University of Chicago Press.

Graetz, Michael J., and Jerry L. Mashaw. 1999. *True security: Rethinking American social insurance*. New Haven, Conn.: Yale University Press.

Grandin, Greg. 2006. *Empire's workshop: Latin America, the United States and the rise of the new imperialism*. New York: Henry Holt and Company.

Greider, William. 2009. Obama's false reform. *The Nation*. July 13.

———. 2010. Battling the banksters. *The Nation*. July 19.

Hale, Robert L. 1952. *Freedom through law: Public control of private governing power*. New York: Columbia University Press.

Handler, Joel F., and Yeheskel Hasenfeld. 1997. *We the poor people: Work, poverty and welfare*. New Haven, Conn.: Yale University Press.

Kessler-Harris, Alice. 2001. *In pursuit of equity: Women, men, and the quest for economic citizenship in 20th-century America*. New York: Oxford University Press.

Klare, Michael T. 2009. Global crime wave? A syndrome of crime, violence, and repression on the way. *The Huffington Post*. April 8.

Lochner v. New York, 198 U.S. 45 (1905).

Muller v. Oregon, 208 U.S. 412 (1908).

Mankiw, N. Gregory. 2009. The pitfalls of the public option. *New York Times*. June 28.

McCluskey, Martha T. 2003. Efficiency and social citizenship: Challenging the neoliberal attack on the welfare state. *Indiana Law Journal* 78:783–876.

———. 2005. The politics of economics in welfare reform. In *Feminism confronts homo economicus*, ed. Martha A. Fineman and Terence Dougherty, 193–224. Ithaca, N.Y.: Cornell University Press.

———. 2007. Thinking with wolves: Left legal theory after the right's rise. *Buffalo Law Review* 54:1191–297.

Mead, Lawrence M. 2001. The politics of conservative welfare reform. In *The new world of welfare*, ed. Rebecca M. Blank and Ron Haskins, 201–22. Washington, D.C.: The Brookings Institution.

Moyers, Bill. 2009. Madoff was a piker: America's big banks are a far larger fraudulent Ponzi scheme (interviewing William K. Black). *Alternet*, April 6. http://www.alternet .org/economy/135161/moyers_journal:_maddoff_was_a_piker_--_america%27s _bigbanks_are_a_far_larger_fraudulent_ponzi_scheme/.

NLRB v. Jones & Laughlin Steel Corp., 332 U.S. 823 (1947).

Neubeck, Kenneth J., and Noel A. Cazenave. 2001. *Welfare racism: Playing the race card against America's poor*. New York: Routledge.

Nice, Julie A. 2008. No scrutiny whatsoever: Deconstitutionalization of poverty law, dual rules of law & dialogic default. *Fordham Urban Law Journal* 35:629–71.

Personal Responsibility and Work Opportunity Reform and Reconciliation Act of 1996, Pub. L. No. 104-193, U.S.C.C.A.N. (110 Stat.) 2105.

Phillips-Fein, Kim. 2009. *Invisible hands: The making of the conservative movement from the New Deal to Reagan*. New York: W. W. Norton.

Posner, Richard A. 2009. *A failure of capitalism: The crisis of '08 and the descent into depression*. Cambridge, Mass.: Harvard University Press.

Scahill, Jeremy. 2009. 238 bases, 170,000 pieces of equipment, 140,000 troops, and an army of mercenaries: The logistical nightmare in Iraq. *Alternet*, March 30. http://www.alternet.org/story/133676/.

Solinger, Rickie. 2002. *Beggars and choosers: How the politics of choice shapes adoption, abortion, and welfare in the U.S.* New York: Hill and Wang.

Steinfels, Peter. 1979. *The neoconservatives: The men who are changing America's politics*. New York: Simon and Schuster.

Sunstein, Cass R. 1987. Lochner's legacy. *Columbia Law Review* 87:873–919.

———. 2006. *The second bill of rights: FDR's unfinished revolution and why we need it more than ever*. New York: Basic Books.

Yergin, Daniel, and Joseph S. Stanislaw. 2002. *The commanding heights: The battle for the world economy*. New York: Free Press.

CHAPTER TWO

Poverty as an Everyday State of Exception

JULIE A. NICE

THE WAR ON WELFARE

Among developed nations, the United States boasts one of the highest rates of per capita income, while maintaining the highest child poverty rate and one of the highest overall poverty rates (whether measured in relative or absolute terms). Income inequality is widening, as our national policies over the last three decades have doubled the share of after-tax income going to the top one percent of households and have tripled the income gap between rich and poor.[1] Economic insecurity is widespread, with two-thirds of all Americans turning to welfare at some point between the ages of twenty and sixty-five, and 90 percent of those seeking out welfare more than once (Rank 2004, 104–05). Yet, lawmakers have surrendered their brief war on poverty and instead declared war on welfare, demonizing impoverished mothers who fail to secure sufficient income for their children through either work or marriage (Handler and Hasenfeld 2007). In short, the metaphor of war has reversed its aim, no longer focused on ending poverty, but now targeting welfare dependence as the greater danger.

By its own terms, the war on welfare has been an astounding success, with the average number of recipients reduced by approximately 70 percent over the last fifteen years.[2] This dramatic elimination of over ten million recipients from the welfare rolls has challenged the canonical thesis advanced by Piven and Cloward (1971) that the state keeps poor people within its ranks to regulate their behavior. While the less than four million recipients who remain on the welfare rolls continue to be subjected to comprehensive regulation and surveillance of their work and family lives, the reality is that most impoverished families have been abandoned by the state (Gilliom 2001). They are left to the disciplining vagaries of the low-wage labor market, where one quarter of American workers receive low wages (which is double the average percentage of low-wage workers in other developed nations). Yet, the American commitment to neoliberalism appears to have survived the recent stress test provided by the longest and deepest recession since the Great Depression. Perhaps more surprisingly, only a few constitutional law scholars identify anything extraordinary or invidious about the American treatment of poor people (e.g., Forbath 1999; Hershkoff 1999; Loffredo 1993, 2007). Rather, the mainstream consensus perpetuates the belief that poor people have been included within the constitutional regime in standard fashion.

This chapter is grounded on two observations departing from this mainstream consensus: first, the interests of poor people are largely absent from discourse within the realms of law, policy, and politics in the United States; and second, meaningful concern about the plight of poor people specifically, and about economic justice generally, is virtually unintelligible within American law. I have characterized this elsewhere as a "dialogic default" on the issue of economic justice (Nice 2008). More specifically, poor people lack meaningful constitutional protection, legal entitlement, policy consideration, or political mobilization, leaving them to eke out a meager subsistence that brings into stark relief the "bare life" in the state of abandonment so provocatively imagined by Italian philosopher Giorgio Agamben. This chapter explores how American law has accomplished the abandonment of poor people in ways Agamben theorized, particularly through excluding by including ("inclusive exclusion") and by treating poverty as an *everyday* "state of exception" that both constitutes and legitimates abandonment. Agamben's analysis thus brings into focus what otherwise remains blurred in the background, namely, how the inclusive exclusion of poor people traps them in a perpetual relation of abandonment. Agamben's analysis seems to predict no relief for the dire straits of poor people precisely because the ambiguity of the relation of abandonment makes it so very difficult, if not impossible, to break.

The first part of this chapter briefly summarizes some of Agamben's pertinent insights, and the second part uses his conceptualization to consider the specific juridical mechanisms that accomplish the abandonment of poor people. These methods include: first, the doctrinal deconstitutionalization that has created dual rules of law based on economic status; second, the legislative disentitlement effectuated by welfare reform; third, the political economy of welfare policy experimentation that has culminated in "reverse capture" of researchers by government policymakers; and, finally, the general political demobilization of those most impoverished. The chapter's third part offers a foray into a comparative perspective, highlighting two prominent social welfare rights cases from outside the United States. Finally, the fourth part reconsiders how rights matter to poor people.

The ultimate conclusion is two-sided. First, on the downside, what the state has secured through law is not only the abandonment of those most vulnerable, but also their perpetual exposure to bare life in a state of economic insecurity. Second, on the upside, insisting on a dialogue about rights for poor people might open the very space Agamben imagines for what he calls "human action, which once claimed for itself the name of 'politics'" (Agamben 2005, 88).

AGAMBEN AND THE STATE OF EXCEPTION

Interest in Agamben's (1998, 2005) ideas has intensified since the September 11, 2001 attacks and the government's reactive "war on terror," defended on the basis of the purported necessity of making exceptions to the normal rule of law. Persistent questions regarding the legitimacy of these governmental reactions correspond well with Agamben's deep concern about the risks associated with the historical pattern in which the "state of exception" tends to become the norm.[3] The boldness of Agamben's analysis is accentuated by his allegorical use of the concentration camp to represent what happens when the exception becomes the rule.[4] Understandably, some critics have condemned Agamben's analogy to the unique horrors of Nazi genocide. But, for Agamben, his allegorical use of the concentration camp is part of his larger project to understand how it became possible for the state to protect life, on the one hand, and to authorize killing on the other. Agamben positions himself as disagreeing with Foucault's thesis that modern politics commenced with the shift to a biopolitical model of disciplinary power, and instead traces biopolitics back to classical times by invoking the figure of *homo sacer* (sacred man or sacred life) or "bare life" (Agamben 1998, 88). *Homo sacer* was the figure from Roman law who was cast out from the community and could be murdered with impunity, but could not be killed for sacrifice, presumably because his life was no longer deemed worthy. In speaking of *homo sacer*, Agamben is not simply speaking of natural life, but of "life exposed to death." For his purpose, what is especially important is that, from as far back as Roman law, *homo sacer* or bare life was included in the legal regime only for the purpose of being excluded.

He argues that the state of exception not only accomplishes the exclusion of bare life, but also captures bare life within the political order. As the borders between exclusion and inclusion begin to blur, bare life becomes both subject and object of political order. In Agamben's view, modern democracy began when the state made human life into its object and, correspondingly, when people began to present themselves as the subject, rather than the object, of political power. Moreover, modern politics is founded on this paradox—that bare life may be killed (without committing homicide), yet not sacrificed (by sanctioned forms of execution). It is not the social contract, but rather the exclusive inclusion of bare life on which sovereign violence and power are founded (Agamben 1998, 106–09). The modern paradox in which bare life finds itself is possible precisely because the state of exception has become the dominant paradigm of government.

As examples of "profane and banal" exercises of modern political power, Agamben compares government experiments conducted on Jews in Germany with those on death row prisoners in the United States. He queries how it came to be that the lack of an ethical limit for such experiments in the totalitarian Nazi regime could also occur within American democracy. Agamben rejects the theory-of-state explanation, which posits that the type of political system explains these atrocities. Rather, he argues that the particular status of the groups was decisive in both cases. Most relevant for the purpose here, he emphasizes the fact that both Jews in Germany and death row prisoners in the United States were excluded from their political communities by the lack of rights. Agamben specifically identifies the deprivation of or lack of rights as marking what he calls the "state of abandonment." He prescribes that what must be investigated are "the juridical procedures and deployments of power by which human beings could be so completely deprived of their rights and prerogatives that no act committed against them could appear any longer as a crime" (Agamben 1998, 171).

As this brief overview reveals, rights turn out to play a central role in Agamben's analysis. The paradox of modern politics, in his view, is that bare life's exposure to abandonment and death functions both as the foundation for establishing sovereign power, which includes the power to deny rights, and also as the basis for leveraging rights to oppose sovereign power. Even when individuals seek to secure rights in an attempt to liberate them from sovereign power, they further inscribe their lives within the state order, thus simultaneously securing sovereign power. Understanding this rights paradox is necessary to understanding how democracy is forced into "complicity with its most implacable enemy" (Agamben 1998, 10).

Mirroring the paradox of modern politics that he examines, a rights paradox emerges within Agamben's own reasoning. On one hand, it seems axiomatic to read Agamben as rejecting rights as a meaningful solution to the problem of state power. He argues straightforwardly that rights serve as the very means for subjecting the lives of individuals to sovereign power. On the other hand, Agamben identifies the deprivation of rights as the very marker and means of state oppression. He views the absence or deprivation of rights as constructing the relation of abandonment of individuals by the state. In sum, Agamben treats both granting rights and denying rights as problematic, creating what appears to be a rights paradox of his own.

What I identify as a rights paradox within Agamben's analysis might be understood alternatively as merely exemplifying his conceptualization of the state of exception. In other words, the state uses the granting of rights as a means to secure power over the lives of individuals, and simultaneously reserves the power, thus secured, to deprive individuals of those rights. But the question remains: if rights are at least part of the problem, are they too tainted to be part of the solution? In other words, can rights function only as a constraint and not as a resource? Or, to put the question in terms closer to Agamben's, if rights are the means for distinguishing between inclusion and exclusion, and if identifying the point of distinction between inclusion and exclusion is essential to avoid the horrors of state-sponsored violence, then might rights serve as a mechanism for resisting the state of exception?

Agamben does not appear to directly answer the question of whether rights retain the capacity to protect against the dangers inherent in the state of exception. What he clearly conveys is a sense of the potential for, and urgency of, human action to invent a new politics no longer founded on the exclusion of bare life. Implicit in Agamben's analysis is a rejection of the notion that progress will inevitably protect against such dire predictions. He appears to believe, rather fervently, that humans must choose between either continuing the state of exception that legitimates violence or imagining a new politics.

In the meantime, Agamben generously leaves space for others to fill in the gaps, which nicely matches the nature and methodology of his own work. This leaves the task of imagining what this new politics might be. Specifically, can legal rights and/or political action as we currently know them be used to protect against the subjection of bare life to state power? Agamben paints a stark image of the negative response. In describing law's abandonment of bare life, Agamben often invokes Kafka's image of life subsisting in the village at the foot of the castle on the mountain. By evoking Kafka's image, Agamben brings to the foreground the treatment of a group that seems to be trapped in an everyday state of exception, namely, poor people. The possibility of applying his theory to the treatment of those most impoverished is not lost on Agamben, who specifically notes that the elimination of poor people through development is an example of abandonment in the "zone of indistinction" between life and law. Moreover, Agamben especially emphasizes the nebulousness of the relation of abandonment, which makes it virtually impossible to escape and which seems to both predict and ensure a virtual rule of perpetuity for poverty.

POVERTY AS AN EVERYDAY STATE OF EXCEPTION

Poor people in the United States struggle to subsist everyday, with their eyes on the castles built with American wealth. As John Gilliom describes welfare families, "They are frightened, often lonely, women and children who live on the edge of hunger and homelessness and in fear of their caseworkers and their neighbors. . . . They lack a knowledge of the system of rules and procedures that engulfs them. . . . They lack effective political or legal representation and they even lack the formal legal position that might lead to a mobilization of rights. Without the knowledge, the forum, or the resources to wage any sort of battles about what bothers them, they are stuck in a cycle of powerlessness" (2001, 90). I turn now to identifying how each avenue for redress has been closed to those most impoverished, beginning with constitutional law.

Deconstitutionalization

The American judiciary has failed to provide equal constitutional protection for poor people. While poor plaintiffs prevailed in several early and outlier decisions, their claims have received the weakest form of constitutional review for nearly forty years. Yet, most constitutional experts appear to believe that poor people's claims are treated in a standard manner. As a technical matter, their claims are included in the sense of being subjected to what looks like normal judicial review. Upon closer examination, the courts effectively exclude poor people from judicial protection by employing a sort of categorical immunization that instead protects the government's social or economic policies from judicial invalidation (Nice 2008). This seeming contradiction between following the rule and making an exception exemplifies what Agamben identifies as "inclusive exclusion."

While mainstream constitutional law scholars appear to treat this effective exclusion of poor people from constitutional protection as natural, history demonstrates that this doctrinal treatment is not the only plausible interpretation of the United States Constitution. During the mid-twentieth century, the

Supreme Court managed to frame economic justice in constitutional terms (Goluboff 2007). These historic case examples demonstrate the critical point that, contrary to most contemporary constitutional orthodoxy, it is in fact possible for courts to imagine and to enforce meaningful protection and inclusion of poor people.

INCLUDING FOR INCLUSION'S SAKE. In 1941, the Supreme Court refused a state's request to declare an exception that would have denied poor people regular constitutional protection. In *Edwards v. California*, the Court overturned the criminal conviction of Fred Edwards, who by transporting his indigent brother-in-law from Texas to live with him and his wife in California, violated the state's law that criminalized bringing an indigent person into the state. Writing long before the Court had developed its contemporary doctrinal scheme for protecting individual rights under the Due Process and Equal Protection Clauses of the Fourteenth Amendment, the Court ruled that California's barrier against poor people imposed an unconstitutional burden on interstate commerce. The Court, recognizing that it was being asked to depart from the constitutional norm, explicitly rejected California's request for an exception that would allow the state to protect against what it called the "moral pestilence" of poverty and paupers.[5]

The following year, in a well-known decision not typically associated with rights for poor people, the Court heard an appeal brought by Jack Skinner challenging Oklahoma's decision to sterilize him based on that state's early version of a three-strikes law for habitual criminals. Skinner was convicted of stealing chickens, followed by two other armed robberies, and the state subsequently ordered his sterilization. What troubled the Supreme Court was that the state did not authorize sterilization for white-collar criminals who embezzled funds, but instead limited sterilization to those convicted three times of crimes involving "moral turpitude." Emphasizing the "clear, pointed, unmistakable discrimination" between someone who embezzled funds as compared with someone who stole chickens from a coop, the Court in *Skinner v. Oklahoma* for the first time invoked "strict scrutiny"—its strong form of judicial review—and invalidated the state's discrimination as a violation of the Equal Protection Clause.[6]

Perhaps the most well-known decisions protecting poor people involved indigent criminal defendants who could not afford court fees required for pursuing their defense. In the path-breaking case regarding equal access to the courts, Judson Griffin and James Crenshaw asked to appeal their armed robbery convictions but could not afford the cost of preparing the required trial transcript. Illinois refused to waive the fee for preparation of the trial transcript.

Griffin and Crenshaw argued that this denial of appellate review was because of their poverty, and that such an invidious discrimination violated the Due Process and Equal Protection Clauses. In its 1956 decision in *Griffin v. Illinois*, the United States Supreme Court agreed.[7] The Court reasoned that the Constitution, like the Magna Carta, requires the government to strive constantly to achieve "equal justice for poor and rich, weak and powerful alike." Although the Illinois transcript requirement applied equally to all criminal defendants, the Court ruled that it must invalidate even a neutral law when it is "grossly discriminatory" against poor people in operation. Conceding that Illinois had no constitutional duty to provide any criminal appellate review, the Court held that, once Illinois chose to provide appellate review, it could not discriminate based on poverty because the inability to pay costs is irrelevant to guilt or innocence, just as race is irrelevant.

The Court later extended its protection of poor people from the context of criminal law into the realms of both political and procedural rights. In 1966, the Supreme Court held that Annie Harper should not be deprived of the opportunity to vote in state and local elections simply because she was unable to pay the state poll tax. In *Harper v. Virginia State Board of Elections*, the Court reasoned that wealth is irrelevant to voter qualifications and, therefore, requiring a fee for voting constituted an invidious discrimination. In support, the Court emphasized that lines drawn on the basis of wealth—like those of race—have been "traditionally disfavored."[8]

Perhaps emboldened by this momentum, John Kelly and other welfare recipients challenged New York's policy of terminating welfare benefits without a prior opportunity for recipients to be heard. In its landmark 1970 decision in *Goldberg v. Kelly*, the Supreme Court held that a statutory entitlement to the ongoing receipt of welfare benefits constituted a type of property interest that the government could not deprive without satisfying procedural due process requirements. As a result, the Court held that the government must afford a welfare recipient an opportunity to be heard prior to termination of benefits.[9]

INCLUDING FOR EXCLUSION'S SAKE. Perhaps the progressive logic of these victories served as a sort of wake-up call for some sleeping neoliberal giant. Shortly after holding that welfare recipients must be afforded procedural due process protections in *Goldberg*, the Supreme Court immediately retrenched and announced the exception for poverty to which it has adhered ever since. *Dandridge v. Williams* established the Court's contemporary doctrinal rule that courts should apply only the weak form of rationality review to challenges of governmental regulation in the social or economic arena. The case involved a constitutional challenge brought by Linda Williams against Maryland's law setting a maximum grant amount for families receiving welfare benefits, which denied any additional allotment for any child born after the family's first two children. Williams argued that the maximum grant discriminated against larger families compared to smaller ones. Maryland argued the maximum family grant served two governmental interests: first, encouraging welfare recipients to work; and second, ensuring welfare families would not be treated more favorably than working poor families (who do not usually receive a wage increase upon the birth of an additional child, as lawyers for the state emphasized).

The Supreme Court upheld the maximum grant, even though there was no evidence that Maryland's purported purposes were the actual purposes (which appeared to be merely reducing welfare costs). Nor was there evidence that the maximum grant directly advanced the government's purported purposes. In other words, there was no evidence that family size was actually relevant to the goal of encouraging employment, or that the amount of the maximum grant was actually related to the amount of minimum wages earned by low-wage workers. The Court invoked the weak form of judicial review and established the general rule that a social welfare regulation would be upheld, even if "illogical" and "unscientific," so long as courts could conceive any legitimate governmental interest to which the regulation might rationally relate. This lenient test for welfare regulations apparently served to alleviate the Court's structural concerns about respecting the horizontal separation of national powers as well as the vertical nation-state balance of federalism, as reflected in the Court's emphasis that the Constitution does not empower federal courts to second-guess social policy choices made by the states.

Forty years later, *Dandridge* is still cited as the primary precedent for allowing only the weak form of judicial review for social and economic legislation. This weak review typically means poor people will not receive judicial protection from governmental policies and practices that disadvantage them. The *Dandridge* declaration has become boilerplate: "the intractable economic, social and even philosophical problems presented by public welfare assistance programs are not the business of this Court." [10]

Although the *Dandridge* decision certainly came close, it did not go so far as to declare that challenges to discrimination against poor people fail to state any cognizable constitutional claim. Nor did it deem such poverty-based challenges to be nonjusticiable and therefore excluded from judicial review. Thus, one effect of *Dandridge* is that such claims are technically included within the system of constitutional adjudication. But, *Dandridge* establishes the presumption that most, if not all, claims of discrimination or disparate impact based on poverty should be rejected. In applying only its weak form of judicial review, the Supreme Court established a standard that protects social welfare regulation from judicial invalidation and thereby denies judicial protection for those most impoverished. It is as if the Court welcomed poor people through the front courthouse door, only to whisk them out through the back door. In other words, in Agamben's terms, it includes poor people so as to exclude them. *Dandridge* thus appears to be a paradigmatic example of inclusive exclusion.

Following *Dandridge*, the Court has routinely used the weak form of judicial review for claims involving poverty. In doing so, the Court has adeptly avoided applying its normal doctrinal test for determining whether a governmental action either affecting a disadvantaged class or relying on an irrelevant classification might justify more searching judicial scrutiny. Whether or not targeting poor people as a class or relying on poverty as a classification would be deemed suspicious or "suspect" matters a great deal for normal constitutional analysis. If targeting a class or relying on a classification is deemed suspect, then courts typically heighten judicial scrutiny of the government's action. This heightened scrutiny effectively requires the government to meet a higher level of justification and more frequently results in protection of those affected.

After mandating "strict scrutiny" as a strong form of judicial review for governmental actions based on race, the Court developed criteria for considering whether higher judicial scrutiny is needed when the government acts on the basis of other characteristics, such as sex, disability, and age.[11] To determine whether targeting a class or relying on a classification is suspect, the Supreme Court has identified factors for consideration, including: (1) whether the affected group has suffered historical discrimination, (2) whether the affected group lacks sufficient political power to protect itself, (3) whether the classification of the group is based on a characteristic which is immutable or difficult to change, and (4) whether that characteristic is irrelevant to an individual's abilities.

Applying the standard doctrinal test to poverty, the basic question would be: are disadvantages imposed by the government upon poor people or governmental classifications based on poverty sufficiently "suspect" as to deserve heightened judicial scrutiny? Challenging the orthodox belief among constitutional scholars, I have argued the Court has never applied the normal criteria in any case deemed to involve discrimination based on poverty (Nice 2008). If the Court actually considered these factors in a case directly affecting poor people, one wonders how the justices could deny that poor people have suffered historical discrimination and are powerless to influence the political system without financial resources, and also that they are defined by a characteristic which is difficult to change and which is irrelevant to an individual's actual abilities.[12]

IDENTIFYING JUDICIAL MANEUVERS AND SCHOLARLY COMPLICITY. A close examination of the full text of the post-*Dandridge* decisions—rather than merely the summaries or edited excerpts typically included in mainstream law textbooks—reveals various doctrinal sleights of hand that accomplished and perpetuated the inclusive exclusion of poor people from equal judicial protection of their constitutional rights. For example, in the leading case of *San Antonio Independent School District v. Rodriguez*, residents of a San Antonio public school district claimed that the school financing system disadvantaged students based on the low property tax base of the school district. Specifically, plaintiffs claimed that, within the city of San Antonio, the wealthier school district spent two-thirds more dollars per pupil than the poorer school district. Based on its examination of the record, the Court found no evidence that poor people were concentrated in poorer school districts, and it therefore *refused* to treat the challenge as one based on discrimination against poor people as a group. The Court instead treated the challenge as based on discrimination against residents of poorer school districts, and it then applied the normal criteria and squarely held that discrimination based on school district residency was not sufficiently "suspect" to warrant heightened judicial protection.[13]

Although the Court refused to treat the *Rodriguez* claim as either based on discrimination against poor people as a class or based on poverty as a classification, constitutional scholars nonetheless extracted several key statements from the opinion (which were extraneous to the Court's holding), and used these dicta to interpret the decision more broadly. Admittedly, the Court in *Rodriguez* opined that absolute equality is not required where wealth is concerned, and also noted that wealth discrimination alone had never been deemed sufficient for invoking its strict form of judicial scrutiny. After putting these few sentences back into the context of the entire decision, however, it is clear that these points were not necessary to the Court's actual holding and also were contradicted by more specific findings in the decision. Such dicta normally would not be treated as part of a decision's formal holding. Nonetheless, the *Rodriguez* decision is frequently cited for the purported holding that poor people are not a suspect class and that governmental discrimination against poor people must receive only the weak form of judicial review.[14] In fact, the Court had refused to treat the case as involving discrimination based on poverty. Thus, in effect, scholars picked up where the Court left off and thereby completed the task of excluding poor people from constitutional protection, all the while insisting—again, quite correctly as a technical matter—that poor people have been included in the constitutional regime.

Soon after *Rodriguez*, another maneuver in a pair of abortion funding cases closed a remaining loophole. In *Maher v. Roe*, decided in 1977, the Court upheld the federal ban on Medicaid funding for an elective abortion, explaining that it "had never held that financial need alone identifies a suspect class for equal protection analysis."[15] Three years later, in *Harris v. McRae*, the Court upheld the federal ban on Medicaid funding even for an abortion medically necessary to protect the health or life of the mother. Here, the Court worded the critical statement differently, asserting that the Court had "held repeatedly that poverty, standing alone, is not a suspect classification."[16] Noting that it had *never held* that poverty *is* a suspect classification is a very different claim than later claiming that it had *held* that poverty *is not* a suspect classification. No case decided between these two statements explicates or justifies this pertinent difference.[17] Moreover, poverty was not standing "alone" in these cases, but was linked with the fundamental right to choose whether to continue or terminate a pregnancy, which, at that time, could have served as an independent basis for triggering heightened judicial scrutiny.

The Supreme Court and commentators thus appear to agree that relying on poverty as a classification or targeting poor people as a class will not be treated as "suspect" and, therefore, will receive only the weak form of judicial review. In short, in Agamben's terms, while constitutional jurisprudence appears to include poverty within its regular doctrinal analysis, it effectively excludes poor people from substantive constitutional protection.

ESTABLISHING DOUBLE STANDARDS FOR HAVES AND HAVE-NOTS. What ultimately emerges from this inclusive exclusion of poor people within the American constitutional regime are dual rules of law; in other words, two different systems of legal rules that treat those who are wealthier more favorably than those who are poorest. The path-breaking work of the late constitutional and poverty law scholar Jacobus tenBroek identified dual systems of family law for the haves and have-nots. Meticulously documenting the differences between the two family law systems, Professor tenBroek described them as "different in origin, different in history, different in substantive provisions, different in administration, different in orientation and outlook." He described the family law system regulating underprivileged families as "heavily political and measurably penal" while the family law system managing more fortunate families remains private, nonpolitical, and less penal (tenBroek 1964, 257–58).

Maintaining dual systems of law frequently requires disregarding the normal level of judicial protection for a constitutional right. In one particularly striking example in 1987, the Supreme Court refused to apply its usual protection of property from governmental taking when the property was child support received by a child living in an impoverished family. The issue in *Bowen v. Gilliard* was whether the state could take child support from one child to repay welfare benefits needed by other members of the child's family. Because state law required child support payments to be used for the child, such child support clearly constituted the child's property. But, welfare rules required child support received for any child living with family members who requested welfare benefits to be assigned to the state. Under its normal doctrinal analysis for a governmental taking of property, the Court would have applied heightened scrutiny to determine whether the government's taking was justified. The Court instead ratcheted its level of scrutiny down to its weak form of rationality review precisely because welfare benefits were involved. The Court once again cited the *Dandridge* exception to the constitutional norm, repeating the now familiar mantra: "the intractable economic, social, and even philosophical problems presented by public welfare assistance programs are not the business of this Court."[18]

CONSIDERING CONTEMPORARY CASES. The *Dandridge* deference to the government for social and economic legislation remains the default standard for constitutional claims brought by poor people today. Several recent decisions highlight the extent of this inclusive exclusion of poor people. Consider, for example, what has occurred when the maximum grant has been combined with the assignment of child support. Following federal welfare reform in 1996, some states imposed maximum grants in the form of a family cap, which denies any welfare benefits for children born after the family began receiving welfare benefits. Some states, nonetheless, required the assignment of child support received for the capped child even though this child was not receiving welfare benefits, thus effectively taking the capped child's support payments so as to repay the government for welfare benefits provided to the child's other family members. In its 2003 decision in *Williams v. Martin*, a federal district court in Georgia combined *Dandridge*'s upholding of a maximum grant with *Bowen*'s upholding of assignment of child support to justify its holding that the assignment of child support payments for capped children is not an unconstitutional taking.[19]

Another recent example from the Ninth Circuit Court of Appeals (usually perceived to be one of the more liberal federal courts) extends the now-familiar dual rules of law for the haves and have-nots within the realm of criminal procedure. In *Sanchez v. County of San Diego,* the Ninth Circuit ruled that San Diego County could require welfare applicants to be subjected to a home "walk-through" conducted by badge-carrying officials trained to search for evidence of welfare fraud, contraband, child abuse, or any other criminal violations. An applicant's failure to give her express consent for such a search would trigger the denial of her welfare application. The Ninth Circuit rejected concerns about any coercive effect on a welfare applicant, reasoning that "a person's relationship with the state can reduce that person's expectation of privacy even within the sanctity of the home."[20] The court's assertion that one's dependence on welfare alters one's constitutional rights was remarkably candid.

The dissenting judges characterized the decision as "nothing less than an attack on the poor," noting that the Fourth Amendment normally protects against unreasonable searches by prohibiting the government from conducting generalized fraud investigations without individual suspicion when the recipients of government benefits are not poor.[21] Nonetheless, the United States Supreme Court refused to review the case, thus allowing the Ninth Circuit decision to stand.[22]

The extreme deference courts afford to the government's social and economic legislation has become routine. The days are long gone when dissenting members of the Supreme Court denounced this weak review as "no scrutiny whatsoever" or as "only the most perfunctory examination."[23] Regardless of how well established it is, this standard makes a mockery of rationality. For example, consider the recent Seventh Circuit Court of Appeals decision in *Turner v. Glickman.* Henry Turner challenged a federal statute prohibiting any individual convicted of a drug-related felony from receiving welfare benefits and food stamps. Mr. Turner argued the prohibition permanently deprived him of welfare and food stamps, despite his financial and nutritional need, solely to further punish him for his prior conviction for drug possession.

The Seventh Circuit rejected Mr. Turner's claims, emphasizing that he had failed to meet his "heavy burden" to "negate every conceivable basis which might support it . . . whether or not the basis has a foundation in the record." Remarkably, the judges found that the prohibition would deter drug use since individuals "would undoubtedly consider potential disqualification from federal benefits before engaging in crimes involving illegal drugs." The judges further found that denying food stamps and welfare to those convicted of a drug felony would decrease fraud. Because they were applying only the weak form of judicial review, the judges did not need, nor did they cite, any empirical support for their assumptions that permanent welfare disqualification following a drug conviction would deter drug use or reduce the incidence of fraud. The "highly-deferential rational basis" standard allowed the court to dodge the need to cite evidence to support its assumptions and to deny both the Equal Protection and Substantive Due Process claims. The court also rejected Mr. Turner's double jeopardy claim because it found both the intent and the effect of the permanent disqualification from welfare benefits to be merely a "civil sanction" rather than criminal punishment.[24]

These recent examples illustrate the broader pattern: courts apply a standard of judicial review that affords great deference to the government and little constitutional protection to those most economically vulnerable. This unequal enforcement of constitutional rights constructs dual rules of law—one more protective of the haves and one less protective of the have-nots. In these and many other instances, the American judiciary appears to have accomplished exactly what Agamben theorized. It has included poor people within its constitutional regime and then excluded them from judicial protection.

The next section reveals how the legislative branch of government has joined the judiciary in subjecting poor people to inclusive exclusion.

Disentitlement

The most recent tactic in the war on welfare has been systematic legislative disentitlement. While a complex set of benefit programs make up the tattered American safety net, welfare typically refers to the primary program for single mothers with children, now known as Temporary Assistance for Needy Families. For over sixty years, Congress jointly funded the basic welfare program with the states, which was known originally as Aid to Dependent Children and subsequently Aid to Families with Dependent Children. The former and current welfare programs differ in key respects, but what has been constant is that such aid provided to those typically deemed "undeserving" has remained politically controversial, which has provided constant fuel for the war on welfare.

Not surprisingly, welfare requirements have always been administered in a discriminatory manner, for example, by denying benefits to women who harbored a "man in the house" or failed to keep a "suitable home," which were applied disproportionately to disqualify racial minorities (e.g., Abramowitz 1988; Gordon 1994; Bell 1965). Similarly, welfare benefit levels have always been miserly, typically providing barely enough, or in fact not enough, for a family to survive (Edin and Lein 1997). In part because of the low benefit levels, welfare has never been a substitute for work, and, while the specific mechanisms have differed over time, the welfare system has always imposed some work requirement.

The unpopularity of welfare remained ripe for the political taking when Bill Clinton centered his presidential campaign on his promise to "end welfare as we know it." After several years of jockeying with Republicans, President Clinton signed into law sweeping changes enacted by Congress with broad bipartisan support in 1996. In the Personal Responsibility and Work Opportunity Reconciliation Act, Congress expanded its goals beyond assisting needy families to encompass promoting work and marriage, preventing nonmarital pregnancies, and encouraging two-parent families. Congress specifically imposed a lifetime limit of sixty months for welfare assistance and increased sanctions for both individuals and states for failure to comply with work and other requirements (Nice and Trubek 1997, 93–5).

The welfare reform of 1996 effectively dismantled the federal floor, below which states were not allowed to fall, and replaced it with a federal ceiling, above which states are not allowed to rise. The new legislation specifically removed the statutory entitlement for all eligible individuals to receive benefits and replaced it with block grants to states to be disbursed largely based on state priorities so long as the state complied with federal restrictions on benefits. The federal statute's repeated "no entitlement" proclamation signified congressional desire to deny constitutional due process protection for welfare recipients.

In their comprehensive study of the effects of welfare reform, Joel Handler and Yeheskel Hasenfeld have documented in great detail how most poor people have played by the rules but still have not earned enough to escape poverty (Handler and Hasenfeld 2007). Economic growth has not eliminated poverty, in part because wages in the low-wage labor market have remained stagnant, and in part because the American welfare state distributes most benefits to those who are better off, thus actually reinforcing social stratification (Handler and Hasenfeld 2007). Even the so-called "near poor" (whose wages keep them just above the poverty line) frequently do not earn enough to avoid experiencing hunger or to afford adequate housing and proper health care (Newman and Chen 2007).

Behind the celebrated dismantling of the always-tattered welfare safety net lurks another level of disentitlement. In addition to the constitutional guarantee of equal protection, another basic individual right in many developed legal systems is statutory protection from discrimination. Within the United States, federal, state, and local antidiscrimination laws have extended protection beyond race and sex to various categories (such as prohibitions against discrimination based on marital status or military service) and also have extended protection against actions taken by the private sector (such as prohibiting private employers and landowners from discriminating against individuals in employment and housing). Yet, again, the notion that poor people should enjoy comparable protection from discrimination remains unintelligible within this statutory civil rights scheme.

While few courts have considered the question, the California Supreme Court in *Harris v. Capital Growth Investors* confronted the question of whether California's broad civil rights statute, the Unruh Act, protects individuals from discrimination based on poverty. The state Supreme Court determined that the state legislature did not intend to protect individuals from economic discrimination. In this case, Tamela Harris and Muriel Jordan sued a real estate company for refusing to rent to them because their welfare checks were not sufficient to meet the company's requirement that a tenant's income be three times greater than the amount of the rent. Harris and Jordan believed they could afford the rent, but they were rejected because their income did not meet the company's requirement. Like most states, California's antidiscrimination statute listed specified categories of prohibited discrimination, such as race and sex. Also, like other states, California's list did not include poverty or wealth discrimination among its prohibitions.

California's highest court, however, had never limited protection from discrimination to such specified categories but instead had reasoned that the legislature intended to protect individuals from any "arbitrary" discrimination (interpreted in other cases, for example, to include discrimination based on unconventional appearance or sexual orientation). Harris and Jordan argued that the income requirement constituted a type of arbitrary discrimination. But the California Supreme Court rejected their claim, explaining that its prior decisions had only extended protection from discrimination to "personal characteristics," that economic circumstances are not such personal characteristics, and that relying on economic circumstances to select a "responsible consumer" as a tenant rationally served the company's legitimate business interest. The Court emphasized: "Plaintiffs have cited no federal or state constitutional or statutory provision (nor are we aware of any) that would place financial or economic status on the same footing with the specified categories of discrimination the legislature has chosen to include in the Unruh Act."[25] The state legislature could have amended the statute to include protection from economic discrimination, but it did not.

In short, economic discrimination is not considered arbitrary but instead has been deemed categorically reasonable or rational. A claim of economic discrimination is simply not cognizable as a claim of discrimination within the American civil rights regime. The legislative branch not only has stripped poor people of their meager statutory entitlements, but also has failed to protect them from discrimination based on their poverty.

Policy Experimentation

Although it may not be too surprising that legislators are more beholden to the haves than the have-nots, one might expect the scholarly community to provide independent analysis and knowledge about poverty to policymakers. Instead, all too often, academic researchers appear to have been captured by the government-funded research agenda. The result is that welfare policy research has tended to reinforce entrenched political interests.

For several decades, states were granted waivers from federal requirements to test pilot welfare projects with little federal oversight. As Bennett and Sullivan revealed, welfare waivers were routinely granted by the Secretary of Health and Human Services without regard to standards normally followed in administrative decision-making, without requiring rigorous evaluation of experimental results, and without due regard for the hardships imposed on recipients (Bennett and Sullivan 1993). Soon after their study appeared, the Ninth Circuit Court of Appeals ruled in *Beno v. Shalala* that the Secretary's decision to grant a waiver to California to experiment with cutting welfare benefits below federal requirements was subject to judicial review to ensure the Secretary had evaluated the merits of the project and considered its impact on welfare recipients.[26] It appeared that courts might begin to scrutinize welfare waivers. But shortly thereafter, Congress launched the 1996 welfare overhaul, which itself was a national experiment based largely on selective results from various questionable state experiments and which built state flexibility to continue such experimentation into the block grant structure.

At a pivotal point in the national debate about how to reform welfare, attention was focused on Florida's early pilot program to determine whether welfare families participating in a "work-first" program would fail to find private sector jobs before they reached their time limit despite their good faith efforts. Florida and the media reported with great fanfare that all recipients were able to find private sector jobs and that no creation of public sector jobs was needed. As sociologist Robin Rogers-Dillon has revealed, however, Florida's success depended in part on a detail hidden in the administrative system: Florida simply defined as noncompliant any recipient who had failed to find a job, thus effectively excluding such person from the program's public job guarantee. Even the outside researchers who were hired to conduct an independent evaluation of Florida's pilot program failed to reveal Florida's convenient circularity (Rogers-Dillon 2004, 90, 174). Instead, Florida's program was touted as proof that a work-first time-limited approach would help welfare recipients without harming them, and it was soon copied by other states as well as by the federal government in its 1996 overhaul of welfare.

In other instances, the government pressure on researchers has been direct and visible, such as the apparently retaliatory termination of a contract to evaluate the effects of Wisconsin's Learnfare program when researchers found no increase in school attendance (Rogers-Dillon 2004, 172). Scholars from various social science disciplines have examined welfare policy research and confirmed that the problem of capture is systemic. They have found, for example, most research is driven by the government agenda that is focused on reducing welfare costs, welfare policy is less a result of rigorous science and more a football used for political and ideological purposes, and researchers themselves have been complicit in focusing on ending welfare rather than ending poverty (Schram 1995; Epstein 1997; O'Connor 2001).

The problem of scholarly complicity is not limited to the government's capture of the research agenda or researchers' participation in experiments of dubious design. Serious constitutional and ethical concerns are implicated by subjecting welfare recipients to extensive governmental experimentation with their work and family lives. For example, the United States Constitution protects various fundamental rights in the realm of family law, including marriage, sexual privacy, and parental control over education, custody, and decisions regarding raising children. Yet the private lives of poor women are subjected to routine surveillance and regulation (Gilliom 2001). They also are subject to questionable experimentation, as illustrated by federal funding of an initiative designed to promote marriage as a solution to poverty. The relevant data have shown that poor women already place marriage on a pedestal, suggesting no need for a promotional campaign on behalf of marriage (Edin and Kefalas 2005). Moreover, data thus far have not supported a causal link between marriage and the reduction of poverty. The federal government nonetheless funds educational campaigns to promote the benefits of marriage for poor people, and also funds major longitudinal research to evaluate whether marriage promotion results in more marriages of impoverished individuals (Nice 2007). Reducing welfare dependency, rather than reducing poverty, again seems to be the metric against which the experimentation is measured. If not for the

Dandridge exception to our constitutional norms, surely treating those most vulnerable among us as social science guinea pigs with regard to constitutional rights would not be allowed.

Political Demobilization

If poor people cannot count on courts or legislatures or scholars for protection of their interests, then direct political mobilization becomes their last resort. Yet successful social movement mobilization typically requires lawyers and advocacy organizations (Epp 1998). There seems no way around the reality that wielding political influence requires money, which is precisely the weapon poor people lack. The problem is made that much more difficult by the extraordinary restrictions that Congress has imposed on lawyers for poor people. Adding insult to injury, the Supreme Court also has upheld various burdens that disadvantage poor people in the political process.

To be clear, poor people have demonstrated the desire to change the political economy that supports economic stratification. For example, in one in-depth study of the largest national movement for welfare rights, historian Felicia Kornbluh described those historic 1960s participants as "energetic, eager to engage in collective action, concerned about their own and their children's futures, passionate about political affairs, and both strategically and analytically astute" (Kornbluh 2007, 183). Other anthropological studies have confirmed that poor people continue to engage in strategies both to survive and also to change the structural conditions of poverty (Goode and Maskovsky 2001). For example, John Gilliom's recent study of welfare recipients described in detail how they engaged in "everyday resistance" against the routine surveillance and control of their lives (Gilliom 2001, 12). However, except in pockets and spurts, no sustained antipoverty social movement has registered on the national political radar screen for nearly four decades.

Rather than assisting poor people in assuring meaningful access to political participation, the United States Supreme Court has upheld barriers disproportionately burdening poor people while invalidating barriers that tend to burden other interests. For example, California voters approved an amendment to the state constitution mandating that no low-rent housing could be constructed without first obtaining the approval of a majority of local voters. In *James v. Valtierra*, the Supreme Court refused to frame the case as disadvantaging poor people who need low-income housing, instead describing those affected as "persons advocating low-income housing." The Court then reasoned that the mandatory referendum requirement ensured that the people of a community would have a voice in decisions affecting their tax expenditures and future. The Court held that such "democratic decision-making" did not violate equal protection of the laws.[27]

When similar voter initiatives enacted barriers against open-housing laws that prohibited racial discrimination, however, the Supreme Court invalidated those barriers.[28] At the most basic level, this different outcome highlights the enormous practical difference between the strong judicial review applied to discrimination based on race, which requires the government to prove its actions were necessary to achieve a compelling government purpose, and the weak judicial review applied to discrimination based on poverty, which requires the government merely to identify any conceivable legitimate government to which its actions might be rationally related. The different standards of review led to opposite results: the Court invalidated voter-approval barriers that thwarted efforts to end housing discrimination based on race, but upheld voter-approval barriers that thwarted efforts to end housing discrimination based on low income.

At a more nuanced level, these cases reveal the judiciary's insistence that each type of discrimination be treated separately rather than acknowledging the myriad ways in which race and class are interrelated. The Court in *James v. Valtierra* emphasized that there was no evidence that the political barrier to low-income housing was actually based on racial discrimination. More recently, the Court issued a unanimous decision that provided extraordinary protection to those who sought to block a low-income housing complex. The result of the rather technical analysis was that the Court refused even to allow the case to go to trial, thus preventing the nonprofit developer from attempting to prove that the city had given effect to the racial bias reflected in public opposition to the low-income housing project.[29] Thus, not only has the judiciary refused to protect poor people from barriers erected against them, but it also has refused to recognize the intertwinement of race and class bias.

A more prominent recent case dealt with barriers to participation in the political system by exercising the right to vote. In *Crawford v. Marion County Election Board*, the Supreme Court upheld Indiana's requirement of a government-issued photo identification to vote. The challengers to Indiana's law argued this requirement would disparately impact impoverished voters who might have difficulty affording the travel and fees necessary to obtain either the required birth certificate or the substitute affidavit. Rather than requiring Indiana to justify the burden this law placed on an individual's ability to vote, the Court instead imposed a "heavy burden of persuasion" on the challengers. The Court ultimately concluded the challengers had failed to demonstrate that Indiana had placed any excessive burden on impoverished voters. The Court allowed whatever deterrent effect on impoverished voters the voter identification requirement might impose, thus making it that much more difficult for poor people to participate in the political process.[30]

Because poor people have difficulty exerting direct political influence, the task of asserting the interests of poor people before the courts and the political branches frequently falls to their advocates, especially their lawyers. Soon after the federal government began funding lawyers for poor people during the 1960s, legal services lawyers achieved remarkable success in constitutional litigation (Bussiere 1997; Davis 1993; Lawrence 1990). But a powerful backlash against legal services lawyers ensued. Congress stymied legal services lawyers with severe funding cutbacks and subsequently tied their hands by imposing stringent restrictions on their advocacy. One set of restrictions prohibits legal services lawyers from representing certain types of clients, including undocumented immigrants, incarcerated persons, persons seeking abortions, and persons seeking a defense from an eviction based on alleged illegal drug activity by any member of the household. Another set of restrictions prevents legal services lawyers from engaging in particular types of advocacy, including seeking to influence legislation, administrative rulemaking, and ballot measures. Legal services lawyers are also prohibited from filing class actions—the primary legal device for seeking collective judicial relief—and from seeking attorneys fees after a successful outcome, even when otherwise authorized by statute (Nice and Trubek 1997, 211–12). Such restrictions prevent lawyers for poor people from engaging in zealous advocacy, which is what lawyers are ethically required to provide their clients.

It is not only the lawyers for poor people whose activities are closely scrutinized. Consider the recent example made of the Association of Community Organizations for Reform Now ("ACORN"), apparently the largest organization of low-income families within the United States. The ACORN organization came under attack for allegedly misusing governmental funds to support partisan election activity and also for some embarrassing videos taken by hidden camera that showed ACORN employees advising a couple about how to engage in illegal activities and evade law enforcement. Congress responded by passing a highly unusual continuing resolution that specifically prohibited ACORN from receiving any federal funding, which the Obama administration promptly implemented. A federal district court recently ruled that this extraordinary targeting of ACORN by the federal government violated the Constitution's prohibition against a "bill of attainder," which prohibits legislative punishment of specific individuals without the protection of a judicial adjudication of guilt.[31]

Compare these systemic barriers that burden the political participation of poor people to the recent constitutional protection afforded to corporate interests. In *Citizens United v. Federal Election Commission*, the Supreme Court struck down federal limitations on political expenditures by corporations. Perhaps the most striking portion of the decision was the Court's concern that the government had muffled "the voices that best represent the most significant segments of the economy" and thus had prevented corporate "voices and viewpoints from reaching the public and advising voters on which persons or entities are hostile to their interests."[32]

In sum, effective political advocacy by or on behalf of poor people seems neither affordable, nor welcome, nor tolerated. Yet, the courts frequently advise poor people to turn to the political branches, rather than the courts, for protection. As former Justice Sandra Day O'Connor explained, the reason the judiciary defers to economic legislation is because the Constitution presumes the political process will rectify unwise decisions.[33] With no protection from either the legal or political systems, however, poor people are caught between a rock and a hard place. They are abandoned and trapped in the nebulousness of inclusive exclusion, precisely as Agamben feared.

A COMPARATIVE FORAY

While this critique focuses on American law, the concerns raised here apply to many, if not most, other constitutional regimes. It is true that, unlike the United States Constitution, many more recent constitutions drafted since World War II have included textual provisions that either explicitly or implicitly provide protection of social and economic rights. Yet, these protections have rarely been judicially enforced. For example, Canada's Charter of Fundamental Rights and Freedoms includes at least two provisions that might support welfare rights. Section 7 protects every individual's right to life, liberty, and security of the person against deprivation except in accordance with the principles of fundamental justice. Section 15 contains a robust substantive equality provision that protects the right to equal protection and equal benefit of the law without discrimination. However, the Supreme Court of Canada's 2002 decision in *Gosselin v. Quebec (Attorney General)* refused to apply these provisions to invalidate Quebec's refusal to provide equal welfare benefits to younger adults as provided to older adults. The Court squarely rejected the appellant's novel interpretation of the Charter as positively obligating the government to guarantee adequate living standards.[34]

South Africa appears to sit at the opposite end of the spectrum both because social and economic rights are explicitly protected in the text of the Constitution and because they are judicially enforceable. Such enforcement remains limited, however, to considering whether the government has taken reasonable measures within available resources to achieve the progressive realization of such rights. In *Republic of South Africa v. Grootboom*, the Constitutional Court held that the government's dismal attempt to house the homeless was unreasonable and therefore unconstitutional. The Court, nonetheless, rejected Irene Grootboom's broader request to enforce a "minimum core" right to shelter. As a result, the Court granted declaratory relief that the government had failed to take reasonable measures and ordered the government to develop a new plan, but refused to grant injunctive relief that might have required the actual provision of housing.[35]

While this foray makes no attempt to comprehensively survey the global constitutional scene, two general comparative points emerge in some tension with one another. The first point is that the United States seems to be out of step with other developed nations in its refusal to recognize social and economic rights. The second point is that the difficulty in obtaining meaningful constitutional protection does not appear to be unique to the United States. Even where constitutional texts explicitly protect social and economic rights and where courts are authorized to enforce them, obtaining meaningful judicial protection for poor people remains elusive. However, even if weak judicial enforcement is a widespread problem, this does not directly constrain the impact of such rights in the political arena.

RECONSIDERING RIGHTS

The inquiry thus returns to the foundational questions. How does the lack of legal rights for poor people matter? Do poor people need legal rights, or do they just need more money? And what are the societal effects of their lack of rights? One of the leading American scholars opposing a rights-based approach is political scientist Gerald Rosenberg who has argued that seeking judicial enforcement of rights "almost never" produces significant social change (Rosenberg 1991, 338). While rights most certainly are no panacea, poor people provide a stark example of what happens when a group is included within law but excluded from any right to substantive protection. For poor people, the result has been a dialogic default on the question of economic justice, leaving their claims for protection virtually unintelligible within law and society.

This dialogic default reverberates precisely because law and society are mutually constitutive, with each shaping, and being shaped by, the other. In one direction, the refusal of American lawmakers and courts to provide substantive protection permits and exacerbates the extraordinary vulnerability of poor people within society. In the other direction, the lack of a sustained societal demand for economic justice perpetuates the absence of substantive rights protection within law. In short, neither law nor society is exerting much pressure toward achieving economic justice. Poor people have been mired in the resulting stagnation for over forty years.

The effects of a dialogic default are felt with particular valence within constitutional discourse. Much recent constitutional theory builds on an emerging understanding that constitutional interpretation is shaped by the ongoing dialogue between the courts, the political branches, and the people (Nice 2008, 657–59). Thus, without a dialogic demand for economic justice, constitutional interpretation is unlikely to offer substantive protection.

Changing the law is not the only, or even the most important, end. As with other social movements, the demand for rights may serve as a device for mobilizing and empowering poor people. For example, during the national welfare rights movement of the 1960s, the demand for legal fair hearings was a primary organizing tactic, and access to lawyers and legal information were specific benefits provided by the movement (Kornbluh 2007, 81). The welfare rights activists "did not believe they had to choose between direct action and legal action; they saw the two as mutually supportive" (Kornbluh 2007, 86). In the words of one of the Brooklyn organizers, "People began to understand that they could do a whole lot more if they knew a lot more. And the basic, basic, basic thing they needed to know was welfare law" (Kornbluh 2007, 83).

The literature about social movement mobilization provides additional support for this understanding. While advancing the critique of rights as failing to produce social change, Stuart Scheingold nonetheless conceived of a "politics of rights" by which social movements might leverage rights as a means of mobilizing political support for social change (Scheingold 1974). Twenty years later, Michael McCann's pioneering work on the role of rights in social movement mobilization provided strong empirical evidence of the role of rights in developing consciousness of inequality, creating a common identity among those affected, organizing and mobilizing them to assert rights as remedies, and cultivating a greater sense of inclusion and empowerment (McCann 1994, 304). Beyond the role of rights claims in seeking to win legal victories, McCann emphasized the importance of the indirect effects of rights claims. Even if rights continue to be "limited, contingent, uncertain," they remain one of the few resources for leveraging against "overwhelming systemic inequalities" (McCann 1994, 309).

Gilliom's study of welfare recipients reminds us that recipients rarely speak in the language of rights today (Gilliom 2001, 10). Perhaps this should not be surprising, given the deeply entrenched resistance to rights for poor people. After all, as Engel and Munger have explained, legal consciousness "emerges from the continual interplay of law, everyday life, and individual experience" (Engel and Munger 1996, 14). While rights are not the only way to frame one's thought, speech, or action, rights can serve as a powerful resource, especially for those who have so few other resources to harness.

American law makes an everyday exception for poverty, denying its standard protections to those most economically vulnerable. Courts have not given equal protection to their constitutional claims, legislatures have stripped them of their legislative entitlements, researchers have subjected them to welfare experimentation that reinforces an anti-welfare agenda, and various barriers to political participation hinder efforts to overcome their inherent political disadvantage. Poor people are thus required to play by the rules of American law, while being saddled with disadvantages in each forum.

Law includes poor people so as to exclude them, trapping them in an everyday state of abandonment, as Agamben theorized. If making exceptions to rights is the everyday means by which the law secures such abandonment, then perhaps the demand for rights holds some potential to open the space Agamben simultaneously imagined for a new politics no longer founded on the bare life, otherwise known as the state of poverty. At the very least, there seems to be little risk of harm in demanding rights, as poor people have little left to lose.

NOTES

1. These and other poverty data from the Census Bureau and the Congressional Budget Office are available from the Center on Budget and Policy Priorities.

2. According to data from the United States Department of Health and Human Services, the average monthly number of total Aid to Families with Dependent Children (AFDC) recipients in 1994 was 14 million, while the average monthly number of total Temporary Assistance for Needy Families (TANF) in 2007 was 4 million.

3. Agamben himself identifies the American tactics in the war on terror as, in many ways, exemplary of the dangers of the state of exception. He argues that President Bush's order authorizing indefinite detention of those suspected of terrorist activities made such detainees "the object of a pure de facto rule," subjecting them to detention indefi-

nite both in time and in nature and removed from law and judicial oversight (Agamben 2005, 3–4).

4. Agamben's use of the concentration camp as his paradigm for exploring the modern state of exception evokes Foucault's use of Jeremy Bentham's circular prison, the panopticon, as his paradigm for exploring disciplinary power. Foucault examined the panopticon as representative of a governmental disciplinary regime; Agamben examines the concentration camp as representative of a governmental suspension of the rule of law.

5. *Edwards v. California*, 314 U.S. 160, 177 (1941).

6. *Skinner v. Oklahoma*, 316 U.S. 535, 541 (1942).

7. *Griffin v. Illinois*, 351 U.S. 12 (1956).

8. *Harper v. Virginia State Board of Elections*, 383 U.S. 663 (1966).

9. *Goldberg v. Kelly*, 397 U.S. 254 (1970).

10. *Dandridge v. Williams*, 397 U.S. 471 (1970).

11. See, for example, *Frontiero v. Richardson*, 411 U.S. 677 (1973) (examining whether burdens based on sex are suspect); *City of Cleburne v. Cleburne Living Center*, 473 U.S. 432 (1985) (examining whether burdens based on disability are suspect); and *Massachusetts Board of Retirement v. Murgia*, 427 U.S. 307 (1976) (examining whether burdens based on age are suspect).

12. Data show that children born to the poorest 10 percent of families will likely end up in the poorest 20 percent of families as adults (Bowles, Gintis, and Osborne Groves 2005).

13. *San Antonio Independent School District v. Rodriguez*, 411 U.S. 1 (1973).

14. For example, in his treatise, Erwin Chemerinsky claims the Rodriguez decision "held that discrimination against the poor does not warrant heightened scrutiny." In his very next sentence, he concedes that the Court had "rejected the claim that the law should be regarded as discriminating against the poor as a group" (Chemerinsky 2006, 786). Normally, any reasoning extraneous to the facts of the case would be treated as dictum and not part of the holding or ruling.

15. *Maher v. Roe*, 432 U.S. 464, 471 (1977).

16. *Harris v. McRae*, 448 U.S. 297, 323 (1980), rehearing denied, 448 U.S. 917 (1980).

17. Interestingly, in a recent concurring opinion, Justice Antonin Scalia cited to *Harris* as having decided that a class defined by poverty is not protected. *Crawford v. Marion County Election Board*, 553 U.S. 181, 207 (2008).

18. *Bowen v. Gilliard*, 483 U.S. 587, 609 (1987).

19. *Williams v. Martin*, 283 F.Supp.2d 1286 (N.D. Ga. 2003).

20. *Sanchez v. County of San Diego*, 464 F.3d 916, 927 (9th Cir. 2006).

21. *Sanchez v. County of San Diego*, 483 F.3d 965, 966 (9th Cir. 2007) (dissenting from denial of rehearing).

22. 552 U.S. 1038 (2007).

23. *James v. Valtierra*, 402 U.S. 137, 145 (1971) (Marshall, J. dissenting); *Blum v. Yaretsky*, 457 U.S. 991, 1014 (1981) (Brennan, J. dissenting).

24. *Turner v. Glickman*, 207 F.3d 419, 424–26, 431 (7th Cir. 2000).

25. *Harris v. Capital Growth Investors*, 805 P.2d 873, 883 n. 9 (Cal. 1991).

26. *Beno v. Shalala*, 30 F.3d 1057, 1068 (9th Cir. 1994).

27. *James v. Valtierra*, 402 U.S. 137 (1971).

28. *Reitman v. Mulkey*, 387 U.S. 369 (1967); *Hunter v. Erickson*, 393 U.S. 385 (1969).

29. *City of Cuyahoga Falls, Ohio v. Buckeye Community Hope Foundation*, 538 U.S. 188 (2003).

30. *Crawford v. Marion County Election Board*, 553 U.S. 181 (2008).

31. *Association of Community Organizations for Reform Now v. United States*, 692 F.Supp.2d 260 (E.D.N.Y. 2010). Despite numerous statements by members of Congress assailing ACORN as "crooked," "corrupt," "criminal," and the like, the Second Circuit Court of Appeals quickly overturned the district court, finding insufficient evidence to establish that Congress intended to punish ACORN. *ACORN v. United States*, 2010 WL 3191442 (2nd Cir. 2010).

32. *Citizens United v. Federal Election Commission*, 130 S.Ct. 876, 907 (2010) (internal citations omitted).

33. *Lawrence v. Texas*, 539 U.S. 558, 579–80 (O'Connor, J., concurring) (2003).

34. *Gosselin v. Quebec (Attorney General)*, [2002] 4 S.C.R. 429, 2002 SCC 84 (Can).

35. *Republic of South Africa v. Grootboom*, 2001 (1) SA 46 (CC) (S. Afr.).

REFERENCES

Abramowitz, Mimi. 1988. *Regulating the lives of women: Social welfare policy from colonial times to the present*. Boston: South End Press.

Agamben, Giorgio. 1998. *Homo sacer: Sovereign power and bare life*. Stanford, Calif.: Stanford University Press.

———. 2005. *State of exception*. Stanford, Calif.: Stanford University Press.

Bell, Winifred. 1965. *Aid to families with dependent children*. New York: Columbia University Press.

Bennett, Susan, and Kathleen A. Sullivan. 1993. Disentitling the poor: Waivers and welfare "reform." *University of Michigan Journal of Law Reform* 26:741–84.

Bowles, Samuel, Herbert Gintis, and Melissa Osborne Groves. 2005. *Unequal chances: Family background and economic success*. Princeton, N.J.: Princeton University Press.

Bussiere, Elizabeth. 1997. *(Dis)entitling the poor: The Warren court, welfare rights, and the American political tradition*. University Park, Pa.: Pennsylvania State University Press.

Chemerinsky, Erwin. 2006. *Constitutional law: Principles and policies*. 3rd ed. New York: Aspen Publishers.

Davis, Martha F. 1993. *Brutal need: Lawyers and the welfare rights movement, 1960–1973*. New Haven, Conn.: Yale University Press.

Edin, Kathryn, and Maria Kefalas. 2005. *Promises I can keep: Why poor women put motherhood before marriage*. Berkeley: University of California Press.

Edin, Kathryn, and Laura Lein. 1997. *Making ends meet: How single mothers survive welfare and low-wage work*. New York: Russell Sage Foundation.

Engel, David M., and Frank W. Munger. 1996. Rights, remembrance, and the reconciliation of difference. *Law and Society Review* 30:7–53.

Epp, Charles R. 1998. *The rights revolution: Lawyers, activists, and supreme courts in comparative perspective*. Chicago: University of Chicago Press.

Epstein, William M. 1997. *Welfare in America: How social science fails the poor*. Madison, Wis.: University of Wisconsin Press.

Forbath, William E. 1999. Caste, class and equal citizenship. *Michigan Law Review* 98:1–91.

Gilliom, John. 2001. *Overseers of the poor: Surveillance, resistance, and the limits of privacy*. Chicago: University of Chicago Press.

Goluboff, Risa L. 2007. *The lost promise of civil rights*. Cambridge, Mass.: Harvard University Press.

Goode, Judith, and Jeff Maskovsky, eds. 2001. *The new poverty studies: The ethnography of power, politics, and impoverished people in the United States*. New York: New York University Press.

Gordon, Linda. 1994. *Pitied but not entitled: Single mothers and the history of welfare 1890–1935*. New York: Free Press.

Handler, Joel F., and Yeheskel Hasenfeld. 2007. *Blame welfare: Ignore poverty and inequality*. New York: Cambridge University Press.

Hershkoff, Helen. 1999. Positive rights and state constitutions: The limits of federal rationality review. *Harvard Law Review* 112:1131–96.

Katz, Michael B. 1986. *In the shadow of the poorhouse: A social history of welfare in America*. New York: Basic Books.

Kornbluh, Felicia. 2007. *The battle for welfare rights: Politics and poverty in modern America*. Philadelphia: University of Pennsylvania Press.

Lawrence, Susan E. 1990. *The poor in court: The legal services program and Supreme Court decision making*. Princeton, N.J.: Princeton University Press.

Loffredo, Stephen. 1993. Poverty, democracy and constitutional law. *University of Pennsylvania Law Review* 141:1277–389.

———. 2007. Poverty, inequality, and class in the structural constitutional law course. *Fordham Urban Law Journal* 34:1239–67.

McCann, Michael. 1994. *Rights at work: Pay equity reform and the politics of legal mobilization*. Chicago: University of Chicago Press.

Minow, Martha. 1990. *Making all the difference: Inclusion, exclusion, and American law*. Ithaca, N.Y.: Cornell University Press.

Newman, Katherine, and Victor Tan Chen. 2007. *The missing class: Portraits of the near poor in America*. Boston: Beacon Press.

Nice, Julie A. 2007. Promoting marriage experimentation: A class act? *Washington University Journal of Law & Policy* 24:31–45.

———. 2008. No scrutiny whatsoever: Deconstitutionalization of poverty law, dual rules of law, & dialogic default. *Fordham Urban Law Journal* 35:629–71.

Nice, Julie A., and Louise G. Trubek. 1997. *Cases and materials on poverty law: Theory and practice*. St. Paul, Minn.: West Publishing.

O'Connor, Alice. 2001. *Poverty knowledge: Social science, social policy, and the poor in twentieth-century U.S. history*. Princeton, N.J.: Princeton University Press.

Piven, Frances Fox, and Richard A. Cloward. 1971. *Regulating the poor: The functions of public welfare*. New York: Vintage Books.

———. 1979. *Poor people's movements: Why they succeed, how they fail*. New York: Vintage Books.

Rank, Mark Robert. 2004. *One nation, underprivileged: Why American poverty affects us all*. New York: Oxford University Press.

Rogers-Dillon, Robin. 2004. *The welfare experiments: Politics and policy evaluation*. Stanford, Calif.: Stanford University Press.

Rosenberg, Gerald N. 1991. *The hollow hope: Can courts bring about social change?* Chicago: University of Chicago Press.

Sarat, Austin. 1990. ". . . The law is all over": Power, resistance, and the legal consciousness of the welfare poor. *Yale Journal of Law and the Humanities* 2:343–79.

Scheingold, Stuart. 1974. *The politics of rights: Lawyers, public policy, and political change*. New Haven, Conn.: Yale University Press.

Schram, Sanford F. 1995. *Words of welfare: The poverty of social science and the social science of poverty*. Minneapolis: University of Minnesota Press.

tenBroek, Jacobus. 1964. California's dual system of family law: Its origin, development, and present status. *Stanford Law Review* 16:257–317.

Trattner, Walter I. 1999. *From poor law to welfare state: A history of social welfare in America*. New York: Free Press.

Tushnet, Mark. 2008. *Weak courts, strong rights: Judicial review and social welfare rights in comparative constitutional law*. Princeton, N.J.: Princeton University Press.

CHAPTER THREE

Beyond Displacement

Gentrification of Racialized Spaces as Violence—Harlem, New York, and New Orleans, Louisiana

PAULA C. JOHNSON

The collusion among state, private, and institutional actors generates insecurity between primarily poor and working-class Black people in U.S. urban centers and secures accumulation among mostly economically affluent White populations through the practice of gentrification. Beyond the acquisition of property and accumulation of wealth on the one hand, and massive displacement of Black residents on the other hand, this chapter emphasizes the physical, psychological, cultural, and political traumas that are consequent from the forced removal of long-term residents of gentrified communities. The notion of gentrification as a benign and natural population shift that benefits all members of the community belies the realities of forced displacement. As Jonathan Wharton writes, "[g]entrification is part of man's continual obsession with conquering, disempowering, politicizing and capitalizing over other individuals for their own gain" (Wharton 2008, 7).

As argued in this chapter, gentrification must properly be perceived as the perpetration of violence—both direct and structural. In 1969, Johan Galtung, who pioneered the discipline of peace studies, developed the concept of structural violence to define constraints on human potential and deprivation of basic human needs resulting from economic and political structures (Galtung 1969, 167). Galtung's definition has assumed broad disciplinary and practical application and encompasses the circumstances that are the focus of this chapter; namely, that structurally embedded race and class inequality constitutes violence that results from the deliberate and avoidable denial of fundamental human needs—in this instance, housing and protection from displacement caused by gentrification (Galtung 1969, 167; Galtung 1990, 291).

In light of the neoliberal state's role in propagating housing insecurity by conspiring in global capital-inspired gentrification practices, it is legally and morally responsible for violence against populations who experience the severe harms of gentrification. Legally, such violence must not be viewed solely through the lens of the U.S. domestic legal regime, but must be recognized as human rights violations for which the state incurs responsibility to rectify the harms it has created (Farmer 2004, xiii).

Gentrification is not a practice that is unique to the United States, the West, or the Global North. Indeed, as anthropologist and urban geographer Neil Smith demonstrates, it is rapidly becoming a worldwide phenomenon (Smith 2002). While Smith's work highlights the present generalized nature of gentrification across global milieus, with its prioritization of global capitalist production over social reproduction and human need, he also recognizes that gentrification must be understood in the specific societal context in which it occurs (Smith 2002, 440). This necessitates examining the intersectionality of racial, gender, class, and spatial dimensions of gentrification in the United States.

As Iris Young has observed, "Without such a critical stance, many questions about what occurs in society and why, who benefits and who is harmed, will not be asked, and social theory is liable to reaffirm and reify the given social reality" (Young 1990, 5). Critical race theory, Black geographies, and Black feminist theory provide useful frameworks to examine the power dynamics that facilitate gentrification (see Crenshaw et al. 1995; McKittrick and Woods 2007; Soja 1989; Collins 1990; James and Sharpley-Whiting 2000). Thus, these critical analytical constructs that examine the ways in which race, gender, class, and space are deployed to maintain subordination and inequality in American society inform my examination of gentrification in the U.S. context.

Trends in Harlem, New York, and New Orleans, Louisiana, exemplify the pervasiveness and detrimental impact of gentrification occurring in Black communities across the United States. Harlem and New Orleans share distinctions as iconic centers of Black people's long-standing historical, cultural, social, economic, and political roots. In the Harlem community of greater New York City, gentrification has been an ongoing process of public and private development and real estate market speculation for over twenty years, and has accelerated since the mid-1990s. In New Orleans, gentrification was precipitated by the putative recovery and rebuilding efforts following Hurricane Katrina in

2005. Fundamentally, the causes and effects of gentrification in the racialized communities of Harlem in New York City, and the Lower Ninth Ward in New Orleans are much the same, despite recognized contrasts.

The chapter begins by describing the central terms "gentrification" and "racialized spaces." The next section discusses the creation of racialized spaces, including de jure and de facto policies of racial segregation and discrimination that maintain such spaces and foster gentrification and applies these terms to the contexts of Harlem and New Orleans. The third section focuses on the effects of gentrification, including an examination of "root shock"—the trauma experienced by long-term residents who are forced from their homes, communities, and cultural moorings (Fullilove 2004, 11).[1] This section argues that the effects of root shock fit within Galtung's definition of state-sponsored structural violence. The final section examines resistance efforts to the gentrification of poor and working-class communities of color. Housing activists, in coalition with others who are justice-minded, are engaged in vigorous resistance efforts against gentrification to demand that the state meet its obligation to enact and enforce greater protections on behalf of vulnerable dislocated and disenfranchised populations and bring an end to the commodification and exploitation of people's fundamental need and right to housing. Such efforts work to realize Chester Hartman's call for legal and societal recognition of a "right to stay put" movement to protect vulnerable communities from gentrification and displacement (Hartman 1984). In its conclusion, this chapter espouses this view as well.

GENTRIFICATION OF RACIALIZED SPACES

This section begins with definitions of "gentrification" and "racialized spaces." A Black resident of Chicago public housing explained the gentrification of racialized spaces this way: "You know how they say the white people moved all the way to the suburbs because they don't want to be around us? So now they building all these homes knowing damn well most of us can't afford them. So they trying to get the white people back in. And that's the system."[2]

My aim in this section is not to explicate the entire complex, nuanced, and sometimes conflicting definitions of these terms (cf. Marcuse 1995, 1999; powell 2000; Cashin 2004).[3] Rather, I put forth a fundamental understanding of these key concepts to illustrate the legal, social, and political dynamics that perpetuate traumatic dislocation of Black people from their homes and communities in the interest of capital accumulation. The effects of gentrification on the racialized communities of Harlem and New Orleans will be explored from the foundation established by these basic and contextualized meanings.

Racialized Space

Initially, critical analysis of space is important because as Michel Foucault states, "A whole history remains to be written of *spaces*—which would at the same time be the history of *powers* (both these terms in the plural)—from the great strategies of geo-politics to the little tactics of the habitat . . . passing via economic and political installations" (Foucault 1980, 146, 149). In this particular context, the "racialization of space" is the process by which residential location and community are based on racial identity (Calmore 1995). Audrey McFarlane adds, "Racializing space effectively demarcates particular areas not only based on racial identity but also imposes popular stereotypes, anxieties, and concerns on these places. The role of these places in the popular imagination justifies their subordination and oppression" (McFarlane 1999, 295, 340).

Thus, racialized spaces are not merely concentrations of members of racial groups who live in proximity to each other based on similar identity, experiences, and cultural affinity; rather, racialized spaces are creations of the state whereupon the state has implemented policies to isolate and contain Blacks to the social and economic benefit of Whites. These economic benefits are derived from the devaluation of the spaces where Black people live, irrespective of their income level. This is typically the case in areas that are racialized Black and classified poor, but it is also true in areas where moderate and higher-income Blacks reside. This is because blacks earn, on average, much less than Whites, in part because of their historical isolation from the resources and job opportunities available in wealthier and socially privileged White communities (Ford 1994, 1841, 1850. See also Roberts 2009).[4] Hence, the same spaces that have been racialized as Black and poor, and where the forces of global capital transform and dismantle local labor markets and employment opportunities, become ripe for gentrification (Sassen 2007).[5]

Gentrification

Sociologist Ruth Glass coined a widely adopted definition of gentrification in 1964 based on her study of homogenous London neighborhood districts in which working-class residents were displaced by upper and lower middle-class residents. According to Glass, "Once this process of 'gentrification' starts in a district it goes on rapidly until all or most of the original working-class occupiers are displaced and the whole social character of the district is changed" (Glass 1964, xviii–xix).

While Glass's definition aptly describes the class dimensions of the phenomenon in the United States, the definition of gentrification must reflect the interlocking dynamics of race and class that result in the displacement of poor and working-class people of color from urban communities by more affluent Whites. With increased housing prices elsewhere, White potential homeowners and renters find inner city areas more attractive and private investors find the formerly spurned areas more lucrative. Richard Ford recognizes the larger consequences of the exercise of economic and social power in this way, stating, "Racial segregation is more than a social distance; it is political fragmentation and economic stratification along racial lines"(Ford 1994, 1844).

Smith denotes further limitations of Glass's original definition of gentrification upon expounding on the political economy of gentrification in light of late-capitalist formation. In this regard, in the 1960s Glass identified a localized and rather idiosyncratic manifestation of gentrification by "hipper professional classes unafraid to rub shoulders with the unwashed masses" (Smith 2000, 439). As it has evolved, however, the contemporary process of gentrification has become systematized on a grand scale and has become the central goal of urban policy in the United Kingdom, the United States, and elsewhere. This newest phase of gentrification is characterized by "the reach of global capital down to the local neighborhood scale," which distinguishes it from earlier iterations (Smith 2002, 441; See also Smith and DiFilippis 1999; Sassen 1998).[6]

Further, in the strategic process of gentrification, positive sounding exhortations for regeneration and renaissance, UK planners, economists, and politicians cynically call for "social balance" in predominantly Black neighborhoods such as London's Brixton. In reality, this is an appeal for White middle and upper-middle classes to retake control of the political and cultural economies, as well as the geographies, of the largest cities. As Smith astutely observes, "Advocates of 'social balance' rarely, if ever, advocate that White neighborhoods should be balanced by equal numbers of people of African, Caribbean, or Asian descent" (Smith 2000, 445).

Thus, as a global urban strategic planning phenomenon, gentrification represents the infusion of global capital into local neighborhoods on a large, systematized scale that facilitates Whites' exercise of economic, legal, and political prerogatives to occupy whatever spaces—including previously devalued racialized spaces—for their greater security and greater wealth accumulation and for the greater disadvantage and insecurity of Blacks. As discussed in the next section, in Harlem and New Orleans, law, public policy, and private investment exemplify the manifestation of White capital accumulation through gentrified development of racialized urban spaces resulting in the forced removal of people of color from their communities and social and cultural roots.

The Causes of Racialized Spaces: History, Law, and Policy

Racialized spaces in American society do not result solely from the function of private market forces or people's decisions to live among those with whom they share certain characteristics, including race and culture. Historically, laws expressly demarcated areas where Blacks and members of other racial groups could live, imposing racial segregation in housing and all other areas of American life, denoted as "American Apartheid" by Massey and Denton (Massey and Denton 1993). Thus, Richard Ford is correct in noting "the history of public policy and private action in the service of racism reveals the context in which racialized spaces were created" (Ford 1994, 1849).

The U.S. Government had promised "adequate housing within their means for all Americans" with the passage of the Housing Act of 1937. However, despite the 1937 Act, civil rights activism, and successful legal challenges that eroded the injustices of the Jim Crow era, governmental and private sector housing policies continued to disadvantage people of color and advantage Whites. Even in the modern era, with the passage of the Civil Rights Act of 1968 (the Fair Housing Act), discriminatory practices including isolated public housing, urban renewal, redlining, discriminatory mortgage lending, exclusionary zoning, and empowerment zone designation remained pervasive. Hence, the legal, social, and political structures that historically created segregated racialized spaces remain essentially in effect today.[7]

SPACES IN POINT: HARLEM, NEW YORK, AND NEW ORLEANS, LOUISIANA

Harlem, New York—Black Mecca

Harlem has long been viewed nationally and internationally as the cultural and political epicenter of Black life in America. Robin Kelley captures the meaning and concerns about the future of Harlem as a Black community:

> For Black residents the glory that was Harlem was more than just a colorful backdrop to enhance neighborhood charm. On the contrary, the past has always been about charting a new future. After all, this place has been labeled "the Negro Mecca." . . . It offered hope for a new beginning in an age of scientific racism

barely two generations removed from slavery. It promised the flowering of a Black intelligentsia and culture, a symbol of what sophisticated, urbane Black people can become if they held power and were left alone. Indeed, it is precisely this sense of hope, possibility, dreams unrealized, that explains why every generation since the early twentieth century laments the loss of "the old Harlem." But what was really lost and what will the new Harlem bring? To answer these questions, we need to dig even deeper beneath the surface . . . and figure out how Harlem evolved from mecca to market. (Kelley 2003, 9-10)

Harlem has one of the largest concentrations of Black working-class and poor residents in the United States, and significant middle-class and upper-income populations. Black residents arrived in great numbers in Harlem from the South during the Great Migration in the early twentieth century. Many African Americans left the lynch-prone Jim Crow South for safety, employment, and educational opportunities in the industrial North generated by World War I.

Situated within greater Manhattan, Harlem is physically located above Central Park up to the South Bronx, and extends to 96th Street on the east and to 125th Street on the west. As perceived racialized space, author Ralph Ellison famously quipped, "Wherever Negroes live uptown is considered Harlem" (Ellison in Sverdlik 1993, 6). Central Harlem is considered the heart of the community. Between 1920 and 1930, the Black population of central Harlem grew from 33 percent to just over 70 percent. This era also heralded the great Harlem Renaissance cultural epoch and Harlem's renown as "the spiritual home of the Negro protest movement," which included rent strikes and protests that urged, "Don't Buy Where You Can't Work" (Clarke 1971).

White flight to the suburbs became contemporaneous with Black migration to Harlem. In the decade between 1920 and 1930, as roughly 88,000 Blacks arrived mostly from the South and the Caribbean, nearly 119,000 Whites simultaneously left the area. Although Black migration slowed during the Great Depression in the 1930s, it resurged during World War II and continued during the 1950s and 1960s (Appiah and Gates 2003). However, there was little new construction and housing investment since World War II except for public housing and other mostly state-funded undertakings.

In addition to leaving the area when Blacks arrived, White owners and landlords engaged in blockbusting, refused to rent or sell to Blacks, entered racially restrictive covenants, practiced redlining, and employed discriminatory mortgage lending policies. Landlords charged higher rents to Black tenants, even as the housing condition was poorer. The 1960 census revealed that only half of the housing in Harlem was in habitable condition, compared to 85 percent habitability rates elsewhere in New York City. As housing in Harlem fell into deep disrepair, many owners simply abandoned the properties, leaving Black tenants to pay disproportionately higher rents for unsound, unsafe structures.

By the 1960s, Harlem had become infamous as a symbol of Black deprivation in America, as has been characterized by poor quality housing, disproportionately high unemployment, and high mortality (see Schaffer and Smith 1986). Harlem also has one of the highest asthma rates in the United States, largely attributable to poor housing conditions and excessive exposure to diesel exhaust. The infectious disease rate likewise exceeds national averages.

GENTRIFICATION IN HARLEM: HELLO/GOODBYE. Gentrification in Harlem became full-fledged by 1995 when more affluent White residents, national and multinational corporate entities, and public and private institutions encroached deeper into Harlem neighborhoods. Census reports from 2008 reveal that the Black population of greater Harlem is at its lowest level since the 1920s, and finds that Blacks no longer constitute a majority of the greater Harlem population. The number of Black Harlem residents declined steadily between 1980 and 2000. Further, between 1990 and 2000, the number of housing units in Harlem increased 14 percent, and property values in Central Harlem increased nearly 300 percent during the 1990s, compared with only 12 percent increases in the rest of the city (Beveridge 2009). These changes have accelerated in recent years causing widespread displacement of long-term Black residents, irrespective of income (McFarlane 1999), and an alteration of Harlem's racial, cultural, and physical cityscape.

Some have dubbed the recent flurry of speculation, investment, and development the "second Harlem renaissance." Yet, as Robin Kelley writes, new White residents to Harlem "have put a completely different spin on 'White flight'":

> Fleeing the more expensive parts of Manhattan, whites are integrating Harlem in large numbers. Unlike the integration of African Americans into white neighborhoods, where fear of declining property values compels white residents to fight (burning crosses, burning houses, mob violence) or flee altogether, White moving into Black communities tends to push property values up, thus pricing many longtime Black residents out. (Kelly 2003, 11-12)

Gentrification in Harlem was facilitated by local and federal policies, including aggressive, militaristic police practices that targeted drug users, drug dealers, and small-scale street vendors alike. Furthermore, infusions of capital were directed to external individuals and entities rather than local residents and enterprises. In 1994, Harlem was designated an Empowerment Zone and the Upper Manhattan Empowerment Zone (UMEZ) channeled millions in federal grants and tax credits for commercial development of the retail corridor on 125th Street (see McFarlane 1999). Lloyd Williams, president of the Greater Harlem Chamber of Commerce, observed, "The number of people from this community who own anything on 125th Street you can count on one hand and still have a number of fingers left" (Olivo 2001, 49).

The New York City Council also approved major commercial development, including office towers, luxury housing, hotels, and retail enterprises across Harlem. In one development, of 1,100 luxury housing units, only 200 were designated low income. Similarly, local government entities like the New York Housing Preservation Department (HPD) have implemented policies that encourage high-end purchasers to the exclusion of low or moderate-income buyers.

Columbia University's planned $7 billion expansion into central and west Harlem was approved by state and local leaders, as well. The New York City Council voted on the plan a week before Christmas in December 2007 to avert "a bitter battle in a community of color stretching out into the New Year" (Michaud 2007, 1). Touting an economic and employment boon for the community, city officials announced that Columbia had "tentatively" agreed to spend $150 million as part of a community benefits agreement that would contribute to providing low- to moderate-income housing and expanded educational opportunities. However, University President Lee Bollinger did not rule out the possibility of obtaining additional desired property through eminent domain (Moynihan 2007).[8] These developments prompted Nellie Bailey, Director of the Harlem Tenants' Council, to observe "zoning and rezoning have become our 'Katrina' for Harlem's ethnic cleansing" (Bailey 2008b).

As gentrification accelerated in Harlem, law and policy continued to operate detrimentally to poor and moderate-income tenants of color. In 2003, for example, the state enacted legislation allowing landlords to demand market rent from tenants whose rent had been stabilized. Valerie Orridge, president of the Delano Village Tenants Association, a seven building complex of 1,800 units in Harlem commented, "Our new owners purchased the complex a year ago for $175 million only to refinance several months ago for $350 million! Some tenants upon lease renewal had increases upward to a thousand dollars! We are working people, where are we to go?" (*Workers World* 2007). Photographer Alice Attie ruefully surmised, "In a community such as Harlem, where a sense of place and a sense of having access to public space is essential to the concept of community itself, the process [of gentrification] becomes one of *erasure.*" As Attie further recalled, "In March 2003, two years after my project began, traveling up to Harlem to look at the sites I had photographed I found more than half of them were gone. There are losses that signify not merely the transitory nature of the urban landscape but threats to the very concept of ethnic diversity" (Attie 2003, 117).

New Orleans—Black Crescent City

After the deluge and devastation, the Black experience in New Orleans is typically viewed through the prism of Hurricane Katrina, which struck in August 2005. However, it is important to remember the continuum of New Orleans Black heritage, which, like Harlem, has been a primary locus of Black artistic, spiritual, political, and protest movements. Indeed, New Orleans's large free and bonded Black communities actively resisted slavery and racial subordination, including upon passage of the United States Slave Trade Act of 1807 when enslavement became an internal rather than international enterprise, with New Orleans as "the most important trading center of the lower South."[9] New Orleans is where Blacks notably challenged their unequal status, albeit unsuccessfully, to the U.S. Supreme Court in *Plessy v. Ferguson*.[10] Black diasporic communities from Africa, the Americas, and the Caribbean infused New Orleans's cultural mélange with Black musical traditions that gave rise to the blues, jazz, gospel, and zydeco. The community found information in publications such as the New Orleans *Crusader* and found strength in indigenous African religions and other major religious traditions. As Cornel West states:

> New Orleans has always been a city that lived on the edge . . . with Elysian Fields and cemeteries and the quest for paradise. When you live so close to death, behind the levees, you live more intensely, sexually, gastronomically, psychologically. Louis Armstrong came out of that unbelievable cultural breakthrough unprecedented in the history of American civilization. The rural blues, the urban jazz. It is the tragicomic lyricism that gives you the courage to get through the darkest storm. Charlie Parker would have killed somebody if he had not blown his horn. The history of black people in America is one of unbelievable resilience in the face of crushing white supremacist powers. (West 2005, 19)

In the South, as elsewhere, Black people gravitated to emerging cities in search of better opportunities. By 1900, there were 77,000 blacks in New Orleans. And as elsewhere, the forces of racial discrimination and disadvantage were entrenched in the social structure of Louisiana broadly and New Orleans specifically. In the aftermath of slavery, Blacks seeking better lives in urban centers were constrained by the Louisiana Black Code of 1865, Jim Crow laws, employment discrimination, and housing segregation. In New Orleans, these repressive measures demarcated racialized spaces that contained Blacks within predetermined areas and constrained Black people's literal and social mobility.

The federal government helped to establish the racially stratified spaces and conditions that continually imperiled Black people's lives by man-made and natural forces. Public housing in New Orleans was segregated since its inception in 1937, for instance, and funding under the American Federal Housing Act of 1949 was used to expand existing housing projects in situ rather than expand the geographical areas in which low- and moderate-income Blacks could reside (see Mahoney 1990).

Economically, as one of the nation's largest ports, New Orleans has been important to domestic and global transportation of goods, particularly regarding the petroleum-chemical industries. However, relocation of the petroleum industry to other Gulf Coast cities witnessed the decline of this economic sector. Moreover, New Orleans's historically anemic manufacturing sector declined even further during the post–World War II period. Between 1970 and 2000, New Orleans lost 13,500 manufacturing jobs, while low-paying service and retail sector jobs grew by 136 percent and 76 percent, respectively (see Brookings Institution 1, 2005). New Orleans subsequently adopted tourism as its primary economic industry.

During these economic transformations, Whites left the city for employment opportunities that grew in surrounding St. Tammany, Jefferson, and St. Charles parishes. With the loss of major industries and their replacement with low-paying jobs, and lack of transportation access to suburban areas, Blacks faced greater unemployment, underemployment, and consequent need for housing assistance. As the city got blacker, it got poorer: The New Orleans Black population grew from 37 percent in 1960 to nearly 70 percent in 2000; and, in 2000, the median household income for Black families was $21,461 compared to $40,390 for White families (see Dyson 2006; Brookings Institution 2, 2005b).

"The waters came in 2005, but the state did not, at least for the Ninth Ward" (James 2007, 162). On August 29, 2005, Hurricane Katrina struck the U.S. Gulf Coast, affecting nearly one million people and causing millions of dollars in destruction across Louisiana, Mississippi, and Alabama. By far the greatest damage, injury, and loss of life occurred in New Orleans. The Congressional Research Service (CRS) estimated that 77 percent of Orleans Parish, where New Orleans is located, was affected by the storm (Gabe et al. 2005). The CRS further estimated that about half of all the people displaced by the hurricane lived in New Orleans, and that the storm most heavily impacted the poor, elderly, young, and African Americans.

Blacks were especially vulnerable to the vicissitudes of natural disasters within the racialized dimensions of the particular geographical topology of New Orleans (Ducre 2005). The legacy of legal and de facto segregation meant that Blacks across income levels lived in the lowest and most marginalized areas of the city. Federal, state, and local policies assured suburban sprawl through the location of highways with easy exit from the inner city. It would later become painfully clear that a third of residents in the city's flooded areas lacked access to automobiles, which included about half of all poor Black residents and half of the children and elderly who were affected (Brookings Institution 1, 2005a; see also Neville 2007).[11]

Government at all levels also failed the people of New Orleans by failing to prepare for the storm and ignoring repeated warnings to repair the dangerous levee systems that were to protect the city from Lake Pontchartrain and the Mississippi River (U.S. House of Representatives, Bipartisan Committee Report 2006). Eighty percent of people of color in New Orleans lived in areas flooded by Hurricane Katrina, while only 54 percent of Whites were similarly affected. The majority of residents in the Lower Ninth Ward were Black. Historically, the Lower Ninth Ward was the only place where Blacks could buy homes. Thus, in addition to one-third of Black residents who lived below the poverty level, there was a significant population of Black middle class, educated, and professional residents who owned their homes and passed them down from generation to generation (Quigley 2008). By virtue of the racialization of space, as Kalamu Ya Salaam points out, "[A]ll strata of the Black community were wiped out by the flooding . . . Those who had nothing, lost everything. Those who had everything, lost everything" (Salaam 2007, xiii).

Legal scholar Kimberlé Crenshaw developed the theory of "intersectionality," which expounded on the multidimensionality of Black women's lives and revealed the manners in which Black women were vulnerable or erased in gendered spaces (typically perceived as White) and racial spaces (typically perceived as male) (Crenshaw 1989, 1991). In this regard, Black women were further victimized after Katrina by sexual violence perpetrated by officials of the state (such as the police, the National Guard, and the FBI) and by men and boys of the New Orleans community. Janelle White, a member of INCITE! New Orleans wrote, "The bottom line that this catastrophe painfully demonstrates is, yet again, how women and girls of color are at the intersection of violence perpetrated upon marginalized communities, both by external social forces and by those within our communities" (Bierra et al. 2007, 34).

Nearly as catastrophic as, and more enduring than, the natural effects of the hurricane were the hideous governmental responses to it. Besides the patent racism, it represented "the corporatization, criminalization, and militarization, and privatization of relief" (Flaherty 2007, 100). Black victims and survivors were maligned in life and in death. They were racially constructed as criminals and enemies as private paramilitary groups roamed the city's streets prepared to shoot to kill. Mindy Fullilove and colleagues state plainly:

> [T]he actions of the Federal Emergency Management Agency (FEMA) [among others] created chaos, rather than calming it, with the results that hundreds of thousands of poor people, many black, were left in dangerous waters, without food, water to drink, medicine, or succor. When help arrived, it was often callous and random, dispersing survivors of the flood throughout the forty-eight contiguous states without a plan for their arrival or their return home. (Fullilove et al. 2005, 304)

THE "NEW" NEW ORLEANS. The determinants of racialized space in New Orleans dictated not only who would be disproportionately affected by Hurricane Katrina, but also who would be able to return after the waters receded. By August 2008, only 11 percent of families who previously lived in the Lower Ninth Ward had returned home. In contrast, Whites who previously fled majority Black neighborhoods like the Lower Ninth Ward seized the opportunity to return to the city. Greater New Orleans is now 70 percent White. Such opportunism has altered the socio-demographics of New Orleans and has resulted in a city that is "older, Whiter, and more affluent" (Brookings Institution 2, 2005b). As Darwin Graham observed, "In other cities, it's simply called gentrification. But in post–Katrina New Orleans, it [is] called 'logical,' the 'return of nature,' 'opportunity,' and 'market forces'" (Graham 2005, 28). New Orleans political officials have endorsed several major projects in the new tourism-based economy and racial composition of the city. These initiatives include conglomerate-spawned multimillion-dollar tourist and residential developments geared toward affluent visitors and residents. Polling on the subject reveals that a majority of white New Orleans voters do not support rebuilding flooded areas such as the Lower Ninth Ward.[12] The Associated Press trenchantly noted, "Hurricane Katrina [may] prove to be the biggest, most brutal urban-renewal project Black America has ever seen" (Sexton 2007, 126).

While state legal, political, and economic apparatus have supported real estate speculation and corporate development, poorer New Orleans residents have been deprived of even meager legal protections to uphold their leases and prevent summary evictions. Many displaced renters' efforts to return to New Orleans were thwarted by unscrupulous landlords/owners who doubled or tripled rents, and instituted mass evictions. Bill Quigley has described how renters returned "to find furniture on the street and strangers living in their apartments at higher rents," despite the governor's order halting evictions after the storm (Quigley 2008; Lovett 2009).

Governmental policies create the conditions of poverty, with disproportionate race, gender, and class effects. These state-sponsored policies are manifest, for example, in the destruction of affordable housing, denial of health care, lack of environmentally safe public schools, and lack of other critical community services. In this vein, as the state creates the conditions of poverty, it enforces these conditions by punishing those who were most affected by also engineering their displacement and removal from their communities. As such, the conditions of many Black women's lives generated by these state-sponsored policies made it particularly difficult for low-income Black women to return home to New Orleans (Bierra et al. 2007). The Institute for Women's Policy Research found that before Katrina, women made up 56 percent of the local workforce, but comprised only 46 percent after the storm (Bierra et al. 2007). The government's active participation in perpetuating inequality and conditions of impoverishment through social policy, legal rulings, and economic deprivation resonate under Galtung's theory of state-sponsored structural violence, creating forced migration and displacement of people of African descent and other people of color from New Orleans, with disparate impact on Black women and children.

EFFECTS OF GENTRIFICATION: COMMUNITY TRANSFORMATION AND TRAUMA

As discussed in this chapter, racialized spaces such as Harlem and Black neighborhoods in New Orleans are not accidental creations and are not total functions of individual agency. Indeed, despite incredible resilience and innovative methods of self-sustainability, it is difficult for the poor to come out from under formidable constraints precisely because state-sponsored and endorsed practices of gentrification, destruction of affordable housing, and eminent domain are purposely established by law and custom to concentrate predominantly poor Black populations in areas marked by official and social disparity and neglect (Phillips and Sillah 2009). The subsequent gentrification of such neighborhoods is fueled by the same forces of their creation: racist and classist systems that prioritize wealth and property accumulation through national and global capital infusions over the fundamental shelter and security needs of citizens, families, and communities of color.

Gentrification, as with earlier eras of leveling Black communities through urban renewal, is called progress.

> Root shock, at the level of the individual, is a profound emotional upheaval that destroys the working model of the world that had existed in the individual's head. Root shock undermines trust, increases anxiety about letting loved ones out of one's sight, destabilizes relationships, destroys social, emotional, and financial resources, and increases risk for every kind of stress-related disease, from depression to heart attack. . . . Root shock, at the level of the local community . . . ruptures bonds, dispersing people to all the directions of the compass. . . . Root shock goes even further than one city, linking a local tragedy to events around the globe (Fullilove 2004, 14–16).

Yet, as Mindy Fullilove notes, "For the people whose homes and districts were bulldozed . . . [urban renewal] *was nothing short of assault*" (Fullilove 2004, 7). Speaking about post–Katrina New Orleans, Fullilove states, "The idea that maybe we will do something with the Ninth Ward that won't include poor people in New Orleans is really an assault on somebody who has been evacuated from a disaster and then told, 'Well, maybe you can never go home'" (Fullilove 2006). In law and common parlance, assault is understood as threatened or actual violence. When it is propagated by government policy, it is also state-sponsored structural violence. As posited in this chapter, gentrification must be viewed accordingly as direct and structural violent assaults on Black people and Black communities.

Gentrification, the Centers for Disease Control and Prevention (CDC) notes, "is a housing, economic, and health issue that affects a community's history and culture and reduces social capital" (U.S. Department of HSS 2009). The health consequences include shorter life expectancy, higher cancer rates, more birth defects, greater infant mortality, and higher instances of asthma, diabetes, and cardiovascular disease, which are all diseases that register statistically higher in Black communities. The CDC also noted greater incidence of injuries, violence and crime, mental health, and social and environmental justice concerns. These ills are predictable, preventable, and known to occur in conjunction with the displacement that stems from gentrification. In this light, therefore, these effects must be viewed as intentional infliction of harm against poor people of color by the state and private actors who profit from deracinating communities like Harlem and New Orleans and transforming them from places of Black cultural security into sites of ever-increasing White presence and concomitant economic and political power. U.S. governmental entities must be held accountable for these acts of structural violence that result from persistent inequities in the housing situation in this country (Galtung 1990, 1969; Farmer 2004).

In their extensive study of gentrification and displacement in seven New York City neighborhoods, including Harlem, urban studies scholars Kathe Newman and Elvin Wyly found that in 2002 about 225,000 renters with incomes below the poverty line had moved at least once and cited cost pressures among their reasons (Newman and Wyly 2005). Nearly 43 percent of those respondents were directly displaced either by private landlord or government actions, and many people described unprecedented pressure from landlords who pushed tenants out in order to obtain higher rents (Newman and Wyly 2005).

Newman and Wyly's research refutes claims by other researchers that minimize the relationship between gentrification and displacement of long-term residents and its ensuing harms (cf. Freeman and Braconi 2004; Vigdor 2002).[13] In Fort Greene (Brooklyn) and Harlem (Manhattan), two communities with large Black populations, Newman and Wyly found that displaced residents moved great distances from the city to Long Island, New Jersey, and upstate New York; others engaged in the reverse Great Migration to the South. Still other displaced renters doubled up with family or friends, moved into shelters or onto the streets. As Newman and Wyly ruefully note, however, "Those who are most vulnerable to displacement, and those who must endure its greatest hardships, are invisible in the dataset" (Newman and Wyly 2005, 142).

For residents who manage to stay, the advent of improved conditions and services draws mixed feelings, and often exacerbates their anxiety about the changes in their neighborhoods. Many residents, of course, long advocated for improvements in their communities. For example, Ms. Walker, a long-term resident of the General Grant public housing complex in Harlem and her neighbors expressed concern about their future in three to five years: "Change is good, and progress is inevitable. But the feeling is, 'What are we going to do? Where are we going to go?'" (Williams 2008).

Another important consequence of displacement is the impact on a community's political voice. When one examines the evidence, one is compelled to ask: is this the ultimate intent of state policies? For example, there were 46,000 fewer African American voters in New Orleans in the 2007 Louisiana gubernatorial election than in the 2003 gubernatorial election. In 2005, the Federal Emergency Management Agency (FEMA) denied funding to inform displaced New Orleans residents that they could cast absentee ballots in critical elections after the storm. Many local activists viewed FEMA's refusal to support the voting rights of evacuees as consistent with the larger objective to discourage Black residents' return to the city (Davis 2005).

In the changed post–Katrina political order, in which White residents have gained more political power in New Orleans, effectively electing the first White-majority city council since 1985 and Mitch Landrieu as mayor, some have suggested that the new political landscape heralds a "post-racial" New Orleans. Even if the post-racial concept were fathomable, such pronouncements seem premature or unfounded, as Landrieu himself acknowledged upon recognizing that his election may evince "an uneasy moment" for Black residents who still feel politically and economically disenfranchised (Mock 2010).

Five years after Katrina, Black residents in New Orleans remain disproportionately affected by laggard recovery efforts. Anxiety over diminished population and tenuous political voice is a realistic concern for citizens in racialized communities who have fought and died for political inclusion and governmental responsiveness since, historically, the redrawing of political boundaries has often been used to disenfranchise or dilute the voting strength of communities of color (See Ford 1994; Clarke 2005).[14] As the preceding discussion demonstrates, the health and social effects of gentrification and displacement are severe and seriously compromise physical and mental well-being, community connections, and political voice. In the face of such threats, residents are coalescing and rallying to save their neighborhoods.

RESISTANCE TO GENTRIFICATION

Michèle Alexandre described a powerful lesson upon assisting an elderly African American woman in the post–Katrina cleanup:

> I was assigned to help clean, gut, and restore a public housing unit. . . . My first instinct was to throw away all of the contents of the house. I was in the process of implementing this agenda when I met the owner of the housing unit. She was a small, frail woman who could have been my mother. As she watched me place her clothes and her other belongings in a "throw away" pile, her eyes began to water. Finally, she stopped me and told me: "This [is] all I have. I had to leave everything when the storm came and I have been away from my home for a year and a half. Please, let's look to see if we can salvage anything." At that moment, I was forced to step out of my efficiency-motivated mindset and had to remind myself that for Ms. Jackson . . . this was a last attempt at salvaging any remnant of her life pre-Katrina. Ms. Jackson, like many others, did not want her pre-Katrina life to be discarded as no longer useful or relevant. (Alexandre 2009, 157–8)

As a parable of our times, Ms. Jackson refused to have her life discarded and tossed in the "throw away" box. So, too, the resistance against the gentrification and displacement of Black geographical, cultural, and political communities such as New Orleans and Harlem. As Nellie Bailey, director of the Harlem Tenants Council insists:

> Harlem has the right to remain as the historic African-American community. And that it wasn't just a matter of Blacks coming to Harlem, but it was a matter of public policy predicated on race and class that created the largest concentration of people of African descent in one location in the city of New York. And what came out of that was not pity but a rebirth. And as they said at the time of the Harlem Renaissance, the New Negro, and that is worth fighting for as part of community, and that is the community of historic Harlem (Bailey 2008a).

Currently, countless long-term Black residents of Harlem and New Orleans are vulnerable to the violence of root shock. The present era of increased housing costs, luxury commercial development, massive displacement, and drastically reduced legal protections for low and moderate income homeowners and renters requires sustained, informed, and inventive activism by grass-roots organizations to effect what Chester Hartman has called a "right to stay put" movement that is predicated on the belief that "moving people involuntarily from their homes or neighborhoods is wrong" (Hartman 1984, 306). Such activism is well underway. In August 2008, for example, a broad coalition of groups participated in a "call to action, day of unity" to demonstrate against the shared struggles of gentrification and displacement in New York City and New Orleans (Make the Road Staff 2008). In both cities, communities and organizations have held public forums, sued to stop demolition of existing and repairable housing, protested the use of eminent domain for private profit, advocated for greater public support for low and moderate income homeowners and renters, demanded mandatory inclusionary zoning practices, boycotted "big box" stores, and lobbied Congress and local governments to stop cutting housing programs.

Whether the discussion is urban renewal, gentrification, or foreclosure, poor and moderate income Black people are under tremendous assault with respect to housing in iconic Black neighborhoods in Harlem and New Orleans, and across the United States. Having established racialized communities, policies that engender poverty, and other conditions for gentrification, the state bears the greatest responsibility to remedy the violent manifestations of the extant housing crises. Law and social justice values in the United States must be oriented to meet fundamental human needs against the expedient interests of local and global capital accumulation and the insecurity it engenders. This view must eschew parochial domestic legal schemes and embrace international law, which recognizes the *right*, not just the *privilege*, of decent, affordable housing for citizens (Wing 2006; Edwards 2006).

Surely, as Mindy Fullilove correctly states, "We have the possibility of preventing further damage by nurturing the world's neighborhoods instead of destroying them" (Fullilove 2004, 7). As New Orleans activist Kalamu Ya Salaam further insists, "We who live below the water line have no choice. Our first priority is to survive. Our second priority is to struggle. Our ultimate responsibility is to win. Survive. Struggle. Win" (Salaam 20007, xviii).

NOTES

1. Mindy Fullilove, M.D., a psychiatrist, described "root shock" as "the traumatic stress reaction to the destruction of all or part of one's emotional ecosystem" experienced by those who had been displaced through urban renewal and other forms of forced dislocation.

2. Black resident of public housing in Chicago quoted in Patillo (2007, 11).

3. For instance, Peter Marcuse insists that critical distinctions be drawn between "abandonment" and "development" regarding gentrification. In contrast, john powell calls attention to the relationship between sprawl, concentrated poverty, and the need for regional responses to gentrification. Mary Patillo and Sheryll Cashin focus on the dynamics when the "gentrifiers" in poor and working-class communities of color are themselves people of color, albeit more affluent. I am aware of these distinctions and debates and do not intentionally gloss over them. However, while salient, I do not find them essential to illuminate the core issues and harms pertaining to gentrification that are the subject of this chapter.

4. Roberts notes Andrew Beveridge's finding that "racial isolation is increasing for blacks, falling slightly for whites" and that "income level has very little impact on the degree of residential racial segregation experienced by African-Americans."

5. Saskia Sassen explicates the global dynamics noting, "The evidence shows that under specific conditions the massive spatial dispersal of economic activities at the metropolitan, national, and global levels we associate with globalization has actually contributed to new forms of territorial centralization of top-level management and control operations. On the one hand, large cities concentrate a disproportionate share of corporate power and are one of the key sites for the overvalorization of the corporate economy; on the other hand, they concentrate a disproportionate share of the disadvantaged and are one of the key sites for their devalorization" (Sassen 2006, 107, 126).

6. Smith cites, for example, a sixty-one-unit condominium in New York's Lower East

Side, two miles from Wall Street, where every apartment is wired with the latest high-speed Internet connections. This is a small development by global city standards, but it was built by nonunion immigrant labor, the developer is Israeli, and the major source of financing comes from the European American Bank. Sassen also speaks to the unprecedented scale, stating, "Inequality in the profit-making capabilities of different sectors of the economy has always existed. But what we see happening today takes place on another order of magnitude and is engendering massive distortions in the operations of markets, from housing to labor" (Sassen 1998, 89).

7. For instance, after decades of opposition to racial integration, Westchester County, New York, recently entered a settlement with the Department of Housing and Urban Development (HUD), and agreed to create hundreds of houses and apartments for moderate income people in overwhelmingly White communities and market them to people of color in Westchester and New York City. Blacks comprise only 1 percent of the population in twelve of the more affluent overwhelmingly White Westchester communities (See Roberts 2009; also see Applebome 2009).

8. See also, Hollis (2007), discussing *Kelo v. City of New London*, 125 U.S. 2655 (2005), in which the Supreme Court ruled that the government could seize private property for economic development, that is, for public use, without violating the Fifth Amendment.

9. New Orleans had a large population of free Blacks since the early 1700s. Professors Franklin and Moss note, "Revolts, or conspiracies to revolt, began with the institution and did not end until slavery was abolished," further noting uprisings in Louisiana, and New Orleans in particular (See Franklin and Moss 1994, 115, 144–5). Also, even with passage of the 1807 Act, the illicit international slave trade continued in the United States. "New York merchants as well as those of New Orleans were benefiting from the illicit traffic" (Franklin and Moss 1994, 120).

10. *Plessy v. Ferguson*, 163 U.S. 537 (1896) (upholding the "separate but equal" doctrine of Black racial subordination).

11. Evidence of the disparate lack of transportation and mobility is reflected in Charmaine Neville's searing description of the desperate and successful commandeering of a school bus to rescue abandoned neighbors in the Ninth Ward.

12. "Whites Oppose Reviving Flood-Ruined Black Areas," *Syracuse Post-Standard*, May 31, 2009, A4.

13. Freeman and Braconi conclude that living in a gentrifying neighborhood in New York City made it less likely a poor resident would move; Vigdor concludes that gentrification drives comparatively few low-income residents from their homes in Boston.

14. In *Gomillion v. Lightfoot*, 364 U.S. 339 (1960), for example, the city of Tuskegee, Alabama, redrew district boundaries to exclude Blacks, while in *Shaw v. Reno*, 509 U.S. 630 (1993), the Supreme Court struck down a district in North Carolina that created a majority Black district to enable the election of a Black representative in Congress. In both cases, the Supreme Court noted the "bizarreness" of the shapes of the districts: one (Ala.), a twenty-eight-sided figure drawn to exclude Black political participation, and the other (N.C.) traversed a long stretch of Interstate-85 drawn to rectify the exclusion of Black political participation. Despite the Court's recent decision upholding the constitu-

tionality of the Voting Rights Act (VRA), it has shown increasing antipathy toward race-conscious remedies for racial discrimination generally, and in the voting rights context in particular. See *Northwest Austin Municipal Utility District v. Holder*, 557 U.S. (2009) (upholding the VRA, but questioning the future vitality of its race-conscious rationale). See also, Kristen Clarke's discussion of the 2006 New Orleans election in Marable and Clarke (Clarke 2005).

REFERENCES

Alexandre, Michèle. 2009. Navigating the topography of inequality post-disaster. In *Law and recovery from disaster: Hurricane Katrina*, ed. Robin Malloy, 157–58. Burlington, Vt.: Ashgate.

Appiah, Kwame A., and Henry Louis Gates Jr., eds. 2003. *Africana: The encyclopedia of the African and African-American experience*. New York: Basic Civitas Books.

Applebome, Peter. 2009. Integration faces a new twist in the suburbs. *New York Times*. August 23.

Attie, Alice. 2003. Afterword. In *Harlem on the verge*, ed. Alice Attie, 117–18. New York: Quantuck Lane Press.

Bailey, Nellie Hester. 2008a. Growing pains come to Harlem. *Weekend Edition Saturday*, National Public Radio. November 1.

———. 2008b. Juneteenth march and rally in Harlem against gentrification. Accessed June 1, 2008. http://www.assatashakur.org/forum/new-york-city/31104-juneteenth-march-rally-harlem-ny.

Beveridge, Andrew. 2009. An affluent, white Harlem? *Gotham Gazette*. August 27. http://www.gothamgazette.com/print/2620.

Bierra, Alisa, Mayaba Liebenthal, and INCITE! Women of Color against Violence. 2007. To render ourselves visible: Women of color organizing and Hurricane Katrina. In *What lies beneath* 31–47. Cambridge, Mass.: South End Press.

Brookings Institution. 2005a. *Key indicators of entrenched poverty*. Washington, D.C.: Brookings Institution. http://www.brookings.edu/~/media/Files/Metro%20Simple%Pages/20050920_povertynumbers.pdf.

Brookings Institution Metropolitan Policy Program. 2005b. *New Orleans after the storm: Lessons from the past, a plan for the future*, (October). http://www.brookings.edu/reports/2005/10metropolitanplicy.aspx.

Calmore, John O. 1995. Racialized space and the culture of segregation: "Hewing a stone from a mountain of despair." *University of Pennsylvania Law Review* 143:1233–73.

Cashin, Sheryll. 2004. *The failures of integration: How race and class are undermining the American Dream*. New York: Public Affairs.

Clarke, John Henrik. 1971. *Harlem USA*. New York: Collier Books.

Clarke, Kristen. 2005. Race-ing the post-Katrina political landscape: An analysis of the 2006 New Orleans election. In *Seeking higher ground: The Hurricane Katrina crisis, race, and public policy reader*, ed. Marable, Manning, and Clarke, 33–38. New York: Palgrave MacMillan.

Collins, Patricia Hill. 1990. *Black feminist thought: Knowledge, consciousness, and the politics of empowerment.* New York: Routledge.

Crenshaw, Kimberlé. 1989. Demarginalizing the intersection of race and sex: A black feminist critique of antidiscrimination doctrine, feminist theory and antiracist politics. *University of Chicago Legal Forum* 139:139–68.

———. 1991. Mapping the margins: Identity politics, intersectionality and violence against women of color. *Stanford Law Review* 43 (6): 1241–300.

Crenshaw, Kimberlé, Neil Gotanda, Gary Peller, and Kendall Thomas, eds. 1995. *Critical race theory: The key writings that formed the movement.* New York: New Press.

Davis, Mike. 2005. Gentrifying disaster. *Mother Jones.* October 25.

Ducre, Kishi A. 2005. Hurricane Katrina as an elaboration on an ongoing theme: Racialized spaces in Louisiana. In *Seeking higher ground: The Hurricane Katrina crisis, race, and public policy reader,* ed. Marable, Manning, and Clarke, 65–74. New York: Palgrave MacMillan.

Dyson, Michael Eric. 2006. *Come hell or high water: Hurricane Katrina and the color of disaster.* New York: Basic Books.

Edwards, George E. 2006. International human rights law violations before, during and after Hurricane Katrina: An international law framework for analysis. *Thurgood Marshall Law Review* 31:353–426.

Farmer, Paul. 2004. *Pathologies of power: Health, human rights, and the war on the new poor.* Berkeley: University of California Press.

Flaherty, Jordan. 2007. Corporate reconstruction and grassroots resistance. In *What lies beneath* 100–19. Cambridge, Mass.: South End Press.

Ford, Richard T. 1994. The boundaries of race: Political geography in legal analysis. *Harvard Law Review* 107:1841–920.

Foucault, Michel. 1980. The eye of power. In *Power/knowledge,* ed. Colin Gordon, 146–65. Trans. Colin Gordon, Leo Marshall, John Mepham, and Kate Soper. New York: Pantheon Books.

Franklin, John Hope, and Alfred A. Moss Jr. 1994. *From slavery to freedom: A history of African Americans.* New York: Knopf.

Freeman, Lance, and Frank Braconi. 2004. Gentrification and displacement: New York City in the 1990s. *Journal of the American Planning Association* 70:39–52.

Fullilove, Mindy. 2004. *Root shock: How tearing up city neighborhoods hurts America, and what we can do about it.* New York: One World/Ballantine Books.

———. 2006. Interview in WBHM-FM/NPR, Making Sense of Mental Health. Radio Segment is Hurricane Katrina: Root Shock. http://www.wbhm.org/News/2005/rootshock.html. January 30.

Fullilove, Mindy, Fred Bosman, Henk Bakker, Pieter de Wit, Eric Noorthoorn, and Robert Fullilove. 2005. Envisioning "complete recovery" as an alternative to "unmitigated disaster." In *Seeking higher ground: The Hurricane Katrina crisis, race, and public policy reader,* ed. Marable, Manning, and Clarke, 303–11. New York: Palgrave MacMillan.

Gabe, Thomas, Gene Falk, Maggie McCarty, and Virginia Mason. 2005. *Hurricane Ka-*

trina: Social-demographic characteristics of impacted areas. Virginia Cong. Research Service report for Congress, November 4.

Galtung, Johan. 1969. Violence, peace, peace research. *Journal of Peace Research* 6 (3): 167–91.

———. 1990. Cultural violence. *Journal of Peace Research* 27 (3): 291.

Glass, Ruth, University College London, Centre for Urban Studies, et al. 1964. *London: Aspects of change.* London: MacGibbon & Kee.

Graham, Darwin Bond. 2005. The New Orleans that race built: Racism, disaster, and urban spatial relationships. In *Seeking higher ground: The Hurricane Katrina crisis, race, and public policy reader,* ed. Marable, Manning, and Clarke, 17–32. New York: Palgrave MacMillan.

Grassroots/Low-Income/People of Color-led Hurricane Katrina Relief, November 2005, http://katrina.mayfirst.org.

Halpern, Robert. 1995. *Rebuilding the inner city: A history of neighborhood initiatives to address poverty in the United States.* New York: Columbia University Press.

Hartman, Chester. 1984. The right to stay put. In *Land reform American style,* ed. Charles C. Geisler and Frank J. Popper, 302–18. Totowa, N.J.: Rowman and Allanheld.

Hollis, Adrienne L. 2007. Eminent domain and compensation—From the Trail of Tears to Hurricane Katrina: Is it just? *Rutgers Race and Law Review* 8:349–85.

James, Joy. 2007. Afterword: Political literacy and voice. In *What lies beneath: Katrina, race, and the state of the nation,* ed. South End Press Collective, 157–66. Cambridge, Mass.: South End Press.

James, Joy, and T. Denean Sharpley-Whiting. 2000. *The black feminist reader.* Malden, Mass.: Blackwell Publishers.

Kelley, Robin D. G. 2003. Introduction. In *Harlem on the verge,* ed. Alice Attie, 9–17. New York: Quantuck Lane Press.

Lovett, John A. 2009. Property and radical change: Observations on property relationships from Post-Katrina New Orleans. In *Law and recovery from disaster: Hurricane Katrina,* ed. Robin Paul Malloy, 7–36. Burlington, Vt.: Ashgate.

Mahoney, Martha. 1990. Law and racial geography: Public housing and the economy in New Orleans. *Stanford Law Review* 42:1251–76.

Make the Road Staff. Over 300 community activists commemorate 3rd anniversary of Hurricane Katrina. Accessed August 29, 2008. http://www.maketheroad.org/article_print.php?

Marcuse, Peter. 1995. Gentrification, abandonment, and displacement: Connections, causes, and policy responses in New York City. *Washington University Journal of Urban and Contemporary Law* 28:195–248.

———. 1999. Comment on Elvin K. Wyly and Daniel J. Hammel's "Islands of decay in seas of renewal: Housing policy and the resurgence of gentrification." *Housing Policy Debate* 10:789–97.

Massey, Douglas S., and Nancy A. Denton. 1993. *American Apartheid: Segregation and the making of the underclass.* Cambridge, Mass.: Harvard University Press.

McFarlane, Audrey G. 1999. Race, space, and place: The geography of economic development. *San Diego Law Review* 36:295–340.

McKittrick, Katherine, and Clyde Woods, eds. 2007. *Black geographies*. Cambridge, Mass.: South End Press.

Michaud, Anne. 2007. City council approves Columbia expansion. *Crain's New York Business.com*. Accessed December 19, 2007. http://www.crainsnewyork/com/apps/pbos.d11/article?AID=/20071219/FREE/1210356333/1058/newsletter01.

Mock, Brentin. 2010. Breaking news: Landrieu elected mayor of New Orleans. Accessed February 5, 2010 at http://www.theroot.com/views/breaking-news-landrieu-elected-mayor-new-orleans.

Moynihan, Colin. 2007. Columbia announces deal on its 17-acre expansion plan. *New York Times*. Accessed September 27, 2007. http://www/nytimes.com/2007/09/27ny region/27columbia.htm?pagewanted=print.

Neville, Charmaine. 2007. How we survived the flood. In *What Lies Beneath: Katrina, race, and the state of the nation*, ed. South End Press Collective, 28–30. Cambridge, Mass.: South End Press.

Newman, Kathe, and Elvin Wyly. 2005. Gentrification and resistance in New York City. *National Housing Institute*. July/August. http://www.nhi.org/online/issues/142/gen trification.html.

Olivo, Antonio. 2001. As Clinton moves in, Harlem rents go UP. *Chicago Sun-Times*. July 22.

Patillo, Mary. 2007. *Black on the block: The politics of race and class in the city*. Chicago: University of Chicago Press.

Phillips, Sandra, and Marion Sillah. 2009. A house is not a home: Effect of eminent domain of the poor, African Americans, and the elderly. *Housing and Society* 36: 111–33.

powell, john a. 2000. Race, poverty, and urban sprawl: Access to opportunities through regional strategies. Institute on Race and Poverty. Accessed August 29, 2008. http://www.umn.edu/irp/publications/racepovertyandurbansprawl.html.

Quigley, Bill. 2008. New Orleans: Leaving the poor behind again! *Counterpunch*. October 11. http://www.counterpunch.org/quigley10112005.html.

Roberts, Sam. 2009. Westchester County agrees to desegregate housing in mostly white towns. *New York Times*. August 11.

Salaam, Kalamu Ya. 2007. Introduction: Below the water line. In *What lies beneath: Katrina, race, and the state of the nation*, ed. South End Press Collective, ix–xviii. Cambridge, Mass: South End Press.

Sassen, Saskia. 1998. *Globalization and its discontents: Essays on the new mobility of people and money*. New York: The New Press.

———. 2007. *A sociology of globalization*. New York: W.W. Norton.

Schaffer, Richard, and Neil Smith. 1986. The gentrification of Harlem? *Annals of the Association of American Geographers* 76 (3): 347–65.

Scott, Janny. 2001. White flight, this time toward Harlem; newcomers and good times bring hope, and fears of displacement. *New York Times*. February 25.

Sexton, Jared. 2007. The obscurity of black suffering. In *What lies beneath: Katrina, race, and the state of the nation*, ed. South End Press Collective, 120–32. Cambridge, Mass.: South End Press.

Smith, Neil. 2002. New globalism, new urbanism: Gentrification as global urban strategy. *Antipode* 34 (3): 427–50.

Smith, Neil, and J. DiFilippis. 1999. The reassertion of economics: 1990s gentrification in the Lower East Side. *International Journal of Urban and Regional Research* 23:638–53.

Soja, Edward W. 1989. *Postmodern geographies*. London: Verso Press.

Sverdlik, Alan. 1993. Take the a-train; heart of Harlem starts where the subway stops. *Chicago Tribune*. November 7:6C.

Syracuse Post-Standard. 2009. Whites oppose reviving flood-ruined black areas. May 31.

Thompson, Richard F. 1997. Geography and sovereignty: Jurisdictional formation and racial segregation. *Stanford Law Review* 49:1365.

U.S. Department of Health and Human Services, Centers for Disease Control and Prevention. Health effects of gentrification. Accessed August 25, 2009. http://www.cdc.gov/HEALTHYPLACES/healthtopics/gentrification.htm.

U.S. House of Representatives. *A failure of initiative: Final report of the Select Bipartisan Committee to investigate the preparation for and response to Hurricane Katrina*. Accessed August 25, 2008. http://www.gpoaccess.gov/katrinareport/fullreport.pdf.

Vigdor, Jacob. 2002. Does gentrification harm the poor? *Brookings-Wharton Papers on Urban Affairs* 134–73. http://muse.jhu.edu/login?uri=/journals/brookings-wharton_papers_on_urban_affairs/v2002.1vigdor.html.

West, Cornel. 2005. World: Hurricane aftermath: Exiles from a city and from a nation. The Observer. September 11:19, quoted in Walters, Joanna. *Tikkun Magazine Online*, September. http://files.tikkun.org/current/article.php?story=20061028140331323.

Wharton, Jonathan L. 2008. Gentrification: The new colonialism in the modern era. *The Forum on Public Policy* 2:1–12. http://www.forumpublicpolicy.com/summer08papers/archivesummer08/wharton.pdf.

Williams, Timothy. 2008. Mixed feelings as change overtakes 125th Street. *New York Times*. June 13.

Wing, Adrien K. 2006. From wrongs to rights: Hurricane Katrina from a global perspective. In *After the storm: Black intellectuals explore the meaning of Hurricane Katrina*, ed. David D. Troutt, 127–45. New York: New Press.

Workers World. 2007. Harlem, N.Y. conference held on housing crisis. June 18.

Young, Iris. 1990. *Justice and the politics of difference* Princeton, N.J.: Princeton University Press.

CHAPTER FOUR

Schooled In/Security

Surplus Subjects, Racialized Masculinity, and Citizenship

DEBORAH COWEN and AMY SICILIANO

In 1986, Attorney General Felix Nunez instituted the nation's first program of "zero tolerance," impounding all seagoing vessels found carrying any trace of drugs in American waters. Soon after, the language and spirit of zero tolerance pushed inland to become a chief technology in the United States' War on Drugs. Spearheading an era of unprecedented penality, zero tolerance policies have been central in the radical reshaping of life trajectories for African American men, prompting their incarceration rates to soar during the 1980s.[1] Zero tolerance policies demand automatic and severe punishment for a wide range of infractions. They resonate with the individualist and revanchist sentiments circulating at a time of social and economic upheaval, quickly infiltrating a sweeping range of policy arenas. Perhaps the most powerful impact of zero tolerance has been in the field of education where it is now in place in 80 percent of the nation's public schools (Heaviside et al. 1998). As a strategy of school discipline, zero tolerance has similar impacts as the "war" that spawned it: starkly racialized social violence enacted through the criminalization of young men of color. Flaherty captures this well in sharing the words of a student at John McDonogh High School in New Orleans, "Being at John Mac feels like I'm in prison . . . The bus ride to school feels like a trip from court to jail" (Flaherty 2006).

Not long after zero tolerance was transferred from the national border to the public schools, another geopolitical force invaded the classroom. In inner city neighborhoods across the United States since the late 1990s, military academies began *replacing* public schools altogether. In Chicago alone over 10,000 students now wear military uniforms to class, suggesting a startling pace of growth since the opening of the first military high school in that city in 1999. Perhaps even more striking is the highly targeted nature of this militarization. Young men of color constitute 92 percent of the cadet/student body, leading one critic to ask, "why are they good schools for low income African American and Latino students and not good schools for affluent white kids?" (Public Broadcasting Service 2007). Indeed, the classed racialization of this militarization of education is no accident; it is part of a deepening crisis of military recruitment and an official response that targets particular groups for enlistment. The replacement of public schools with military academies in poor communities of color is a sign of the military's growing reliance on so-called surplus populations to fill the ranks.

Both zero tolerance education policies and public military academies can be understood as part of a securitization of the lives of young men of color in conjunction with their widespread shedding from the formal economy. On the one hand, zero tolerance aggressively *produces* delinquency, establishing the means for securitization and the conditions for exceptional exploitation. Zero tolerance in schools helps engineer the rise of a carceral economy and society with sharply racialized contours. According to a recent study, 72 percent of black males in their twenties without high school diplomas were either unable to find work or incarcerated, while 60 percent of those in their thirties who had not finished high school had spent time in prison (Eckholm 2006). Critical scholars emphasize the fungible nature of criminality, highlighting the ways in which prisons and policing systems expand even as crime remains constant or declines. The expansion of carceral institutions has been identified as a leading political and economic response to deindustrialization, absorbing populations that are thereby made redundant by changing regional and global patterns of uneven development (Body-Gendrot 2000; Gilmore 2007; Wacquant 2002). The prison system has become a means of warehousing a racialized reserve army of predominantly young male labor. Zero tolerance in the schools criminalizes entire populations and constitutes them as undeserving citizens, a status that thereby circumscribes future incarceration.

On the other hand, military academies provide a route for devalorized subjects to resuscitate their social standing and social security by enlisting into the service. The explicit militarization of public education is part of this same story of the securitization of surplus subjects. With its housing and health care, college tuition and long-term contracts, the military makes redundant lives "productive," offering what are increasingly rare opportunities of stable work and employment benefits in a precarious economy. It is not only activists and critical scholars, but also libertarian think tanks that have deemed the military a highly potent form of *workfare* (Cowen 2008).[2] But the military offers more than just a regular paycheck to personnel; it extends a route to deserving citizenship through sacrifice and service for surplus populations.

In this chapter we explore this securitization of citizenship with a focus on the institutional and geographic site that plays a key role in sorting young people's trajectories through this mode of re/production: the schools. The racialized and classed demographics of urban schools in the United States, when considered alongside the role of schools in the production and control of knowledge, values, and ideas, makes them particularly constructive sites to consider security as the assemblage of a means of reproducing human lives. We suggest that the dual role of schools in cultivating future citizens and training future workers has made schools constitutive sites of what we term "securitized social reproduction." Indeed, the securitization of childhood is particularly significant as it propels the possibility of lives lived wholly within institutions and discourses of security. However, as the cases of zero tolerance and military academies suggest, the logistics of this securitization relies on sorting surplus populations into categories of deserving and undeserving citizens. Securitization is definitive of both of these trajectories; the space of the school is increasingly definitive in ordering circulation, and so, too, accumulation, through each route.

As key institutions of social reproduction, schools play a pivotal role in the pervasive securitization of economy and society. But before turning to this topic, we first outline in the next section three trajectories that we argue constitute the move toward securitized social reproduction. Following this, we trace the historical and contemporary function of schools in the constitution of modern citizenship. In the final two sections, we bring these two themes together to examine specific practices of criminalization and militarization in schools, in particular the racialized and gendered process of social sorting they engender.

SURPLUS MASCULINITIES AND SECURITY

Looking at the United States today, there is little doubt that urban penality and national militarism are both a means of warehousing reserve armies of labor. However, as we have argued elsewhere,[3] these different forms of the securitization of surplus subjects—criminalization and militarization—are increasingly entangled (Cowen and Siciliano, forthcoming). Rather than separate or competing processes (see Sutton 2000), criminalization and militarization are moments in an evolving assemblage of securitized social reproduction. If social reproduction is "the relationship between how we live at work and how we live outside it" (Mitchell, Marsden, and Katz 2003, 416), then securitized social reproduction is the assembly of a future wherein targeted groups reproduce themselves and are productive within securitized identities, institutions, and industries. Securitized social reproduction relies precisely on the cycling of racialized surplus subjects from criminalization to incarceration to militarization, and with the privatization of prisons, policing and military force offers unprecedented opportunities for accumulation every step along the way. Elsewhere, we have traced some of the changing policies and practices that engineer this cycling from one institution and experience of securitization to another (Cowen and Siciliano, forthcoming). For instance, the growing use of moral waivers to admit felons into the armed forces is one key and explicit instance of this entanglement, providing a direct valve on bulging prison populations, and channeling lives and labor into the arid armed forces.

Securitized social reproduction points not simply toward the expansion of security industries, but entails three more precise trends. First, security operates not only as a means of discipline and social control, but increasingly as a means of accumulation. Prisons and militaries are not simply warehouses for surplus populations, but are increasingly factory spaces. The construction and management of prison facilities, as well as the hyperexploitation of inmates as captive labor, are clear signs of the expansion of capitalist accumulation through incarceration (Gilmore 2007; LeBaron 2008). Warfare, too, is wide open for business. The military industrial complex is hardly a new phenomenon, but the pace and extent of the marketization of warfare is stark (Klein 2007; Scahill 2007).

Second, the expansion of this economy must be situated within the massive transformations in the gendered division of paid labor. The decline of traditional industrial employment in advanced capitalist economies over the last four decades has also characterized the redundancy of the forms of masculinity typically associated with blue-collar work—machismo, strength, and physicality (McDowell 2003). At the same time, the rise of service sector work and other forms of immaterial labor rely ever more on emotional and affective labor. These transformations and others have led scholars to diagnose an ongoing process of labor market "feminization" (Vosko 2000).

Labor restructuring is tightly interwoven with education systems. Perhaps unsurprisingly, we have seen sustained attention pivoting on boys' underachievement in a range of subjects and socialization skills in comparison to their female counterparts (McDowell 2003; Connell 2000). In recent years, performative failures that have long stigmatized the lives of boys of color have burst their racialized boundaries swelling into a so-called "crisis of masculinity" (see Moynihan 1965). Yet, rather than developing progressive pedagogy that responds to gendered shifts in labor dynamics, primary and secondary schools have increasingly embraced disciplinary tactics—in forms of criminalizing and militarizing policies—to combat surges in disruptive, degenerative, and antisocial antics. In contrast to scholarship that posits the redundancy of working-class masculinities within post-Fordist labor markets and gender norms, this response suggests that such securitization practices work instead to rejuvenate these devalorized masculinities (McDowell 2003). When our viewpoint expands to consider the centrality of men and boys to an expansive web of security industries and the gendered performances that constitute their reproduction, it is hard to deny that masculinity matters. As the target of both security policies and the labor force for security industries, zero tolerance policies and military academies provide specific address to masculine attributes of discipline, physical force, and even violence while simultaneously constructing femininity as out of place.

Finally, the increasing entanglement of different forms of securitization, most notably the entangling of police and military forms, is indicative of a blurring of the boundaries of inside and outside state authority. Thus, while criminalization and militarization usher in distinct transformations in the schools, their simultaneous presence in this space reveals the weakening boundary between these two domains. The range of ways that these institutions—their technologies and jurisdictions—are explicitly and deliberately entwined is chilling. This entanglement is significant precisely because the separation of police and military authority inside and outside national space is a hallmark of the modern nation-state (Mignolo and Tlostanova 2006). While the trespass of the border is not only a frequent but foundational experience of nation-states in the context of colonial violence, trespass was typically managed as an exception to everyday practice. Today, this entanglement provides solutions to the problem and opportunity of surplus populations.

Schools have long been crucial institutions of liberal citizenship for the production of *both* discipline and delinquency. They carry the authority to discipline children, but the flip side of this authority entails casting children who are unsuccessfully disciplined as delinquent. Mandatory schooling in liberal states emerged precisely for the purpose of cultivating citizens and workers for industrial capitalist society. Today, however, the culture of militarism and the politics of fear fuel profound transformations at the intersection of education and security. Zero tolerance and military academies are part of a reorientation of education toward a system of securitized social reproduction where surplus populations of largely young men of color are sorted into different trajectories of securitization: *de*valuation through criminalization, or *re*valorization through militarization.

SCHOOLS AND THE MAKING OF MODERN CITIZENS

If young people are an object of desire for security industries and institutions, they are also critical to the whole enterprise of modern citizenship, both sustaining and undermining liberal subjecthood. Modern childhood is that category of persons who are not-yet-citizens, who can never be full liberal subjects but remain in a perpetual state of protection, and who require training and transformation until they can act as sovereign liberal individuals. According to Sue Ruddick, the child is a *limit condition* of liberal citizenship, "an impossible subject since, by liberal definition, the child cannot speak for him or herself without adult authorization" (Ruddick 2007, 514). It is through mandatory education that liberal states transform children into citizens. This critical role of education in the political and economic life of modern citizenship has a history. Indeed, while the securitization of citizenship through schools takes on particular urgency today, education has long played a vital role in the making of citizens.

Modern childhood is certainly real, but it was an invention of the industrial revolution. In the European context, young people went from being "pocket sized adults who were mostly involved in employment" to something quite different over the course of the nineteenth century, when romantic philosophers and social reformers began to criticize this role for young people and argue instead for the protection of childhood (Jans 2004, 33). In a parallel fashion, Zelizer (1985) argues that the late 1800s saw dramatic transformation in the ontology and socioeconomic organization of childhood. Whereas young people had previously been economic actors and contributors to household livelihoods, with the increased mechanization of industry their labor largely became surplus. Along with women, children were retired from the formal economy. As Nast argues, this was at once a political and economic transformation, and a reorganization of intimate life, "the withdrawal of children was reckoned through the passing of various laws in tandem with a profound sentimentalization of child persons. Children were socially re-situated, re-framed, and re-valued in powerful ways that held economic, emotional, and psychical consequences" (Nast 2006, 898).

The creation and cultivation of childhood was not simply a benevolent act on the part of states and social reformers. Rather, "by restraining child labor and introducing compulsory education, the government did not only want to achieve the ability to read, write and calculate for children. It also wanted to teach them virtuousness and patriotism—in other words, to educate them as exemplary citizens. As a consequence, citizenship became the exclusive territory of adults. For children, it was the final destination of their childhood" (Jans 2004, 32). Indeed, compulsory education is what separated adults from children, thus helping to constitute the very meaning of childhood and also providing the material and institutional *space* where children can become adults and, so, citizens.

The nineteenth century was the century of schooling and "as education became increasingly formalized through public funding and governance . . . the state began to have a greater influence in the lives of individual citizens through education" (Harris 2008, 68). This political role for schooling was also thoroughly economic, as its role in the reorganization of both production and social reproduction for industrial society suggests. Indeed, as Samuel Bowles emphasizes, schooling was an institutional response to the social crisis of industrial capitalism. Bowles argues that "an ideal preparation for factory work was found in the school: specifically its emphasis on discipline, punctuality, acceptance of authority outside the family, and individual accountability for ones work" (Bowles 1982, 29, 30). Schooling was critical to the real subsumption of labor as it also cultivated liberal citizens. "Economic progress required civil order, and schools had a key role to play in ensuring political stability," thus schools were meant to "cultivate the students' sense of citizenship, loyalty, respect for property, and deference to authority" (Axelrod 1997, 25).

SCHOOLS AND SOCIAL SORTING

If education plays such a critical role in transforming children into citizens and workers, it also plays a crucial role in sorting to-be-citizens into particular kinds of workers. Schools have long played a role in reproducing classed and racialized futures, organizing young people into distinct occupations. Schools have been deeply implicated in social stratification through the cultivation of different skills and expectations in young people. Almost three decades ago, Bowles argued that the relative lack of financial support devoted to schools serving working-class communities means that children in these schools are treated "as raw materials on a production line," with emphasis placed on obedience and punctuality and few opportunities for "independent, creative work or individualized attention by teachers" (Bowles 1982, 35–6). This is in strong contrast to schools that serve elite children, which offer opportunities for the "development of the capacity for sustained independent work" and other skills that are required for success in the professional occupations. Bowles also points out that within mixed schools, class stratification takes place through "tracking" and streaming of students, through participation in extracurricular activities, and through the active steering of students toward anticipated career outcomes by teachers and guidance counselors.

This form of targeting to stream and steer students has very clearly worked to corral people of color, particularly African American young men, into low wage work. We can go back to the turn of the last century and the classic work of W.E.B. Dubois to see how longstanding this practice is. In his classic work *The Philadelphia Negro*, Dubois (1899) outlines how black boys and girls are discriminated against in the schools and steered to become waiters and maids. But today we are seeing young racialized men streamed in some very particular ways. The possible trajectories of such steering have become quite stark; a majority of African American men are now given the choice of prison or military futures. As a series of recent and disturbing reports have documented, there are far more African American men in prison and the military than in postsecondary education. Dr. Reginald Wilson, senior scholar at the American Council on Education in Washington, D.C., speaks to this narrowing field of opportunities when he questions why so few black men are finding their way into teaching as a profession: "A growing number of Black men are going into the military services, which is a positive choice. Black servicemen have told me they went into the services to 'save their lives and get off the streets. With few jobs out here and Black unemployment rate twice as high as Whites, they are going into the military which has good benefits.'" He stresses, however, that the most negative reason for the low number of black male teachers is that too many "young men are inordinately represented in the prison population. More Black men are in prison than in college dormitories," he notes (quoted in Waldron 1995).

While Wilson laments the narrow field of possibilities extended to African American young men, he simultaneously reproduces the valorization of the military as the positive choice of the two. This valorization of the soldier is part of an increasingly potent distinction between deserving and undeserving citizens.

Since the 1970s, renewed emphasis on obligation and capacity over rights and entitlements in the realm of citizenship has meant, in practice, that some people become deserving of rights while other people do not. If neoliberal citizenship valorizes those able to perform service in exchange for rights, it also revives nineteenth century moral appraisals of the urban poor's penchant for criminality. Poor as a consequence of individual failures and cultural dysfunction, these citizens are constructed as "high needs" or "high risk," substituting economic insecurity with latent criminality and, thus, undeserving of the rights and benefits awarded by the state. Their casting as criminal is produced and reproduced through heightened regulation and sweeping surveillance in schools, housing projects, streets, and through a range of other governmental institutions (Wacquant 2002; Krinsky 2008). Within this framework, if the problems of marginality are to be overcome, the solutions rest almost exclusively on the individual's capacity to overcome them. This logic, at times powerfully propagated by men of color encouraging others to "pull up their bootstraps," suggests that military service becomes the either/or option for poor black men; a choice they must make—as Wilson suggests—in order to "save their lives and get off the streets." There is no better example than Bill Cosby's recent advocacy for black men to get "on the path from victims to victors." His recent book with Alvin Poussaint *Come on, People!* implores its readership, "We can change things we have control over if we accept personal responsibility and embrace self help" (Cosby and Poussaint 2007, xviii). Cosby acknowledges the long histories of systemic violence that constitute our racialized present, but he recasts the problem as one of personal responsibility: specifically as one of rebuilding black masculinity.

Indeed, as Rose argues, citizenship has largely transformed from a "possession or a right of persons-in-general, to a capacity to be performed through acts of choice" (Rose 2000, 99). This model of citizenship has helped galvanize support for a "workfarist" model of rights, contingent on labor market participation and a revival of the distinction between a deserving and undeserving poor. To be part of the deserving poor and worthy of public assistance, one must be productive in the narrowest sense; employed in the formal labor force. Workfare thus substitutes economic participation for political belonging and has the effect of making basic rights *contingent* on contribution.

While neoliberalism has intensified distinctions between deserving and undeserving, poverty has long been associated with criminality in the liberal tradition, and both the poor and the criminal are often cast as undeserving (cf. Linebaugh 2003). We can go back to the early liberal thinkers to find this logic operative. After describing the poor as "the foster children of the country," Bentham (1843, 420), for example, argued that a system of pauper workhouses would have a "collateral benefit of a most important nature" providing "nursery—a supplement—and in part a succedaneum—to the existing system of national defense" (420). For Bentham, "national force" could be strengthened "without effort—without disbursement—without expense to anybody" by having paupers who live in workhouses serve in national defense on weekends and labor in the factories during the week (420). The poor could, in fact, redeem themselves through national service. Indeed, as Bentham's logic suggests, soldiering has intimate connections to notions of deserving citizenship. Contribution to society may allow the poor to be deemed deserving; however, when society is nationalized, contribution takes its highest form in military service. In the contemporary period, as social entitlement is shrunk back into the military, soldiering is once again emerging as a form of work and citizenship for the deserving poor.

The intimate connection of soldiering to citizenship takes particular form when woven through the racialized legacy of U.S. political and cultural economy. Perhaps its most influential articulation dates back to the 1965 Moynihan Report. Trained as a sociologist, employed as a politician and assistant secretary of the U.S. Department of Labor under Johnson, Daniel Patrick Moynihan's ideas traveled widely in the midst of racialized urban uprisings across America. His report, "The Negro Family," argued that the failure of the black family caused African American welfare dependency, and this failure of the family was more specifically a failure of black masculinity. Scarred from a legacy of emasculating slavery, Moynihan argued that black men failed to assert themselves in the labor market and failed to assert patriarchal power over African American women. These failures resulted in the "almost complete breakdown" of "the Negro family, leaving the Negro community . . . forced into a matriarchal structure which, because it is too out of line with the rest of the American society, seriously retards the progress of the group as a whole" (Moynihan 1965). Moynihan warns that most Negro youth are in *danger* of being "caught up" in a whole "tangle of pathology," and like Cosby, he acknowledges the central role of structural racist violence but reassigns responsibility to black men to rebuild their masculinities and, so too, "natural" familial forms. The report identifies an important solution to the problems of African American men. *Military service* provides not only the "largest and most important education and training activities of the Federal Government" and "the largest single source of employment in the nation," Moynihan points out, but there is "another special quality about military service for Negro men: it is an utterly masculine world" (1965, chapter 4).

SCHOOLED IN/SECURITY

During the 1980s and 1990s, in the racialized climate of anxiety that nurtured John DiIulio's wildly influential juvenile "superpredator" thesis, zero tolerance policies became the hallmark of a range of security and disciplinary measures introduced in the nation's public schools. The American Bar Association traced the movement of zero tolerance during this period from "a Congressional response to students with guns," to "the gamut of student misbehavior, from 'threats' in student fiction to giving aspirin to a classmate" (Martin 2001). According to a landmark U.S. Department of Education study, under zero tolerance policies, one in eight black students was suspended compared to one in thirty white students, and a third of students permanently expelled from school were black (Center on Juvenile and Criminal Justice 2000; see also Civil Rights Project, Harvard University 2000). Rates of expulsion and suspension skyrocketed for young men of color such that zero tolerance has since engineered a de facto withdrawal of these young men's right to education.

During the same period, an unprecedented expansion of incarceration, correctional supervision, and criminal conviction rates—like rates of school suspensions and expulsions—disproportionately came to bear on African American men and boys. These two trends are intimately intertwined: a recent study reveals that "the lifetime risk of incarceration is increasingly stratified by education"; those with less than a high school diploma are far more likely to end up imprisoned (Pettit and Western 2004, 151). The mounting transparency of what some call the "Schools-to Prison-Pipeline" now means that prison time, more "than patterns of military enlistment, marriage or college graduation . . . differentiates the young adulthood of black men from the life course of most others" (Pettit and Western 2004, 165).

As a newly securitized social milieu transforms the socialization of children and youth, public discourses of criminality meld with school disciplinary practices ushered in under the banner of safety. Cast as dangerous spaces that threaten safety and security, a range of exceptional surveillance and policing practices are thus deployed (Brown 2003). The media contributes heartily to the production of insecurity within these problem places: when principals in over 1,300 public schools were asked in a recent national survey to explain the reason they chose a law enforcement and security presence in schools, the most common reason was not actual violence, but *national media attention to violent crime in schools*. To be sure, this same report found that the majority of principals reported zero incidents of violent crimes (82 percent), sexual harassment (67 percent), firearms or sharp objects possession (92 percent and 52 percent), and possession or distribution of drugs (68 percent and 81 percent) (Travis and Coon 2005). These statistics align with a wealth of data from law enforcement agencies that together reveal schools as one of the safest places from crime and violence for young people in the United States. School securitization might thus be better understood by looking to its effects: the forging of a path to imprisonment for the country's racialized urban poor.

Thus, for instance, soon after Mayor Bloomberg of New York City took over the city's ailing public school system, he partnered with the New York Police Department and the Department of Education to openly import a "Broken Windows" model of policing that had been wildly successful in "sweeping the city's streets clean" of repeat offenders. Like the policing model, Operation Impact employed Geographic Information Systems (GIS) crime data to target high crime areas in the city for intensive policing. "Impact Schools" targets were selected on the basis of criminal incidents, safety violations, and "early warning problems" including school absences and "disorderly behavior" (Drum Major Institute 2005, 2). The program not only doubles the number of police in these Impact Schools, it introduces a range of surveillance measures, requires all adults—from teachers to administrators—to impose order, and mandatory auditing aimed at enforcing the practice of security under the philosophy of zero tolerance.

Like New York City, the Louisiana legislature has also acquired and centralized public schools performing at or below the state average. Students, in what are now called Recovery School Districts, repeatedly report their everyday educational experiences as "prison like." One of these, John McDonogh, an inner city high school in New Orleans serving predominately African American students and those with special needs, currently has a ratio of thirty-one to forty security officers plus two to four New Orleans Police Department (NOPD) officers for twenty-one to thirty teachers. Each day, students:

> After standing in long lines to enter the building . . . pass through metal detectors staffed by seven security guards and one officer from the New Orleans Police Department. Students are scanned with a hand-held metal detector while the contents of their book sacks are searched. Cell phones, oversized jewelry and belts with certain buckles are confiscated. Students who set off the metal detectors three times with no item found are sometimes sent away at the door. On various days, students who are not in their classrooms by 9:00 a.m. are locked out of their classrooms while . . . security guards on staff perform a "sweep." Students rounded up in the sweep are brought to the auditorium and suspended. According to the principal, 52 students were suspended in one day for tardiness. (Tuzzolo and Hewitt 2006, 66).

Zero tolerance policies and heightened surveillance in schools are installed as a technological response to both tightened budgets for education and infrastructure and the growing polarization and segregation that define globalizing cities. Across the country, the level of law enforcement activities and police presence in schools positively and significantly correlates with racial, ethnic, ability minority populations, and the percentage of students benefiting from free lunch programs (Travis and Coon 2005). An independent review of Impact Schools found they were more "overcrowded than the average city high school, were far larger than most city high schools, received less funding per student for direct services . . . and served a student body that was disproportionately comprised of poor and black students as compared to the average New York City public high school" (Drum Major Institute 2005, 2).

The securitization of schools creeps in from both sides of the military/police divide. Indeed, the military presence in schools is long-standing as programs like Reserve Officer Training Corps (ROTC) suggests, but it has nevertheless been resuscitated. This is not entirely surprising given the role of schools in cultivating citizenship and the central role of military service to national belonging. At the same time, a series of recent changes to education and recruitment policy are actively and aggressively transforming schools into recruitment centers. In addition to the outright replacement of public schools with military academies in poor communities of color, the military targets remaining public schools as prime spaces for recruitment. As Tyler Wall (2010) describes, U.S. recruiter's "geographic assignment is solely informed by the location of schools" in districts across Midwestern states. The military is also highly selective about the methods and resources it devotes to recruitment in different schools depending on the class makeup of the student body. Kurt Gilroy, recruiting policy director for the Office of the Secretary of Defense, explains that although the military strives "to give everyone an opportunity to enlist," it devotes resources primarily to places most likely to "maximize return on the recruiting dollar" (Savage 2004). Indeed, the military targets the $2.6 billion it spends on recruitment and retention in highly selective ways that are officially rationalized by cost benefit analysis, and informally rationalized in ways that reinforce the choice between prison and the military. Sergeant Isaac Horton, Army recruiter for the working-class D.C. school of McDonough sees "enlisting is a way to improve the lives of young people with few options. In his pitches to recruits, he uses his life as an example, talking of returning home to find many of his high school friends either dead or in jail. 'If I had to do it over again, I would do it. . . . Look at the crime rate in D.C.—I'll take my chances in the military'" (Savage 2004). Furthermore, Wall suggests that within targeted schools there is a further social targeting that takes place as recruiters deliberately zero in on kids without cash: "most of 'em has holes in their shoes" one recruiter reports (Wall 2010).

This kind of targeted recruitment and access to the schools for recruiters is made possible through former President Bush's No Child Left Behind (NCLB) education initiative, which makes funding of local education agencies contingent on their release of student information to Department of Defense (DoD) recruiters. Schools are also required to offer military recruiters the same access to the schools as college recruiters (No Child Left Behind Act 2001). This initiative is part of a much broader strategy to recruit low income African American and Latino youth for the military to fill its quotas. In a letter promoting the Act to public school boards, Secretary of Education Rod Paige and Secretary of Defense Donald Rumsfeld noted that military service "[f]or some of our students, may be the best opportunity they have to get a college education" (Paige and Rumsfeld 2002). Institutionalizing standardized testing and punitive sanctions, the NCLB narrows the options for those unwilling or unable to conform (Furumoto 2005). This increasing supply of "delinquents" has in turn been met by decreasing prerequisites for military service. By 2004, enlistment standards had dropped considerably:

> The number of high school dropouts allowed to enlist will rise 25 percent—accounting for 10 percent of recruits this year, compared with 8 percent last year. The percentage allowed to enlist despite borderline scores on a service aptitude test will rise by 33 percent—from 1.5 percent last year to 2 percent this year. (Savage 2004)

TARGETING SURPLUS

Far too many young men today are extended a choice between prison or military futures: the targeting practices of zero tolerance and military academies shape how and for whom that "choice" unfolds. With support from state educational institutions, both the military and police now inform targeting practices in schools to constitute and then govern surplus subjects through criminalization and militarization. Targeting is a key means through which security agendas are reterritorialized across these jurisdictional domains.

The very practice of targeting has a military genesis. But even as targeting is imported into domestic space, it rarely betrays its battlefield genesis. Kaplan argues that civilian targeting borrows much more than metaphor from military practice (Kaplan 2006). Like its military counterpart, civilian targeting operates through the logic of "precise positioning" of a problem: containment in absolute space. Kaplan outlines the history of precision targeting as part of the rise of airpower leading up to World War II, but she also looks at the subsequent spread of the language and technologies into civilian practices like target marketing. For Kaplan, the migration of the *language of targeting* is indicative of the migration of militarized political and spatial logics, information gathering, and surveillance practices into civilian life.

If targeting is a means of securitization, it also plays a constitutive role in the broad reorganization of citizenship in post-welfare states. Indeed, targeting is understood as a key element of post-welfarist citizenship, and central to the shift from Keynesian universalism to selective social policy that distinguishes deserving from undeserving citizens (Rose 1996). An explicitly spatial form of governmentality, targeting contrasts with the implicit, typically national geography of welfarism, and transforms the said goal of government from collective welfare and development to managing spatially bounded problems (Cowen 2005).

Today, in the racialized architecture of advanced capitalist urbanism, these concentrations of "problem citizens" are corralled, on the one hand, through targeted social policies such as zero tolerance and heightened surveillance in public school systems. Targeting the undeserving poor by criminalizing the institutional spaces charged with educating them, these practices ensure that bulging rates of incarceration take on such social specificity. On the other hand, the military targets the same surplus populations for recruitment with promises of employment and social security in exchange for service. Even more important, the military offers surplus populations the means to deserving citizenship while avoiding a life of criminalization and incarceration.

Targeting surplus subjects as security problems in schools garners widespread support by building on extended legacies of racialization to renew practices of domination and subjectification. It sanctions a flood of new policy making, programming, and experimentation in governmentality, as well as novel forms of accumulation that rely on a remasculinization of subjects as both the object of security and the labor force for security work. We are, to be sure, particularly concerned with how the rise of this entangled security assemblage culls forms of masculinity made surplus through gendered shifts in industrial restructuring. The U.S. military's moral waivers liberate surplus masculine subjects from one institution of securitization, propelling them right into another—one of the most direct links between processes of criminalization and militarization. Whether subjects are placed on one side or the other of that divide, or as is increasingly the case, *cycled between them*, they are part of the assembling of a broad future of securitized social reproduction.

NOTES

1. Black incarceration rates soared from 329,821 in 1980 to 627,402 in 1990 (Lusane 1991, 44).

2. Brink Lindsay, senior fellow at the Cato Institute and author of *Against the Dead Hand*, runs a weblog. This quote is drawn from a December 12, 2002, posting of his titled "World View Archives." http://www.brinklindsey.com/archives/003056.php.

3. Please see the article of the same name, Cowen and Siciliano, forthcoming, for a more elaborate discussion.

REFERENCES

Axelrod, P. 1997. *The promise of schooling: Education in Canada, 1800–1914*. Toronto: University of Toronto Press.

Bentham, J. 1843. Pauper management improved. In *The Works of Jeremy Bentham*, vol. 8, ed. J. Bowring. Edinburgh: William Tait.

Body-Gendrot, S. 2000. *The social control of cities?* Malden, Mass.: Blackwell.

Bowles, S. 1982. Education and the reproduction of the social division of labour. In *Education policy and society*, ed. B. Cosin and M. Hales, 27–50. New York: Routledge.

Brown, E. 2003. Freedom for some, discipline for "others": The structure of inequity in education. In *Education as enforcement: The militarization and corporatization of schools*, ed. K. Saltman and D. Gabbard, 127–52. New York: RoutledgeFalmer.

Center on Juvenile and Criminal Justice. 2000. School house hype: Two years later. http://www.cjcj.org/pubs/schoolhouse/shh2.html.

Civil Rights Project, Harvard University. 2000. Opportunities suspended: The devastating consequences of zero tolerance and school discipline policies. *Report from a national summit on zero tolerance*. (Washington, D.C., June 15–16). http://www.law .harvard.edu/groups/civilrights.

Connell, R. 2000. *The men and the boys*. Berkeley: University of California Press.

Cosby, B., and A. Poussaint. 2007. *Come on people! On the path from victims to victors*. Nashville, Tenn.: Thomas Nelson.

Cowen, D. 2005. Suburban citizenship? The rise of targeting and the eclipse of social rights in Toronto. *Social and Cultural Geography* 6:335–57.

———. 2008. *Military workfare: The soldier and social citizenship in Canada*. Toronto: University of Toronto Press.

Cowen, D., and A. Siciliano. Forthcoming. Surplus masculinities and security. *Antipode.* Hoboken, N.J.: Wiley-Blackwell.

Drum Major Institute. 2005. A look at the impact schools. http://www.drummajorinstitute.org/library/report.php?ID=18.

Dubois, W.E.B. 1899. *The Philadelphia Negro.* Philadelphia: University of Pennsylvania Press.

Eckholm, E. 2006. Plight deepens for black men, studies warn. *New York Times.* March 20.

Flaherty, J. 2006. Continuing crisis in New Orleans' schools. October 16. http://www.dissidentvoice.org/Oct06/Flaherty16.htm.

Furumoto, R. 2005. No poor child left unrecruited: How NCLB codifies and perpetuates urban school militarism. *Equity and Excellence in Education* 38:200–10.

Gilmore, R. 2007. *Golden gulag: Prisons, surplus, crisis and opposition in globalizing California.* Berkeley: University of California Press.

Harris, G. 2008. Learned citizenship: Geographies of citizenship in Ontario schools. Ph.D. diss. University of Toronto, Toronto, Ontario.

Heaviside, S., C. Rowand, C. Williams, and E. Farris. 1998. Violence and discipline problems in U.S. public schools: 1996–97. (NCES 98030). Washington, D.C.: U.S. Department of Education, National Center for Education Statistics.

Jans, M. 2004. Children as citizens: Towards a contemporary notion of child participation. *Childhood* 11:27–44.

Kaplan, C. 2006. Precision targets: GPS and the militarization of U.S. consumer identity. *American Quarterly* 58:693–713.

Klein, N. 2007. *The shock doctrine.* New York: Metropolitan Books.

Krinsky, C., ed. 2008. *Moral panics over contemporary children and youth.* London: Ashgate.

LeBaron, G. 2008. Captive labour and the free market: Prisoners, production and the state. *Capital and Class.* 95:59–81.

Linebaugh, P. 2003. *The London hanged: Crime and civil society in the eighteenth century.* London: Verso.

Lusane, C. 1991. Pipe dream blues: Racism and the war on drugs. Boston: South End Press.

Martin II, R.C. 2001. Zero tolerance policy report. American Bar Association. http://www.abanet.org/crimjust/juvjus/zerotolreport.html.

McDowell, L. 2003. *Redundant masculinities.* Malden, Mass.: Blackwell Publishing.

Meiners, E. 2007. *Right to be hostile: Schools, prisons, and the making of public enemies.* New York: Routledge.

Mignolo, W., and M. Tlostanova. 2006. Theorizing from the borders: Shifting to geo- and body-politics of knowledge. *European Journal of Social Theory* 9:205–21.

Mitchell, K., S. Marsden, and C. Katz. 2003. Introduction: Life's work: An introduction, review, and critique. *Antipode* 35:415–42.

Moynihan, D. P. 1965. *The Negro family: The case for national action.* Washington, D.C.:

Office of Policy Planning and Research, United States Department of Labor. http://www.dol.gov/oasam/programs/history/webid-meynihan.htm.

Nast, H. 2006. Critical pet studies? *Antipode* 38:894–906.

No Child Left Behind Act, 2001. Pub. L. No. 107–110. 115 Stat. 1425, 20 U.S.C.

Paige, R., and D. Rumsfield. 2002. Recruiting letter. U.S. Department of Education. http://www.ed.gov/news/pressreleases/2002/10/recruitingletter.html.

Pettit, B., and B. Western. 2004. Mass imprisonment and the life course: Race and class inequality in U.S. incarceration. *American Sociological Review* 69:151–70.

Public Broadcasting Service (PBS). 2007. Chicago's military academies raise education debate. Online Newshour Report. December 26. http://www.pbs.org/newshour/bb/education/july-dec07/military_12–26.html.

Rose, N. 1996. The death of the social? Refiguring the territory of government. *Economy and Society* 25:327–56.

———. 2000. Governing cities, governing citizens. In *Democracy, citizenship and the global city*, ed. E. Isin, 95–109. New York: Routledge.

Ruddick, S. 2007. At the horizon of the subject: Part one. *Gender, Place and Culture* 14:513–26.

Saltman, K., and D. Gabbard, eds. 2003. *Education as enforcement: The militarization and corporatization of schools*. New York: Routledge.

Savage, C. 2004. Military recruiters target schools strategically. *Boston Globe*. November 29.

Scahill, J. 2007. *Blackwater: The rise of the world's most powerful mercenary army*. New York: Nation Books.

Sutton, J. 2000. Imprisonment and social classification in five common law democracies: 1955–1985. *American Journal of Sociology* 105:350–96.

Travis III, L. F., and J. K. Coon. 2005. *The role of law enforcement in public school safety: A national survey*. Final Report For The National Institute of Justice (Center for Criminal Justice Research University of Cincinnati).

Tuzzolo E., and D. Hewitt. 2006. Rebuilding inequity: The re-emergence of the school-to-prison pipeline in New Orleans. *The High School Journal* 90:59–68.

Vosko, L. F. 2000. *Temporary work: The gendered rise of a precarious employment relationship*. Toronto: University of Toronto Press.

Wacquant, L. 2002. *Prisons of poverty*. Minneapolis: University of Minnesota Press.

Waldron, C. 1995. Why we don't have more black male teachers. *Jet*. http://findarticles.com/p/articles/mi_m1355/is_n10_v88/ai_17263158/.

Wall, T. 2010. School ownership is the goal: Military recruiting, public schools, and rronts of war. In *Schools under surveillance: Cultures of control in public education*, ed. T. Monahan and R. Torres, 104–122. Piscataway, N.J.: Rutgers University Press.

Zelizer, V. 1985. *Pricing the priceless child*. New York: Basic Books.

CHAPTER FIVE

Dispossessing Law

Arbitrary Detention in Southern Thailand

TYRELL HABERKORN

At 3:30 A.M. on June 23, 2007, a group of ten police and army officials rattled the gate outside the house of M., a young father, Muslim, and Thai citizen living in Narathiwat. Along with Yala, Pattani, and four districts of Songkhla, Narathiwat is one of the southernmost border provinces of Thailand under martial law and emergency rule. Once M.—and his wife, mother-in-law, and two children— were awake, the officials asked him to open the gate and then for permission to search the house. After half an hour, the officials concluded that there were no illegal items or suspects present. They asked M. to sign a statement certifying this. M. signed, because there was nothing to implicate him in any wrongdoing, and the officials seemed to agree. The police and army officials left, and the family went back to sleep.

After morning prayers the next day, M. went to eat breakfast at a local restaurant. As he was finishing his meal, his mother-in-law came to find him because the police were looking for him. There was a problem with the statement he signed and he needed to sign a new statement. M. didn't think anything was wrong, so he went with the police. They took him to see their commander, who told him that he was 50 percent innocent. M. was confused, and asked the commander why he needed to sign again, and if anything was wrong. The commander told him not to worry, and then told the soldiers present to take M. to a nearby school-turned-temporary detention center. M. asked the officials why he needed to go to the school. They told him that he would be able to sign the new statement there, and then return home.

When M. arrived at the school, he saw thirty or so of his neighbors. There were old people, teenagers, including a few younger than eighteen, as well as three or four women, two of whom had babies less than a year old with them. It became clear to M. that he was not going home anytime soon. After a few hours at the school, M. and many of the others there were sent to Ingkayuthboriharn Army Camp in Pattani province, where hundreds of individuals arrested under suspicion of being "terrorists" across southern Thailand have been detained since 2004.

On his third night at Ingkayuthboriharn, army officials told M. that he would be leaving the camp very soon. M. assumed that this meant that he would be going home imminently. M.'s hopes were dashed when he realized that he and other detainees were being sent to a different army camp in Hat Yai district, Songkhla province. During the trip to Hat Yai, M. was afraid because he didn't know what would happen at the new camp. For the first two days after arriving in Hat Yai, M. was interrogated each day, but he was never accused of any crimes. Three weeks passed, and M. was still not charged with any crimes. A low-ranking army officer told him that whatever happened, he would be able to go home on July 24.

On July 24, M.'s family came to pick him up at the camp in Hat Yai to return home. But before he had a chance to see his family, police and army officials came into the room and told him he had two choices "if he wanted to go home one day." M. could attend a four-month "occupational training" course, for which he would receive 12,000 baht, or approximately $350 USD, upon completion as well as assurance that he was completely innocent. His slate would be wiped clean. *Or*, if he did not want "occupational training," the police could bring official national security charges against him, and he would spend at least two years in jail without bail before his case even made it to the first court hearing. M. chose the first option. He was one of close to four hundred detainees who did so and in late July and early August 2007 traveled outside the southern provinces under emergency rule to begin occupational training programs in Chumpon, Ranong, and Surat Thani provinces.[1]

The decision to move the detainees out of the three southernmost provinces for the occupational training course caused tremendous hardship for the families of the detainees. Yet the location of the camps also provided the basis for the detentions to be challenged within the Thai judicial system. Once the detainees were moved out of the area under emergency rule, the official provisions permitting administrative detention up to thirty-seven days no longer applied.[2] Families of detainees along with human rights advocates, including the Thai-based Working Group on Justice for Peace and the Hong Kong–based Asian Human Rights Commission, brought parallel cases challenging the legality of the occupational training in the provincial courts in Chumpon, Ranong, and Surat Thani. On October 30, 2007, all three courts ruled that "the Army's actions in sending residents to the camps may not have been unlawful, but the men taking part in the job-training schemes could return home if they wished."[3] When he was arrested, M. was told that he was 50 percent innocent. One might say that in this moment, the courts were 50 percent just.

Even after the court decision, however, M. and the others could not return home. Citing an army order containing a list of 399 prohibited individuals dated July 22, 2007, one month after the sweep leading to the arrests began, Lieutenant-General Viroj Buacharoon, the Fourth Region Army Commander, said that those on the list could not return to Pattani, Yala, Narathiwat, or Song-khla provinces for six months. The names of all of those who participated in the occupational training were on the list.[4] Following queries from human rights advocates and the families of the detainees, on November 17, 2007, Lieutenant-General Viroj nullified his order and allowed M. and the others to return home.

INTERVENTION

The three southern border provinces—Yala, Pattani, and Narathiwat—were placed under martial law in January 2004, and have been under emergency rule since July 2005. The reason given by the central Thai state for the abrogation of rights under martial law, and then the intensification of repression under emergency rule, has been the need to curb rising Islamic insurgency. In contrast to the other seventy-four provinces of Thailand, where the majority of residents are Buddhist, the majority of the residents of the three southernmost provinces are Muslim. Five years after the declaration of martial law, actions by insurgents show no signs of abating.[5] In September 2008, the International Crisis Group reported, "while the attacks are declining in quantity, the insurgents seem to be attempting more spectacular operations."[6] Amnesty International echoed this concern in April 2009, citing particular concern around five recent beheadings of civilians likely carried out by insurgents.[7]

Simultaneously, the forms of violence used by different state actors against citizens have developed, morphed, and multiplied in official as well as increasingly hidden, unofficial forms. In a January 2009 report, Amnesty International stated that despite Thailand's accession to the United Nations (UN) Convention Against Torture, state forces in southern Thailand systematically use torture against civilians.[8] The Yala-based Muslim Attorney Center (MAC), and the Bangkok-based Accessing Justice Project of the Cross Cultural Foundation reported that between January and September 2008, reported instances of torture, disappearance, and arbitrary detention were on the rise. For example, the MAC documented over fifty cases of torture of national security detainees between January and September 2008.[9] Perhaps the most notable is the case of Imam Yapa Kaseng, who was arrested as a suspected insurgent in Narathiwat province on March 19, 2008. Imam Yapa died on March 21, 2008, from wounds inflicted from being tortured while interrogated. The autopsy ruled that he died from blunt force trauma.[10] While the Narathiwat Provincial court ruled in December 2008 that military officers carried out the torture that killed Imam Yapa, there has not yet been a criminal prosecution.[11] In an attempt to challenge the impunity surrounding Imam Yapa's death, his family has decided to file for damages in civil court.[12]

Yet, as I try to make sense of the constellation of violence in southern Thailand, it is the case of M. and others like him, rather than that of Imam Yapa, that is most confusing—and compelling—to me. The detentions—and how quickly detainees were released (and even would have possibly been released without intervention by human rights advocates)—are unusual within the context of state repression in southern Thailand. Along with rapid release, unlike other simultaneous cases of detention, most detainees did not report torture or other ill-treatment during the period of occupational training, but rather many cited the banality of their detention. To be clear, this banality was accompanied by arbitrary detention without charge and forced occupational training. In addition, some of those who attended the occupational training reported torture or coercion by the army or police at their preliminary points of detention. While the case of Imam Yapa is a clear indication of the use of extrajudicial violence with impunity by state actors against individuals identified as enemies of the state, M.'s experience challenges what is known about the diversity of ways that law and violence can intersect, disconnect, or remain opposed in order to produce repression.

M.'s unexpected search, reassurance of no wrongdoing, and then subsequent detention immediately brings to mind the situation of Josef K. in Franz Kafka's novel *The Trial*. Josef K. awakes one morning to find strangers, who he learns are officers of the Law, knocking at his door. They have come to inform him that proceedings, a trial, against him are taking place. The subject of Kafka's novel is the Law, cast as a nameless, unquestionable authority. Despite his continuous attempts to learn of the charges against him so that he can refute them, Josef K. is never able to do so. The Law—and the guards, lawyers, judges, and other officers of the court—constrains Josef K., yet consistently refuses him the knowledge of the cause of his constraint. Throughout the novel, he is reassured of a positive outcome if he goes along with the proceedings. Yet, at the close of the novel, Josef K. is killed by two men affiliated with the proceedings against him. His never-spoken sentence was death. His crime remains unstated, but one wonders if his transgression was his questioning of the Law and the very attempt to learn the charges against him. The cause of Josef K.'s unexpected death seems clear—one man plunges a knife into his heart and the other encircles his neck with his hands. Yet this material violence can be read as a culmination of the violence done throughout the novel by the arbitrary proceedings against Josef K. and the consistent denial of information about the charges against him. The Law's murder of Josef K. began when two strangers first appeared in his flat.[13]

Unlike Josef K., M. was not killed and was released a few months after his arrest. Yet what makes Kafka's imagination of Josef K.'s pursuit of and by the Law compelling in the context of M.'s detention is the place of the lack of knowledge of wrongdoing in structuring the experiences of both. This lack of knowledge— and the accompanying insecurity and circulation of fear—are constitutive of the emerging contemporary human condition and its concomitant inhumanity. What is accomplished by the army and police forces who conduct arbitrary detention in southern Thailand? What are the effects on the individuals that are detained? What are the effects on their families and communities? How might these effects be assessed? How is this kind of detention—and forced occupational training—part of a range of forms of violence used against citizens in southern Thailand? What happens to the law—and the relationship of the law to justice—when these detentions take place? Unlike the unnamed, fictional country of *The Trial*, these questions are urgently material ones in southern Thailand.

Questions of historical and global comparison are significant here as well. How are the strategies used today in southern Thailand resonant—or not— with arbitrary detention strategies used in earlier periods by different parts of the Thai state? The propagation of fear, arbitrary adherence or discard of the law, and threatened or actual torture by state actors are not new practices— in Thailand or elsewhere. What is new—or at least resurgently dangerous—is the seeming normalization of this practice. Can the strategies used in southern Thailand be seen as part of a broad frame of the abrogation of rights of those who come under suspicion in the U.S.-led global "War on Terror"? In *Tearing Apart the Land: Islam and Legitimacy in Southern Thailand*, Duncan McCargo criticizes analysts who see the conflict in southern Thailand as part of the War on Terror. McCargo argues that rather than jihad, the conflict in southern Thailand is a struggle over legitimacy, broadly conceived in his analysis as the state's right to morally rule, and the citizens' willingness to accept that rule.[14] I agree with McCargo that the conflict in southern Thailand is not resonant with the

War on Terror, at least from the perspective of those challenging the central Thai state. What resonates instead are concerns about the long-term effects of widespread arbitrary detention, the conditions faced by detainees, and the relationship among different kinds of detention in producing fear and constituting repression.

Writing about fear and the development of mistrust within Buddhist and Muslim communities in southern Thailand since 2004, Marc Askew examines the effects of unannounced home searches by state authorities, such as the one that preceded M.'s detention. He cited one Muslim villager who noted that, "these sudden searches were a very bad thing that frightened villagers and made them mistrust the authorities."[15] Despite his criticism, the villager did not identify another method for finding hidden insurgents. This idea that there is no other alterative strategy for fighting insurgency is also reflected in the policies of the Thai internal security apparatus. Even when forced to look for alternatives to arbitrary detention in the context of criticism of the detention of M. and others, state officials simply reinvented arbitrary detention under another name. In the remainder of this chapter, I examine how coerced occupational training is one of multiple strategies through which the Thai state represses by, in Judith Butler's formulation, simultaneously containing and dispossessing citizens.[16] The danger of this simultaneous containment and dispossession becomes most visible when arbitrary detention is evaluated as a policy both cynical and sincere.

OUTSIDE THE JUDICIAL SYSTEM

In 2007, authors of a document of the Internal Security Operations Command, or ISOC, Thailand's military-police-civilian internal security coordinating agency, raised concerns that Thailand was getting an international reputation for mistreating, repressing, and terrorizing Muslim people in the South.[17] This was not a desirable image to cultivate, so a new strategy needed to be developed. Ideally, the author noted, a strategy would be developed that would be amenable to observers outside Thailand but would also eliminate the problems in the three southernmost border provinces by removing the culprits of unrest from the area. An idea was proposed that "training" programs would produce peaceful, state-abiding Thai citizens. Incorrect thinking would be corrected, pride in being citizens under the system of democracy with the king as head of state would be fostered, and a group of people to serve as "good examples" for others would be created.

Who was to be eligible for this program? Who were the targeted actors? To answer this, I step back to the broader frame of categories of individuals identified as in need of state attention by the ISOC, and a three-point typology that recurs across ISOC documents outlining problems and possible strategies for resolving unrest:

- GROUP 1 was comprised of individuals who break serious laws and for whom there is clear evidence of wrongdoing. These are individuals who should be prosecuted using the justice system to the fullest extent, with a transparent and just prosecution.
- GROUP 2 was comprised of individuals who are involved in wrongdoing, but for whom there is not enough evidence to bring a case. If a case is brought, the people will go free. This, the authors of the ISOC document alleged, will be bad for the justice system and will have serious psychological warfare consequences as well.
- GROUP 3 was comprised of individuals who commit a little bit of wrongdoing [*kratam pid lek lek noy noy*] and who could go either way—to support the state or the militants.

Members of groups 2 and 3 were those who were seen as appropriate to target and invite/arrest for training *outside* the three southernmost border provinces. *Physical removal* of individuals was articulated as central to the strategy. While it deserves more attention than I can give it here, to use the word "invite," or *churn*, rather than "arrest," or *chap*, significantly elides the arrestees' lack of agency or ability to refuse the invitation to detention. Cases in which there is strong evidence against the accused are urged to go through the justice system—transparently and justly. Those cases without clear evidence cannot—and must be resolved outside. In other words, those who were placed in the greyest legal area were those who may or may not have done anything wrong. One was *almost* safer, at least from unclear, arbitrary arrest, if there was clear evidence that could be marshaled against one.[18] *Almost* because individuals in the first category still face thirty-seven days of administrative detention before evidence needs to be presented to continue their arrest.

Duncan McCargo notes that supporters of the existing judicial system highlight the relatively small number of suspects prosecuted in the courts as evidence of its justness. As a result, he explains that it is difficult "for critics of the system to identify substantive miscarriages of justice."[19] Yet this typology of individuals in need of state attention by the ISOC indicates that the sheer position of the judicial system is in crisis. The real indictment of the criminal justice system may not be in the cases processed through it, but those forced outside it.

MULTIPLE FORMS OF VIOLENCE AND DISPLACEMENT

Arbitrary detention and various forms of compulsory training, or "reeducation," are not unique to Thailand or to the present moment. While the indefinite internment at Guantánamo Bay of individuals suspected of being terrorists in the context of the U.S.-led War on Terror may be the most analytically and politically visible case currently, arbitrary detention is a strategy of control and violence used by many different kinds of rightist, leftist, and centrist repressive governments, including Chile under General Augusto Pinochet and Cambodia under the Khmer Rouge. In Thailand, arbitrary detention was used against individuals identified as *anthaphan* or "hooligans" between 1958 and 1974, against individuals deemed to be a *phai thaw sangkhom* or "danger to society" between 1976 and 1979, and against those identified as Communists at various points between the 1950s and the 1980s.

Yet despite its ubiquitous use in Thailand, relatively little is known about the varieties of violence possible under arbitrary detention, the relationship of arbitrary detention to the law, and how arbitrary detention works together with other strategies of repression to instill fear and control in a given population.[20] Martial law, in force since January 2004, permits detention for seven days before charges need to be brought against someone being held under suspicion of threatening national security. The emergency decree, in force since July 2005, adds another thirty days before charges need to be brought against a suspected individual. The International Crisis Group notes that during the first seven days detainees are often held in temporary sites of detention and cannot see family members or other visitors during the first ten days of detention, which means that the risk of torture is greatest during this period. Detainees do not have access to lawyers during the initial thirty-seven-day period of detention.

The Krue Se and Tak Bai massacres in 2004, and the relative impunity of state officials involved, indicate that the lives of southern Muslims presumed to be terrorists may be seen as unworthy of protection.[21] The torture and disappearance of national security detainees while under administrative detention indicate the existence of a space in which anything—including actions leading to death as in the case of Imam Yapa—can be done to the bodies of individuals under suspicion. One way to understand the state murder of Imam Yapa and other similar cases is by thinking through Giorgio Agamben's *homo sacer*; that is, ones who can be killed with impunity because they have ceased to be understood as human.[22] Derek Gregory explains that Agamben's *homo sacer* exists "in a zone not merely of exclusion but a zone of abandonment . . . What matters is not only those who are marginalized but also, crucially, those who are placed beyond the margins."[23] The space beyond the margins is a space of exception, one whose existence paradoxically makes possible the security of the boundaries of those inside the margins, and ensures that those dwelling in it are both unsafe and often unaccounted for.

Upon initial examination of the conditions of arrest and the murky legal basis for the detention and occupational training of M. and the hundreds of other individuals detained between July and October 2007, it could potentially be understood as taking place in a space of exception as well. Yet, even before considering how their detentions were ultimately resolved within the judicial system *outside* the three southern border provinces, it is important to note that M. and the other detainees were not *homo sacer*. Unlike Imam Yapa, those who were killed at Krue Se and Tak Bai, and some of the national security detainees, the intention of the occupational training program did not seem to be to kill those detainees who were compelled to participate in it. The daily schedule for those detained included time for eating, prayers, and sports. Seminars on Thainess, the correct way to read the Koran, and great religions of the world were part of each week, as well as optional courses in job-training skills.[24] In the court decision about the release of the detainees there is a comment from a detainee noting that aspects of the training were useful, but that he objected to being unable to leave the camp or go home. Other complaints from those who attended the occupational training were that it was boring and caused their families hardship.

M. was meant to return to his community after occupational training and the expiration of the six-month ban on returning to the three southern border provinces. Instead of being placed *outside* the Thai nation, M. was instead displaced within it, metaphorically and materially. Expressing the critique that Agamben's ideas may limit critics' ability to theorize power and the varieties of violence visited upon those who become enemies of the state, Judith Butler and Gayatri Spivak are concerned that critics may "become unable to take on the representational challenge of saying what life is like for the deported, what life is like for those who fear deportation, who are deported, what life is like for those who live as *gasterbeiters* in Germany, what life is like for Palestinians who are living under occupation. These are not undifferentiated instances of 'bare life' but highly juridified states of dispossession."[25]

They pose a further question that is useful in relation to the case of M. and the other detainees. They ask, "What does it mean to be at once contained and dispossessed by the state?"[26] I identify containment as the process of being confined within boundaries determined by the state.[27] To be dispossessed is to be deprived or denied (of space, of thought, of control over one's life) by the state.

The idea of simultaneous containment and dispossession is apt for the case of M. and the other occupational training detainees. For a period of time, M. and the others were internally displaced persons, or IDPs. They were denied the legal protections offered by the polity to its members, but then allowed, even expected, to return to the polity. More significant, the detention of M. and the others is simultaneous containment as Thai citizens who can do good for the nation, and dispossession, as Thai citizens who might not do good for the nation. The double action compels me to ask who and what is produced through this process? Rather than the docile, state-loving citizens ISOC hoped to produce, my contention is that this produced fear and insecurity on the part of citizens. Recalling M's story with which I began—he, and those around him, learned that it is possible to be arrested, threatened with long-term detention, and forced to undergo training, even if the police search your house and confirm that they find nothing. Like Kafka's Josef K., M. was never apprised of his alleged wrongdoing. Unlike Josef K., M. returned to his village to continue *living* with this lack of knowledge. How these strategies might convince citizens to join the side of the state is perplexing—how could citizens even find agents of the state trustworthy after such an experience? To return to McCargo's prescient argument: if the conflict in southern Thailand is understood as a struggle for legitimacy, the compulsory occupational training programs contribute to producing the illegitimacy of the Thai state.

SINCERE DISPOSSESSION

I first learned about M.'s experience of detention in a collection of eight testimonies of occupational training detainees gathered by human rights activists in late 2007. The other testimonies contained similar stories of confusion upon arrest (and confused arrest practices), the stark (and unusual) choice of four months of occupational training or being charged as a national security threat, fear at what might happen at each point, and distress at being separated from one's family. Some detainees reported physical violence or coercion prior to attending this training.

The writers appealed to the United Nations to listen to what they endured and survived, to recognize their detention as constituting a violation of their rights, and to end fear and create justice for people in southern Thailand.

What is at stake—analytically and politically—is specifying M.'s experience as a form of violence existing in the same time and space with torture, disappearance, and the deaths of other individuals suspected of insurgency in southern Thailand. Rather than collapse these differing forms of violence into one another, or try to rank them in terms of severity, the challenge that I explore here and in my broader project about twentieth-century histories of extrajudiciality and arbitrary detention in Thailand is to understand how they work together to affect the lives of those directly subject to them as well as the broader context of daily life.

When I first presented one of my questions in this project—of how to understand widely differing conditions of detention in existence under the same legal instrument—a question that recurs in my work about detentions in the late 1970s, a journalist colleague dismissed it. He alleged that the variation in strategies of detention and the use, or nonuse, of physical violence was politically insignificant and simply about the preferences of the different state agents involved. The variation may be personal; I am not suggesting that there is an exceptionally well-planned conspiracy. But even if the variation is accidental, it raises questions about producing and sustaining fear and uncertainty. Writing about the operations of fear in Guatemala during and after the civil war, Linda Green argues that "Repression is used selectively: to threaten, intimidate, disappear, or kill one or two labor leaders, students, or campesinos is to paralyze everyone else with fear. If one crosses the arbitrary line, the consequences are well known; the problem is that one cannot be sure where the line is, nor when one has crossed it, until it is too late."[28]

Yet in M.'s case, not only did he not know where the line was located, he also lacked prior knowledge of what the consequences were for crossing it. Even after his release and return home in November 2007, M. still did not know the precise reason why he came under suspicion of the police and army authorities. Recent reports indicate that state officials working in the southernmost provinces may have already forgotten the ruling of the courts in Chumpon, Surat Thani, and Ranong that individuals could not be forced to undergo occupational training. In April 2008, army and police officials began "inviting" villagers to undergo training in "creating understanding." Here I share part of the text of the letter issued to villagers inviting them to this endeavor:

> The situation in the south of Thailand has created daily violence continuously, causing loss of lives including increasing insecurities about life and property. Peaceful livelihood of peoples in the southern-most provinces continue to be

threatened. Suffering, loss of lives and injuries are being caused by the insurgency. There are some groups of people who have been building movements and creating propaganda including threatening and intimidating villagers to act against state agencies that have been trying to provide assistance to affected villagers. Therefore the affected areas are underdeveloped and undergoing unrest. As per information received from our intelligence services, together with information received from those people who have surrendered, we have learnt that you have been named amongst those who are considered to possibly be involved in some movement, some infraction or trouble in your respective area. We would like to create better understanding and also add more information to our database. We want to have opportunities to learn and exchange opinions from each other. This process will help us in arriving at a peaceful means to solve the situation in the South. Therefore we would like to invite you to join the program from 1 May–15 May 2008 . . .[29]

The letter continues with further information about the training session and how to proceed. Although I agree that the situation in southern Thailand is grave, it is unclear to me if the policy proposed in this letter will help resolve the crisis or not. While this is an invitation, refusal is difficult when said invitation comes from the security forces in an area under martial law and emergency rule. If villagers have no choice as to whether to attend or not, *can this create understanding within Thailand? And if so, whose Thailand?*

This question creates a final articulation of simultaneous dispossession and containment. Through compulsion to attend training, villagers are contained. They are marked as outside and dispossessed at the moment they are identified as being in need of detention and training in order to "create understanding." The occupational training program—an alternative to more visibly brutal methods of repression that tarnished Thailand's international reputation—and its transformation into a program of training to create understanding suggests two possible interpretations of the logic of the programs. The first is cynical and pragmatic: these programs are simply one more way to repress, through dispossession and containment, Thai citizens who come to be seen as enemies of the state. Yet, an interpretation of the programs as sincere is ironically far more sinister. What if, instead, the logic of containment and dispossession is imagined by those who construct and administer the programs as a way to actually create understanding and improve the situation in southern Thailand? If so, then it suggests that it is not only displacement, but also belonging, that is shot through with violence in Thailand.

NOTES

I would like to thank Shelley Feldman, Gayatri Menon, and Charles Geisler for their comments and criticism of this chapter.

1. M. is the pseudonym of a resident of the three southernmost border provinces. The preceding paragraphs are based on my summary and translation of a testimony he wrote in December 2007.

2. For the provisions of administration detention under the Emergency Decree, see Article 11 in the Decree, *Ratchakitchanubeksa*, 16 July 2548 [2005], Book 122, Part 58 Koh, pages 1–9. For the provisions providing for immunity for state actors, please see Article 17 of the same Decree. For analysis of the implications of the Decree, please see International Commission of Jurists (2005).

3. Asian Human Rights Commission (2007b).

4. Asian Human Rights Commission (2007a).

5. According to the report of the National Reconciliation Commission, "Over the course of 11 years, from 1993 to 2003, a total of 748 violent incidents occurred in Pattani, Yala, and Narathiwat (including Songkhla and Satun at certain times), an average of 68 incidents per year. However, in 2004 and 2005 the frequency of such violent incidents escalated at an alarming rate: there were 1,843 and 1,703 violent incidents in 2004 and 2005 respectively, a total of 3,546 incidents in the two years combined. These occurrences resulted in 1,175 deaths and 1,765 injuries. On average, there were 1,773 violent incidents per year over the last two years, or 148 per month. It may be said that the frequency of incidents between 2004–2005 increased 26-fold compared to the number of violent incidents during the previous 11 years." See National Reconciliation Commission (2006, 9). Please also see International Crisis Group (2005, 2008).

6. International Crisis Group (2008).

7. Amnesty International (2009b).

8. Amnesty International (2009a).

9. Cross Cultural Foundation (2008).

10. The inquest further noted "including rib fractures from the front, side, and back that punctured his lungs. Bruises and wounds were found all over his body, including his eyes, forehead, and lips. Imam Yapa also had long abrasion marks on his back, indicating he may have been dragged on his ankles across a hard and rough surface." See Human Rights Watch (2009).

11. Ministry of Foreign Affairs (2009).

12. Cross Cultural Foundation (2009).

13. Kafka (1925/1998).

14. McCargo (2008).

15. Askew (2009, 75).

16. See Butler and Spivak (2007, 5–6).

17. ISOC document (confidential source).

18. Hannah Arendt's analysis of the vulnerability of stateless people living outside

the law is relevant here. She writes "Since he was the anomaly for whom the general law did not provide, it was better for him to become an anomaly for which it did provide, that of the criminal." She later notes, "If a human being loses his political status, he should, according to the implications of the inborn and inalienable rights of man, come under exactly the situation for which the declarations of such general rights provided. Actually the opposite is the case. It seems that a man who is nothing but a man has lost the very qualities which make it possible for other people to treat him as a fellow-man. This is one of the reasons why it is far more difficult to destroy the legal personality of a criminal, that is of a man who has taken upon himself the responsibility for an act whose consequences now determine his fate, than of a man who has been disallowed all common human responsibilities." See Arendt (1951/1973, 286, 300).

19. McCargo (2008, 89).

20. According to the UN Working Group on Arbitrary Detention, there is no clear definition of arbitrary detention in international law. The Working Group therefore developed the following three categories of detention that is arbitrary: (1) when there is no legal basis for the deprivation of liberty; (2) when a person is deprived of liberty guaranteed either by the Universal Declaration of Human Rights (UDHR) or the International Covenant on Civil and Political Rights (ICCPR); and (3) when a person has been deprived of their liberty without the benefit of a fair trial. Please see United Nations Working Group on Arbitrary Detention (2000).

21. In what has become known as the Krue Se mosque massacre, or simply "Krue Se," on 28 April 2004, only two days before the Study Group meeting, clashes between state forces and Muslim militant men left 106 Muslim men and five members of state forces dead. What is clear is that while the militants did launch initial attacks on state forces in some locations, there were out-numbered and out-armed. Many of the militants were armed only with machetes, while the army soldiers were well-equipped with automatic weapons, grenades, and other hardware. Although the largest number of people was killed at Krue Se mosque (thirty-two men), there was fighting between Muslim men and Thai army forces in various locations in the South, including Saba Yoi district in Songkhla province and Krong Pinang district in Yala province.

Eighty-five people died in the Tak Bai massacre on 25 October 2004. Seventy-eight of this number died when over 1500 protestors were arrested and stacked, in horizontal layers, in trucks and transported to the Ingkayuthboriharn military base six hours away from the Tak Bai police station, where the protest took place. The 1500 citizens were protesting what they believed was the unjust arrest of six villagers on charges of allegedly stealing guns from the local defense forces. At an event commemorating the two-year anniversary of the massacre, one survivor of the massacre recalled that in his truck, there were four layers of people; everyone on the bottom layer died.

22. Agamben (1998, 2005).

23. Gregory (2004, 62).

24. Fourth Army Region and ISOC documents (confidential source).

25. Butler and Spivak (2007, 40–41).

26. Ibid., 5–6.

27. In *Who Sings the Nation-State*, Butler articulates the relationship between containment and expulsion as follows: "What distinguishes containment from expulsion depends on how the line is drawn between the inside and the outside of the nation-state. On the other hand, both expulsion and containment are mechanisms for the very drawing of that line. The line comes to exist politically at the moment at which someone passes or is refused rights of passage." See Butler and Spivak (2007, 34).

28. Green (1999, 67).

29. Fourth Army Region invitation (confidential source). Translation is my own.

REFERENCES

Agamben, G. 1998. *Homo sacer: Sovereign power and bare life*. Trans. D. Heller-Roazen. Palo Alto, Calif.: Stanford University Press.

———. 2005. *State of exception*. Trans. K. Attell. Chicago: University of Chicago Press.

Amnesty International. 2009a. "Thailand: Torture in the southern counter-insurgency." AI Index: ASA 39/001/2009. January 13. http://www.amnesty.org/en/news-and-updates/report/thai-security-forces-systematically-torture-southern-counter-insurgency-2AI report.

———. 2009b. "Thailand: Insurgents abusing human rights with attacks on civilians." AI Index: ASA 39/003/2009. April 1. http://www.amnesty.org/en/library/asset/ASA39/003/2009/en/aa877e58-c6b7-4441-8928-d4908226a635/asa390032009en.html.

Arendt, H. 1951/1973. *The origins of totalitarianism*. New York: Harvest Books, Harcourt.

Asian Human Rights Commission (Hong Kong). 2007a. UPDATE (Thailand): Hundreds released from army detention prevented from going home. UP-143-2007. November 2. http://www.ahrchk.net/ua/mainfile.php/2007/2641.

———. 2007b. UPDATE (Thailand): Hundreds of detainees released from "vocational training" camps. UP-154-2007. November 20. http://www.ahrchk.net/ua/mainfile.php/2007/2667.

Askew, M. 2009. Landscapes of fear, horizons of trust: Villagers dealing with danger in Thailand's insurgent south. *Journal of Southeast Asian Studies* 40 (1): 59–86.

Butler, J., and G. C. Spivak. 2007. *Who sings the nation-state? Language, politics, belonging*. Oxford, U.K.: Seagull Books.

Cross Cultural Foundation (Thailand), Accessing Justice and Legal Protection Program. 2008. Statement on the use of torture and inhumane methods one year after signing the UN Convention Against Torture: Evidence under martial law and emergency decree in the three southern provinces (1 November). Bangkok: Cross Cultural Foundation.

———. 2009. Family of Imam Yapa Kaseng sue the military, army and police for damages (18 March). Bangkok: Cross Cultural Foundation.

Green, L. 2004. *Fear as a way of life*. New York: Columbia University Press.

Gregory, D. 2004. *The colonial present*. Oxford, U.K.: Blackwell.

Human Rights Watch. 2009. Thailand: Inquest blames soldiers for imam's death. January 7. http://www.hrw.org/en/news/2009/01/07/thailand-inquest-blames-soldiers-imam-s-death.

International Commission of Jurists. 2005. More power, less accountability: Thailand's new emergency decree. 17 August. http://www.icj.org/IMG/pdf/More_power_less_acco_D4033.pdf.

International Crisis Group. 2005. Thailand's emergency decree: No solution. Asia Report N°105, 18 November. http://www.crisisgroup.org/home/index.cfm?id=3795&l=1.

———. 2008. Thailand: Political turmoil and the southern insurgency. Asia Briefing N°80, 28 August. http://www.crisisgroup.org/home/index.cfm?id=5640&l=1.

Kafka, F. 1925/1998. *The trial*. Trans. B. Mitchell. New York: Schocken Books.

McCargo, D. 2008. *Tearing apart the land: Islam and legitimacy in southern Thailand*. Ithaca, N.Y.: Cornell University Press.

Ministry of Foreign Affairs. 2009. MFA spokesperson comments on Amnesty International's report concerning southern Thailand. January 15. http://www.mfa.go.th/web/35.php?id=21560.

National Reconciliation Commission. 2006. *Report of the national reconciliation commission: Overcoming violence through the power of reconciliation*. Bangkok: National Reconciliation Commission.

United Nations Working Group on Arbitrary Detention. 2000. Fact sheet #26 of the office of the high commissioner for human rights: The working group on arbitrary detention. May 15. http://www.unhchr.ch/html/menu6/2/fs26.htm.

PART TWO

Fugitive Corporeality

CHAPTER SIX

Spectacle of Terror,
Spectacle of Security

NICHOLAS DE GENOVA

In his "Address to the Nation" on the evening of September 11, 2001, and persistently reiterated thereafter, George W. Bush enunciated the self-congratulatory litany by which we were to understand that "the terrorists" were obsessed with "America" and targeted it because it is "the brightest beacon for freedom and opportunity in the world." Soon this claim was embellished with the contention that "these people can't stand freedom; they hate our values; they hate what America stands for" (Bush 2001a). The events of September 11, 2001, enabled the Bush administration and the full mass-mediated panoply of spectacular public discourse to repeatedly and extravagantly insist to the world that "everything changed"; indeed, that nothing would ever be the same again (De Genova, n.d.). In the years following these events, there has indisputably been a radical and rigorous material and practical overhaul of the U.S. sociopolitical order, predicated upon precisely this elaborate scaffolding of distinctly *metaphysical* premises, propositions, and inferences about "terror" and its changeling, counterterror, which were now purportedly engaged in nothing less than a total global war, without limit, without borders, and apparently without end. That the Homeland Security State, by its own account, entails "the most extensive reorganization of the federal government in the past fifty years," according to the *National Strategy for Homeland Security*, is merely the material and practical verification of the more decisive strategic reconfiguration, which has proclaimed: "The U.S. government has no greater mission" than "securing the American homeland . . . from terrorist attacks," a new mandate that has furthermore been confirmed as "a permanent mission" (USOHS 2002, vii, 1, 4). The ascendancy of the Homeland Security State therefore signals a momentous new and ongoing process of state formation in the United States (De Genova 2007).

Indeed, in its essentials, this metaphysics of antiterrorism has in fact been re-iterated and reanimated under the presidency of Barack Obama. In the Obama administration's *National Security Strategy*, we are reminded that the events of September 11, 2001, revealed "the dark side of this globalized world" and authorized "fighting a war against a far-reaching network of hatred and violence" (White House 2010, 1, 4; see also De Genova 2010b).[1]

SECURITIZING EVERYDAY LIFE

However, in the face of this new "war"—this monumental struggle against evil itself, in Bush's phrase—the commander-in-chief's injunctions to the citizenry from the outset were consistently and remarkably quotidian. "Americans are asking: What is expected of us?" Bush ventriloquized, with the immediate re-ply, "I ask you to live your lives, and hug your children" (Bush 2001f, September 20, 2001). He went on to list a series of other modest, even pedestrian, re-quests: do not single out anyone for "unfair treatment or unkind words because of their ethnic background or religious faith"; make charitable donations for the victims of the attacks; cooperate with the FBI; be patient with delays and incon-veniences caused by more stringent security measures, for a very long time to come; continue to "participate" confidently in the U.S. economy; and pray for the victims, for the military, and "for our great country." In short, leave the war in the hands of the experts (including the prosecution/persecution of suspected enemies [see De Genova 2007]), submit to the authority of the antiterrorist security state, combine religious devotion with nationalist and militaristic ac-quiescence, work hard, spend money without inhibitions, and above all, just "live your lives"—which is to say, conform to the dreary lifeless conventions of an already alienated everyday life.

The demand for a dutiful and docile (and now, patriotic, even heroic) sub-mission to the terrifyingly mundane business-as-usual of alienated labor and joyless consumption has to be recognized as the covert yet resplendently overt "truth" of the spectacle of terror, the antiterrorist regime of the new Home-land Security State, and its official "state of emergency" (promulgated by Bush on September 14, 2001, and never subsequently discontinued; see De Genova 2010b). The spectacle of "terrorism," however, electrified the overall sense that the everyday—if consistently disappointing, universally dissatisfying, and in general, excruciatingly boring—was now to become a sign that could trigger both a nostalgia for a putatively "lost" sense of safety and comfort, and a perma-nent if ineluctable sense of being imperiled by an elusive menace. Baudrillard notes incisively:

[The terrorists] have even—and this is the height of cunning—used the banality of American everyday life as cover and camouflage. Sleeping in their suburbs, reading and studying with their families, before activating themselves suddenly like time bombs. The faultless mastery of this clandestine style of operation is almost as terroristic as the spectacular act of September 11, since it casts suspicion on any and every individual. Might not any inoffensive person be a potential terrorist? . . . So the event ramifies down to the smallest detail—the source of an even more subtle mental terrorism. (2001/2002b, 19–20; cf. 2001/2002a, 409–10)

Furthermore, Baudrillard adds, "If *they* could pass unnoticed, then each of us is a criminal going unnoticed . . . and, in the end, this is no doubt true" (2001/2002b, 20). Here, indeed, is the most profound possible meaning to Baudrillard's contention that "a globalized police state of total control" is being actualized through "a security terror" (Baudrillard 2001/2002a, 414).[2]

This subtle terrorizing that apparently disrupts and destabilizes the somnolence of the everyday, which Baudrillard attributes to the cunning of "the terrorists," is figured as an effect of a larger "vertiginous cycle" in which the death of the terrorist is "an infinitesimal point," a kind of miniscule puncture "that provokes a suction, a vacuum, a gigantic convection" around which power "becomes denser, tetanizes itself, contracts and collapses in its own superefficiency." He goes on to claim that "all the visible and real power of the system" is virtually helpless against the merciless and irreducible potency of the minute but symbolically supercharged suicides of a few individuals—exactly because their deaths challenge power to match their exorbitant audacity and determination by doing what the system could never do (destroy itself), thus leaving it with no possibility of a symbolically adequate reply (Baudrillard 2001/2002b, 19–20; 2001/2002a, 409–10). Yet, in all of this, Baudrillard never parts company with the official story, by which we are instructed to believe—based on the "intelligence" of the police and secret police, the veracity of which may strictly never be demonstrated and is therefore never strictly verifiable—the unquestionable and irrefutable "truth" of what is finally a conspiracy theory *par excellence* about a handful of fanatics.[3]

The "shock and awe" publicity campaign for the obscenely asymmetrical and ruthlessly indiscriminate aerial bombardment of Iraq (to say nothing of the less trumpeted assault on an already prostrate Afghanistan before it, or the subsequent protracted military occupation of both countries) surely never matched the palpable symbolic momentousness of the collapse of the World Trade Center's twin towers. Nonetheless, that spectacular "originary" moment indubitably did provide the ensuing onslaught of global militarism with the necessary (and arguably adequate, if not sufficiently persuasive) symbolic "cause."[4] And if these spectacular events have indeed ensured that we are all now suspects (De Genova 2007), each a potential "criminal going unnoticed," then the securitization of everyday life that has ensued from the gigantic convection generated by those events may itself be their supreme achievement. For the "terrorist" menace is the state's pronouncedly evil changeling, its most perfect and ideal enemy, whose banal anonymity and phantasmagorical ubiquity prefigure and summon forth the irradiation of the everyday by the security state as our savior and redeemer. The ascendancy of the reanimated security state may even be an expression of the would-be superefficiency of the system of power, precisely not reeling from a symbolically mortal assault and careening toward an implosive collapse, but rather meticulously refortifying its foundations by seeking to assiduously secure and perpetuate what Raoul Vaneigem calls "the everyday eternity of life" with all its "abundant and bitter consolations" (1991/1994, 7, 8).

It is instructive here to revisit some of the critical insights of the critique of everyday life postulated by Henri Lefebvre (1947, 1961, 1968, 1981, 1992). In *Everyday Life in the Modern World* (1968), his boldest reformulation of that critical itinerary, which he ultimately continued to elaborate and refine over the greater part of a long and remarkably prolific intellectual lifetime, Lefebvre arrives at an arresting conclusion: the outcome of an excessively bureaucratitized capitalist society of controlled consumption and regimented everyday life is, precisely, *terrorism* (Lefebvre 1968/1971, 148). Beginning from the premise that publicity and advertising have acquired an eminently ideological role (106) and serve to communicate "a whole attitude toward life" (107), assuring the consumer, "you are being looked after, cared for, told how to live better, how to dress fashionably, how to decorate your house, in short how to exist," Lefebvre identifies the peculiar contradiction of this form of social control: "you are totally and thoroughly programmed, except that you still have to choose among so many good things, since the act of consuming remains a permanent structure." Hence, advertising commands: "Use this After-Shave, or you will be nobody and know it" (107). Beginning from the "carefully organized confusion" of the use-value and exchange-value of commodities (107), Lefebvre interrogates a kind of terrorism predicated upon a repressive social order "that, in order to avoid overt conflicts, adopts a language . . . that deadens or even annuls opposition . . . a certain type of (liberal) democracy where compulsions are neither perceived nor experienced as such," which "holds violence in reserve . . . [and] relies more on the self-repression inherent in organized everyday life" (146). In *a terrorist society* (in emphatic contradistinction with the reign of political terror and its extravagant and convulsive recourse to outright violence to terrorize a polity),

Lefebvre continues, "compulsion and the illusion of freedom converge . . . terror is diffuse, violence is always latent, pressure is exerted from all sides."

The putative "values" of such a society, Lefebvre continues, "need no explaining, they are accepted, they are compelling, and any desire to understand or question them savours of sacrilege" (147). In a terrorist society, "each individual trembles lest he ignore the Law . . . everyone feels guilty and is guilty— guilty of possessing a narrow margin of freedom and adaptability and making use of it by stealth in a shallow underground darkness, alas, too easily pierced" (159). Hence, "moral discipline [is] the insignia of terrorist societies . . . the façade exhibited for the benefit of a well-governed everyday life" (161). This sort of terror defines for itself a pure, formal, abstract, unified societal space of everyday life as the arena of its power, from which time—and thus, history and historicity—as well as original speech and desire, must be unrelentingly evicted. Here, human actions are merely "catalogued, classed, and tidied away," isolated, estranged, and kept in order. Rather than a space of "false consciousness," therefore, it is one of a true consciousness of a crippled reality—one severed from the sheer open-endedness of radical possibility and unscripted creativity—which renders terror *normal* (179).

T'ERROR IS HUMAN (BUT TERROR IS SUBLIME)

In the immediate aftermath of September 11, 2001, amidst the cacophony of heightened security alerts and the proclamations that we were living now in an altogether "different world" (Bush 2001f, September 20, 2001), there were also immediately discernable calls summoning ordinary U.S. citizens to demonstrably enact with patriotic fervor the "the steel of American resolve" and not allow those "despicable" terrorist bullies to intimidate "a great nation" (Bush 2001a, September 11, 2001). What was the precise content of this relentless flattery of "American resolve"? Anything less than a dazzling display of collective will to be "open for business" would be tantamount to conceding that the enemy had succeeded in their mission of depriving "Americans" of "our way of life, our very freedom." The day after September 11, 2001, Bush appeared for a media "photo opportunity" with his National Security "team" to announce that the prior day's events were indeed "more than acts of terror. They were acts of war." He assured the public that the state was there to protect "the nation" and deliver it from darkness, that the federal government was fully operative, that all of its agencies were indeed "conducting business." "But," he continued, "it is not business as usual" (Bush 2001b, September 12, 2001). Evidently in a spirit of magnanimity that inadvertently confirmed that "our way of life, our very freedom" was not in fact to be confused with free time, however, when Bush officially proclaimed Friday, September 14, 2001, to be a "National Day of Prayer and Remembrance for the Victims of the Terrorist Attacks on September 11, 2001," he "encourage[d] employers to permit their workers time off *during the lunch hour* to attend noontime services to pray for our land" (Bush 2001c, September 13, 2001; emphasis added).

Five days after the events, on the same occasion when President Bush notoriously announced that the so-called war on terrorism was a "crusade" in which "we will rid the world of evil-doers," the complementary and truly emphatic message of his prepared remarks was nonetheless that it was time to "go back to work" and "work hard like you always have" (Bush 2001e, September 16, 2001). In this brief outdoor press conference, for which the prepared opening statement consisted of only five short paragraphs, Bush remarkably uttered the words "work" or "job" fifteen times. In a subsequent media event, staged in an airport to shore up confidence in the ailing airline industry, Bush ventriloquized the air travelers in attendance by proclaiming "their" clear message to the "American public": "get about the business of America . . . we must stand against terror by going back to work" (Bush 2001g, September 27, 2001). In the face of increasing evidence of an economic recession, these ham-fisted injunctions to collectively shake off the proverbial posttraumatic stress syndrome and return to productive labor were also coupled with tinny bids to go shopping. However uncannily, Bush even declared it "one of the great goals of this nation's war . . . to restore public confidence in the airline industry . . . to tell the traveling public: Get on board. . . . Fly and enjoy America's great destination spots. Get down to Disney World in Florida. Take your families and enjoy life, the way we want it to be enjoyed." On the one hand, one could scarcely miss the spectacular code-switching between the commander-in-chief's millenarian scenarios of "a new type of war" against an elusive network of "evildoers" "who know no borders," whose intent was to "terrorize America," and the chief executive cheerleader's feeble pleas for what Dana Heller has called "the promise of closure through consumption" and "America-as-cure marketing," on the other, luridly strung together in absurd dissonance, alternating currents within the same speech (Heller 2005, 20, 21). Hence, the message: Be scared, be very, very scared . . . but don't neglect your patriotic duty in the war against terrorism to get on board . . . and enjoy life; just be mindful to do so "the way we want it to be enjoyed."

As if to verify that his own incessant labor "to rout out and destroy global terrorism" was enough to work up a beastly appetite, Bush opened his remarks on September 27, 2001, with mention that Chicago's mayor, who was on hand, had reportedly promised to buy him lunch. Bush predictably pandered to what Benjamin DeMott (1990) has called "the imperial middle": "I like my cheese-burger medium." It should suffice to say nothing more of Bush's mediocrity other than it supplies only the most perverse instance that cynically confirms, indeed *displays*, nothing so much as the veritable status of *all* U.S. presidents—precisely, as mere speech-making devices. They simulate a voice for power in a manner akin to the metallic communiqués of an electrolarynx responding to the twitching of throat muscles, but instead of the otherworldly estrangement effects of the mechanical fabrication of speech, they instead provide human expression—more or less persuasive, more or less sympathetic, even visibly fallible—for the soulless machinery of power, dissimulating its message. Bush's oh-so-human cheeseburger cravings, however, offer a revealing instance of just what kind of theatrical work is required of those who come to serve as such prominent devices in the larger spectacle.

In his retrospective *Comments on the Society of the Spectacle* (1988), Guy Debord offers crucial insight into precisely the deep connections between this sort of spectacular politics and the spectacle of terror, as such. He contends:

> This perfect democracy fabricates its own inconceivable enemy, terrorism. It wants, actually, *to be judged by its enemies rather than by its results*. The history of terrorism is written by the State and it is thus instructive. The spectating popula-tions must certainly never know everything about terrorism, but they must al-ways know enough to convince them that, compared with terrorism, everything else seems rather acceptable, in any case more rational and democratic. (The-sis IX 1988, 2005 transl.)

Especially in light of this bold and arresting, if not entirely unthinkable or im-plausible, proposition, our present and unrelenting moment of crisis summons forth reanimated considerations of the enduring explanatory power of Guy Debord's austere theoretical formulation of *spectacle*.[5] In the *Comments*, Debord provides a concise summation of the society of the spectacle as he had origi-nally depicted it in 1967: "the autocratic reign of the market economy, which had acceded to an irresponsible sovereignty, and the totality of new techniques of government that accompanied this reign" (Debord 1988/2005). Debord fur-ther elaborates upon his original formulation, however, calling attention to "five principal features: incessant technological renewal; fusion of State and economy; generalized secrecy; forgeries without reply; a perpetual present" (Debord 1988/2005).[6] Among the new techniques of government that Debord emphasizes, state power itself has come to rely, both intensively and extensively, on the propagation of mass-media public discourse. Debord argues that "the social requirements of the age . . . can be met only through their mediation," and that "the administration of society . . . now depends on the intervention of such 'instant' communication." This is fundamentally because all such instantaneously circulated mass mediation is "essentially *one-way*" (Debord 1967/ 1995, 19; emphasis in original). Variously notorious or celebrated for his awkward but folksy manner of speech, his clumsy inarticulateness, and his malapropisms (see, e.g., Miller 2001), Bush's language perfectly enacted this sort of spectacular unidirectional garrulousness—what Lawrence Schehr has depicted as not merely a dialogue of the deaf but in fact a monologue of the deaf, an utter "abandonment of principled dialogue in favor of affect" through a use of "empty rhetoric and gesture politics" that obfuscate "nonmeaning and insidious action behind nice expression" (Schehr 2006, 139, 143, 144, 147). "The simple fact of being without reply," Debord elucidates further, "has given to the false an entirely new quality. At a stroke it is truth which has almost everywhere ceased to exist or, at best, has been reduced to the status of pure hypothesis that can never be demonstrated" (Debord 1988/2005). Uncertainty, ambiguity, equivocation, dissimulation, intransigent secrecy, inconceivable enemies, falsehoods without reply, truths that cannot be verified, hypotheses that can never be demonstrated—these have truly become the hallmarks of our (global) political present.

In order to adequately theorize the society of the spectacle, then, Debord's critique invites us to comprehend its rampant fetishism as, in effect, a fusion of the fetishism of the commodity with the fetishism of the state. The brazenness of the spectacle—its reliance on unrelenting mass mediation, publicity, advertising, and exuberant display in order to manifest itself as a specious unity, "an enormous positivity, out of reach and beyond dispute" (Debord 1967/1995, 15)—remains, as in Marx's classic account of the thing-like reification of relations between people, inevitably accompanied by the *invisibility*—hidden in plain sight, as it were—of the real social relations of (alienated, exploited, and subjugated) life. Prefiguring the spectacle indeed, the "secret" of the commodity, as Giorgio Agamben notes in his reflections on Debord, was one that capital sought to most effectively conceal "by exposing it in full view" (2000, 74). "The self-movement of the spectacle consists in this," Debord clarifies, "it arrogates to itself everything that in human activity exists in a fluid state so as to possess it in a congealed form—as things that, being the *negative* expression of living value, have become exclusively abstract value. In these signs we recognize our old enemy the commodity, which appears at first sight"—very much like the cheeseburger that the mayor is going to *buy* for the president—"a very trivial thing, and easily understood, yet which is in reality a very queer thing, abounding in metaphysical subtleties" (1967 [1995, 26]).

Bush's seemingly trite and ephemeral remark about an apparently trifling cheeseburger, which he was so performatively eager to consume, abounds in the sort of metaphysical subtleties that command immanent critique. Indeed, the gesture recalls Andy Warhol's famous observation about the metonymic relation between "America," the illusory egalitarianism of the market, and the absolute supremacy of the commodity:

> You can be watching TV and see Coca-Cola, and you know the President drinks Coke, Liz Taylor drinks Coke, and just think, you can drink Coke too. A Coke is a Coke and no amount of money can get you a better Coke than the one the bum on the corner is drinking. All the Cokes are the same and all the Cokes are good. Liz Taylor knows it, the President knows it, the bum knows it, and you know it.[7]

Bush's cheeseburger thus signaled both his fatuous equality (his primacy among equals, we might say) with the citizens and denizens alike who comprise the U.S. populace and are routinely interpellated into varying degrees of subjection by his discourse. The cheeseburger's prospective consumption promised to consummate what would be, by implication, the well-deserved but emphatically humble reward for Bush's tireless labor of protecting "the American people" by waging and winning the so-called War on Terror.

Earlier during the media event, in an awkward effort to strike a measured balance between the potentially competing demands of compassion and "resolve," tragedy and opportunity, mourning and war-making, Bush had remarked: "I am a loving guy, and I am also someone, however, who has got a job to do—and I intend to do it" (Bush 2001g, September 27, 2001). The middle-brow, "Middle America," and compulsively "middle-class" (reactionary) populism of U.S. politics aside, and its egalitarian ethos of wholesome and unpretentious sameness notwithstanding, the message was clear. The president was simply and dutifully doing *his* job, just as he urged everyone else to get back to work and do theirs.

> And we have got a job to do—just like the farmers and ranchers and business owners and factory workers have a job to do. My administration has a job to do, and we're going to do it. We will rid the world of evil-doers (Bush 2001e, September 16, 2001).

The just reward for each and every hardworking drone (as patriotic citizen-bystanders in the larger passion play of "America" versus evil) would also be "at first sight an extremely obvious, trivial thing," which upon closer inspection is revealed to be "a very strange thing, abounding in . . . theological niceties" (Marx 1867/1976, 163)—the sublime and otherworldly commodity—in this instance, dressed down in the homely and diminutive garb of so many unassuming cheeseburgers, all the same, and all good.

Or, at least, as good as anyone should have any right to expect.

THE SPECTACLE OF SECURITY

If the fetishism that conjures the image of the commodity as an alien power is deeply imbricated in the fetishism of the state itself—the ultimate manifestation of "power" as an alien "thing" beyond our reach—then the force of the spectacle must always refer also to coercive force of the state. Likewise, the spectacle of terror is inseparable from a spectacle of security. If the spectacle is "the self-portrait of power," quintessentially characterized by its incessant monological tyranny and voluble redundancy, "a sort of eternity of non-importance that speaks loudly," such a spectacular self-portrait nevertheless dissimulates state power (Debord 1967 [1995, 19]; cf. 1988/2005). The spectacle of security, conjured by all the ideological apparatuses and governmental techniques of the antiterrorist security state, must produce—above all else—the state's most precious and necessary political resource, and must advance what may likewise be its most politically valuable end; namely, heightened *insecurity*. Thus, unprecedented securitization and the more general militarization of everyday life on an evermore expansive scale and intensity conjures the permanent spectacle of its own purported insufficiency, preemptively supplying the justificatory rationale for still more state power.

In the wake of the events of September 11, 2001, the antiterrorism regime needed to generate and intensify the fetish of a "terrorist" menace as a "fact" of the contemporary sociopolitical moment. Thus, immigration law enforcement was deployed selectively, "preventively" (indeed "preemptively") in the production of pretexts for surveillance and detention. Immigration law provided the perfect matrix through which to mobilize minor violations of what were often mere procedural technicalities to serve as pretexts for the *indefinite* detention of "suspect foreigners" who could then remain "under investigation" indefinitely (Cole 2003). Selectively targeted indefinite and protracted detentions directed against an identifiable "foreign" minority (almost entirely comprised of Arab and other Muslim noncitizen men) have operated to uphold and sustain racialized suspicion, and apparently confirmed that minority's more general susceptibility for detention—their *detainability*. Thus, the antiterrorist security state disclosed its crucial role as an apparatus that *produces the specter of "guilt,"* which presumptively hovers over these migrants' mere detainability. Whereas detainability was contingent upon nothing more than *susceptibility to suspicion*, actual detention appeared to confirm *susceptibility to culpability*. The enforcement spectacle generated by these selective detentions involved a staging of presumptive "guilt" that, in effect, *produced culprits*. The distinctly secretive spectacle of these protracted detentions then sustained and enhanced what I have called *the "terrorism" effect*. Antiterrorism's requisite phantom menace of elusive "evildoers" ultimately commands a *material* enemy. The detention dragnet rendered the detained "suspects" collectively to be de facto "enemy aliens" and still more important, at least by implication, it has appeared to substantiate the allegation of a palpable and imminent threat of terrorism in the "homeland." Whereas border enforcement conventionally provides a highly *visible* spectacle of what appears to be an "illegal alien invasion," the antiterrorist security state's tedious, unrelenting, and above all secretive enforcement of inconspicuous technicalities produces the rather more mysterious, indeed terrifying, spectacle of an *invisible* infiltration of "sleepers" (the War on Terror's "secret agents")—and serves to justify increasingly invisible government (De Genova 2007).

Thus, in the wake of September 11, 2001, any public discussion of immigration reform, much less any suggestion of a prospective "legalization" of the undocumented, became for a significant period, at the level of official legislative and policy debate, literally unspeakable. In addition to the detention of Arab and other Muslim "terror suspects," approximately ten thousand airport screeners were summarily fired from their jobs and refused rehire on the singular grounds that they were not U.S. citizens, as the federal government took over the screening of travelers' luggage.[8] In the highly publicized Operation Tarmac, the INS raided 106 airports and arrested 4,271 migrants—overwhelmingly Latino service workers—deporting hundreds of them (USGAO 2003). Recall, however, that by 2002, an estimated 20.3 million migrant workers constituted 14 percent of the U.S. workforce, of whom an estimated 6.3 million were undocumented. Over the ensuing years and in the subsequent "immigration debate," the continuously circulated estimate of the number of undocumented migrants has been inflated to 11 million. The numbers, of course, are not pertinent here, except inasmuch as they verify a truly unanimous and ubiquitous explicit acknowledgment that undocumented migrants and their "unauthorized" labor are in fact a perfectly mundane and routine feature of the U.S. social formation. Nonetheless, the spectacle of security has fixated upon the fetish of the "illegal alien" as the embodiment of nebulous "foreign" menaces and the icon of borders perceived to be woefully violable, signaling a putative border crisis synonymous with a nation-state in the throes of a veritable "invasion." Thus, migrants came to be easy stand-ins for the figure of "terrorism," generally. Indeed, the purportedly antiterrorist security state stages transnational mobility as a menacing figure of transgression, and fashions "immigration" in general as an utterly decisive material site where the ostensible War on Terror may be practically and physically realized (De Genova 2007, 2009, n.d.; cf. Fernandes 2007).

During the spring of 2006, forcefully galvanizing widespread public awareness of the U.S. Senate's ongoing deliberations in response to the House bill that sought to criminalize all undocumented migrants, truly unprecedented mass protest mobilizations in defense of the "rights" of "immigrants"—especially the undocumented—took the United States by storm (De Genova 2009; 2010c). Ultimately, the Border Protection, Antiterrorism, and Illegal Immigration Control Act proved to be politically untenable, and no significant federal immigration legislation has been passed subsequently. Nevertheless, the parties to the legislative debate finally did approve a similarly punitive but dramatically more limited and perfunctory law, the Secure Fence Act of 2006, ostensibly providing for further fortification of the U.S.-Mexico border with hundreds of miles of new physical barriers to be added to the existing 125 miles of fence. This, after all, is the standard fallback position of all U.S. immigration politics: when in doubt or at a loss for some other sort of resolution, further militarize the U.S.-Mexico border. Furthermore, state-level lawmaking has responded to the Congressional stalemate with a new proliferation of more local immigration laws. Of 1,562 bills introduced nationally during 2007 alone, 240 were enacted in forty-six states. In the first quarter of 2008, another 1,100 bills were introduced across forty-four states. A new law in the state of Mississippi, for instance, made it a felony for an undocumented migrant to hold a job. In Oklahoma, it became a felony to provide an undocumented migrant with shelter. Accompanying these legislative tactics has been an ensuing and unrelenting campaign of intensified immigration enforcement. Indeed, by the end of 2008, the number of U.S. Border Patrol agents was legally mandated to have more than doubled since 2001, to a record high of 20,000 by the end of 2009.[9] In addition, an unprecedented profusion of local police departments are now being deployed to enforce immigration violations (a distinctly post–September 11, 2001, phenomenon) (Cave 2008). In 2010, Arizona notoriously passed a law effectively sanctioning racial profiling by authorizing police officers to detain and verify the immigration status of anyone whom they suspected might be undocumented.

As an intimidation tactic in anticipation of the May 1, 2006, rallies, and evidently in response to the audacious upsurge in migrant labor and community organizing, the Department of Homeland Security announced on April 20, 2006 (a few days after what at the time had been the largest workplace enforcement raid operation against undocumented workers in recent memory), the initiation of a new "aggressive" and "hard-hitting" campaign of raids and deportations to "[reverse] the growing tolerance for . . . illegal immigration" (USDHS-ICE 2006b), and to ensure that undocumented workers "not be allowed to think *they* [are] *safe* once they [are] inside the country" (BBC News 2006; emphasis added). On that occasion, immigration authorities had arrested 1,187 employees of a single company across twenty-six states as an explicit warning to put "employers and workers alike . . . on notice that *the status quo has changed*"(USDHS-ICE 2006a; emphasis added). Numerous raids followed in locales across the country, and only subsided in 2009 with the introduction under the Obama administration of a revised policy of "silent raids" by which immigration authorities audit workplace records and then compel employers to fire undocumented workers en masse (Preston 2010). This strategy of *not* deporting the undocumented workers identified through these audits, of course, merely *circulates* undocumented migrants in the labor market, and likewise introduces still more severe conditions of protracted precariousness to their already manifold vulnerabilities. As the alternating current of these enforcement policies reveal, and as I have argued in considerable detail elsewhere, U.S. immigration authorities have almost never even pretended to try to achieve the presumed goal of a mass deportation of all undocumented migrants (De Genova 2005). On the contrary, it is *deportability*, and not deportation as such, that ensures that *some are deported in order that most may remain* undeported as workers, whose pronounced and protracted legal vulnerability may thus be sustained indefinitely.

Nevertheless, with the advent of the Homeland Security State and its characteristic expansiveness, aggressiveness, and general bombast, U.S. immigration authorities in the DHS's Office of Detention and Removal did indeed enunciate a ten-year "strategic enforcement plan" (called "Endgame"), whose express mission was to promote "national security by ensuring the departure from the United States of all removable aliens" (USDHS-ICE 2003, ii). The avowed commitment to eventually "developing full capacity to remove all removable aliens" plainly sustained and vigorously reaffirmed the conventional goal of "removal" that has long distinguished the regime of deportability. Now however, there has been a significantly new tactical emphasis on *targeted* policing, and its predictable capacity for generating a spectacle of law enforcement "results."[10] Thus, the

U.S. immigration authorities could regularly trumpet their "successes" in highly publicized sweeps that dredged up hundreds and even upwards of a thousand undocumented migrants, and which simultaneously allow them to conflate the great mass of humdrum "illegal alien" workers with so-called "criminal" and "fugitive aliens," who were the officially designated targets of the raids. Commonly, the utterly mundane and pervasive practice of working with fraudulent documents came to be routinely depicted as "identity theft" or "fraud" and increasingly prosecuted as a criminal (rather than a mere immigration) violation—fuelling the more general moral panic surrounding this newfound phantom, and conflating it with the despised and unsettling "foreignness" of the migrant working poor (Cole and Pontell 2006).

Similarly, those who have evaded deportation orders now came to be characterized as "criminal fugitives." Thus, on May 12, 2008, an immigration raid on Agriprocessors, Inc., a meatpacking plant in Iowa—which led to the arrest and detention of 389 migrant workers, culminating in federal criminal convictions for 270 of them—was distinguished for being "the largest criminal enforcement operation ever carried out by immigration authorities at a workplace" (Preston 2008a). There have, of course, been larger workplace raids. What made this one so special was that the prosecutions were strictly focused on federal *criminal* charges (almost entirely for the use of fraudulent Social Security cards or immigration documents), leading not to immediate deportations but rather to prison sentences in federal penitentiaries (to be followed later by deportations). Thus, 297 undocumented migrants, mainly from Guatemala, were marched with hands and feet in shackles in groups of ten into a makeshift court room staged in a dance hall, adorned for the occasion with black curtains, as well as adjacent mobile trailers, on the fair grounds of the National Cattle Congress. The proceedings went from 8:00 A.M. until late at night, over several days, with the undocumented workers, who had been threatened with much harsher penalties, pleading guilty in rapid succession and being summarily sentenced to five-month prison terms. In one instance, they set the record for the highest number of sentences issued on any single day in that judicial district. As one of the convicted migrants, Isaías Pérez Martínez, resolutely and repeatedly replied in response to the efforts of lawyers to explain his putative legal options in the case: "I'm illegal, I have no rights. I'm nobody in this country. Just do whatever you want with me" (Preston 2008b). The U.S. attorney for the district who oversaw the spectacle called the whole affair an "astonishing success."[11]

THE GHOST IN THE MACHINE

Heightened terror for undocumented migrant workers came to be offered frankly as the necessary price of a kind of publicity campaign. This more stringent enforcement regime, unquestionably the most severe crackdown in at least two decades, was distinguished by a remarkably candid, if seemingly paradoxical, strategy to compel more widespread acquiescence with the proposed *expansion* of guestworker schemes for the importation of migrant labor. Former Secretary of Homeland Security, Michael Chertoff, remarked candidly, "It would be hard to sustain political support for vigorous work-site enforcement if you don't give employers an avenue to hire their workers in a way that is legal, because you're basically saying, 'You've got to go out of business'" (quoted in Hsu and Lydersen 2006). Chertoff continued, "We are not going to be able to satisfy the American people on a legal temporary worker program until they are convinced that we will have a stick as well as a carrot" (quoted in Preston 2008). Indeed, in their newfound and increasingly vocal enthusiasm for expanded guestworker arrangements as a peculiar and distinctly circumscribed recipe for the "legalization" of undocumented migrants, employers rallying behind the fig leaf of legality have adopted an ironic but revealing rallying cry. In reply to anti-immigrant lobbies, demanding "What part of 'illegal' don't you understand?", an employers' coalition in the state of Arizona promoted a state-level guestworker program, with the slogan: "What part of *legal* don't you understand?"(Preston 2008a).

The deep continuities of this "new" antiterrorist regime of migrant "illegality" with that upon which it is historically predicated, therefore, remain to haunt it. Recall that the very title of the House legislation that instigated so much controversy explicitly coupled "Antiterrorism and Illegal Immigration." Migrant labor is plainly the irrepressible ghost in the machine of Homeland Security, and the resurgence of the conventional and pedestrian preoccupations with mundane "illegal alien" workers in the current immigration debate in the United States exposes labor subordination as one of the constitutive if suppressed conditions of possibility for the metaphysics of antiterrorism. Subjected to excessive and extraordinary forms of policing, denied any semblance of supposedly fundamental "human rights" or "civil liberties," and thus, consigned to an always uncertain social predicament, often with little or no recourse to any semblance of protection from the law, undocumented migrant labor-power has increasingly become the commodity of choice for employers in an ever-expanding range of industries and enterprises. But if this is so, it is only *because*, and to the extent that, migrant labor may continue to be subjugated under the stigma of "illegality."

The more profitable it is to exploit undocumented labor, the more bellicose and fanatical must be the sanctimonious political denigration of "illegal aliens." Hence, undocumented migration must be perennially *produced* as a "problem": as an invasive and incorrigibly "foreign" menace to national sovereignty, as a racialized contagion that undermines the presumed national culture, and as a recalcitrant "criminal" affront to national security. Undocumented migrants need not be branded as actual "terrorists." Indeed, given that they are absolutely desired and demanded for their labor, to do so would be counterproductive in the extreme. Rather, it is sufficient to mobilize the metaphysics of antiterrorism to do the crucial work of continually and more exquisitely stripping these "illegal" workers of even the most pathetic vestiges of legal personhood, such that their own quite laborious predicament of rightlessness may be further amplified and disciplined. The more that the figure of the "illegal alien" can be conjured as the sign of a crisis of national security, the more guestworker proposals are promoted as a congenial panacea that satisfies U.S. employers' deeply entrenched historical dependency on, and enduring demand for, the abundant availability of legally vulnerable and ever-disposable (deportable) migrant labor, while simultaneously pandering to the pervasive rhetoric of "securing" borders against nebulous and nefarious threats.

INCONCEIVABLE ENEMIES

In an important sense, "foreign" (and commonly, also racially subordinate) deportable migrant labor presents a striking analogy to racially subjugated "minority" citizens. In their analysis of the Watts rebellion of 1965, the situationists (the political formation around Debord and Vaneigem) posited that impoverished African Americans served as "a perfect spectacular prod," supplying the spectacle of a loathsome "threat of . . . underprivilege [that] spurs on the rat race" (S.I. no. 10, December 1965; in Knabb 1981, 157). In contrast to this sort of tacit threat of permanent marginalization and the subordinate status enforced through protracted un- and underemployment, however, the spectacular prod of the "illegal alien" is that of a predicament of unrelenting and unforgiving overemployment, super-exploitation. What the two have in common, of course, is excessive misery. What they further have in common is the stigmata of racialized *difference*, reassuring the racial "majority" (or, alternately, the racially heterogeneous but still unequal polity of proper "citizens") that their own misery is not so bad after all, while also simultaneously unset-

tling the presumed assurance that such excesses of suffering could ever be reserved only for someone else (the "others"), a population condemned—be it as
an effect of their "natural" (racial) inheritance, their "alien" juridical status, or
both—to an inferior social station.

Deportable (migrant) labor, therefore, conceals within it—and yet, simultaneously *reveals* and proclaims—the universal disposability of *all* labor.
And inasmuch as, under capitalism, labor is but the most commonplace and
ubiquitous objectified, alienated, and fetishized form of *life* itself (in its active
practical expression as open-ended creative capacity and productive power),
so must the *deportable* labor of global capitalism's multifarious transnational
migrant denizens signal the ultimate disposability of human life in general, on
a planetary scale. In her brilliant interpretation of the sniper shootings in the
suburbs of Washington, D.C., shortly after the events of September 11, 2001,
Susan Willis describes how randomly chosen "ordinary people doing ordinary
things were transformed into targets" and "the cloak of uneventful malaise that
passes for security was torn asunder." Willis elucidates how the principal sniper,
a military veteran, "manifests the repercussions of U.S. imperialism on the
home front" by straddling "the blurred boundary between military and civilian
life that is fast becoming every American's common lot. . . . The only common
characteristic of the dead," she clarifies, with regard to the victims, "is their
civilian status"; they were selected "not as collateral damage (people inadvertently killed for their proximity to a designated enemy), but targets chosen for
want of a more clearly defined enemy—or perhaps chosen because the civilian
has become the enemy" (Willis 2005, 51, 52, 65, 68, 69). In the truly terrifying
irruption of random and utterly unpredictable deadly violence in the otherwise
somnolent and unsuspecting realm of the everyday, the logic of U.S. militarism
was ominously exposed: the War on Terror's inconceivable enemies are we, the
empire's sitting ducks.

The spectacle, Debord proclaims, is "the sun that never sets on the empire
of modern passivity" (1967/1995, 15). Bathed in its unforgiving light, we are
subjected to its incessant display of images and its endless monologue of one-
way communiqués, inculcated into "a generalized autism" (153). The passivity
that is such a chief feature of the society of the spectacle, moreover, is inextri-
cable from a social order predicated upon privacy. The egotism of the global
capitalist sociopolitical order operates as the unencumbered reign of private
property and private aggrandizement, but also as the atomizing individuation that ubiquitously accompanies an alienated everyday life, where privacy
is haunted always by privation (cf. Lefebvre 1947/1991, 149; 1961/2002, 70–74).
And as Marx incisively notes, "Security is the supreme social concept of civil

society; the concept of the police. . . . Security is . . . the *assurance* of its ego-tism" (1843/1978, 43]; emphasis in original). If security is the assurance of the generalized poverty, tedium, and humiliation that together comprise the most elementary preconditions of capitalist social relations of both production and consumption, the spectacle of security, like all propaganda, must necessarily take everyday life as its premier object (Lefebvre 1961/2002, 73). The spectacle of security thus entails a strategic campaign to possess everyday life by unre-lenting tactical calculation, to "[smother] it under the spurious glamour of ide-ologies," and to perpetrate and perpetuate "a passive awareness of disaster and gloom" (Lefebvre 1968/1971, 33). Yet, the spectacle finally derives its force from what Marx depicted as the more elemental process through which capital (dead labor) extracts life from the wakeful death of the living, ensconced as we are in the routinized subordination of our work and the subordinated routinization of our everyday life. For the spectacle of security, therefore, our life and labor sup-plies the antiterrorist state with the innumerable and assorted manifestations of its inconceivable enemy, in yet another more fundamental sense: the inexorable antagonism of its denizens.

NOTES

1. Although this revised formulation specifies that "this is not a global war against a tactic—terrorism" (White House 2010, 20), it reaffirms nonetheless that "the United States is waging a global campaign" to "disrupt, dismantle and defeat al-Qa'ida" (19), "a specific network . . . and its terrorist affiliates" (20).

2. If I have relied upon the Turner translation (2002b) in the previous citations, I have opted in favor of the Valentin translation (2002a) here and hereafter as a matter of preference for the suggestiveness of his choice of language in these particular passages.

3. For a more extended critique of Baudrillard, see De Genova (n.d.).

4. For the foundational text proposing the military doctrine associated with "shock and awe," see Ullman and Wade (1996); for a critique, see Goff (2004).

5. Debord would indubitably have had as his principal frame of reference the state repression of "terrorism" associated with the left-wing "armed struggle" movements that emerged in Europe during the 1970s, as well as the various military formations associated with separatist movements demanding national self-determination in Europe, such as in Northern Ireland or the Basque country. Writing in the late 1980s, during the waning years of the cold war, when anti-imperialist national liberation struggles throughout the so-called third world were routinely branded as "terrorist," and in the aftermath of vari-

ous sensational airline highjackings, however, Debord would already have recognized the increasing salience of the figure of "international" terrorism. Thus, in retrospect, we may appreciate his insights with regard to the discourse of antiterrorism, not merely as a commentary on the devolution of the social and political struggles of the 1960s but also as a remarkably prescient anticipation of post–cold war geopolitical realignments.

For more extended elaborations of Debord's conception of the society of the spectacle, see De Genova (2010a, n.d.). For other recent engagements with Debord, see, e.g., Agamben (2000; cf. 1995/1998, 6, 10–11); Hussey (2001); Merrifield (2004, 2005); Retort (2004, 2005, 2008); Rogin (1993); Weber (2002); for critical engagements with Retort (2005), see Balakrishnan (2005); Campbell (2008); Katz (2008); Mitchell (2008); Stallabrass (2006); Tuathail/Toal (2008); for more general invocations of the significance of spectacle, see also the contributions to Garber, Matlock, and Walkowitz, eds. (1993); for a discussion of "the banality of images" for a consolidation of global power through visuality, see Mirzoeff (2005, 67–115).

6. The more prosaic of these themes have already been remarkably prominent in critical scholarship regarding the antiterrorist security state. For work addressing the intersection of "incessant technological renewal" with the operations of state power, see Monahan (2006) and Webb (2007). For work on the fetishization of technology, see Campbell (2006), Johar Schueller (2007), and Parenti (2007). For work on the "fusion of State and economy," see Hughes (2007), Martin (2007), and Wolin (2008).

7. The Andy Warhol Museum, "Andy Warhol: Life and Art." www.warhol.org/educa tion/pdfs/art_and_life.pdf.

8. The Aviation and Transportation Security Act (signed November 19, 2001) mandated that all airport security staff be U.S. citizens, directly employed by the newly created federal Transportation Security Administration, with no legal right to be organized in unions. There were approximately 28,000 baggage screeners working in over 440 commercial airports at that time, with noncitizens comprising as much as 80 to 90 percent in some major airports. By November 2002, one year after the law's passage, there were more than 55,000 newly hired federal security screeners.

9. Over the preceding five-year period, the Illegal Immigration Reform and Immigrant Responsibility Act of 1996 had already mandated a dramatic increase in the numbers of Border Patrol agents (by 1,000 per year), toward what then was the ambitious goal of a total of 10,000 by 2001. With the rapid increase in the Border Patrol, there has been a predictably sharp rise in cases of corruption within the agency, notably including Border Patrol agents deeply implicated in extensive migrant smuggling and trafficking rings (Archibold and Becker 2008).

10. In addition to the initial targeting of undocumented workers employed at airports and military installations, the Immigration and Customs Enforcement bureau (ICE) of the Department of Homeland Security has executed this explicit strategy of "fugitive apprehension" (as in Operation Return to Sender) through well-publicized raids primarily targeting undocumented migrants with final orders of deportation or previous deportations, but coupling these always with the more menacing figure of "criminal aliens" with

pending arrest warrants, alongside any other random undocumented migrant who may be swept up in the course of a raid. In April 2006, in the midst of the immigrants' rights mobilizations, the Identity and Benefits Fraud Unit (established in September 2003) created ten local task forces to perpetrate a campaign of workplace raids targeting undocumented workers for the use of fraudulent documents, which it has publicly depicted as "identity theft" for alarmist effect. The Compliance Enforcement Unit (established in June 2003) is charged with the targeted detection and prioritized apprehension of visa overstayers and other immigration status violators who allegedly "pose national security or public safety threats." Other targeted campaigns have included Operation Community Shield, devised to expedite the deportation of noncitizen alleged street gang members as "criminal aliens," and the Secure Border Initiative, intended to expedite the deportation of (specifically) non-Mexicans apprehended at the U.S.-Mexico border. For broader discussions of targeted policing as a distinctly neoliberal form of governmentality, see Valverde (2003); Valverde and Mopas (2004); cf. Henman (2004).

11. Subsequently, a professional legal interpreter, Erik Camayd-Freixas, revealed that many of the Agriprocessors workers who were convicted could not have knowingly committed the crimes in their pleas. "Most of the clients we interviewed," he wrote, "did not even know what a Social Security card was or what purpose it served." He reported that many of the migrants could not distinguish between a Social Security card and a residence visa, (a.k.a. a "green card"). They said they had purchased fake documents from smugglers, or had obtained them directly from supervisors at the Agriprocessors plant. Most did not know that the original cards could belong to U.S. citizens or "legal" residents, Camayd-Freixas explained. See Camayd-Freixas (2008, 6; cf. 2009); see also Preston (2008b).

The threat of more severe punishments relied upon the prospect of charging the defendants with "aggravated identity theft," which would have required the prosecution to demonstrate that the workers in question had not only used false identification numbers but had known that those numbers belonged, in fact, to other individuals. On May 4, 2009, in the *Flores-Figueroa v. United States* decision, regarding precisely this construal of whether or not the mere use of the identification numbers satisfied the stipulation that it was done "knowingly" (i.e., that the numbers in question were known to belong to other persons), the U.S. Supreme Court ruled unanimously that the federal law concerning "identity theft" could no longer be used to routinely prosecute undocumented workers who have used false Social Security numbers to secure employment.

REFERENCES

Agamben, Giorgio. 1995/1998. *Homo Sacer: Sovereign power and bare life.* Stanford, Calif.: Stanford University Press.

———. 2000. Marginal notes on *Comments on the society of the spectacle.* In *Means without end: Notes on politics,* 73–90. Minneapolis: University of Minnesota Press.

Archibold, Randal C., and Andrew Becker. 2008 As border efforts grow, corruption is on the rise. *New York Times.* 27 May. www.nytimes.com/2008/05/27/us/27border.html.

Balakrishnan, Gopal. 2005. States of war. *New Left Review* 36:5–32.

Baudrillard, Jean. 2001/2002a. L'Esprit du Terrorisme. Trans. Michel Valentin. *South Atlantic Quarterly* 101 (2): 403–15.

———.2001/2002b. *The spirit of terrorism, and requiem for the Twin Towers.* Trans. Chris Turner. New York: Verso.

BBC News. 2006. U.S. detains 1,200 illegal migrants. April 20, 2006, 21:51:19 GMT. http://news.bbc.co.uk/go/pr/fr/-/2/hi/Americas/4928764.stm.

Bush, George W. 2001a. (September 11) Statement by the president in his address to the nation. White House Office of the Press Secretary. www.whitehouse.gov/news/releases/2001/09/20010911-16.html.

———. 2001b. (September 12) Remarks in photo opportunity with the National Security Team. White House Office of the Press Secretary. www.whitehouse.gov/news/releases/2001/09/20010912-4.html.

———. 2001c. (September 13) President pledges assistance for New York in phone call with Pataki, Giuliani. White House Office of the Press Secretary. www.whitehouse.gov/news/releases/2001/09/20010913-4.html.

———. 2001d. (September 14) Declaration of national emergency by reason of certain terrorist attacks. White House Office of the Press Secretary. www.whitehouse.gov/news/releases/2001/09/20010914-4.html.

———. 2001e. Today we mourned, tomorrow we work. Remarks by the president upon arrival, the South Lawn. White House Office of the Press Secretary. www.whitehouse.gov/news/releases/2001/09/20010916-2.html.

———. 2001f. Address to a joint session of Congress and the American people. White House Office of the Press Secretary. www.whitehouse.gov/news/releases/2001/09/20010920-8.html.

———. 2001g. Get on board! Remarks to airline employees at O'Hare International Airport, Chicago, Illinois. White House Office of the Press Secretary. www.whitehouse.gov/news/releases/2001/09/20010927-1.html.

Camayd-Freixas, Erik. 2008. Interpreting after the largest ICE raid in history: A personal account. Unpublished Manuscript, June 13. http://graphics8.nytimes.com/images/2008/07/14/opinion/14ed-camayd.pdf.

———. 2009. Interpreting after the largest ICE raid in history: A personal account. *Latino Studies* 7 (1): 123–39.

Campbell, David. 2006. The biopolitics of security: Oil, empire, and the sports utility vehicle. In *Legal borderlands: Law and the construction of American borders,* ed. Mary L. Dudziak and Leti Volpp, 351–80. Baltimore: Johns Hopkins Press.

———. 2008. Beyond image and reality: Critique and resistance in the age of spectacle. *Public Culture* 20 (3): 539–49.

Cave, Damien. 2008. States take new tack on illegal immigration. *New York Times.* June 9, 2008, www.nytimes.com/2008/06/09/us/09panhandle.html?partner=rssnyt&emc=rss.

Cole, David. 2003. *Enemy aliens: Double standards and constitutional freedoms in the war on terrorism.* New York: New Press.

Cole, Simon A., and Henry N. Pontell. 2006. "Don't be low hanging fruit": Identity theft as moral panic. In *Surveillance and security: Technological politics and power in everyday life,* ed. Torin Monahan, 125–48. New York: Routledge.

Debord, Guy. 1967/1995. *The society of the spectacle.* Trans. Donald Nicholson-Smith. New York: Zone Books.

———. 1988/2005. *Comments on the society of the spectacle.* Trans. NOT BORED! www .notbored.org/commentaires.html.

De Genova, Nicholas. 2007. The production of culprits: From deportability to detainability in the aftermath of "Homeland Security." *Citizenship Studies* 11 (5): 421–48.

———. 2009. Conflicts of mobility, and the mobility of conflict: Rightlessness, presence, subjectivity, freedom. *Subjectivity* 29 (1): 445–66.

———. 2010a. Alien powers: Deportable labor and the spectacle of security. In *The contested politics of mobility: Borderzones and irregularity,* ed. Vicki Squire, 91–115. London: Routledge.

———. 2010b. Antiterrorism, race, and the new frontier: American exceptionalism, imperial multiculturalism, and the global security state. *Identities,* forthcoming.

———. 2010c. The queer politics of migration: Reflections on "illegality" and incorrigibility. *Studies in Social Justice,* forthcoming.

———. n.d. *The spectacle of terror: Immigration, race, and the Homeland Security State.* Unpublished Book Manuscript.

DeMott, Benjamin. 1990. *The imperial middle: Why Americans can't think straight about class.* New York: William Morrow.

Fernandes, Deepa. 2007. *Targeted: Homeland security and the business of immigration.* New York: Seven Stories Press.

Garber, Marjorie B., Jann Matlock, and Rebecca L. Walkowitz, eds. 1993. *Media spectacles.* New York: Routledge.

Goff, Stan. 2004. *Full-spectrum disorder: The military in the new American century.* Brooklyn, N.Y.: Soft Skull Press.

Heller, Dana. 2005. Introduction: Consuming 9/11. In *The selling of 9/11: How a national tragedy became a commodity,* ed. Dana Heller, 1–26. New York: Palgrave Macmillan.

Henman, Paul. 2004. Targeted! Population segmentation, electronic surveillance and governing the unemployed in Australia. *International Sociology* 19 (2): 173–91.

Hsu, Spencer S., and Kari Lydersen. 2006. Illegal hiring is rarely penalized: Politics, 9/11 cited in lax enforcement. *The Washington Post.* 19 June 2006. www.washingtonpost .com/wp-dyn/content/article/2006/06/18/AR2006061800613_pf.html.

Hughes, Solomon. 2007. *War on terror, inc.: Corporate profiteering from the politics of fear.* New York: Verso.

Hussey, Andrew. 2001. Spectacle, simulation, and spectre: Debord, Baudrillard, and the ghost of Marx. *Parallax* 7 (3): 63–72.

Johar Schueller, Malini. 2007. Techno-dominance and Torturegate: The making of U.S. imperialism. In *Exceptional state: Contemporary U.S. culture and the new imperialism*, ed. Ashley Dawson and Malini Johar Schueler, 162–90. Durham, N.C.: Duke University Press.

Katz, Cindi. 2008. The death wish of modernity and the politics of mimesis. *Public Culture* 20 (3): 551–60.

Knabb, Ken. 1981. *Situationist international anthology*. Berkeley, Calif.: Bureau of Public Secrets.

Lefebvre, Henri. 1947/1991. *The critique of everyday life, volume one: Introduction*. Trans. John Moore. New York: Verso.

———. 1961/2002. *The critique of everyday life, volume two: Foundations for a sociology of the everyday*. Trans. John Moore. New York: Verso.

———. 1968/1971. *Everyday life in the modern world*. Trans. Sacha Rabinovitch. London: Allen Lane/Penguin.

———. 1981/2005. *The critique of everyday life, volume three: From modernity to modernism: (Toward a metaphilosophy of daily life)*. New York: Verso.

———. 1992/2004. *Rhythmanalysis: Space, time, and everyday life*. New York: Continuum.

Martin, Randy. 2007. *An empire of indifference: American war and the financial logic of risk management*. Durham, N.C.: Duke University Press.

Miller, Mark Crispin. 2001. *The Bush dyslexicon: Observations on a national disorder*. New York: W. W. Norton and Co.

Marx, Karl. 1843/1978. On the Jewish question. In *The Marx-Engles reader*, 2nd ed., ed. Robert C. Tucker, 26–52. New York: W. W. Norton and Co.

———. 1867/1976. *Capital: A critique of political economy, Volume One*. Trans. Ben Fowkes. New York: Penguin Books.

Merrifield, Andy. 2004. Debord's World. *Environment and Planning D: Society and Space* 22 (3): 325–28.

———. 2005. *Guy Debord*. London: Reaktion Books.

Mirzoeff, Nicholas. 2005. *Watching Babylon: The war in Iraq and global visual culture*. New York: Routledge.

Mitchell, W. J. T. 2008. The spectacle today: A response to RETORT. *Public Culture* 20 (3): 573–81.

Monahan, Torin, ed. 2006. *Surveillance and security: Technological politics and power in everyday life*. New York: Routledge.

Parenti, Cristian. 2007. Planet America: The revolution in military affairs as fantasy and fetish. In *Exceptional state: Contemporary U.S. culture and the new imperialism*, ed. Ashley Dawson and Malini Johar Schueller, 88–104. Durham, N.C.: Duke University Press.

Preston, Julia. 2008a. Employers fight tough measures on immigration (under the presidential administration of Barack Obama and 6 July 2008). www.nytimes.com/2008/07/06/us/06employer.html?pagewanted=1&th&emc=th.

————. 2008b. An interpreter speaking up for migrants. *New York Times*. 11 July, www .nytimes.com/2008/07/11/us/11immig.html?_r=1&th=&adxnnl=1&emc=th&page wanted=1&adxnnlx=1215788426-WJjQYPsHXaINkxApWjKF/Q.

————. 2010. Illegal workers swept from jobs in "silent raids." *New York Times*. July 9, www.nytimes.com/2010/07/10/us/10enforce.html.

Retort (Iain Boal, T. J. Clark, Joseph Matthews, and Michael Watts). 2004. Afflicted powers: The state, spectacle, and September 11. *New Left Review* 27:5–21.

————. 2005. *Afflicted powers: Capital and spectacle in a new age of war.* New York: Verso.

————. 2008. The totality for grownups. *Public Culture* 20 (3): 583–93.

Rogin, Michael. 1993. "Make my day!" Spectacle as amnesia in imperial politics. *Cultures of United States imperialism*, ed. Amy Kaplan and Donald Pease, 499–534. Durham, N.C.: Duke University Press.

Schehr, Lawrence R. 2006. Mr. Malaprop, or, no president left behind. *South Atlantic Quarterly* 105 (1): 138–52.

Stallybrass, Peter. 2006. Spectacle and terror. *New Left Review* 37:87–106.

Tuathail, Gearóid Ó (Gerard Toal). 2008. Pleasures of the polemic. *Public Culture* 20 (3): 561–71.

Ullman, Harlan K., and James P. Wade. 1996. *Shock and awe: Achieving rapid dominance.* Institute for National Strategic Studies. Washington, D.C.: U.S. Government Printing Office.

U.S. Department of Homeland Security, Bureau of Immigration and Customs Enforcement (USDHS-ICE. 2003. *Endgame: Office of Detention and Removal strategic plan, 2003–2012: Detention and removal strategy for a secure homeland.* http://www.ice .gov/graphics/dro/endgame.pdf.

————. 2006a. ICE agents arrest seven managers of Nationwide Pallet Company and 1187 of the firm's illegal alien employees in 26 states. Office of the Press Secretary, ICE Public Affairs, 20 April. http://www.dhs.gov/xnews/releases/press_release _0891.shtm.

————. 2006b. Department of Homeland Security unveils comprehensive immigration enforcement strategy for the nation's interior. Office of the Press Secretary, ICE Public Affairs, 20 April. http://www.dhs.gov/xnews/releases/press_release 0890.shtm.

U.S. General Accounting Office (USGAO). 2003. Homeland security: Overstay tracking is a key component of a layered defense. Washington, D.C.: GAO-04-170T, October 16, www.gao.gov/htext/d04170t.html.

U.S. Office of Homeland Security (USOHS). 2002. *The national strategy for homeland security.* http://www.whitehouse.gov/homeland/book/nat_strat_hls.pdf.

Valverde, Mariana. 2003. Targeted governance and the problem of desire. In *Risk and morality*, ed. Richard V. Ericson and Aaron Doyle, 438–58. Toronto: University of Toronto Press.

Valverde, Mariana, and Mike Mopas. 2004. Insecurity and the dream of taregeted governance. In *Global governmentality: Governing international spaces*, ed. Wendy Larner and William Walters, 233–50. New York: Routledge.

Vaneigem, Raoul. 1991/1994. The everyday eternity of life. (Preface to the first French paperback edition.) In *The revolution of everyday life* (1967), 7–15. Trans. Donald Nicholson-Smith (1994). London: Rebel Press/Left Bank Books.

Webb, Maureen. 2007. *Illusions of security: Global surveillance and democracy in the post–9/11 world*. San Francisco: City Lights Books.

Weber, Samuel. 2002. War, terrorism, and spectacle: On towers and caves. *South Atlantic Quarterly* 101 (3): 449–58.

White House. 2010. *National security strategy* (May). www.whitehouse.gov/sites/default/files/rss_viewer/national_security_strategy.pdf.

Willis, Susan. 2005. *Portents of the real: A primer for post–9/11 America*. New York: Verso.

Wolin, Sheldon S. 2008. *Democracy incorporated: Managed democracy and the specter of inverted totalitarianism*. Princeton, N.J.: Princeton University Press.

CHAPTER SEVEN

Securing Life

Human Trafficking, Biopolitics, and the Sovereign Pardon

CLAUDIA ARADAU

The end of the cold war saw the reemergence of human trafficking on the global political agenda as a new security threat integrated in a continuum of organized crime, illegal migration, drug trafficking, and terrorism. The words of the U.S. Immigration and Customs Enforcement agency (2007) echo this logic: "The threat to the United States posed by criminal organizations engaged in smuggling of any kind cannot be overemphasized. By exploiting vulnerabilities in border integrity, these criminal smuggling organizations, whether they traffic in humans, narcotics, or counterfeit merchandise, are an unquestionable threat to the security of the United States." While the myth of white slavery was reactivated in the public imaginary, security professionals rendered the problem of human trafficking actionable as a security threat (Aradau 2008).[1] In the midst of a context defined by the "War on Terror," human trafficking has never been far from the overarching concerns with terrorism, organized crime, or irregular migration. In Europe, the EU Hague Programme on the area of freedom, security, and justice has reinforced the securitization of human trafficking by enjoining the member states to develop a more effective approach to "cross-border problems such as illegal migration, trafficking in and smuggling of human beings, terrorism and organized crime, as well as the prevention thereof" (Council of the European Union 2004, 3). Placed in this continuum of threats, human trafficking appeared to partake of the sovereign inscription of power that has been characteristic of national security. Anti-trafficking strategies entailed the sovereign abandonment of women whose irregular status removed them from the purview of law while being included as de facto sources of labor. Victims of trafficking were to be deported or criminalized in a sovereign move to reduce vulnerabilities and reinforce the "carapace" of the state against undesirable circulations of people.

Nonetheless, human trafficking has also been integrated within a competing scenario of threat. "Human trafficking is a serious crime that violates human dignity and poses a threat to human security in our societies" (Biaudet 2009). Human security is a newly coined concept—usually attributed to the 1994 UNDP Human Development Report (United Nations Development Programme [UNDP] 1994), which renders visible threats to the individual. This move of expanding the concept of national security has been made possible by taking "life" as the referent object of security. It has also been particularly relevant for human trafficking, as security was increasingly claimed as the "right" of victims of trafficking rather than the survival of the state. Within the broader global shift to human security—"responsibility to protect" and care for life—the lives of victims of trafficking became the sites of the reinscription of life as worthy of protection. Anti-trafficking campaigns have used the mobilizing potential of life to efface the security construction of human trafficking by presenting an image of trafficking victims as suffering lives. Rather than undesirable subjects, potentially risky noncitizens who were to be deported or detained, women were increasingly represented as lives worthy of care, victims worthy of compassion, and bodies deserving of treatment. Their vulnerabilities and behavior became the focus of analysis with the purpose of restoring them to normality.

In International Relations (IR), this move from national security to human security has been analyzed in terms of a shift from sovereign power to biopower. Security as biopolitics takes hold of life, manages its abnormalities, and attempts to prevent "dangerous irruptions" of risk in the future (Aradau 2008; Dillon 2007; Dillon and Lobo-Guerrero 2008). The shift from people to population, noted by Foucault in his lectures, *Security, Territory, and Population* (2007), marks a transformation of governance from sovereign juridico-political rationalities to the rationality of political economy, of utility, and cost-benefit calculations. As Dillon and Lobo-Guerrero (2008, 279) put it, "[s]ecurity mechanisms . . . statistically mapped the contingent behavioral characteristics of populations." This understanding of security that mobilizes knowledge of populations and of the body, anticipatory technologies, and preventive interventions upon the life of subjects has allowed IR scholars to show how security has become a much more pervasive form of governing the lives of populations. Alongside a conceptualization of national security as sovereign punitive power, retaliation, killing, war, and geopolitics, the influence of Foucault's work on biopolitics has led to engagements with the insidious ways in which security permeates the everyday. The biopolitics of security works through technologies of risk management and prevention, whose purpose is to foster self-governing forms of life.[2] It increasingly underpins less violent and more insidious practices than understandings of national security, militarization, and exceptionalism indicate.[3]

However, this Foucauldian reading of the shift from national to human security runs into the problem of periodization. On the one hand, in IR, the shift from national to human security is often considered to be a post–cold war development. On the other, the biopolitics of security as theorized by Foucault is an eighteenth-century development. How does one account for these different periodizations and transformations from securing territories to securing the life of populations? Although several authors have recently attempted to bring together sovereignty and biopolitics together, either by considering life as the proper domain of sovereignty or by supplementing biopolitics with necropolitics, these periodizations make it difficult to understand the reiteration of the shift from sovereignty to biopolitics in current contexts such as human trafficking (Agamben 1998; Mbembe 2003). Taking my cue from Foucault's suggestion that sovereignty and biopolitics coexist, I draw attention to a third element that has been largely overlooked in the theorizations of sovereignty and biopolitics. The sovereign power of pardon allows for the recategorization of subjects and reclassification of abjection in ways that do not challenge other security practices or the edifice of sovereignty. Risky and undesirable lives become deserving lives through the bestowal of the sovereign pardon. Although the sovereign pardon is often considered to be an obsolete juridical form, reducible to rare instances of executive pardon, I show that it is a more encompassing form of power that mediates the relationship between sovereignty and biopolitics.

In order to unpack the role of the sovereign pardon in the biopolitics of human trafficking, I start by exploring some of the strategies of representing victims of trafficking as suffering lives worthy of protection. Second, I consider the forms of power that function in relation to protected/dangerous lives and the role of the sovereign pardon. Finally, I offer a different interpretation of the sovereign pardon in security practices by drawing on Foucault's writings on the *lettres de cachet* and the Bastille archives. Conceived as instruments of punishment and arbitrary power, these infamous letters of the French *ancien regime* expose the function of the sovereign pardon as a different rationality from that of sovereign punishment.

LIVES OF INFAMOUS/INSECURE WOMEN

Donna Hughes, a controversial representative of an abolitionist position in the anti-trafficking struggle, has compared the abuse at Abu-Ghraib with more "familiar" stories of trafficking that remain untold, buried in inconspicuous everydayness (Hughes 2004). In her story, trafficking appears as the Abu-Ghraib of everyday life, the extraordinary violence and abuse rendered ordinary by being embedded in the structures of ordinary, unexceptional existence. Equating human trafficking to torture, slavery, and exceptional violence has been one of the most common strategies of anti-trafficking campaigns. "Let's call sex trafficking by its real name—slavery" enjoined an article in one of the United Kingdom's national broadsheets (Smith 2010). "Slave Britain: the Twenty-First Century Trade in Human Slaves" was the main title of a recent exhibition organized in the United Kingdom by a series of prominent NGOs (nongovernmental organizations) involved in anti-trafficking campaigns. Still in the United Kingdom, a short film commissioned by the Body Shop in which Emma Thompson "stars" as a victim of trafficking who is forced to have sex with forty clients a day ends with the laconic sentence, "Trafficking is Torture" (United Nations Global Initiative to Fight Human Trafficking [UN.GIFT] 2008). Stories of victimhood and terrible suffering, whether narrated through the voice of NGOs or by the victims of trafficking themselves, appear to reenact images of abjection, those who have become politically disqualified by life and have been projected to spaces beyond the law (Agamben 1998). Many NGOs and anti-trafficking organizations pepper their Web sites and reports with stories of trafficking. These stories claim to offer an insight into the hidden violence and exceptional suffering that goes on undetected. The U.S. Department of State "Trafficking in Persons Report" includes stories of trafficking deemed to be "representative":

> Viola, a young Albanian, was 13 when she started dating 21–year-old Dilin, who proposed to marry her. They moved them to Italy where Dilin said he had cousins who could get him a job. Arriving in Italy, Viola's life changed forever. Dilin locked her in a hotel room and left her, never to be seen again. A group of men entered and began to beat Viola. Then, each raped her. The leader informed Viola that Dilin had sold her and that she had to obey him or she would be killed. For seven days Viola was beaten and repeatedly raped. Viola was sold a second time to someone who beat her head so badly she was unable to see for two days. She was told if she didn't work as a prostitute, her mother and sister in Albania would be raped and killed. Viola was forced to submit to prostitution until police raided

the brothel in which she was held. She was deported to Albania. (U.S. Department of State 2005)

The "Slave Britain" exhibition in the United Kingdom tells similar stories of trafficking:

> "Natasha" was 12 when her mother died and her father turned to drink and started to abuse her. She asked a family friend for assistance to escape the abuse. The friend agreed and helped Natasha flee across the border to Serbia and Montenegro.
>
> Once there, her friend turned on her and sold her into prostitution. She was then resold several times and forced to work as a prostitute in Albania and Italy, before ending up in the UK. During Natasha's first six months in the UK she was prostituted and repeatedly raped and beaten by her trafficker. She finally escaped and, with support from the Social Services, was able to bring her trafficker to justice. In 2002, her trafficker was sentenced to 10 years in prison. (Panos Pictures 2007)

The accounts of victims of trafficking render them as bare, depoliticized life, life which exists beyond the law. Their stories unravel ineluctably and women appear as pure marionettes, deprived of any agency and almost inexplicably having events and people "turn" on them. Boyfriends become traffickers and friends turn into exploiters and profiteers in the blink of an eye. This unexpected turn of events appears to propel them toward the exceptional situation. Their existence "beyond the law" renders them vulnerable both to what Butler (2004, 65) has called the "petty sovereigns," the traffickers who can function in this interstitial space, and the "sovereign police" (Agamben 1998, 174). Amnesty International, as many other NGOs involved in anti-trafficking campaigns, has argued that women are "systematically subjected to torture, including rape and other forms of cruel, inhuman and degrading treatment" (Amnesty International 2004). Women's confessionary stories are renditions of "bare life," lived outside the law where life can be sacrificed with impunity:

> He beat and raped me constantly for three days, to the point while I was lying in blood and urine while tied to the bed. He then brought two of his friends who raped me, put out cigarette butts on me, and cut me with razors. (Barbir Mladinovic 2006)

Beaten, fragmented, and suffering bodies make up most of the trafficking stories. "It's a baptism of brutality," states a London newspaper. "In every case, trafficked women are raped and brutalised by their 'owners' and agents before they are put to work, to make them compliant and terrified" *(The Evening Stan-*

dard 2002, 16). The UK Human Trafficking Centre starts stories of trafficking in similar emotional terms: "I have been raped, beaten, sold, cut with knives and threatened. I have scars and I am depressed" (UKHTC 2007).

Emotional accounts of trafficking focus on portraying the evil traffickers who exploit and reduce women to an undignified state of slavery. These stories of human trafficking depict the violence that victims of trafficking suffer at the hands of their traffickers. Representations of human trafficking, formulated in terms of sale, trade, or slavery, rely on the imagination of human insecurity as an intersubjective experience. Love and friendship become interpersonal relations of violence, so that violence remains in the register of the personal, the intersubjective, and the domestic. Insecurities emanating from the state and its agents are not mentioned. Violence and insecurity are exclusively manifest in the relationship between victims and traffickers, a relation that appears to unravel at a distance from the site, in the shadows of brothels, massage parlors, or the night shades of street work. A poster by the Council of Europe celebrating the Convention on Anti-Trafficking is dominated by the "comic novel" figure of an immense villain, whose powers are implicitly overwhelming to the women, who appear minuscule in comparison.

These stories of exceptional suffering also recreate an emotional trial in which exceptional suffering renders victims as innocent. Yet the exceptionality of suffering is also problematic for anti-trafficking NGOs and activists as it risks inscribing the bodies of victims as abject. Therefore, the stories and images of trafficking are grounded in a paradox: they need to render the suffering of victims of trafficking extraordinary, exceptional, and at the same time represent them as "normal," innocent, as everybody else. Victims of trafficking repeatedly say: "I just want to be normal." Anti-trafficking NGOs point out that "anybody can be a victim of trafficking" (IOM 2007). In a USAID (United States Agency for International Development) newsletter in Ukraine, the first myth of trafficking is "Trafficking can never happen to me." Yet, USAID warns,

> Trafficking can happen to anyone. Traffickers use increasingly clever schemes to trick people into cooperating with them for jobs that will never materialize. No one is immune from the threat unless they understand the risk and educate themselves about how to protect themselves. (USAID 2006a, 3)

Through the paradoxical combination of exceptional suffering and "normality," trafficked women are tentatively misidentified from categories of migrants, criminals, or prostitutes. Women who are trafficked into prostitution, the argument goes, should not be deprived of their rights on grounds that they are undocumented migrants. The "guilt" of migrants who cross borders illegally, prostitutes who work irregularly, and criminals who break the law is suspended in the presence of raw suffering and the desire for normality. The transgressions of victims of trafficking are excusable, erasable by the presence of raw suffering. The bodily pain of victims of trafficking also renders them nonculpable, deserving of protection and pardon rather than punishment.

These stories of violence and suffering lead to an implicit invocation of the sovereign pardon. According to Hughes as well as NGOs involved in anti-trafficking campaigns, raw suffering and damaged bodies require sovereign interventions that would suspend the existing state of emergency in which victims of trafficking find themselves. Nonetheless, sovereignty is not simply invoked here through its punitive capacity, but through the capacity for pardon. The demand for pardon is also not simply a request for governing the bodies of victims of trafficking through biopolitical technologies of prevention and regulation. Victims of trafficking cannot ultimately be proven innocent or guilty; they can be neither exceptional nor ordinary. The impasse created is transcended through recourse to pardon. Sovereign power does not decide on the exception, but intervenes to suspend it.

The Council of Europe Convention on Action against Trafficking in Human Beings explicitly integrates a "non-punishment provision" (Council of Europe 2005, Article 26). As victims are rendered as innocent and suffering lives, sovereign power can erase the guilt of legal transgression and protect them. Sovereignty is invoked simultaneously for its punitive power, its protective power, and the power to pardon. As the limits of protection are those of dangerous and undesirable subjects, victims of trafficking are misidentified from risky or dangerous subjects and are represented as worthy of mercy. Their irregular status and involvement in networks of crime has been a temporary coercion or cheating—they have not really broken the law or if they have transgressed it, they should be pardoned. Neither guilty nor not-guilty, their relation to sovereign power can only be mediated through the pardon. Victims are not to be punished because of not being legally proven innocent; given their often irregular status or involvement in criminal activities, they are effectively guilty in the eyes of the law. Yet their guilt can be suspended by the power of the sovereign pardon. The pardon appears to make possible the shift in thinking infamous lives as evil and abnormal to the etymological meaning of "infamous" as simply ordinary, normal.

SOVEREIGN PARDONS

The stories of trafficked victims share numerous similarities to the remission letters addressed to the king, starting from the sixteenth century. Just like the remission letters, the stories of victims attempt to render women as innocent or their transgressions as excusable. Natalie Zemon Davis (1987, 7) has pointed out that "pardon tales were mostly about homicides, claimed to be unpremeditated, unintentional, in self-defense, or otherwise justifiable or excusable by French law." Alongside homicides, pardons could be granted for theft, receiving stolen goods, rape, taking part in a tax riot, resisting royal officers, and heresy. Unlike legal judgements, the claims for sovereign pardon start with personal stories. Every letter of remission had at least two persons involved in it—the royal notary and the supplicant. Women's stories are similarly prepared by NGOs and rely on particular formulas of trafficking stories. These formulas are either differentiated by the type of exploitation (sex work, labor, domestic work) or by the victim's trajectory (war-torn country, love story, desire for a better life).[4] Training manuals for judges, police, or NGOs use these formulas to draw up case studies of stories of trafficking (International Centre for Migration Policy Development [ICMPD] 2004; International Organization for Migration [IOM] 2007).

Despite these similarities, the role of the pardon for victims of trafficking has not been given much attention. Generally, the sovereign pardon has been subsumed under the sovereign's power of death. Foucault has pointed out that the sovereign, "must remain the master, he alone could wash away the offences committed on his person" (Foucault 1991/1977, 53). Thus, the sovereign pardon appears to partake of the same logic of power. In the history of legal and political thought, the sovereign pardon is thought of as an anomaly or subsumed to the state of exception and the sovereign prerogative.[5]

Giorgio Agamben's work on the sovereign exception has reinforced the indistinguishability of pardon and exception. For Agamben, the claim of mercy and its attendant humanitarianism is just another manifestation of the sovereign decision rather than an attempt to suspend or close spaces of exception. Claims to mercy and sovereign protection only extend them. "The 'imploring eyes' of the Rwandan child, whose photograph is shown to obtain money but who 'is now becoming more and more difficult to find alive,'" cautions Agamben, "may well be the most telling contemporary cipher of the bare life that humanitarian organizations, in perfect symmetry with state power, need" (Agamben 1998, 134). In his view, the claim to life reinforces and expands the sovereign moment that delimits bare life from politically qualified life. It is only by being rendered bare that the claim for the protection of life can be voiced. Similar to Agamben's critique of human rights, legal scholars have also seen in the moment of the sovereign pardon the authorization of lawlessness by law and the enactment of sovereign decisions (Sarat 2005b). Whether the sovereign decides to punish or not, what counts is the moment of discretionary decision.

According to Austin Sarat, mercy is not just a moment beyond the law, but also a moment of personal decision and responsibility. Using accounts of governors in cases of clemency, Sarat argues that the narratives indicate "an effort to demonstrate the gravity of the decision making process, and some rhetorical trope that would ground what is in the end a personal choice in larger cultural and political values" (Sarat 2005a, 277).

If Agamben sees in the new humanitarianism the continuation of sovereign exceptionalism, for Foucault biopolitics entailed a change from the sovereign power to "make die and let live." Starting from the eighteenth century, sovereign power has been supplemented by a new form of power, biopolitics, which takes populations and their lives as the object of governance (Foucault 1991, 2007). Biopolitical analyses of security have equally located the transformation of the sovereignty beyond the discernment and implementation of inclusions and exclusions and friend/enemy distinctions (Dillon 1995, 328). The advent of biopolitics brings about a change in the development of the modern state from the "city-citizen" game to that of pastoral care of life and the living (Foucault 2000). The state does not only assign membership in the political community and ensures the survival of the community, but is also in charge of the well-being of individuals (or of categories of the population). Security becomes entwined with the development of the state in heterogeneous ways that go beyond the territorial and geopolitical dominant understanding of security. It functions in ways that complexify and disturb the state's taken-for-granted "right to kill" and the legitimacy of rule.

Rather than working through juridical prohibition and drawing boundaries of life and death, power is deployed in much more insidious ways by disciplining subjects and governing the life of populations. This type of order is concerned with specifying the norm around which deviations can be measured. Individuals or populations are ordered according to a norm against which deviations can be measured. Human trafficking would thus not entail just exclusionary and punitive measures for traffickers and/or women, but would be concerned with governing the behavior of categories of potential victims of trafficking according to norms of social behavior.

As part of this process of governing populations and securing order, boundaries still need to be drawn, creating categories of individuals who are to be protected at the expense of the exclusion and elimination of others. As racial boundaries delimit and divide the life of the species between life worth living and life that is to be curtailed (Foucault 2004), security practices are exposed as inherently *insecuring*, dividing categories of populations and preparing some for elimination, disciplining, or therapy. In Dillon's words, the "continuous biopolitical assaying of life proceeds through the epistemically driven and continuously changing interrogation of the worth and eligibility of the living across a terrain of value that is constantly changing" (Dillon 2005, 41). There is a suggestion here that the biopolitics of security operates in conjunction with the sovereign power to draw boundaries. Nonetheless, there is no indication of how these boundaries could be made more porous and the categorizations challenged. How can dangerous others become victims worthy of protection?

The fragmentation and delimitation of risky and nonrisky, worthy of life and punishable, is not simply dependent upon sovereign decisions that function along the lines of difference and exclusion. Collective mobilization and resistance have often challenged these limits and boundaries, categorizations and classifications. Yet the claim for recategorizing victims of trafficking does not challenge the law. It remains untouched and only demands that women be pardoned. Victims of trafficking move from realms of abjection that prepare them for detention, deportation, and criminalization to the injunction of "non-punishment" as the expression of pardon. The UNODC toolkit on the noncriminalization of victims of trafficking explains this shift:

> An essential element of protection of victims of trafficking and their rights must be that States do not prosecute or punish trafficked persons for trafficking-related offences such as holding false passports or working without authorization, even if they agreed to hold false documents or to work without authorization. Whether prostitution is legal or not, States should not prosecute persons for being trafficked into sexual exploitation, even if the person originally agreed to work in the sex industry. (United Nations Office on Drugs and Crime [UNODC] 2006)

If the sovereign pardon mediates the transformation of abject lives into lives worthy of care, how is it possible that victims of trafficking are never effectively pardoned? Victims of trafficking are eventually *voluntarily* returned home, after having testified against their traffickers and having undergone more or less extended periods of *rehabilitation*. Instead of deportation, voluntary return. Instead of detention centers, rehabilitation shelters. Instead of illegal migrants, victims. Although deployed upon supposedly different categories of subjects, the measures employed do not appear very different. In the shift from illegal migration to an emphasis on the human rights of victims of trafficking—a shift that has been made possible by the mobilization of NGOs in the anti-trafficking struggle—what appears to change is rather the form of incarceration or the mode of normalization. In order to account for the political effects of the sovereign pardon, I turn to Foucault's "minor" texts on the *lettres de cachet*.

FROM SOVEREIGNTY TO BIOPOLITICS

Foucault's writings on the *lettres de cachet* (letters under the seal of the king) reveal a sovereign power that becomes transformed into a humane, biopolitical power by intervening in the quotidian and eliminating minor dangers, threats, and irregularities. Although the *lettres de cachet* have usually been conceived of as instruments of arbitrary royal power used against the enemies of the king, Foucault reveals them as instruments of ordinary governance. In the seventeenth century, for example, one out of every one hundred inhabitants of Paris found themselves confined through *lettres de cachet* within the space of a few months (Foucault 2001, 35).

Despite their brief and geographically restricted history, Foucault notes the importance of the *lettres de cachet* for understanding how power works. Often taken for granted as symbols of the king's discretion and desire to eliminate enemies without any recourse to justice, the *lettre de cachet* was a more mundane and at the same time more pervasive expression of power (Farge and Foucault 1982). The practice of the *lettres de cachet* derived from the king's right of pardon and was an alternative procedure to criminal proceedings. This power inscribes the details of everyday life, gathers knowledge, incites to confession, and is haunted by the question "who are you?" Moreover, it does not arbitrarily intrude into everyday lives, but rather is part of a complex circuit of power that involves different institutions and is invested by various tactics depending on the objectives of those who use it or suffer it. It also does not arbitrarily decide on which subjects to select, but is solicited from within society and in a sense tactically used by dominant social and political forces.

The infamous men of the *lettres de cachet* are anonymous figures, infamous people in the etymological sense, had it not been for their collision with power. Power extracts them from their anonymity and everydayness as they have been named by their families, neighbors, and communities "infamous," evil, and abnormal. Foucault attempts to capture the process through which infamous individuals in the etymological sense become infamous subjects. Ordinary subjects are brought into the limelight as dangerous individuals to be eliminated, neutralized, or constrained. Unlike the sixteenth-century remission letters, these are letters that attempt to persuade the kind to take action against the infamous. "Stifled" is one of the terms that Foucault finds in the archives and that reveal the situation of infamous people toward the end of the *ancien regime*.

Nonetheless, the sovereign power does not stifle them but pardons their transgression by offering the possibility of normalization. The sovereign pardon is the power that effaces the punishment due to law transgressors. Yet the sovereign pardon does not restore normality as juridical accounts tell us. It ultimately does not restore people to their anonymity and everydayness. Rather, the sovereign pardon creates new forms of disciplinary and biopolitical normalization and extends the reach of power. In France, sovereign pardons led to the "great confinement" of the seventeenth and eighteenth centuries. In England, starting from the seventeenth century, the pardon was used to ease labor shortages in the colonies and gave rise to the transportation of felons to the New World (Moore 1989, 19). The pardon was not necessarily based on the evidence of innocence. It could be based on character evidence about the defendant—and information from people who knew the defendant—about whether he or she would reform. Just like transportation in England, internment in France was indicative of the power of sovereign pardons. Defendants could be pardoned if they reformed. Therefore, internment was not simply the rise of a "better" way of punishing, but also emerged in relation to pardon and the extension of sovereign power into a normalizing force for the purpose of protecting pardoned lives.

The sovereign pardon legitimates normalization as merciful action. Although often experienced as punishment, correction cannot be challenged on the same grounds as unjust punishment. Having recourse to pardon leaves the law in place and justifies forms of punishment that do not apply to reformable individuals. The sovereign pardon is not indicative of supreme authority and the arbitrary power of decision on life or death, as in Agamben's conceptualization. As Farge and Foucault's historical inquiries into the archives of the Bastille have shown, the pardon was equally underpinned by the power of patriarchal families. The *lettres de cachet* targeted excesses to the traditional geographies of labor and the family (Farge and Foucault 1982, 30). Those who disturbed the order of the family were to be punished: unfaithful wives, squandering husbands, and disobedient children. Those who did not belong to a family were the beggars and vagabonds who "acted as disturbers in the system of protections and obligations" (Donzelot 1979, 49).

Although offering all these nonaffiliated individuals clemency, the *letters de cachet* and their attendant internment soon became infamous as instruments of patriarchal power.[6] During the French Revolution, the main argument against the *lettres de cachet* was that the king had become an accomplice of private tyranny through public despotism (Farge and Foucault 1982, 350). Not only were the *lettres de cachet* accomplices of domestic tyranny, but they were also accomplices, one could add, of capitalism. Alongside vice, debauchery, and sexual license—the main concerns of patriarchal power—vagabonds and criminals make up the archives of the Bastille.

The French Revolution finally abolished the *lettres de cachet*. Less known, perhaps, is that the revolution also abolished the sovereign pardon for about six months in 1790. The strategic relationship between punishment and pardon in the deployment of sovereign power was thus one of the main targets of the French Revolution. The *lettres de cachet* shed a different light on the functioning of power and its transformation starting from the seventeenth and eighteenth centuries. While biopolitics is related on the one hand with the rise of capitalism, the need to regiment the productive body within relations of production, and with the liberal desire for "better" punishment on the other, this concern with the infamous lives of people is shown in a different light when the sovereign pardon is considered. The sovereign pardon opens a field of force in which different powers struggle over the definition of lives to be protected and lives to be lived in infamy. The pardon also legitimates sovereign power: the *lettres de cachet* attempted to render sovereign power more acceptable than patriarchal or capitalist power. What are the political effects of the power of pardon for victims of trafficking?

CONFESSIONS OF INFAMY

Victims of trafficking can be misidentified from the category of the dangerous through the bestowal of the sovereign pardon. As in the history of the sovereign pardon, the demand for pardon needs to be initiated from within society, namely by those NGOs women have been referred to by lawyers or the police. The clause of nonpunishment regarding victims of trafficking implies that the pardon of their legal transgression is also dependent upon reformability and the test of "normality." Victims of trafficking have to undergo more or less extended periods of *rehabilitation* and *reintegration* (Aradau 2008). To be restored to society, victims of trafficking need to be firstly identified as "genuine" victims. The recourse to the sovereign pardon means that victims of trafficking do not challenge the injustice of the law or the injustice of the offense. What takes place is a "*dematerialization of the offense*," which places women in "a mechanism of interminable investigation, of perpetual judgment" (Donzelot 1979, 110). As Donzelot observed in relation to juvenile courts, the investigation is meant to serve more as a means of access to the minor's personality than as a means of establishing the facts (Donzelot 1979, 111). As the pardon leaves the law in place, women need to be misidentified from categories of the guilty, dangerous, and undesirable. "Real" victims of trafficking need to prove that they have been coerced and cheated. The International Organization for Migration (IOM), for example, has argued that:

It is important to properly screen persons referred as trafficking victims to service delivery organizations for assistance to ensure that they are in fact trafficking victims and not smuggled or other irregular migrants, or other individuals
in an abusive or vulnerable situation who may be in need of assistance and/or
protection. Furthermore, care should be taken to assess whether the presumed
victim is in fact not a victim of trafficking or someone in need of assistance, but
someone actually trying to infiltrate the service organization for other motives.
(IOM 2007, 17)

These distinctions are not easy to make, particularly as there can be a continuum between regular migration and trafficking as well as irregular migration and trafficking. Confession is one of the means of identifying victims of
trafficking. Yet, confession is not enough.[7] As migrants and asylum seekers have
been increasingly met with suspicion, stories are no longer sufficient to identify
victims. The process of identifying victims of trafficking is far from straightfor-
ward recognition—in that sense very different from the ways in which vagabonds and debauched wives or husbands were identified by their community
in the eighteenth century. Coercion and lack of consent are often difficult to
prove and most NGO manuals for the identification of victims of trafficking list
medical and psychological signs that would allow the identification of "genuine" victims.

The situation of trafficking is seen as a prolongation of other situations of
abuse: control tactics used by traffickers, employers, and pimps are similar to
those associated with perpetrators of torture, domestic violence, or child abuse
(IOM 2007, 190). Human trafficking is an acute form of violence against women
that often overlaps with and sometimes is coextensive with other practices of
gender-based violence, in particular domestic violence and sexual assault:

Almost all sex trafficking victims are victims of serial sexual assault. For many,
sexual assault precedes their entry into sex trafficking; the trauma they have
sustained renders them vulnerable to their traffickers, facilitates their traffickers' control, and is exacerbated by the trafficking. For all sex trafficking victims,
the sexual exploitation they are subjected to as an integral part of the trafficking
leaves profound psychic injuries. (Leidholdt 2007)

Significantly, victims are shown to have often experienced "exposure to violence
at home or in a state institution" (Limanowska 2002). Most victims have been
abandoned by parents, friends, and/or husbands, and many have been sexually abused (Centrul pentru prevenirea traficului de femei 2002). They often
come from dysfunctional families (La Strada 2007).[8] The Bulgarian NGO Ani-

mus also indicates that the groups most at risk of being trafficked are women and adolescents who have suffered traumatic experiences; for example, victims of domestic violence, sexual assault, children from orphanages, and children with a large number of siblings and only one parent (Zimmerman 2003). Of the returned women at Animus, 26 percent had been victims of incest or childhood psychological abuse and all of them had untreated psychological trauma (Stateva and Kozhouharova 2004, 112). Diana Tudorache, from the IOM shelter on Kosovo, clearly connects the two types of traumatic events. In her words, "[t]he feelings of vulnerability and emotional pain that are experienced by the VoT [victims of trafficking], combined often with a background of childhood abuse and mistreatment, play a significant role in the occurrence and severity of the acute reactions" (Tudorache 2004, 23).

The family is no longer solely the guarantor of social order, but also the guarantor of individual normality. Disordered individuals are rendered thus by families and close personal environments. Similarly, victims of trafficking become disaffiliated due to disorderly capitalist relations. Their disaffiliation is represented as due to the excesses of capitalism, namely unscrupulous individuals who attempt to make extortionate profits. The UK Joint Committee on Human Rights places traffickers in two main categories: organized crime networks and unscrupulous family or friends (House of Commons 2006).

The sovereign pardon is dependent upon the victims' ability to reintegrate within "normal" family relations and "normalized" working relations. In Ukraine, USAID recounts the trajectory of a "rehabilitated" victim of trafficking: "Today, Lena is married, and she and her husband are expecting their first child. Lena works as an accountant in a small company and earns a comfortable salary" (USAID 2006b). Victims of trafficking are expected to find normal jobs and undertake productive labor. Those who return to sex work are excluded from any help or further NGO programs. The pardon implies that victims of trafficking need to show themselves as self-governing and capable to make proper use of their lives. Thus, in most European countries victims are also expected to testify against their traffickers in court.

The sovereign pardon legitimates all these measures as merciful, responding to the victims' desire for correction and improvement. Making a case for the protection and security of victims of trafficking is possible only if they are willing to participate in NGO-led rehabilitation and reintegration programs. These programs are not rendered as punishment, be it "better" punishment, but as what is implied by the desire for normality, which underpins the possibility of pardon. The normality of family, capitalism, productive labor, and belonging is the protection mercifully offered to trafficked women. They are shifted from the category of dangerous and undesirable others to that of lives worthy of protection only inasmuch as their lives can be reintegrated within regulated normality. This implies, on the one hand, an anatomo-politics of the body (of production and reproduction) and on the other the biopolitical governance of their circulations (migration and labor).

In conclusion, the sovereign pardon appears as a necessary vector of the transition from the sovereign delimitation of abjection and infamy to the bio-political care of life. This transition is not simply one of historical periodization, but it is part of the struggle over the governance of current social and political problems. However, while this transition is reenacted in various contexts, the history of sovereign pardons reveals the care for life as subsumed to the biopolitical imperative of regulated normality. Thus, victims of trafficking are pardonable only inasmuch as they display the desire for normal productive labor, patriarchal family life, and substantive community of belonging.

NOTES

1. On the reactivation of the myth of white slavery, see Jo Doezema (2000).

2. "Biopolitics of security" was coined by Dillon and Lobo-Guerrero (2008).

3. For an analysis of the role of the exception and exceptionalism for understandings of security in IR, see Aradau and van Munster (2009).

4. These are the formulas used by an anti-trafficking comic book designed by the Council of Europe (2006).

5. For a discussion of pardon in legal thought, see Kathleen Dean Moore (1989). The subsumption of the sovereign pardon to sovereign exceptionalism and punishment has also been challenged. For Derrida, the pardon contains the promise of justice. Christoph Menke (2006) has refuted a Schmittian reading of the exception by arguing that Schmitt ignores that sovereign power of pardon.

6. I have borrowed the term "nonaffiliated" from Nikolas Rose (1999).

7. On the limits of confession, see Aradau (2008).

8. La Strada is one of the first NGOs funded by the EU to prevent trafficking in women in Central and Eastern Europe.

REFERENCES

Agamben, Giorgio. 1998. *Homo Sacer. Sovereign power and bare life*. Trans. Daniel Heller-Roazen. Stanford, Calif.: Stanford University Press.

Amnesty International. 2004. "So does it mean that we have rights?" Protecting the human rights of women and girls trafficked for forced prostitution in Kosovo. Accessed 5 August 2006. http://web.amnesty.org/library/index/ENGEUR/700102004.

Aradau, Claudia. 2008. *Rethinking trafficking in women. Politics out of security.* Basingstoke, U.K.: Palgrave Macmillan.

Aradau, Claudia, and Rens van Munster. 2009. Exceptionalism and the "War on Terror": Criminology meets international relations. *British Journal of Criminology* 49 (5): 686–701.

Barbir Mladinovic, Ankica. 2006. Croatia: A human trafficking victim speaks with Rfe/Rl. Accessed 5 August 2006. http://www.thewarproject.org/node/10086.

Biaudet, Eva. 2009. Anti-trafficking. OSCE (Organization for Security and Co-operation in Europe). Accessed 20 March 2009. http://www.osce.org/activities/13029.html.

Butler, Judith. 2004. Indefinite detention. In *Precarious life. The powers of mourning and violence*, ed. Judith Butler, 50–100. London: Verso.

Centrul pentru prevenirea traficului de femei. 2002. *Traficul De Femei in Moldova. Realitate Sau Mit* [Trafficking in women in Moldova. Reality or myth]. Accessed 31 October 2004. http://www.antitraffic.md/materials/reports/cptf_2002_05/.

Council of Europe. 2005. *Convention on action against trafficking in human beings.* Accessed 20 June 2007. http://www.coe.int/T/E/human_rights/trafficking/PDF_Conv_197_Trafficking_E.pdf.

———. 2006. *You're not for sale! Trafficking in human beings.* Accessed 2 April 2008. Available from http://www.coe.int/trafficking.

Council of the European Union. 2004. *The Hague Programme: Strengthening, freedom, security and justice in the European Union.* Accessed 16 January 2006. http://www.eu.int/comm/justice_home/doc_centre/doc/hague_programme_en.pdf.

Davis, Natalie Zemon. 1987. *Fiction in the archives: Pardon tales and their tellers in sixteenth-century France.* Palo Alto, Calif.: Stanford University Press.

Dillon, Michael. 1995. Sovereignty and governmentality: From the problematics of the New World Order to the ethical problematic of the World Order. *Alternatives* 20: 323–68.

———. 2005. Cared to death. The biopoliticised time of your life. *Foucault Studies* 2: 37–46.

———. 2007. Governing terror: The state of emergency of biopolitical emergence. *International Political Sociology* 1 (1): 7–28.

Dillon, Michael, and Luis Lobo-Guerrero. 2008. Biopolitics of security in the 21st century: An introduction. *Review of International Studies* 34 (2): 265–92.

Doezema, Jo. 2000. Loose women or lost women? The re-emergence of the myth of white slavery in contemporary discourses of trafficking in women. *Gender Issues* 18 (1): 23–50.

Donzelot, Jacques. 1979. *The policing of families.* New York: Random House.

Evening Standard. 2002. Saved from the sex slave gangs. October 10.

Farge, Arlette, and Michel Foucault. 1982. *Le Désordre Des Familles. Lettres De Cachet Des Archives De La Bastille.* Paris: Gallimard.

Foucault, Michel. 1991/1977. *Discipline and punish: The birth of the prison.* London: Penguin.

———. 1991. Governmentality. In *The Foucault effect. Studies in governmentality,* ed. Graham Burchell, Colin Gordon, and Peter Miller, 87–104. Chicago: University of Chicago Press.

———. 2000. Omnes Et Singulatim: Toward a critique of "political reason." In *Power. Essential Works of Foucault 1954–1984,* ed. D. Faubion, 298–325. London: Penguin.

———. 2001. *Madness and civilization.* London: Routledge.

———. 2004. *Society must be defended.* Trans. David Macey. London: Penguin.

———. 2007. *Security, territory, population.* Basingstoke, U.K.: Palgrave.

House of Commons. 2006. *Human trafficking. Twenty-sixth report of session 2005–2006.* Joint Committee on Human Rights. Accessed 30 June 2007. http://www.publications.parliament.uk/pa/jt200506/jtselect/jtrights/245/24502.htm.

Hughes, Donna. 2004. Not unfamiliar. Images of sexual abuse and humiliation in Abu Ghraib. *National Review Online.* May. Accessed 18 August 2007. http://www.nationalreview.com/comment/hughes200405060834.asp.

International Centre for Migration Policy Development (ICMPD). 2004. Regional standard for anti-trafficking training for judges and prosecutors in see. Accessed 22 June 2007. http://www.icmpd.org/829.html.

International Organization for Migration (IOM). 2007. Handbook on direct assistance to victims of trafficking. Accessed 10 November 2008. http://www.iom.int/jahia/Jahia/cache/offonce/pid/1674?entryId=13452.

La Strada. 2007. Who are the victims of trafficking? Accessed 30 June 2007. http://www.strada.org.pl/index_en.html.

Leidholdt, Dorchen A. 2007. Successfully prosecuting sex traffickers— Testimony before the Committee on the Judiciary, House of Representatives, United States. Coalition against Trafficking in Women (CATW). Accessed 10 November 2008. http://action.web.ca/home/catw/readingroom.shtml?x=113289&AA_EX_Session=3735a8441bbc69e20700fe6237a7c127.

Limanowska, Barbara. 2002. Trafficking in human beings in South-Eastern Europe: Joint UN, Osce, and Unicef report. Accessed 30 June 2007. http://www.osce.org/publications/odihr/2005/04/13771_211_en.pdf.

Mbembe, Achille. 2003. Necropolitics. *Public Culture* 15 (1): 11–40.

Menke, Christoph. 2006. *Reflections of equality.* Trans. Howard Rouse and Andrei Denejkine. Ed. Mieke Bal and Hent de Vries. Cultural Memory of the Present. Palo Alto, Calif.: Stanford University Press.

Moore, K. D. 1989. *Pardons: Justice, mercy, and the public interest.* New York: Oxford University Press.

Panos Pictures. 2007. Slave Britain: The 21st century trade in human lives. Unicef. Accessed 29 July 2010. http://www.unicef.org.uk/campaigns/slave_britain/index.html.

Rose, Nikolas. 1999. *Powers of freedom. Reframing political thought.* Cambridge, U.K.: Cambridge University Press.

Sarat, Austin. 2005a. Mercy, clemency, and capital punishment: Two accounts. *Ohio State Journal of Criminal Law* 3 (1): 273–86.

———. 2005b. At the boundaries of law: Executive clemency, sovereign prerogative, and the dilemma of American legality. *American Quarterly* 57 (3): 611–31.

Smith, Joan. 2010. Let's call sex-trafficking by its real name—slavery. *The Independent.* 15 August.

Stateva, Milena, and Nadya Kozhouharova. 2004. Trafficking in women in Bulgaria: A new stage. *Feminist Review* 76 (1): 110–16.

Tudorache, Diana. 2004. General considerations on the psychological aspect of the trafficking phenomenon. *Psychosocial Notebook,* Psychosocial support to groups of victims of trafficking in transit situations. Schinina Gugliemo ed., 4 (February): 28–42. IOM, International Organization for Migration, Geneva, Switzerland.

United Kingdom Human Trafficking Centre (UKHTC). 2007. Blue blindfold. Open your eyes to human trafficking. UKHTC. Accessed 29 July 2010. http://www.blueblindfold .co.uk/stories/.

United Nations Development Programme (UNDP). 1994. *Human development report. New dimensions of human security.* Accessed 20 July 2007. http://hdr.undp.org/reports/global/1994/en/.

United Nations Global Initiative to Fight Human Trafficking (UN.GIFT). 2008. Trafficking is torture. Accessed 8 October 2010. http://www.ungift.org/knowledgehub/ multimedia.html?vf=/doc/knowledgehub/resource-centre/Multimedia/Emma _Thompson_Trafficking_is_Torture.flv.

United Nations Office on Drugs and Crime (UNODC). 2006. *Online toolkit to combat trafficking in persons.* Accessed 14 December 2008. http://www.unodc.org/unodc/ en/human-trafficking/electronic-toolkit-chapter-6-victim-identification.html.

United States Agency for International Development (USAID). 2006a. Nine myths about trafficking in human beings. *USAID Insight,* September 2006, no. 9. Accessed 20 March 2009. http://ukraine.usaid.gov/lib/newsletter/september.pdf.

———. 2006b. Success Story. Trafficking victim rebuilds life at home. USAID. Accessed 10 February 2009. http://www.usaid.gov/stories/ukraine/ss_uk_trafficking.pdf.

U.S. Department of State. 2005. Trafficking in persons report. Office to Monitor and Combat Trafficking in Persons. Accessed 29 July 2010. http://www.state.gov/g/tip/ rls/tiprpt/2005/46606.htm.

U.S. Immigration and Customs Enforcement. 2007. Human trafficking fact sheet, 16 January. Accessed 20 March 2009. http://www.ice.gov/pi/news/factsheets/humantraffic _011607.htm.

Zimmerman, Cathy. 2003. *The health risks and consequences of trafficking in women and adolescents: Findings from a European study.* Accessed 24 February 2004. http://www .lshtm.ac.uk/hpu/docs/traffickingfinal.pdf.

CHAPTER EIGHT

Surveillance and Securitization

The New Politics of Social Reproduction

SHELLEY FELDMAN

Surveillance has long been a topic of political, social, and ethical debate. This is no more self-evident than in the aftermath of September 11, 2001, and, more particularly, after the passage of the Patriot Act on October 21, 2001.[1] While current crises, and so-called crises, have reframed the character and practice of surveillance, earlier discussions, too, explored techniques of surveillance. And, like today, they were troubled by the increasingly thin line between the imposition of security measures and the curtailment of civil liberties and personal freedoms, and between public accountability and the erasure of privacy. Well before September 11, 2001, these techniques focused on the body as an anchoring point for the regulation of people. What we learned, and what Foucault helped us imagine more clearly, is that social regulation need not be accomplished primarily through segregation, as in the prison, but rather can be achieved by surveilling bodies as people live their everyday lives. Discipline is now efficiently and effectively produced through the micropolitics of everyday life—the control, not of the space that the body inhabits but rather of the body itself, often without the recognition or acknowledgment of its subjects. As William Staples (1994, 655) reminds us, "It is no longer considered effective or efficient to simply gaze at the body—or train it in hopes of rendering it docile—rather, we must serveil its inner evidence and secrets. And it is the social, cultural, and economic logics of late capitalism that make this pornography of the self possible and perhaps even crucial."[2] This pornography includes producing the obedient, alienated subject whose gaze is increasingly realized in and through consumption. Broadly framed, this consumptive logic of contemporary capitalism, "the latest crisis of overcapacity and the workings of global economic restructuring," suggests new relations of subjection and, importantly, signals an emergent crisis of social reproduction (Pred 2007, 367).

What do we mean by social reproduction? In its broadest sense, social reproduction refers to a historically contingent social process through which we reproduce our bodies, our social relations, and the capitalist order. While these varied relations are coconstitutive, I focus most specifically on how we reproduce our everyday lives, where everyday life includes, but is not limited to, the reproduction of labor power.[3] I also focus on the social relations and conditions that characterize contemporary neoliberalism where politics is, in Foucault's inversion of Clausewitz's dictum, "the continuation of war by other means." In this framing, politics sanction and reproduce crisis and its concomitant relations of power that are expressed as "a sort of silent war" that inscribes relations of force through "institutions, economic inequalities, language, and even the bodies of individuals" (Foucault 2003, 16–17).[4]

Today, as in the past, this force is undergirded by the invocation of fear. But, in the past, "fears of death and damnation were powerful realities, used as a disciplinary tool for children and adults alike," whereas today, fear is generalized and built on what was once, but may no longer be, a sense of surety in the responsibility of the state to protect and secure social reproduction (Stearns 2006, 477).[5] To be sure, this sense of security and animation for its possibility accompanied the expansive and progressive moment of capitalist accumulation, even as its benefits were neither imagined nor realized by much of the world's population, including many who reside in the United States. Nonetheless, this ideological frame enabled us to take for granted the "security of life, property and reputation" that is now threatened alongside the failing welfare state and its promise of securing the conditions of reproducibility (Stearns 2006, 478). It is this middle-class expectation of life "as usual," and the fear of its loss, that provides an animating principle of contemporary rule. This principle is expressed through, on the one hand, support for a war embodied in the protection of the American way of life, and on the other hand, the costs of securing such values, the instilling of "a military spirit into the civilian bodies of American citizens" (Armitage 2003, 1).[6] In its most recent incarnation, following the financial crisis of late 2008, it is posed as the question: Are we to expect a "new normal"?

At this conjuncture, surveillance and security prove to be effective means of regulation that creatively draw on experiences that occurred long before September 11, 2001. It is exemplified, for instance, in efforts to secure support for the cold war or to try to compel complicity in hunting down and exposing "communist sympathizers" during the McCarthy reign. Synergy between surveillance and security is also animated by the use of fear to justify new practices that increasingly characterize the contemporary urban landscape with its increased use of "enclosed defensive enclaves . . . [and] technologically managed system[s] based on automated access and boundary control" (Coaffee 2005, 449–50; see also Harvey 2004, 2006).[7] To be sure, discourses about surveillance systems highlight a concern about the trade-off between forms of control and their democratic and ethical accountability. Surprisingly, however, most scholars emphasize the management of this relation rather than the conditions that create the need for surveillance, why surveillance ought come at the expense of compromising civil rights for public safety, or the possibility that fear is part of a political project to legitimate neoliberal rule. Here, I imagine fear as both framing and legitimating the suspension of law and rights in the service of protection, especially as practices of legitimation operate under the increasing interdependence among military, scientific, and industrial communities. Together, they recast the distinction once understood as civil and political society, exposing how moral authority and technologies of surveillance combine to organize social life but leave decreasing political space for opposition.[8] This is especially so where the judiciary offers less and less possibility for critical opposition.

This institutional reorganization accompanies a growing decline in senses of belonging and community, structured in part by high rates of mobility and a growing expectation that individuals and individualism ought to mark measures of accountability. Nicholas Rose (1996) understands this as replacing the social citizen and common society with the responsible individual and his or her self-governing community. For the poor, the under- and unemployed, and others at risk, what was once assumed to be a temporary status—given an expectation of economic growth, capitalist expansion, and opportunities for mobility—has now become a permanent feature of life. With neither secure employment nor redistribution mechanisms to mediate the costs of neoliberalist production practices, new relations of insecurity emerge, and it is precisely these conditions that contextualize the tensions between the security of rights and the transformation of the conditions of social reproduction.[9] In this context, fear becomes a potent tool governing relations of rule.

For example, a recent strike of New York City taxi drivers over the required use of global positioning systems (GPS) suggests that the strike reflects more about drivers' concerns about protecting their rights as workers and entrepreneurs who struggle to meet their subsistence needs than it does about challenges to their right to privacy. This instance of people fighting to secure their livelihoods offers a window on the constitutive making of moral and bodily regulation, since much of the discussion during the strike focused on the inseparability of securing one's life and livelihood while simultaneously making sense of the fear and insecurity that dominates the lives of South Asian cabbies (Mathew 2005). I then briefly examine the use of nanny cams (cameras that show via the computer, and often at a distant location, what is going on in the locations where they are placed) in middle-class households to exemplify how their use signals a shift in the conditions of social reproduction as mothers struggle to meet their multiple work and domestic responsibilities while also struggling to maintain personal responsibility for their children's welfare, a hallmark of middle-class family relations.[10] I will argue that both examples reveal how security, fear, and threat lay the ground for, as well as mask, a crisis of social reproduction and the growing insecurity that accompanies social life in the current U.S. neoliberal social formation.

The deployment of these technologies also reveals new relations of control that rely on more fully integrating people within the body politic as they live their everyday lives, rather than on practices of segregation, sorting, or exclusion. Such technologies make it possible to shift control practices from the paradigmatic notion of controlled space (and bodies) articulated in the architectural model of the panopticon, to social *inclusion* as the routinization of control through monitoring and surveilling of people's everyday social participation. This is possible by the tracking of people as stationary subjects and "moving targets" (Feldman, Geisler, and Silberling 2003). As "a new episteme of control in state-of-the-art datavallience," tracking people incorporates new technologies but, significantly, it also reconstitutes relations among people that build on fear and mistrust to refashion rights and security between people as well as between collectivities (Levin, Frohne, and Weibel 2002, 10). Today, it is perhaps not surprising that, in addition to more than 30 million surveillance cameras in the United States alone (which shoot about 4 billion hours of footage each year), there are sophisticated technologies that measure vehicle speed, identify and ticket cars at traffic lights and intersections, use bracelets to monitor the movement of those on parole and under house arrest, and use cameras to monitor workers and consumers in the absence of direct human supervision (Klein 2007, 302). While some of these technologies may be obvious, others fall under the radar, their use often unbeknownst to target populations.

Also important to emphasize is that control through inclusion suggests surveillance is a specific relation of rule in which privacy and differences among people are technologically mediated by institutions of the state, government institutions that are contingently linked to changing regimes of authority. According to Philip Abrams (1988) and elaborated by Philip Corrigan and Derek

Sayer (1985, 9–10), the "idea of the state . . . is [to be understood as] a claim to legitimacy, a means by which politically organized subjection is simultaneously accomplished and concealed, and . . . constituted in large part [but not solely] by the activities of institutions of government themselves." Yet, despite this improved and more extensive creep of the means of control and inclusion, what David Lyon (2003) acknowledges as a deepening of the political economies of surveillance, I will argue that this creep simultaneously exposes and creates, perhaps counterintuitively, new relations of social exclusion and expendability that references a population that might never be fully incorporated into the current body politic as they embody, in the words of Hannah Arendt, "superfluous human material [to] be liquidated" (1951/1985, 443).

NEW YORK CITY TAXI DRIVERS AGAINST GPS "ANKLE BRACELETS"

A ubiquitous image in New York City is the yellow cabs that dot the streets 24/7. In most cases, one hails a cab with little thought about how to get to where one is going or about their safety, since New York cabbies are known for getting you to your destination. Notwithstanding Jim Jarmusch's *Night on Earth* exploration of the new immigrant cab driver and his fare as a caricature of NYC life, in most cases, drivers assist in times of distress, help with luggage, provide assistance to the elderly, and offer conversation to tourists and regulars alike in a city known for speed and unfriendliness.[11]

Who are the people who drive NYC cabs? Most remain anonymous, even as passengers are likely to recount a travel tale of which cabbies are a part. Most cabbies lease from fleet owners who control a large number of medallions, each costing upwards of $300,000.[12]

Today, with a significant proportion of drivers unable to afford an individual medallion, most work for a fleet and lease a cab at the cost of between $120 and $160 dollars for a twelve-hour shift. Many are new immigrants, and some are new drivers who secure employment to establish themselves in the city, hacking full or part-time to meet their individual and family needs. Others are longtime drivers whose income makes it impossible to save enough to purchase a medallion. Despite their ethnic diversity, comradeship characterizes relations among drivers, often formed at restaurants or diners where they congregate during breaks over coffee and food. As Mathew (2005) shares in his exploration of South Asian taxi drivers, many leave their old prejudices—Hindu, Muslim, Sikh—behind and organize, instead, along regional and ethnic lines. As drivers reveal in Mathew's thoughtful ethnography, since customers cannot distinguish among South Asians, religious differences that may matter in other circumstances fall apart and thereby help to facilitate organizing collectively as taxi drivers.

Taxi drivers also possess a working-class consciousness that likely contributed to their decision to strike. On September 5, 2007, they organized—in the middle of the New York Fashion Week and the U.S. Open tennis tournament—against the Taxi and Limousine Commission (TLC) to protest a city plan requiring GPS tracking in every NYC taxi. The New York Taxi Drivers Alliance, representing 8,000 members, 60 percent of whom supported the action, called the strike in response to Mayor Michael Bloomberg's requirement that drivers must equip their cars with GPS and machines to process credit cards, partially at their own cost. This strike builds on previous contestations between drivers, the TLC, and the mayor's office.[13] On May 13, 1998, for example, more than 24,000 drivers went on strike to fight the imposition by Mayor Giuliani and the TLC of regulations that would quadruple liability insurance costs, increase fines from $350 to $1,000 for violations such as "reckless driving," increase fines from $25 to $150 for "drivers who are discourteous to passengers or smoke while driving," increase new drivers' six-month probation to a year, and force new drivers to submit to drug and alcohol testing (Mathew 2005; Neeley 1998).[14] Previously, the Alliance won a 2004 rate increase, but this success was split with fleet owners. Both strikes took place well after September 11, 2001, when the city had almost shut down and most drivers lost between 60 and 80 percent of their daily income, a loss that generated individual debt of between $5,000 and $10,000 as a direct result of September 11, 2001 (Alliance 2003). As Bhairavi Desai, the New York Alliance organizer argues, hacking is "one of the few professions in the world where not only are you not guaranteed an income, but you might end a long twelve-hour workday losing the money you started with" (Early 2008).

Yet despite their dramatic loss of income, taxi drivers were almost invisible in the aftermath of September 11, 2001, and perhaps unsurprisingly, were largely unrecognized by FEMA (U.S. Federal Emergency Management Agency) (Mathew 2005, 3). A recent report by the Community Development Project of the Urban Justice Center, *UNFARE: Taxi Drivers and the Cost of Moving the City* (Alliance 2003), found that many drivers are continually unable to access disaster-related benefits for displaced workers. Their survey confirms that narrow eligibility guidelines and the lack of information with respect to available benefits limited accessibility and led to only 7 percent of surveyed drivers applying for disaster assistance. Of those who did apply, 34 percent were denied assistance, 5 percent (two drivers) received disaster aid, and 5 percent (two drivers) received loans from SBA or FEMA.[15] Adding to these dramatic economic consequences, the now largely immigrant, often South Asian drivers became the target of random arrests and detentions given that the profile of the Muslim terrorist was constructed as a brown, bearded man. This experience, coupled with a mass mobilization against FEMA in 2002, contributed to the radicalization of the Alliance against the AFL-CIO that, since the late 1960s, was thought to have sold out workers' interests to the TLC.

Importantly for this account, and contributing to how management orders and rules labor, it is hardly surprising that the TLC has sought to control workers for generations, even as the drivers have resisted efforts to orchestrate a structure of labor control. As Biju Mathew writes:

> A driver did begin and end his shift under the watchful eyes of the fleet owner; however, once that driver was out of the garage and on the streets, he[/she] could not be supervised, nor could his [/her] work be structured. A driver could choose the number and the timing of his or her own breaks. How fast [s/]he drove, and how carefully, were the driver's own choices. After having worked his [/her] first eight hours, a driver could theoretically take his [/her] last four off if [she/] he felt [s/]he'd made enough money. (2005, 80)

The implementation of new technologies that would limit drivers' control over their conditions of work were thus critical in catalyzing drivers' efforts to mobilize against their use. The New York Taxi Workers Alliance called the strike specifically to protest requiring the use of GPS that some cabbies feared could be used to track their movements, reveal their special routes and short-cuts, and make them less competitive on the road.[16] As Hossain Khan, one of the strikers, complained, GPS "would let the taxi commission monitor where taxis went during the day . . . and use that information to send speeding tickets to drivers who drove to the airport in less time than the trip should take" (Barron 2007). Concerns with market competitiveness and independence, the hallmarks of the entrepreneurial initiative required to secure a livelihood as a cabbie, remain a critical focus of the strikers: "Drivers will lose days of income while waiting for GPS repairs . . . [and their] income will be hurt by higher lease rates because of GPS."[17] Or, as articulated by others, "GPS WILL NOT give drivers navigation software or online maps but instead will enable private companies to track drivers' AND passengers' every move" (capitalization in original). Moreover, organizers anticipated that the new equipment would mean additional costs for drivers that would include the cost of credit card transactions and between $15 and $45 per week to rent the machine. According to Desai, because the GPS tracking would be on the meter, it also would delay the activation of the meter and the fare reader, making the whole process much slower. As she claims, "sometimes [drivers] will have to drive two to three blocks without the meter on [waiting for the different technologies to work together while . . .] the fare is in the backseat. That's money directly out of the driver's pocket. Drivers have little money to spare to begin with."

For the TLC, the new technology offers a way to use drivers' anxieties about the dangers of hacking and the fear associated with employment in the sector to legitimate the use of GPS. Similar to discussions in the 1960s, when partitions to separate drivers and passengers were installed to protect drivers during an armed robbery, gunfire, or attempted murder, today, too, technologies are used to assuage the fear of danger among drivers. In addition, similar to debates at the time, there is a tension between the need for security and safety on the one hand, and the conditions of employment and ability to maximize returns among drivers on the other. In current discussions, this tension accepts replacing "the lost art of taxicab conversation" with a concern with passenger comfort (Chan 2005). The debate over GPS likewise trades on this tension, emphasizing the ability the GPS provides in directing taxis to places where they are needed, presumably to increase fares, and to "help recover lost property" rather than addressing the working conditions and concerns of drivers (Moynihan 2007).

Moreover, the TLC enjoys the support of Mayor Bloomberg, who has put the city behind efforts to counteract the effectiveness of the strike. New rules for doubling up on passengers and setting fixed rates from area airports were established, and additional bus service was added to critical routes. Additionally, according to Police Commissioner Ray Kelly, "extra officers will take action to protect taxi drivers who refuse to strike" (Allen 2007). These institutional partnerships between the TLC and the city are not new and convey union-busting politics in the post-Reagan years. Also curiously, but perhaps no longer shocking, is the fact that the contract for the GPS systems was awarded to a company headed by the CEO of the Taxi Garage Association. As Bhairavi Desai, Executive Director of the New York Taxi Drivers Alliance would retort, "How can anyone not think this is a scam when the only ones who'll benefit are the taxi bosses, not drivers and not even the riding public?" (Allen 2007).

Also suggested by the city's effort to "modernize the sector" is how such initiatives refashion urban space, in what Mathew calls the "urban suburbs" and what David Harvey interprets as the suburbanization of the city. This model of urban space and consumption is part of a new landscape for the wealthy characterized by security, convenience, and comfort where the installation of GPS by the TLC and the city secures the wealthy's pleasure at the cost of securing the conditions of reproduction for the working poor (Flusty 2001).

As a strategic response, strikers also emphasize the interests of the wealthy and the costs to passengers as well as to themselves in an industry that depends on service provision:

> Stop GPS Spyware in Taxis! Support Drivers' and Passenger Rights! . . . GPS is a bad deal for riders and for drivers. . . . It will subject you to annoying broadcast ads during your ride (video screens will be installed for passengers) . . . will cause the meter to shut down if the technology fails . . . [and] force you to interrupt your ride and hail another cab.[18]

This response, which is framed as a technical intervention and technical concern, accentuates the connections drawn to mobilize support between the interests of passengers and drivers. But in this instance, it does so in ways that elide three other crucial relations: the role of surveillance technologies in the control of labor, the erosion of rights, and the potential support that technology could conceivably offer those whose work is risky or may be experienced as un-safe under some circumstances (and thus a response to the substantive fear that attends to work in the New York taxi industry). It also renders invisible—and this is the critical point for this discussion—the financial costs to drivers, for whom a challenge to their livelihoods can leave them in an even more precari-ous position than their work generally ensures, without the means to secure their own conditions of reproducibility.

The strikers' call also illustrates the persuasive and pervasive power of a nar-rative that incorporates and normalizes both fear and the needs and interests of the middle classes upon whom the survival of the working poor often depends. But, as the example of the taxi strike shows, any response to drivers' fears and physical insecurity promised by those who require and sell GPS systems is off-set by strikers' loss of control and the disrespect they feel as workers. As one striker, Lea Acey, made explicit, a GPS is "like an ankle bracelet they put on criminals" (Hamblen 2007). What is important here is not the creative ways in which technology augments patterns of so-called safety and rule, or even how it establishes new mechanisms for ensuring worker output and labor control, although these may be critical issues about which we ought to remain mindful. Instead, what we draw from driver resistance to GPS concerns securing their dignity, rights, and livelihoods in situations where new financial costs contrib-ute to their growing sense of political, social, and economic insecurity. The strike reveals as well how a growing population of largely marginal workers is commonly imagined and how their struggles for respect, dignity, and entitle-ment frame opposition to new surveillance even as strikers recognize that their ability to secure their livelihoods is increasingly framed in an idiom of securiti-zation. In short, even as taxi drivers address changes they expect for passengers and for their understanding of the rules of privacy and rights, and despite the dangers that accompany employment as a driver, it is fundamentally their ability to provide for themselves and their families that grounds their protest over being surveilled.

SOCIAL REPRODUCTION AND THE INDIVIDUATION OF SECURITY: THE CASE OF NANNY CAMS

The invisibility of taxi drivers in the FEMA fiasco, coupled with their declining incomes and demands for security, reflect the generalized crisis explored in Piven's *The War at Home: The Domestic Costs of Bush's Militarism*, and are linked, in a seemingly unlikely way, to issues of insecurity reflected in Katz's (2001) discussion of the use of technologies to secure the well-being of middle-class children under conditions of declining public investment in their safety and security. In particular, Katz focuses on the use of nanny cams by primarily middle-class parents, mostly mothers, who seek to protect their children while they work, attend school, or meet demands on their lives beyond those that attend to child care. Nanny cams, similar to other spy technologies, are primarily wireless devices that can be hidden in almost any type of household item, from a plant to a stuffed animal, to enable watching a child or caregiver from afar. This privatized strategy of surveillance is part of a $1.1 billion home surveillance industry that signals new practices that enable working mothers to secure the conditions of social reproduction given their responsibilities as workers and mothers (Katz 2001, 48). This privatization of children's security also can be used in child care facilities to monitor the quality of care, attentiveness of the caregiver, and to watch one's children in attendance. The use of such technologies has expanded in a context that includes the lack of adequate and safe child care facilities requiring that individual families, with sufficient resources to support the use of these new technologies, monitor their own children.

Conversations among mothers using the nanny cam or day care camera systems reveal how they enable parents to monitor their child's safety and maintain a connection with the child that, in the words of one mother, enables her "to watch my daughter and smile while I am at work"(Feldman 2007). Others recognize how this fetishization of children's well-being is a luxury in which only a relatively small proportion of the population can engage, while acknowledging that it can elide the vulnerability and risk of the majority of children of the working poor who were once able to depend on modest public investments to secure their children's safety.[19] Such individualized means of providing for security also can elide the new social relations that develop between employers/mothers and employees—which are now less likely to be premised on trust—and between parents and children, as these relations too are being constituted on the basis of fear and insecurity in ways that can lead to an assumed mistrust. They are also increasingly built on a sense of alienation as people confront the loss of intimacy that attends to current demands on their work and "private" lives as they secure conditions of reproducibility. But what their use makes evident is the existence of "a context of emotional anxiety" constituted, in large measure, by a continuous invocation of fear, which has unsettled how mothers once met their familial responsibilities as child rearers and how some caregivers recognize parents' needs to keep abreast of their children's well-being (Stearns 2006, 477). Thus, while there is some evidence to suggest that care providers may not mind being "on camera," it is nonetheless the case that this represents new relations among care providers and parents.

The example also reveals how insecurity, expressed in an idiom of fear and an "acceptable" loss of privacy, is an increasingly normal response to contemporary relations of social reproduction, since those who employ monitoring devices, and those who work under the camera's eye, experience its anxiety. Importantly, too, the example signals, although I will leave this undeveloped here, emergent relations of alienation as parent's seek solace in "peeking at" their children while at work or out of reach.

A RETREAT FROM SOCIAL RESPONSIBILITY

Both the struggle over GPS and the preference of some families to employ child surveillance devices challenges us to think creatively about how individuals, households, and communities reproduce their conditions of everyday life. Before considering this issue, however, it is crucial to emphasize that September 11, 2001, did not establish the ground for the expansion and consolidation of monitoring labor, gathering intelligence, or surveillance even as it unleashed new opportunities to secure legitimacy for once illegitimate relations between states and subjects. In fact, the Foreign Intelligence Surveillance Act (FISA) prescribing procedures for requesting judicial authorization for electronic surveillance of persons was first passed in 1978 and was delimited to those engaged in espionage or international terrorism against the United States on behalf of a foreign power. This act has since been elaborated and refined alongside a growing crisis of accumulation and achievements in perfecting surveillance technologies whose rapid expansion has been enabled, and opposition to it curtailed, through a politics of fear where public sentiment is constructed, and then construed, as a vehicle of legitimation.[20] As Haggerty and Gazso remind us:

In the aftermath of the 9/11 terrorist attacks politicians have routinely appealed
to "public sentiment" as manifest in various polls to justify hastily developed surveillance policies . . . [that demonstrate] how American policy elites aggressively
worked to label the 9/11 events according to existing policy orientations and how,
in a circular fashion, these typifications were reproduced in opinion polls that
were then used to legitimate new policies. (2005, 174)

Such efforts to define and deploy extant and new surveillance technologies,
policies, and practices expand the space for an illiberal state to commodify terrorism in the interests of securing capitalist production at the moment a crisis
of accumulation makes explicit the alliance between state bureaucrats, elected
officials, and the private sector. This is most obvious in the dramatic growth in
national security-related corporations to enable "social fears [to become] . . . a
constant source of profit" (Lockard 2002, 1). We only need to reiterate this point
here, as extensive commentaries reveal the rise and power of what Singer refers
to as "the evolution of private actors in warfare . . . [and] their modern corporate
business form" (2001/2002, 191, 197; Scahill 2007). As hierarchically organized
registered businesses that trade openly on the international market, private
military firms represent the quintessential "normative shift toward the marketization of the public sphere" and "the ultimate representation of neo-liberalism."
It is consistent with the "prevailing orthodoxy of economic rationalism, with its
emphasis on 'downsizing' government and large-scale privatization" (O'Brien
in Singer 2001/2002, 197; Dinnen in Singer, 198).[21] As a "permanent fixture in
the global economic architecture," the Department of Homeland Security alone
distributed $130 billion to private contractors between September 11, 2001 and
2006. And in 2003 the Bush administration spent $327 billion on contracts to
private companies, an amount that represents nearly 40 cents of every discretionary dollar in the federal budget, or what Naomi Klein calls "disaster capitalism" (2007, 301).

Alongside expanding and often unregulated systems of private control, these
changes reduce political rights as new forms of surveillance and new rules instantiated in executive and corporate power come to reign over constitutional
and legal measures, including individual rights to privacy. In response to numerous challenges to individual freedom[22] as expressed by ACLU and other opposition groups against communication networks for "illegal" wiretapping,[23]
Congressional approval now also ensures "that those companies whose assistance is *necessary* to protect the country will, themselves, be protected from
lawsuits for *past or future* cooperation with the government" (White House
Press Secretary 2009, italics added).[24]

While the Patriot Act set in motion a clear focus on war and what would eventually justify invasion, its extension accompanied a reduction in the political rights of citizens and the affirmation of social freedom as consumer and market freedom. As Bush framed it immediately following September 11, 2001, "fight terrorism and buy American" invoked the notion that the increasing control of social life is not centered in the choice to decide on the right of war or to hold an administration accountable for their decision to subvert international law by invading a sovereign state, or even to completely reallocate public resources away from social spending. Instead, securing popular support for the Patriot Act centered on the right of citizens (and subjects) to consume in a "free" market. This discursive and substantive shift in governance and rule reframed citizen rights in the name of safety and security and increased the numbers of marginalized populations, those in positions that constrained their ability to secure their own sustenance. In this shift, questions of choice and rights are subordinated in the name of the protective powers of surveillance: a technical solution provoked by fear, to a social and political problem, whether this concerns GPS to secure the safety and convenience of taxi passengers, nanny cams to secure child safety, or computer chips in children and dogs promoted in the name of safety and protection. It also includes the use of retinal reading to assure one's true identity in the face of a fear of misrecognition in circumstances where "others" are considered a threat and where the body[25] is envisioned as a source of authenticity and truth.[26] It is a short step from these arguably innocuous, even "positive," uses of technology to a reimagining of what the coordinates of safety and security implicate, a world where individuals have little choice but to protect themselves and secure their own welfare given that the constituent elements of social responsibility are increasingly being eroded.

David Lyon (2003, 666) plainly explains the movements of increased private and government expenditures to contain terror and to control insecurity in the idiom of fear: "What transpired after September 11th is that *companies and government departments that already had an interest in such surveillance systems now had a rationale—and public support—for installing them.* Technological fixes are the common currency of crisis in the later modern societies." The emphasis here is crucial since it highlights not that technology itself is determinant, but rather the need for and subsequent building of popular support and government subsidy to legitimate a transformation in the social relations of control. This transformation includes not only building popular support for an unpopular war, but also diffusing opposition to limits on the competition for "Iraq war contracts" to those companies with a "proven" capacity to provide the resources and skills necessary for success. Challenging the very basis of the free market, this latter proviso signals the emergence of new relations of rule and complicity in the construction of new subjectivities under contemporary neoliberalism.[27]

SURVEILLANCE AS SECURITIZATION: FEAR AND THE CONCEALMENT OF RULE

How does fear animate the experience of social reproduction, including during contestation over rights and security? How are particular populations made superfluous and how does their expendability depend on the ways in which surveillance practices are articulated and challenged in both the accomplishment and concealment of rule? As the exchange between the TLC and the mayor's office confirms, states share a protective interest in the private sector and trade on fear to secure its authority. In this context, fear is normalized in ways that make opposition difficult, often creating multiple and divergent responses to its instantiation. This is exemplified by the collective response of the taxi strikers and the tactics they employ to mobilize support among passengers. Importantly, in this case, fear and efforts to militarize rule are not totalizing experiences; rather, they provide the context in which people create spaces of opposition and mobilize against efforts to discipline their behavior. In contrast, in the instance of nanny cams and their use by those able to afford them, the example draws attention to a sustained if not growing individuation of responses of mothers to insecurity and to an increasing differentiation among families and the conditions of their reproduction. It also reveals how fear—sometimes justified—and insecurity now characterize the everyday lives of families and how the use of technologies can mediate some of its most dramatic effects, including the opportunity to "feel connected" and "peek at" a comforting referent in what may be experienced as an otherwise alienating context.

I suggest that today, fear is made banal as a façade for a generalized threat of physical violence or invasion and to support an environment that is founded on the presumption of an unexpected, but ever-present, need for protection.[28] The dictionary definition of fear is noteworthy since it makes an explicit connection between fear and social reproduction: "an unpleasant emotion caused by the belief that someone or something is dangerous, likely to cause pain, or a threat: *drivers are threatening to quit their jobs in fear after a cabby's murder/ fear of increasing unemployment*; a feeling of anxiety concerning the outcome of something or the safety and well-being of someone: *police launched a search for the family amid fears for their safety*; [or a feeling of] anxiety or apprehension" (MAC Dictionary). Coincidentally, these dictionary examples signal the salience of taxi drivers and safety as critical sites for interpreting social reproduction and the meanings attendant to fear and safety. But whereas fear in these examples is captured in the personal fear of particular employment conditions or exceptional situations, today fear is being crafted and generalized, perhaps making it unsurprising that, in Obermeyer's analysis, the continued monitoring of public transportation, and presumably other public venues, can be interpreted as "inevitable and probably on balance, beneficial" (2007, 361). Here, the question that remains is at what cost and for whom?

Also important, if less well-articulated, particularly in discussions of the costs of securing accumulation, is the regulation of popular imagination, the instantiation of a worldview of "us against them" and "good over evil" to establish the ground for always "thinking through" and "in" an idiom of fear and in/security. This normalization of fear in the popular imagination secures what Haggerty and Ericson (2000) refer to as a "surveillant assemblage," a relation of legibility that extends and deepens forms of population monitoring to include opening to private interests the work of governance. The banalization of this assemblage, its "hidden injuries," provides a mask to instantiate and secure state control over its citizens/subjects and other relations of power. Such an assemblage represents techniques and practices that operate through a "staggering array of agencies and institutions" for "purposes of influence, management, or control" that mark legibility in ways similar to the use of the census and maps—to mark boundaries, sort insiders and outsiders, and monitor population change (Anderson 1991; Mitchell 1991; Scott 1998; Lyon 2004, 135). These practices also make possible the tracking of individuals through the "private" uses of the information highway—what we purchase, what we view, and who we contact. Such efforts to monitor popular curiosity and discussion complement a host of ways that work, disease, and criminal behavior have long been monitored and surveilled (Braverman 1974; Sewell 1998). Today, however, surveillance signals contested juridical and legislative shifts that alter the dynamics of politics as usual whereas surveillance, and responses to its imposition, is less about the rise, consolidation, and demise or transformation of relations of rule than about how rule is always and already an accomplishment. Yet, even as we recognize these new relations as an accomplishment, we must remain mindful that their legitimacy and security are consistently contested, even when new forms of social control are presented in the guise of personal protection.

Pred (2007, 351) reveals that the diffusion, reproduction, and enforcement of fear, difference, and distain for others engages what we assume to be the relatively innocuous, or perhaps necessary, practices of camouflagery, multi-colored security alerts, airport screenings, and other practices that suggest a state in control and rule on exhibition. He suggests that such practices are hardly innocuous since they exhort us to report suspicious activity, people, and things, and in so doing alter relations among people. Such practices, as Abrams might express it, may mask the power of such exhortation but also legitimate violence in the service of securitization, including the violence that attends to withholding, dictating, or shaping what information and resources are available to a citizenry. Crucially, this can include what may be claimed as secret information vital to national security, itself a social construction, but also any claims to secrecy in the name of protection.

In this context, fear and apprehension over security aid in legitimating once illegal surveillance practices and blur understandings of violence, state responsibility, privacy, and entitlements. They open to question whether physical force is the most salient form of violence, or if the normalization of inequality and exploitation secured by fear, which creates forms of economic and social violence, may be its apt replacement. Here, discourses of fear and security legitimate these new surveillance practices that help to sustain a sense of the always-and-already threat of the outsider, a threat that displaces a focus on other forms of insecurity such as that which references security as the surety of the conditions of social reproduction. As a consequence, security is increasingly produced and imagined in terms of autonomous individuals who are responsible for their own reproduction, often in relation to the need for, or acceptance of, the enhanced "sorting" of the body politic.[29] Such sorting, or new relations of marginalization and exclusion, is then justified on the basis of fear, rather than the obligation of liberal states to secure the reproduction of their citizens, including freedom from disease, street violence, and drug crimes. This shift in social and institutional responsibility recasts citizenship and entitlements in the idiom of moral failings and, along with individual responsibility for social reproduction, undermines collective responsibility for social sustenance, including both old and new imaginaries of the welfare obligations of the state under neoliberalism.

As Agamben poses it:

> In the course of a gradual neutralization of politics and the progressive surrender of traditional tasks of the state, security imposes itself as the basic principle of state activity. What used to be one among several decisive measures of public administration until the first half of the twentieth century now becomes the sole criterion of political legitimation. . . . A state which has security as its only task and source of legitimacy . . . can always be provoked by terrorism to turn itself terroristic. (2002, 1)

The normalization of these relations can be captured, like globalization, in deepening and expanding forms of enclosure, insecurity, and constructions of the "other." It marks strangers as well as employees and neighbors as potential threats who can be justifiably monitored and surveilled, establishes new relations of subjection, and sets new normative limits on the conditions of social reproduction.

The emergence of these new relations between states and citizens/subjects gained momentum and prominence during the Reagan administration and was signaled in dramatic cutbacks in institutional support and social spending for the dispossessed. It created conditions to end the draft and to support a volunteer military and institutionalized individual responsibility in the form of "just say no" initiatives centered on individual drug users or victims of drug traffickers, and young and potentially sexually active youth. It also established the conditions for deinstitutionalization that decreased social service support for new forms of independent living for the mentally disabled and the ground for the "zero-tolerance" and "three strikes" criminal laws that make reintegration into society as a full and equal citizen virtually impossible for those convicted (Passavant 2005). These shifts stress individual responsibility under a facade of seeking to make more humane the conditions of "normal" life, but in its practice they alter entitlements, rights, and state responsibility while they build on the availability of new technologies to monitor and control selected individual bodies, behavior, and action on the move (Lyon 2003; 2006).

As the hallmark of such neoliberal reform, recasting the meanings of security builds on what Humphreys and Rappaport (1993, 896) offer in their political critique of the Reagan-Bush administrations: the administration "could not simply ignore the large social control apparatus in mental health, criminology, and social welfare that had been captured by progressives. They needed a way to redefine American social control policies in order to further their broader political aims." The subsequent erosion of the welfare state through policies that stripped public support and accountability was legitimated in a discourse of individual responsibility that was signaled before, as well as after, the Reagan-Thatcher policy reforms (Hall 1988). It was identified as well by Piven and Cloward's insightful analysis in *Regulating the Poor* and *The New Class War* (1971; 1982), and further elaborated in *The Breaking of the American Social Compact* (1997) and Piven's *The War at Home: The Domestic Costs of Bush's Militarism* (2004). Tellingly, these earlier contributions examine how the provision of services acts to regulate the poor as a particular class of citizens, whereas the more recent works highlight the social costs of a war that essentially guts the very possibility of a democratic understanding of social protections and rights.

CONCLUDING REFLECTIONS

What is distinctive about the removal of support for social welfare spending, the turn toward the consumer citizen, and the normalization of fear as an animating principle of social relations is the increasing privatization and individuation of social reproduction that alters social practices within families, in work and management relations, and between states and citizen/subjects. What the taxi drivers' mobilization against the required deployment of GPS and the use of nanny cams by mothers reveal is how insecurity and fear animate our daily lives and how the social wage and social contract are being recast in ways that alter expectations, obligations, and the conditions that secure social reproduction. These cases also reveal how violence, not the political violence that we associate with war and death, but the everyday social and economic violence that attends to securing life and livelihoods, is becoming a constituent aspect of daily life. Today, it is the individuation of social reproduction that is normalized in a palpable fear that shapes new subjectivities and new expectations as to what constitutes social and political rights. What we learn from the taxi drivers' strike is that while some recognize and identify GPS as part of an assemblage of surveillance practices that challenge privacy, others recognize the required use of GPS as a threat to their working conditions and a control on their labor. For those able to afford it, the use of nanny cams transforms how work and child care can come together, even as it casts parenting in an individualized and individuated idiom of locatability. What these examples show, as well, is that new technologies enable us to "govern mobility in such a way as to allow circulation and to sustain the *impression* of securability" (Amoore 2009, 62, emphasis added). In these ways, one is able to control through inclusion, making it possible for mothers to privately follow the movement of "their" children at play or in day care, and for drivers to be monitored by others while on the move and in the privacy of their taxis.

Together, these new practices elide the conditions that generate the need for surveillance technologies and that secure and legitimate their use. This is partly accomplished by promoting a context of anxiety and fear that is embodied in the sustained threat of the terrorist. This partially masks a more generalized anxiety that is embedded in an increasingly individualist notion of survival. These practices make it difficult for people to identify and mobilize collectively for improving the conditions that generate this context of fear, especially since there is the simultaneous creation of a desire for personal control. Said differently, as individual responsibility displaces collective action, as the consumer citizen displaces the producing one, and as the poor and working poor find that they are unable to secure their daily sustenance, we may find that increasing numbers of people are marginalized, even made superfluous, not as a consequence of the banality of death, but of the banality of life. It is a life, I suggest, that is enabled when fear and insecurity are normalized in the public imagination in response to policies that remove social protections and social responsibility for securing the conditions of reproducibility, rather than in response to increasing insecurity brought about by the threat of marked others—the terrorist.[30]

Here Arendt's critique of modernity as characterized by conditions of stateless and rightless individuals who face "acute marginalization" is suggestive (1951/1985, 150). As she poses it, the process of marginalization constitutes a specific contemporary conjuncture and a specific alienated human subjectivity. It presumes a decreasing need for labor power and the problems that attend to conditions that increase the numbers of people who, with a disappearing welfare state to protect this once reserve army of labor, are unlikely to reproduce themselves. Hayden's brilliant deployment of Arendt's notion of "superfluous humanity" is especially apt, when he argues that political evil and violence must include the loss of socioeconomic rights within a frame of increasing global poverty and radical inequality (Hayden 2007, 280; Arendt 1951/1985).[31] The denial of socioeconomic rights as a form of evil, particularly in the age of global terror, can elide understanding the various forms that human superfluousness may take and "the structural conditions of modern society which make assaults on the human status possible" (Hayden 2007, 300).

Arendt's reference to concentration camp inmates who are made superfluous and who have no price, even as they can be used as labor during times of acute labor shortage, can today find a parallel under conditions that depend for their reproducibility, not on temporary needs for labor characteristic of a reserve army, but on a permanent decrease in the need for labor power (1951/1985, 444). In such a conjuncture, suggested by labor markets that can no longer keep apace with the demand for work, and as individual forms of production are not adequate to secure conditions of reproducibility, it is not difficult to imagine that increasing numbers of people will be made superfluous. In the words of Arendt, they will become "superfluous human material [that] must be liquidated," as such people are not only superfluous but also can become "socially burdensome" and "bothersome" (1951/1985, 443, 447, 445). Recognizing excess populations as socially burdensome and bothersome indicates the need for new practices of control, now possible through policies and practices of social control, as people live their daily lives. These new relations of rule are accomplished not through marginalization and exclusion, but through *inclusion*. With new technologies, in other words, there is little requirement to quarantine individuals, as control is now possible through collective and generalized forms of surveillance. But paradoxically, such practices of social inclusion also signal new forms of social exclusion where, as Arendt might claim, superfluous means "not to belong to the world at all" (1951/1985, 475). This occurs when "the crisis of surplus capital [becomes] inseparable from the crisis of 'surplus' people, the human debris that every crisis, following invariably upon each period of industrial growth, eliminated from producing society" (Arendt in Hayden 2007, 280). Yet, and perhaps even more important, even as fear and collective anxiety are normalized, and technologies ably monitor and control people, what the taxi drivers reveal is both the inability to totally secure such an accomplishment of rule and the criticality of continuing to mobilize and struggle to expose and secure circumstances that will enable people to reproduce themselves as they work toward unsettling those conditions that legitimate social and economic violence in the name of a "just fear."

NOTES

1. See Haggerty and Grazso (2005).

2. See the shift from colonial to neocolonial rule.

3. This extends the work of Bezanson (2006); Bezanson and Luxton (2006); and Katz (2008).

4. As Cammack (2002, 4) poses it, the contemporary neoliberal project includes "the recipe for the disciplinary state, and the rhetoric for selling it to the people . . . [and] how discipline was to be spread through the system by building contracts and internal competition into direct public provision, and contracting out to private and nongovernmental providers where possible . . . [and] inducing people to experience tightly controlled and carefully delimited forms of market-supporting activity as empowerment." Here Cammack draws on Marx's identification of two crucial transformations, one where "the social means of subsistence and production are turned into capital, and the [other where] immediate producers are turned into wage-labourers" (Marx, 874 in Cammack 2002, 4). See also Robin (2004).

5. Here I limit my focus to social reproduction, but recognize that fear is constituted through comparisons with difference, both external and internal enemies, where for the

former fear is caricatured as the immigrant (particularly the Muslim), and for the latter, enemies are the poor who are deemed undeserving and criminal.

6. Against this, Weber (1991, 78) offers an understanding of states as "a human community that (successfully) claims the *monopoly of the legitimate use of physical force* within a given territory," where politics "means striving to share power or striving to influence the distribution of power, either among states or among groups within a state."

7. This complements research on the dramatic rise of surveillance techniques and the growth of the surveillance industry, including its academic counterpart and the extensive assessments, organization, use, and relationship of surveillance to changes in housing, police, and urban life.

8. While the distinction between these communities and sites are heuristically separable, the distinction is better understood as a social construction, whether of the public and private, or of the state and civil society.

9. As Ellin, writing about the rise of the city in the mid-nineteenth century frames it, accelerated changes enabled by industrialization incite insecurities among the bourgeoisie, and unreliable and often substandard working conditions of wage-earners relate antagonistically to the small class of owners (1997, 20 in Yesil 2006, 413). These relations, coupled with increased geographic mobility in the "search by people for better wages and by workplaces for greater profits' created a 'new constellation of fear. . .both within the factory and outside of it.'" As she continues, "since the nineteenth century, the culture of fear has transformed public spaces into guarded and controlled places . . . increased the visibility of the ruled but decreased the visibility of the rulers"(2006, 34–35).

10. As Katz (2008, 5) frames it, it is in response to "the rise of ontological insecurity provoked by anxieties around the political-economic, geopolitical, and environmental futures."

11. Contestation between drivers and owners occurred more than twenty years ago over the partitioning of the cab that led to the loss of tips because it limited "personalizing" a relationship between drivers and passengers.

12. See www.nyc.gov/html/tlc/medallion/html/auction/main.shtml.

13. "The NYC TLC is currently in the process of mandating a technological update for all yellow cabs—even if the drivers may not like it." About 200 upgrades are already in place; the Vector 530 Driver Information Monitor to automatically log journeys and the iView 8000 Passenger Information Monitor to display a real-time map of the cab's location, fare information, and video content such as news. The system also offers passengers the ability to swipe their credit card to pay for the fare (Quilty-Harper 2007).

14. See http://www.workers.org/ww/1998/taxi0528.php.

15. "Although FEMA and the U.S. Small Business Administration (SBA) made low-interest loans available to some medallion owners and taxi drivers, it was not until a nearly a year after the disaster that FEMA broadened its guidelines under the MRA program to covered workers in industries hardest hit by the disaster, including the taxi industry" (Alliance 2003, 26).

16. The strike also responded to the demand to have touch-screen monitors installed

to enable passengers to use credit cards, which drivers feared could leave them with the hefty fees charged for credit card processing.

17. Quotes in this section come from http://libcom.org/forums/news/nyc-taxi-strike -against-gps-monitoring-05092007, unless otherwise noted.

18. http://libcom.org/forums/news/nyc-taxi-strike-against-gps-monitoring-0509 2007.

19. I am not making a moral argument here and fully appreciate why parents may choose to use such technologies since all insecurity need not be linked to fear, but what fear does is transform how we express and experience new forms of insecurity and new relations of reproduction, including of low-wage working-class women.

20. It is, of course, impossible to distinguish between cause and effect of support for surveillance, but it is important to recognize that moral panics are rarely sui generis, but instead are accomplishments of specific interpretations that are enabled, if not fully orchestrated, by a media that is increasingly centralized.

21. Private firms need to be distinguished from mercenaries and earlier private military ventures since the private provision of violence has been a routine aspect of international relations well before the twentieth century (Herbst in Singer 2001/2002, 190).

22. Not all decisions oppose constitutional freedoms. In *Boumediene v. Bush*, the Supreme Court ruled that the U.S. Constitution applies to the government's detention policies at Guantánamo Bay, making it clear that detainees are protected against unlawful and indefinite imprisonment and retain habeas corpus rights. As Justice Anthony Kennedy wrote in the decision: "The laws and Constitution are designed to survive, and remain in force, in extraordinary times. Liberty and security can be reconciled; and in our system they are reconciled within the framework of the law." *ACLU Online*, e-newsletter, June 21, 2008. http://www.law.cornell.edu/supct/html/06-1195.ZS.html.

23. The FISA Amendments Act of 2008 not only legalizes the secret warrantless surveillance program approved in late 2001, but also grants telecoms immunity from their aid in the surveillance of Americans' international communications. The ACLU lawsuit was filed on behalf of journalists, human rights organizations, and lawyers (e.g., *The Nation* magazine and two of its contributing journalists, Amnesty International, Human Rights Watch, the Service Employees International Union [SEIU]) whose ability to perform their work was greatly compromised as they believed the new law would disrupt their ability "to talk with sources, locate witnesses, conduct scholarship, and engage in advocacy" (*ACLU Online*, e-newsletter, July 19, 2008).

24. http://www.reuters.com/article/idUSN1929314820080620. 7 September 2008.

25. Witness the criticality of DNA results for unsolved crimes or the imprisonment of the wrong perpetrator.

26. The latter is of special concern at national borders where the techniques of surveillance constitute a multibillion dollar industry with global sales on a scale almost unimaginable. Thus, despite (although it is perhaps because of) the presumed movement of goods and people with globalization, the use of specialized technology to keep "unwanted" people out has increased dramatically with the expanded use of technol-

ogy. In Europe, North America, and in many countries of the South the increase is significant.

27. As Espo (2008) reported the limited outcry for Obama's support of the July 2008 vote on expanding surveillance, "With the general election looming, preventing another terrorist attack trumped fears that privacy rights may be violated." Or, as Obama himself said: "The surveillance program is actually one that I believe is necessary for our national security. . . . So I had to balance or weigh voting against a program that I think that we need—and that had been created so that your privacies were protected—or create a situation in which we didn't have the program in place." http://www.usnews.com/us news/politics/bulletin/bulletin_080711.htm. As the *Washington Post* reported (Murray 2008): "Obama voted in favor of legislation to overhaul government surveillance laws and grant effective immunity to telecommunications companies that participated in a secret Bush Administration eavesdropping program." http://voices.washingtonpost .com/44/2008/07/obamas-fisa-vote-goes-against.html. The Democratic leadership including some of Obama's close allies opposed his vote.

28. The meaning of terror has gained currency since September 11, 2001, although state terror is always an aspect of legitimate rule (see Max Weber).

29. Lyon sees sorting as a key strategy of what might be considered a divide and rule tactic, a tactic that readily leads to marking social groups and establishes the criteria for profiling (2001/2003).

30. Here, Bush's claims at the signing of the Patriot Act are noteworthy: "The changes, effective today, will help counter a threat like no other our nation has ever faced. . . . We've seen the enemy, and the murder of thousands of innocent, unsuspecting people. They recognize no barrier of morality. They have no conscience. The terrorists cannot be reasoned with. . . . The bill before me takes account of the new realities and dangers posed by modern terrorists. It will help law enforcement to identify, to dismantle, to disrupt, and to punish terrorists before they strike . . . [and] *allow surveillance of all communications used by terrorists, including e-mails, the Internet, and cell phones*. . . . This government will enforce this law with all the urgency of a nation at war. The elected branches of our government, and both political parties, are united in our resolve to fight and stop and punish those who would do harm to the American people." http://www .whitehouse.gov/news/releases/2001/10/20011026-5.html.

31. See especially chapter 12, "Totalitarianism in Power," and chapter 13, "Ideology and Terror," in *The Origins of Totalitarianism*.

REFERENCES

Abrams, Philip. 1988. Notes on the difficulty of studying the state (1977). *Journal of Historical Sociology* 1:58–89.

Agamben, Giorgio. 2002. Security and terror. *Theory and Event* 5 (4) online, accessed August 2008. http://muse.jhu.edu.proxy.library.cornell.edu/journals/theory_and _event/v005/5.4agamben.html.

Allen, Zita. 2007. Taxi drivers strike over new tracking system. *New York Amsterdam News* 98:1, 3.

Alliance, New York Taxi Workers. 2003. *UNFARE: Taxi drivers and the cost of moving the city*. Report by the Community Development Project of the Urban Justice Center, New York.

Amoore, Louise. 2009. Algorithmic war: Everyday geographies of the war on terror. *Antipode* 41 (1): 49–69.

Anderson, Benedict. 1991. Census, map, museum. In *Imagined communities: Reflections on the origin and spread of nationalism*, ed. Benedict Anderson, 163–85. London: Verso.

Anderson, Scott J. 2008. Obama's surveillance vote spurs blogging backlash. Retrieved July 24, 2008. http://articles.cnn.com/2008-07-11/politics/obama.netroots_1_fisa -bill-obama-bush-s-terrorist-surveillance-program?_s=PM:POLITICS.

Arendt, Hannah. 1951/1985. *The origins of totalitarianism*. New York: Harvest Books.

Armitage, John. 2003. Militarized bodies: An introduction. *Body & Society* 9 (4): 1–12.

Barron, James. 2007. Cabs are on strike, but are on the street, too. *New York Times*. September 6.

Bezanson, Kate. 2006. *Gender, the state, and social reproduction: Household insecurity in neo-liberal times*. Toronto: University of Toronto Press.

Bezanson, Kate, and Meg Luxton. 2006. *Social reproduction: Feminist political economy challenges neo-liberalism*. Montreal: McGill-Queen's University Press.

Braverman, Harry. 1974. *Labor and monopoly capital: The degradation of work in the twentieth century*. New York: Monthly Review Press.

Cammack, Paul. 2002. Attacking the poor. *New Left Review* 2:125–35.

Chan, Sewell. 2005. Taxi partitions, born of danger, may be set for a makeover. *New York Times*. August 9. Online version. http://www.nytimes.com/2005/08/09/nyregion/ 09taxi.html.

Coaffee, Jon. 2005. Urban renaissance in the age of terrorism: Revanchism, automated social control or the end of reflection? *International Journal of Urban and Regional Research* 29:447–54.

Corrigan, Philip. 2002. Some further notes on the difficulty of studying the state, England and the First Empire, 1975 onwards. *Journal of Historical Sociology* 15:120–65.

Corrigan, Philip, and Derek Sayer. 1985. *The great arch: English state formation as cultural revolution*. London: Basil Blackwell.

Early, Steve. 2008. Teamsters & Taxi Drivers. New Labor Forum. Sunday, May 11. http:// www.zcommunications.org/teamsters-and-taxi-drivers-by-steve-early.

Edkins, Jenny, Veronique Pin-Fat, and Michael J. Shapiro. 2004. *Sovereign lives: Power in global politics*. New York: Routledge.

Espo, David. 2008. Analysis: Obama's vote on surveillance moves him toward bipartisan middle. http://www.kansascity.com/news/nation/story/698977.html.

Feldman, Shelley. 2008. Documentation of a conversation overheard on a city bus in Ithaca, New York (September).

Feldman, Shelley, Charles Geisler, and Louise Silberling. 2003. Moving targets: Displacement, impoverishment, and development: An introduction. *International Social Science Journal* 55:7–13.

Flusty, Steven. 2001. The banality of interdiction: Surveillance, control and the displacement of diversity. *International Journal of Urban and Regional Research* 25:658–64.

Foucault, Michel. 1979. *Discipline and punish: The birth of the prison*. Trans. Alan Sheridan. New York: Vintage Books.

———. 2003. *Society must be defended*. London: Penguin.

Greenwald, Glènn. 2007. The lawless surveillance state. December, 16. www.Salon.com. Retrieved July 3, 2008.

Haggerty, Kevin D. 2006. Visible war: Information war, surveillance and speed. In *The new politics of surveillance and visibility*, ed. K. D. Haggerty and R. V. Ericson, 250–78. Toronto: University of Toronto Press.

Haggerty, Kevin D., and Richard V. Ericson. 2000. The surveillant assemblage. *British Journal of Sociology* 51:605–22.

Haggerty, Kevin D., and Amber Gazso. 2005. The public politics of opinion research on surveillance and privacy. *Surveillance and Society: "Doing Surveillance Studies"* 3 (2/3): 173–80.

Hall, Stuart. 1988. The toad in the garden: Thatcherism among the theorists. In *Marxism and the interpretation of culture*, ed. C. Nelson and L. Grossberg, 35–73. Champaign: University of Illinois Press.

Halperin, Karin. 2007. The ethics of GPS. *PC Magazine* 26:17.

Hamblen, Matt. 2007. N.Y. taxi drivers irked by GPS; strike planned in September. Taxi commission is moving forward with upgrades to 13,000 vehicles. *Computerworld*. July 31. http://www.computerworld.com/s/article/9028519/N.Y._taxi_drivers_irked _by_GPS_strike_planned_in_September.

Harvey, David. 2004. The right to the city. In *The emancipatory city? Paradoxes and possibilities*, ed. L. Lees, 236–39. London: Sage.

———. 2006. The political economy of public space. In *The politics of public space*, ed. S. M. Low and N. Smith, 17–34. New York: Routledge.

Hayden, Patrick. 2007. Superfluous humanity: An Arendtian perspective on the political evil of global poverty. *Millennium: Journal of International Studies* 35:279–300.

Humphreys, Keith, and Julian Rappaport. 1993. From the community mental health movement to the war on drugs: A study in the definitions of social problems. *American Psychologist* 48 (8): 892–901.

Katz, Cindi. 2001. The state goes home: Local hyper-vigilance of children and the global retreat from social reproduction. *Social Justice* 28 (3): 47–56.

———. 2008. Childhood as spectacle: Relays of anxiety and the reconfiguaration of the child. *Cultural Geographies* 15:5–17.

Klein, Naomi. 2007. *The shock doctrine: The rise of disaster capitalism*. New York: Metropolitan Books, Henry Holt and Company.

Levin, Thomas Y., Usula Frohne, and Peter Weibel, eds. 2002. Karlsruhe, Germany and Cambridge, Mass.: ZKM/Center for Art and Media and MIT Press.

Lewis, Tyson. 2006. Critical surveillance literacy. *Cultural Studies, Critical Methodologies* 6:263–81.

Lockard, Joe. 2002. Social fear and the commodification of terrorism. *Bad Subjects*:1–4. www.bad.eserver.

Lyon, David. 2001/2003. Surveillance after September 11, 2001. In *The intensification of surveillance: Crime, terrorism and warfare in the information age,* ed. K. Ball and F. Webster, 16–25. London: Pluto Press.

———. 2003. Technology vs. "terrorism": Circuits of city surveillance since September 11th. *International Journal of Urban and Regional Research* 27:666–78.

———. 2004. Globalizing surveillance: Comparative and sociological perspectives. *International Sociology* 19:135–49.

———. 2006. Theorizing surveillance: The Panopticon and beyond. Culompton, Devon: Willan Publishing.

Mathew, Biju. 2005. *Taxi! Cabs and capitalism in New York City.* New York: New Press.

Mitchell, Timothy. 1991. *Colonizing Egypt.* Berkeley: University of California Press.

Moynihan, Colin. 2007. Rival drivers' groups disagree on the likelihood of a taxi strike over new technology. *New York Times.* August 24. http://query.nytimes.com/gst/full page.html?res=9E00E2DC123AF937A1575BC0A9619C8B63.

Murray, Shailagh. 2008. Obama's FISA vote goes against Dem leadership grain. *Washington Post.* July 9. http://voices.washingtonpost.com/44/2008/07/obamas-fisa-vote -goes-against.html.

Neeley, Lyn. 1998. NY cab drivers strike. *Workers World.* http://www.workers.org/ww/ 1998/taxi0528.php.

Obermeyer, Nancy J. 2007. Moving violations: Data privacy in public transit. *Geographical Review* 97:351–64.

Passavant, Paul A. 2005. The strong neo-liberal state: Crime, consumption, and governance. *Theory & Event* 8. Online version. http://muse.jhu.edu.proxy.library.cornell .edu/journals/theory_and_event/v008/8.3passavant.html.

Piven, Frances Fox. 2004. *The war at home: The domestic costs of Bush's militarism.* New York: New Press, distributed by W. W. Norton.

Piven, Frances Fox, and Richard A. Cloward. 1971. *Regulating the poor: The functions of public welfare.* New York: Pantheon Books.

———. 1982. *The new class war: Reagan's attack on the welfare state and its consequences.* New York: Pantheon Books.

———. 1997. *The breaking of the American social compact.* New York: New Press, distributed by W. W. Norton.

Pred, Allan. 2007. Situated ignorance and state terrorism: Silences, WMD, collective amnesia and the manufacture of fear. In *Violent geographies: Fear, terror, and political violence,* ed. D. Gregory and A. Pred, 363–84. New York: Routledge.

Quilty-Harper, Conrad. 2007. Digital dispatch's TLC SmartCab GPS taxi solution. www
.engadget.com.

Robin, Corey. 2004. *Fear: The history of a political idea*. New York: Oxford University
Press.

Rose, Nicholas. 1996. Governing "advanced" liberal democracies. In *Foucault and political reason*, ed. A. Barry, T. Osborne, and N. Rose, 37–64. London: UCL Press.

Scahill, Jeremy. 2007. *Blackwater: The rise of the world's most powerful mercenary army*.
New York: Nation Books.

Scott, James C. 1998. State projects of legibility and simplification. In *Seeing like a state:
How certain schemes to improve the human condition have failed*. New Haven, Conn.:
Yale University Press.

Sewell, Graham. 1998. The discipline of teams: The control of team-based industrial
work through electronic and peer surveillance. *Administrative Science Quarterly*
43:397–428.

Singer, Peter Warren. 2001/2002. Corporate warriors: The rise of the privatized military industry and its ramifications for international security. *International Security*
26:186–220.

Staples, William G. 1994. Small acts of cunning: Disciplinary practices in contemporary
life. *Sociological Quarterly* 35:645–64.

Stearns, Peter N. 2006. Fear and contemporary history: A review essay. *Journal of Social
History* 40:477–84.

Weber, Max. 1991. Politics as vocation. In *From Max Weber: Essays in sociology*, edited
with an Introduction by H. H. Gerth and C. W. Mills, with a new Preface by B. S.
Turner, 77–128. London: Routledge.

White House. 2009. Fact Sheet: Doubling financial resources for agricultural development. Obama calls on Congress to increase support for developing countries. Accessed June 6. http://www.america.gov/st/texttrans-english/2009/April/2009040217
0952xjsnommis4.413348e-02.html.

Yesil, Bilge. 2006. Watching ourselves: Video surveillance, urban space and self-
responsibilization. *Cultural Studies* 20:400–16.

PART THREE

Displacement of Politics

CHAPTER NINE

Securing the Market of War

The Middle East Partnership Initiative[1]

ZAKIA SALIME

The rhetoric of war and terror is the hallmark of George W. Bush's administration.[2] Even the most serious skeptics would agree that President Obama's Cairo speech marked a shift in presidential tone (see Nordland 2009). Yet this shift was already initiated by the Bush administration when Bush announced his umbrella program of reform: the Middle East Partnership Initiative (MEPI), aimed at an area stretching from Morocco to Pakistan. Established in December 2002, MEPI followed a political rationality of "soft" reforms through enhancement of citizen-entrepreneurship, women's empowerment, and capacity building of "civil society," as a means to uproot "terrorism" and spread "democracy."

Touching every aspect of organization of life in the Middle East, MEPI has so far monitored a wide range of "partnership" programs crafted by the Department of State in Washington and monitored through Regional Offices in Tunis and Qatar. It has also mobilized funds to support NGOs and provide training for women, youth, entrepreneurs, and political players. In George W. Bush's terms, MEPI "expands" the United States' "engagement with governments and people of the Middle East to promote economic growth, education, and political freedom" (Bush 2003). The goal is to "build a more peaceful and prosperous Middle East . . . so democracy can spread, education can thrive, economies can grow, and women can be empowered. (U.S. Dept. of State 2003). Anthony Wayne, U.S. Assistant Secretary for Economic and Business Affairs, highlights the most important goal of MEPI by defining this program as "a means of sharing experience and opening trade opportunities to create free and dynamic economies that can boost prosperity in the Arab world" (Wayne 2003). Within this market logic, governments, people, and civil society are brought together in a new "social contract" (see Bush 2004) as imagined by Washington, and new modes of governance are enacted by players in the Middle East and North Africa (MENA).[3]

Since its inception, MEPI has fascinated a wide range of players including academic institutions, corporate business, human rights organizations, feminist groups, think tanks, and research foundations as well as key figures from both the Republican and Democratic parties, including Liz Cheney (in charge of supervising MEPI), Hilary Clinton, and Laura Bush.[4] Condoleezza Rice described MEPI as "transformational diplomacy in action"; that is, the "use of America's diplomatic power to help foreign citizens to better their *own* lives and to build their *own* nations" (Carpenter 2006).

As the substantial increase in its budget under the Obama administration shows, MEPI continues to be imagined as the place for pacifying the social body in the Middle East through both "diplomatic action" and market opportunity (Cofman Wittes and Masloski 2009; McInerney 2009).[5] The questions provoked by this initiative include: what are the assumed connections and tensions between its three levels of social engineering and political intervention—state, civil society, and global capital? What are the assumptions and truths informing MEPI's understanding of civil society and women's empowerment?

As these questions indicate, I will use MEPI as a site to explore the connections between the free market as a regime of capitalist accumulation through *pacification,* and the war on terror as a regime of control and *normalization* of "civil society" players. What are the assumptions informing the MEPI's definition of civil society? How is civil society positioned in this juncture of war and neoliberal reforms? One might argue that war rhetoric is losing its appeal under the Obama administration, despite its extension to Pakistan and probably Somalia. However, for people in the MENA (Middle East and North Africa) region it continues to shape the very way dissent is branded and dealt with by local governments. Beyond rhetoric, the fight against terror continues to materialize under MEPI's various programs that aim at shaping the fabric of the MENA politics and societies.

For these reasons, I do not view MEPI as a short-term program with no significant outcomes, despite well-known shortcomings (Yacoubian 2005; Carothers 2005, 2007). I see it as a discourse of power that generates new institutions, changes the way in which state and societies in the Middle East relate to each other, and shapes subjectivities by creating *objects* of discipline and *subjects* of "freedom" (see Benin 2008). I argue that MEPI is both enabled and constrained by neoliberal regimes of "global governance" and local authority and by a normative understanding of civil society and women's empowerment as pacifying sites. As a political program for pacification, MEPI is embedded in global processes of control, discipline and normalization (see Salime 2007) and circumscribed by the much contested U.S "imperial sovereignty" in the Middle East (see Hardt and Negri 2000, 298).

I pursue these arguments through a content analysis of MEPI's programs and the official discourses that initiated it. This material is available on the MEPI's old and new web site at the U.S. Department of State, Bureau of Near Eastern Affairs. My interest in MEPI started in 2004 when I was finishing an ethnographic study about the interactions among feminist and Islamist women's movements in Morocco (Salime forthcoming). The MEPI, a new site of contention in civil society, was dismissed by both movements as yet another failed attempt by the U.S. government to co-opt women's organizations and create consent about the war on terror. The controversies raged even more when the Moroccan government decided to host MEPI's first sponsored event: the Forum for the Future, in December 2004.[6] The Forum for the Future was launched at the G8 Sea Island Summit in June 2004 and became a yearly discussion platform "for change" that benefits from the involvement of the MENA governments, private investors, and civil society with G8 members (see Cofman Wittes 2004).

Like the women I worked with, I dismissed MEPI at first, seeing it as an attempt to ease social tensions and diminish the widening gap between governors and governed after the U.S. invasion of Iraq. However, as I started following MEPI's "success stories," press releases, official discourses, and programs since its inception in 2002, I saw instead a widening of the scope of intervention. Meanwhile I tracked the controversies and literature—including news reports, political analyses, and web sites—linked to its implementation. In addition, I had the opportunity to be part of two MEPI-sponsored events, notably meetings with "delegations of Arab women" participating in the MEPI's MEET US programs at U.S. institutions including Michigan State University, where I held a faculty position between 2005 and 2008.

While these informal discussions do not constitute ethnographic fieldwork, they did direct my attention to the growing scope of intervention of MEPI and to the implications of identifying women as a main category of interest. It should also be emphasized that this is an exploratory undertaking, which needs to be supported by ethnographic investigation of the "beneficiaries'" perspectives and their use of the various programs of MEPI on the ground. While it might be too early to assess the real impact of MEPI on "democracy building," it is important to understand the problems of MEPI's assumptions about civil society, peace, democracy, and women's empowerment.

THE PILLARS

The MEPI rests on four "pillars": "economic, political, educational, and women's empowerment" (U.S. Dept. of State 2002). With the economic pillar, MEPI aims at creating "the necessary framework for a market-driven, private sector-led economy" (U.S. Dept. of State 2003) .William Burns, Assistant Secretary for the Bureau of Near Eastern Affairs further explains:

> We will support those who are working to open up their economies and expand opportunities for all their citizens . . . we will be strong advocates for enhancing private sector involvement, diversifying economies, and preparing the region's workforce for the global economy." (Burns 2003)

Hence, if democracy seems to be mostly rhetorical to the Arab state (Zayani 2008), market reforms are not. They rely on the creation of concrete economic, legal, and financial institutions that include but are not limited to Middle East Entrepreneur Training, the Middle East Finance Corporation, the Partnership for Financial Excellence, and the Commercial Law Initiative. These institutions facilitate the shift from a "welfare state" (see Bush 2004) to a "market state" (Sivanandan 2004, 45), shifts that are endorsed by an increasing number of governments and expansive bilateral free trade agreements with the United States (Jordan in 2000, Morocco in 2004, and Bahrain in 2004).

Through the political pillar, MEPI "seeks to develop institutions and processes that are essential to active citizenries and accountable, representative governments."[8] The goal is to support "an expanded public space where democratic voices can be heard in the political process." Civil society is central to this process. The MEPI describes it within a "liberal maxim" (Mercer 2002, 7) as the place where the articulation of citizens' demands from the state are mediated by nongovernmental organizations (NGOs):

> Civil society provides an avenue for the governed to advocate to the government for change and to take peaceful action to effect change for themselves. The creation of non-government organizations is central to the building of educated citizenry actively participating in their own governance.[9]

The goal of enhancing civil society is pursued through discussion forums, internship programs, and the training of NGO leaders both in the United States and the region. More than half of the MEPI budget goes directly to NGOs. The economy and politics are brought together both implicitly and explicitly under the educational pillar.

When speaking of education, Anthony Wayne primarily uses economic rationales:

> It will be important for host governments to establish strategies to increase infrastructure deployment and foster use of information and communications technologies, including appropriate commercial and regulatory frameworks that spur investment, competition, and innovation. (Wayne 2003)

Not only the pedagogies of dissemination of knowledge, but also the contents of education come under close scrutiny and are opened wide to market intervention. Increased "funding and private sector incentives" are central to the educational reforms that currently sweep the Middle East (Wayne 2003). In MEPI, knowledge acquisition is expressed in the technical terms of "managerial" capacities, leadership, "skills," "English proficiency," and "digital readiness," with a particular focus on "distance learning" and virtual communication (Wayne 2003). While USAID took over as a G8 cochair of the Broader Middle East and North Africa (BMENA) Literacy Task Force, corporations such as Intel and CISCO System, among others, took charge of developing infrastructure.[10]

This packaging of knowledge entails further shifts from public education and state-sponsored training and employment, enabling "American and regional private sectors" to step in and provide "skills for which there is clear market demand" (Wayne 2003).[11] Here we must keep in mind the U.S.'s drive for the creation of Free Trade Zones and the need for a highly skilled, locally trained managerial class. The latter is recruited from a rising "global middle class" (see Cohen 2005) whose subjectivity has been shaped by the state discourse of citizen-entrepreneurship, and by a desire to transcend the boundaries of the nation-state through the accumulation of personal privileges; that is, visas, recognition, free circulation of bodies, and transnational networking (see Cohen 2005; also Ong 1999). The MEPI responds to these rising aspirations by offering workshops, textbooks, and library books to schoolchildren and high school students, with a focus on private enterprise, citizenship, and good governance.[12] Education is also the site where U.S. academic institutions come powerfully into play through internships, scholarships, and "partnership" projects.[13]

The last pillar of MEPI is women's empowerment. Referring to the first ever UNDP Arab Human Development Report (AHDR 2002), MEPI asserts that the oppression of women is "a major barrier to progress" (Bush 2003). Thus MEPI places a special emphasis on the needs of women as students, entrepreneurs, and advocates for political change.[14] Because of the centrality of women's empowerment and civil society in MEPI, I will focus on these two pillars in the following sections.

MEPI, THE RATIONALE

The MEPI could be seen as the entry into the shifts of the current U.S. administration's rhetoric about the Middle East. Unfortunately, this program received little or no attention in academic writing and was dismissed by a few commentators as a short-term strategy with uncertain political outcomes (Satlof 2002; Windsor 2003). Coming from Washington circles of interest groups and think tanks, these commentaries have been dominated by a pragmatic agenda that seeks to enhance U.S. intervention with more resources, following a donor/ recipients development model (Davidson 2006; Blecher 2003). Embedded in naturalized modernist categories of gaps, deficiencies, progress, and liberty (Bush 2003), most of these studies fall short of questioning the basic assumptions informing the U.S. discourse of democracy and freedom for the Middle East.

To Middle Eastern scholars and activists, MEPI was a desperate attempt to create consent on George W. Bush's wars and to co-opt local calls for true democratic reforms.[15] Many have argued that MEPI's focus on civil society holds the latter hostage to programs that diminish the spheres of contestation rather than enlarge the scope of freedoms (see MEMRI 2004; Baroudi 2004). Their point is that the emergence of true democratic institutions, though a desirable goal, is also feared on both sides. In the Middle East, this is due to a belief that the motives of the United States relate to hegemony rather than democracy (University of Maryland 2007).[16] In political circles in Washington the ambivalence relates to the fear that the rise of true representative institutions would put constraints on local governments' support to the "war on terror" at the least, and might at the worst bring the "wrong" players, Islamists, into formal political institutions. Now that the war on terror is openly franchised to local governments (i.e., Iraq, Pakistan, the Palestinian Authority), democracy is growing even more questionable (University of Maryland 2007).

Neither of these two perspectives questions, however, the place of the market nor on what a focus on civil society means given the way the war on terror conditions the global economic regime. They do, however, question the conflicting agendas of spreading democracy through the support of "civil society" on the one hand, and fighting terrorism by sustaining authoritarian governments on the other (Cofman Wittes 2004; Hawthorne 2003). As President Obama's speech in Cairo bears witness, the goal is not necessarily to compromise alliances with the latter, but rather to solidify them through people's participation. The MEPI is very explicit about the importance of Arab regimes to its mission. It even rewards those most resilient to change by applauding their "leading" role in democracy-building, as William Burns claims:

> Saudi Arabia's Crown Prince Abdullah recently seized on the Arab Human Development Report's challenge to issue a proposed "Arab Charter." The Charter document calls for internal reform, enhanced political participation, and economic revitalization based on free market principles. We need to encourage this ambitious and hopeful vision, and support it. (Burns 2003)

Finally, MEPI was also the site where global capitalist interests that clashed over the Iraq War renegotiated their relationships with each other. The United States was able to settle disputes arising with its European partners over the handling of the war in Iraq by adopting a revised initiative that better responded to the anxieties expressed by the G8 members during their Sea Island, Georgia, summit in June 2004. The more aggressive tone of the United States was tempered by European perspectives on the "social specificities" of the Middle East, and the European interests in the MENA region (see Cofman Wittes 2004). These discussions resulted in the Broader Middle East and North Africa Partnership Initiative (BMENA) granting Europe its share of the cake and further legitimizing capitalist interventions through the framework of "global governance." The latter was exemplified by the first Forum for the Future, hosted by Morocco in 2004.[17] This annual discussion forum brings together the G8 members, the MENA governments, the private sector, and "civil society" around questions of political and economic reform. Finally, MEPI has also allowed the United States to push for the inclusion of "civil society" without alienating Arab partners, a key demand of European players (see Cofman Wittes 2004).

CIVIL SOCIETY, THEORETICAL SHIFTS

Civil society remains one of the most controversial notions in political theory. Within the liberal tradition, civil society is viewed as a space of freedom from both the market and the state, in which citizens' demands are channelled and needs negotiated (Cohen and Arato 1994; Lewis 2004). More importantly, civil society not only creates the necessary space for political participation but also provides government accountability by guarding against excesses of state power (see Mercer 2002; Fisher 1997). In the 1980s, political and economic transitions in Eastern Europe and Latin America enabled a conceptual conflation of civil society and NGOs (see Alvarez 1998). The latter are seen as "the realm of organized social life that is 'voluntary, self-generating, (largely) self-supporting, autonomous from the state, and bound by a legal order or set of shared rules'" (Diamond in Mercer 2002, 9). Hence, in this liberal matrix the proliferation of NGOs is an indicator of the vivacity of civil society and the level of freedoms enjoyed by people (Cohen and Arato 1994; Fukuyama 2001).

The representation of NGOs as autonomous and separate from the state and the market has been critiqued by scholars as a normative liberal conception of bourgeois civil society that is specific to Western political theory and formations (Mamdani 1995; Kamali 2001). Once liberal assumptions about civil society are exposed to dialectical and historical analyses, the proliferation of NGOs becomes representative of new modes of governance operative in a global economy, at the same time regulating and being regulated by market rationalities (Jaggar 2005; Kamat 2004). In these studies the role of civil society seems to be circumscribed by market demands and restricted to administrative and managerial tasks (Pratt 2004; De La Barra 2006).

As development discourse shifts from governments to global governance (Kamat 2004; Vogel 2006) and from megaprojects to microfinance (Elyachar 2002), there is a corresponding shift in theorizing civil society as a site of "neoliberal governmentality" (Ferguson 2006; Goldman 2005). Hence, the creation of "pluralized," "depoliticized" (Kamat 2004) civic arenas becomes the place for generating domestic contractors for global donors (Hanafi and Tabar 2003; Feldman 1997).

Hence, under neoliberal regimes of governance, the contradictions between liberalism and democracy are blatantly exposed. As Held rightly argues, liberalism "promotes self-determination for the individual, protecting the individual from state and societal regulation whereas democracy involves the state and its people actively constructing public institutions and a public sphere that guarantees the welfare of the majority" (Held 1996 in Kamat 2004, 164–65). The state is only necessary as long as it creates the proper climate for the transformation of public good into private property (Kamat 2004; Sassen 1999). Obviously, this raises questions about resistance/violence in the free market and whether these are external, "cultural," and dysfunctional (Huntington 1993; Friedman 2000), or rather inherent to the neoliberal state and its everyday practices (Harvey 2005; Sassen 2002).

But aren't both civil society and the neoliberal state missing in the Middle East? From Bernard Lewis to Paul Wolfowitz, most "private" architects of the war on terror would agree that the Middle East is distinguished not only by the weakness of its civil society, but also that of its market (see Blecher 2003; also see Davidson 2006). No one could put it more blatantly than Daniel Pipes, the founder of the Middle East Forum, a Washington-based neoconservative think tank. He called the Middle East "a region which marches to its own beat" and that is "immune to such happy global developments as democratization, increased respect for human rights and greater scope of the market" (Pipes in Blecher 2003).

This conflation of people's freedom and market freedom not only marks a neoliberal shift in the definition of civil society, but is also essential to the governmentality of the war on terror, since the market is endowed with both a democratizing and a pacifying force. Thus, the current scholarship on the importance of civil society for the governmentality of neoliberal globalization is limited as long as it does not encompass, first the legitimating power of the war on terror and second, the tensions and contradictions between the U.S. discourse of democratization of the Middle East and the widening scope of its war on terror.

I have elsewhere argued that the connection between the war on terror and neoliberalism is not a simple one (Salime 2007). While the war on terror could be viewed in Foucauldian terms, as a technology of power that enables further political and economic interventions in the BMENA, neoliberalism has been viewed as a cultural intervention that aims to shape subjectivities through practices of rights and individual agency taking the form of consumerism, but also expressed under new modes of belonging to a "global middle class" (Cohen 2005) and new modes of sociability—for instance, women as an entrepreneurial group and agent of modernization (see Schild 2002).

In the MEPI these freedoms are expressed under the general goal of political participation and market opportunity. However, as we will see, the relationship between the free market and the war on terror is tricky. While neoliberalism requires a minimized state and a vibrant "entrepreneurial" civil society that will mediate the market's demands—rather than people's demands—to the state, the war on terror requires an inflated state security apparatus and a docile, normalized civil society, from which the "freedom" component is neutralized and even removed (see Hartman 2005).

CIVIL/UNCIVIL SOCIETY

The central role of the market in MEPI betrays these tensions between a liberal understanding of a "free citizenry" that informs its various programs and the need to discipline the "uncivil" society (Kean 1998) through strengthening the security state. The MEPI's framing of "terrorism" as located in the social body (Bush 2003; Lewis 1990) enables modalities of interventions that aim to pacify this body through the creation of "objects" of law and discipline in "states of exception," and subjects of market rewards (Agamben 2005; see also Mbembe 2003). The pacifying forces of the market are reiterated by George W. Bush in his 2003 address in South Carolina:

> The bitterness of that region can bring violence and suffering to our own cities. The hateful ideology of terrorism is shaped and nurtured and protected by oppressive regimes. Free nations, in contrast, encourage creativity and tolerance and enterprise. And in those free nations, the appeal of extremism withers away. (Bush 2003)

As this quotation makes clear, the Middle East poses two levels of threat to the United States: "bitter" masses on the one hand, and authoritarian governments "inciting hatred" on the other. While governments are disciplined through the example set in Iraq (regime change) and normalized through personal privileges—becoming business partners in the transformation of public good into private property—civil society is held hostage to two categories: the enlightened reformers and the terrorist hardliners. The first are the "subjects of freedom" or "subject peoples" in Fouad Ajami's terms and are rewarded with funds, visas, internship programs, visit tours, scholarships, and membership in global governance forums, such as the Forum for the Future (Ajami in Blecher 2003).[18] Under this category the MEPI melds together youth, women, students and entrepreneurs and acknowledges their importance to its mission:

> People in the broader Middle East seek greater freedom and opportunity, and a growing community of reformers in the region has emerged . . . The United States strongly supports the reformers who are working to build a more peaceful and prosperous Middle East. (U.S. State Department 2002)

The creation of the category of reformers serves to simultaneously announce and denounce the other category, of hardliners, or "bad Muslim," to borrow Mamdani's terminology (2004). They are objects of state surveillance and are disciplined through antiterrorism legislation. As suspected "Islamic Terrorists" they invite the suspension of the law and are circulated within the global prison complex or off-shored to police states for further screening. Other modes of punishments come under economic and political sanctions directed to rogue government and state players (i.e., Hamas and Hezbollah). Here again, President Bush's inaugural speech of MEPI articulates this polarization:

> America and a large coalition of nations are waging a global and unrelenting war against the terrorists. . . . The terrorists of that region are now seeing their fate,

the short, unhappy life of the fugitive. . . . Across six continents, America, and our friends and allies have been hunting down the terrorists one by one and bringing them to justice. (Bush 2003)

On the other hand, Bush praises the "reformers":

Reformers in the Middle East are gaining influence, and the momentum of freedom is growing. . . . America is working with governments and reformers throughout the Middle East. We are strengthening ties through our Middle East Partnership Initiative. (Bush 2003)

It is clear that this discourse has planted the seeds for the current polarization of the political fields in Palestine, Lebanon, Iran, and Iraq along the lines of "moderate reformists" (those the United States will speak to), and hardliners (those it will not speak to). The latter are excluded from MEPI's definition of civil society and from participation in its programs. The MEPI works through a selective participation of individuals brought together in meetings or trainings under the assumption that these individuals will "bring home" the "tools" and "skills"—to use MEPI's terminology—learned in the United States (Burns 2003). The process of selection is overseen by governments and supervised by the U.S. Embassy and its various cultural and economic services. Obviously people's profiles are cleared before being proposed by governments and prior to receiving their visa privileges. Gershman comments on this conception of democracy arguing that when "contestation is removed democracy becomes an aspect of development policy, divorced from politics and largely taken over by professionalized bureaucracies, often tied to developments and multinational agencies" (2007, 19). But again, in the case of the Middle East, not only is contestation removed but participation becomes a means for fragmenting social agents, individualizing economic actors, and depoliticizing political players.

This conception of reform is very limited for many reasons. First, the reformers loosely defined as youth, women, students, and entrepreneurs are considered free riders with no ties to particular communities, political parties, or religious groups. The MEPI does not acknowledge the fact that the "reformers" may operate within and across economic, political, and religious lines and may have conflicting interests in seeing state institutions dismantled by the free market (see Cohen 2005). This view also ignores the level of doubt raised by every move from the United States among people in the region, including those calling for reforms (see University of Maryland 2007).

Second, MEPI's perception of "participation" is very problematic since it constantly conflates governments' interests with people's and businesses' interests.

This conflation of interests follows neoliberal assumptions about the rationalizing, homogenizing, and pacifying forces of the free market, not only at the level of civil society but also at the level of interstate relations (see Friedman 1999, 2000; Fukuyama 1992). Hence, though democratization is articulated in a discourse of free elections and free associational life, the most significant expression of "freedom" is delivered to the region under the form of Free Trade Agreements, Free Trade Zones, and microcredit programs:

> Across the globe, free markets and trade have helped defeat poverty, and taught men and women the habits of liberty. So I propose the establishment of a U.S.-Middle East free trade area within a decade, to bring the Middle East into an expanding circle of opportunity, to provide hope for the people who live in that region. . . . We're determined to help build a Middle East that grows in hope, instead of resentment. Because of the ideals and resolve of this nation, you and I will not live in an age of terror. We will live in an age of liberty (Bush 2003).

Through MEPI, the United States is promoting a new "social contract" between governments and people in which the *market* becomes the *regulator* of the conflicting agendas of spreading democracy while fighting "terrorism" with the help of undemocratic governments (Bush 2004). In this process, many venues are created for normalizing and institutionalizing global capitalist interventions, placing them outside the control of relatively representative political institutions, such as unions, political parties, parliaments (when they exist), and political opposition.

Third, MEPI remains silent on political opposition in the Middle East, namely by Islamists, students, the unemployed, and antiglobalization street protests (see Cohen 2005; also see Bayat 2003). The focus on civil society aims in fact to diminish the role of political players, notably the Islamist dissent. Driven by a "normative" understanding of civil society, MEPI is still not clear about how it considers Islamist activism and the type of civil society it has generated. As Kamali argues, any discussion about civil society in Muslim countries requires "that we recognize Islam not only as a religion, but also as a political theory and the major source of a legitimization of political power" (Kamali 2001, 457). Not only political power but the economy too, I would add.

For instance, MEPI ignores the role played by the Islamic morality of social solidarity and ethics of interest-free transactions in shaping entrepreneurial practices in Muslim countries. It does not recognize the role played by the Islamist entrepreneurship in responding to the social crisis created by structural adjustment programs in the 1980s, through alternative yet capitalist—and increasingly popular forms of Islamic banking—Islamic funds and Islamist philanthropy. While the "war on terror" has enabled states to considerably limit "Islamic funds" and control the circulation of money within Islamist networks, MEPI enables global/U.S. capital to compete with these funds by co-opting a fraction of civil society through programs designated for younger generations of elementary and high school children, and through microcredit programs designated for women.

In William Burns's terms MEPI has been looking for ways "to expose young people to entrepreneurship and market-based economics through education and skill-development programs like Junior Achievement" (Burns 2003). Most of these programs are couched in the liberal framework of women's empowerment.

WOMEN AS FREE RIDERS

How does women's empowerment serve the agenda of political and economic change in the Middle East? In every one of its program, MEPI devotes part of the funds to women's empowerment. Defined in terms of political and economic participation, the empowerment of women is viewed as the entry to reforming Middle Eastern societies. As early as 2002, the MEPI was inviting delegations of—rather already empowered—Arab women. The first delegation is described by William J. Burns, Assistant Secretary for the Bureau of Near Eastern Affairs:

> Last fall, we brought 50 Arab women leaders to the U.S. to observe mid-term elections and meet with U.S. political professionals. We plan to expand this effort, establishing regional campaign schools in the Gulf, North Africa, and the Levant, to provide political leaders with the tools to take advantage of new opportunities for democratization. . . . We will soon bring to the U.S. our first group of Arab entrepreneurs, many of them women, to participate in our Middle East Entrepreneur Training program in the U.S., or MEET U.S. (Burns 2003)

Burns suggests that though these are "short-term programs" their "impact will last a lifetime." He claims that "the mutual professional and business relationships forged on the corporate and personal levels will be a platform for the Middle East's economic future—a future shaped with American partners" (Burns 2003). This rhetoric is completely at odds with the MEPI's own definition of Arab women's lack of agency and participation:

> The Middle East presents many obstacles to the advance of freedom [. . .]. Recently, a group of 30 Arab scholars issued a report describing a freedom deficit

in Arab countries. . . . They also identified the social oppression of women as a major barrier to progress. And they are correct. No society can succeed and prosper while denying basic rights and opportunities to the women of their country. (Bush 2003)

The MEPI legitimates its intervention on behalf of Arab women through the "facts" provided by the very controversial 2002 Arab Human Development Reports (AHDR) (for a critique see LeVine 2002). The Report "identifies the women's empowerment deficit as one of three key obstacles holding back the entire region" (Burns 2003). The Department of State builds on the AHDR to describe women's multiple marginalizations as follows:

The facts are sobering. More than half of Arab women are still illiterate. Women lack equal citizenship and legal entitlement. Their participation in the workplace and public life is minimal, as evidenced by a very limited range of representation in parliaments, cabinets, and the work force.[19]

To address these deficiencies, MEPI devotes funds and a wide array of programs for the empowerment of women.[20] The former Secretary of State, Condoleezza Rice, took her words from the mouth of "a Muslim woman" in her 2005 Cairo speech: (Condoleeza Rice's Cairo speech 2009)

There are those who say that democracy is for men alone. In fact, the opposite is true: half a democracy is not a democracy. As one Muslim woman leader has said, "Society is like a bird. It has two wings. And a bird cannot fly if one wing is broken." [21]

Before analyzing the importance of women's empowerment for the U.S. war on terror I would like to make few points. First, the rhetoric of "women's empowerment" is not totally foreign to liberal feminism in the Middle East. Composed of urban, highly educated middle-class activists, liberal feminism has been using development discourse, notably through the WID programs (Women in Development), to speak to governments' agencies and secure transnational funds. This connection between "gender development categories" and "middle-class third world feminisms" has been extensively explored (Mendoza 2002, 8; Poster and Salime 2002; Kriemild 2002). Focusing on individual women, rather than structures of power, this discourse serves capitalism not only as a mode of accumulation but as a "cultural" intervention to change the fabric of "traditional" societies and break the bonds that hold certain communities together (see Eisenstein 2005). The discourse of women's empowerment is grounded in the assumption that if individual women gain economic independence they will have more decisional power over their lives and therefore will create change from within. This brings me to my second point.

Despite their depiction as oppressed, the war on terror is constructed on other layers of meanings about gender and the importance of Arab women as modernizing forces. Feminist theory has already unveiled the centrality of gender in setting the war on terror on a "civilizing mission" (Enloe 2005; Abu-Lughod 2002). The claim to liberate Muslim women also helps to rally feminist sentiments and mobilize funds and private contractors to survey Arab women's needs (Freedom House is an example). Furthermore, the implication of Congresswomen and Department of State officials such as Hilary Clinton and Condoleezza Rice in discussion forums and meetings with "Arab women" helps legitimize the involvement of high-profile women from the Middle East in public events around MEPI. Egypt's First Lady Suzanne Mubarak and Qatar's Sheikha Mozah Bint Nacer have been closely involved in programs and events related to MEPI since its very inception.[22]

For instance, as early as May 2003, the "Arab Women's Forum" took place in Cairo and was coordinated in cooperation with the U.S. Agency for International Development (USAID) and the state-sponsored Egyptian Center for Women's Rights. According to a U.S. State Department (2003) release, "[t]he Forum explored the political and economic challenges facing the empowerment of women in the Arab world." While plans for substantive follow-on projects were underway, Freedom House was "working on a study of women's needs in the region, which will help implement additional programs."[23] A group of twenty-five women from twelve Arab countries joined these discussions (Arab Reform Bulletin 2003). These "transnational" forums become highly legitimated sites for building consent, while serving as alternatives to the grass-roots mobilization by Islamist activists and women's groups across the Middle East.

Besides their impact on the deradicalization of feminist agendas in the Middle East, which have been embedded in geopolitical struggles against colonialism and imperialism, these forms of monitored transnationalism are grounded in the fragmentation and stratification of women's groups, further dividing them along modernist and traditionalist lines (see Karam 1998; Abdulhadi 1998). The MEPI inscribes its programs in this cultural paradigm about the business woman's reformative power in presumably antimodern Middle East. For instance, MEPI describes the "first ever Business Women's Summit for the Middle East and North Africa," which "drew more than 200 women from 15 countries in the region, plus American entrepreneurs and government officials" to discuss this category's needs.[24]

The MEPI's programs also engage schoolgirls through a variety of programs such as "the U.S.-funded ACCESS English-language micro-scholarships (for relatively disadvantaged youth), My Arabic Library, the Jordan Education Initiative (JEI), and Student Leaders project."[25] In some of these programs there is a focus on democracy building through training and participant observation, as the following description illustrates:

> Last fall, 50 women from Arab countries visited the United States to gain practical campaign skills and experience and observe the U.S. mid-term elections first-hand. The Initiative will build upon this success by establishing regional campaign schools to provide training in leadership and organizational skills for women seeking elective office across the region.[26]

What is the problem with these modes of inclusion? First, women are brought to these programs in scattered groups, with no linkages. These individuals are supposed to represent *uniquely* their gender interests in the overly patriarchal Middle East. As a category, the individual woman is very important for the MEPI's construction of development as the individual responsibility of citizens. As political players, women are important to the agenda of fighting terrorism. Their "practical interests" are perceived by the U.S. Department of State as antithetical to those of the Islamist movements and "traditional" societies at large (Molyneux 1985). Women have been portrayed as the first "victims" of Islamic "fundamentalism" and as docile bodies rather than active participants in Islamist politics. The MEPI's assumption is that to empower women is to diminish the appeal of conservative forces in Arab society, while helping the social body become immune to the Islamist influence. Commenting on MEPI's focus on women, Lapidot-Frilla (2006) called Arab women "the West's last line of defense" against Islamism.[27] I have illustrated elsewhere the importance of gender to the positioning of MENA governments within the U.S. war on terror (Salime 2007). I have shown how the Moroccan government managed to co-opt Islamist women's activism in the mosques by inviting women to training programs and appointing them as preachers (*morshidates*) in state-controlled mosques. In the case of the Moroccan state, women are considered the insider voices of "moderation" of the Islamist movements.

The empowerment of women serves another goal for both the U.S. and Arab governments. This is my second point. Confronted with the limits of rhetorical democracy on changing Arab states, MEPI finds in the empowerment of women a concrete place to make a few and more immediate breakthroughs. Arab governments, on the other hand, welcome MEPI's intervention on behalf of women as the least painful endorsement of the U.S. call for democratization. To Arab governments, a few reforms in the arena of women's rights, though salutary, are the best way to enhance their records in the arena of human rights without compromising their hold on power too much. Hence, women's empowerment becomes a place for containing the U.S. push for democratization by Arab governments, and one privileged site for the governmentality of the war on terror by the United States.

Yet unlike most governments in the Middle East and North Africa, the MEPI does not recognize the importance of political Islam for women and the way the Islamist politics has enabled more, not less, political and economic inclusion and participation of women (Salime 1997; Moghadam 2002). The MEPI does not see women as true political challengers holding alternative societal projects, its rhetoric of empowerment notwithstanding. Thus, while it does acknowledge women as "reformers" and agents of change, it fails to see them as advocates of alternative modes of governance and development regimes. For MEPI, women seem to be located at the nexus of these overlapping regimes of securitization and normalization.

SECURING THE MARKET OF WAR

I have shown how MEPI positions the market as a *mediator* between a presumably violent social body and undemocratic governments. The importance of the market follows the assumption that neither the state nor civil society—if left alone—are capable of reaching the goals of democracy, development, and peace. If the state is viewed as authoritarian at best, and failed at worst, civil society is perceived as "weak," yet it is "feared" as potentially violent (see Bayat 2003). It is then through global capital, rather than civil society or the state, that pacification can be achieved. In this context, both the state and civil society are made accountable to the forces of the market rather than to the people whose interests are presumably being represented.

Yet the state, necessary to this transition (Sassen 1999), needs to be monitored through market forces and through the accumulation of material and symbolic resources by its elites. While most studies have looked at the withdrawal of the state as a prerequisite to neoliberalism, it is important to explore the ways in which the state has returned as a private investor. Therefore, the accumulation of material and symbolic privileges by state agents and individual players renders their desire to implement true democratic changes less, not more, likely.

I have also shown how MEPI's intervention is meant to invent the presumably missing bond between "authoritarian" governments and their oppressed citizenry. Though MEPI delineates state authoritarianism as the main obstacle to democracy, it does not go so far as to claim a radical change in the structure of political power, and remains silent about the way Arab governments are waging their own war on terror.[28] The latter requires the invention of the right type of civil society, one pacified not only through capitalist regimes of incorporation but also by the acquisition of individual and symbolic privileges.

The question remains: how could civil society become an agent of democratization if it is put under siege by authoritarian states and oppressive regimes of neoliberalism and war? If liberal democracy is based on the idea of negotiating diverse community interests through a representational electoral system, then the assumption of homogenous interests of governments, civil society, and global corporate business are antithetical to this liberal definition.

NOTES

1. A similar version of this chapter appears in *Sociological Forum* (Salime 2010); the author thanks that journal for permitting the reproduction of those materials here.

2. Typical of President Bush's rhetoric connecting the interests of the United States and the Middle East was this 2003 assertion: "In an age of global terror . . . what happens in the Middle East greatly matters to America. The bitterness of that region can bring violence and suffering to our own cities. The advance of freedom and peace in the Middle East would drain this bitterness and increase our own security" (White House 2003).

3. Ray Bush (2004) pursues the claim that "the MENA has indeed had relatively low levels of poverty and good income distribution." The author argues that "the characterization of autocracy and the west's attempt to promote political liberalization is likely to impact adversely on the social contract that autocratic rulers have enforced regarding the delivery of basic services"(673).

4. To name only a few: the National Republican Institute, the National Democratic Institute, Freedom House, the National Endowment for Democracy, the USAID, the U.S. Institute for Peace, the Carnegie Program, many academic institutions, and American Enterprise Institute.

5. The Obama administration is requesting "$1.54 billion for democracy and governance programs [in the MENA] more than double the amount in President Bush's annual request for Y09" (McInerny 2009).

6. See Randi Mouad (2004).

7. Bureau of Near Eastern Affairs (2003a).

8. Bureau of Near Eastern Affairs (2003c).

9. Bureau of Near Eastern Affairs (2003b).

10. U.S. Department of Homeland Security (2007).

11. Since 9/11 many U.S. universities have created branches in Arab countries, espe-

cially in the Gulf. These branches are not only self-sufficient financially but part of the tuitions and fees is used to fund academic programs and departments in the United States.

12. Programs have been established in Morocco, Jordan, Egypt, and Lebanon among others, to teach school girls the principles of democratic governance and entrepreneurship.

13. Bureau of Near Eastern Affairs (2003a). I have not included governmental reforms in Islamic education, text books, and their monitoring of traditional training in mosques.

14. Bureau of Public Affairs (2009).

15. These calls materialized in transnational forums and declarations in 2004. The most important are the Arab NGOs' Beirut Summit (March 2004), the Doha Declaration (June 2004), the Alexandria Charter (March 2004), the Sana'a (Yemen) Declaration (January 2004), the Arab Business Council Declaration (2004), and the Egyptian Muslim Brothers' Reform Initiative (March 2004).

16. For a survey of these commentaries, see Salime (2010, ff.15).

17. For a description and reaction in Morocco about the Forum, see Salime (2010, ff.16).

18. See Salime (2010, ff.17).

19. Bureau of Near Eastern Affairs (2003b).

20. For instance, in 2005, 13 percent of the $293 million that the United States Congress committed to MEPI went to programs for women's empowerment with the percentage rising that year to 20 percent. (Salim 2010, ff.19).

21. Ibid.

22. Salim (2010, ff.21).

23. Salim (2010).

24. Salim (2010).

25. Salim (2010).

26. See Salim (2010, ff.25).

27. See Salim (2010, ff.26).

28. See Benin (2008).

REFERENCES

Abdulhadi, Rabab. 1998. The Palestinian women's autonomous movement: Emergence, dynamics and challenges. *Gender and Society* 12 (6): 647–39.

Abou Khalil, As'ad. 2002. Women in the Middle East. *Foreign Policy in Focus* 5 (30) 1:3.

Abu-Lughod, Lila. 2002. Do Muslim women really need saving?: Anthropological reflections on cultural relativism and its others. *American Anthropologist* 104 (3): 783–90.

Achar, Gilbert. 2004. Fantasy of a region that does not exist. Greater Middle East: The U.S. plan. *Le Monde Diplomatic*, April. http://mondediplo.com/2004/04/04world.

Agamben, Giorgio. 2005. *State of exception*. Chicago: University of Chicago Press.

Alvarez, Sonia E. 1998. Latin American feminisms "Go Global"; Trends of the 1990s and challenges for the new millennium. In *Culture of politics/politics of culture: Re-Visioning Latin American social movements*, ed. Sonia Alvarez, Evelyn Dagnino, and Arturo Escobar, 293–324. Boulder, Colo.: Westview Press.

Arab Human Development Report (AHDR). 2002. New York: United Nations Publications.

Arab Reform Bulletin. 2003. A Women's conference to design MEPI projects, July 2008. http://www.carnegieendowement.org/arb/?fa=show&article=21595.

Baroudi, Sami E. 2004. The 2002 Arab human development report: Implications for democracy. *Middle East Policy* 11 (1): 1–12.

Bayat, Asef. 2003. The street and the politics of dissent in the Arab world. *Middle East Report*. December 17, 2010. http://www.merip.org/mer/mer226/226_bayat.html.

Benin, Joel. 2008. Underbelly of Egypt's neoliberal agenda. *Middle East Report*. December 17, 2010. http://www.merip.org/mero/mero040508.html.

Blecher, Robert. 2003. "Free people will set the course of history": Intellectuals, democracy and American empire. *Middle East Report*, December 17, 2010. http://www.merip.org/mero/interventions/blecher_interv.html.

Brinkley, Joel, and Steven R. Weisman. 2004. U.S. slows bid to advance democracy in the Arab world. *New York Times*. December 5. http://query.nytimes.com/gst/fullpage.html.

Bureau of Near Eastern Affairs. 2003a. The U.S.-Middle East partnership initiative: Expanding political opportunity fact sheet, 18 June. Accessed December 17, 2010. http://www.state.gov/p/nea/rls/22251.htm.

———. 2003b. Middle East partnership initiative to place emphasis on women fact sheet, 18 June. Accessed December 18, 2010. http://www.america.gov/st/washfile-english/2--3/July/20030707125002namfuakso.6972402.html.

———. 2005. "U.S. commitment to women in the Middle East fact sheet, 6 September. Accessed September 13, 2007. http://www.state.gov/g/wi/rls/52487.htm.

Burns, William. 2003. Political and economic goals of a new generation in the Middle East. Testimony before the House International Relations Committee, Subcommittee on the Middle East and Central Asia. Washington, D.C. March 19, 2003. Retrieved September 8, 2007: http://www.state.gov/p/nea/rls/rm/19351.htm.

Bush, George. 2003. "President Bush presses for Middle East democracy." Speech. White House Office of the Press Secretary. http://www.state.gov/p/nea/rls/rm/20497.htm.

Bush, Ray. 2004. Poverty and neo-liberal bias in the Middle East and North Africa. *Development and Change* 35 (4): 673–95.

Carothers, Thomas. 2005. A better way to support Middle East reform. *Policy Brief*. Washington, D.C.: Carnegie Endowment for International Peace. 33:1–7.

———. 2007. The democracy crusade myth. *The National Interest* 8 (12): 8–12.

Carpenter, J. Scott. 2006. Transformational diplomacy in action: Remarks to Detroit Council for World Affairs. Washington, D.C., June. http://2002-2009-mepi.state.gov/68167.htm.

Cofman Wittes, Tamara C. 2004. The new U.S. proposal for a greater Middle East initiative: An evaluation. In *Saban Center for Middle East Policy, memo no. 2: The Brookings Institute.* http://www.brookings.edu/papers/2004/0510middleeast_wittes .aspx.

Cofman Wittes, Tamara C., and Andrew Masloski. 2009. Democracy promotion under Obama: Lessons from the Middle East Partnership Initiative. Middle East Memo: No. 13.

Cohen, Shana. 2005. *Searching for a different future: The rise of a global middle class in Morocco.* Durham, N.C.: Duke University Press.

Cohen, Jean, and Andrew Arato. 1994. *Civil society and political theory.* Cambridge, Mass.: MIT Press.

Davidson, Lawrence. 2006. Privatizing foreign policy. *Middle East Policy* 13 (2): 134–47.

De La Barra, Ximena. 2006. Who owes and who pays? The accumulated debt of neo-liberalism. *Critical Sociology* 32 (1): 125–61.

Diamond, L. 1994. Rethinking civil society: Toward democratic consolidation. *Journal of Democracy* 5:4–18.

Eisenstein, Hester. 2005. A dangerous liaison? Feminism and corporate globalization. *Science and Society* 69 (3): 487–518.

Elyachar, Julia. 2002. Empowerment money: The World Bank, non-governmental orga-nizations, and the value of culture in Egypt. *Public Culture* 14:493–513.

Enloe, Cynthia. 2005. *The curious feminist: Searching for women in new age of empire.* Berkeley: University of California Press.

Feldman, Shelley. 1997. NGOs and civil society: (Un)stated contradiction. *Annals of the American Academy of Political and Social Science* 554:46–65.

Ferguson, James. 2006. *Global shadows: Africa in the neoliberal world order.* Durham, N.C.: Duke University Press.

Fisher, F. William. 1997. Doing good? The politics and antipolitics of NGO practices. *Annual Review of Anthropology* 26:439–64.

Friedman, Thomas. 1999. *The world is flat: A brief history of twenty-first century.* New York: Farrar, Straus, and Giroux.

———. 2000. *The Lexus and the olive tree.* New York: Farrar, Straus, and Giroux.

Fukuyama, Francis. 1992. *The end of history and the last man.* New York: Avon Books.

———. 2001. Social capital, civil society and development. *Third World Quarterly* 22:7–20.

Gershman, Carl. 2007. Surviving the democracy backlash. *Washington Post.* June 8.

Goldman, Michael. 2005. *Imperial nature: The World Bank and struggles for social justice in the age of globalization.* New Haven, Conn.: Yale University Press.

Hanafi, Sari, and Linda Tabar. 2003. The Intifada and the aid industry: The impact of the new liberal agenda on the Palestinian NGOs. *Comparative Studies of South Asia, Africa and the Middle East* 23 (1–2): 205–14.

Hardt, Michael, and Antonio Negri. 2000. *Empire.* Cambridge, Mass.: Harvard Univer-sity Press.

Hartman, Yvonne. 2005. In bed with the enemy: Some ideas on the connections between neoliberalism and the welfare state. *Current Sociology* 53 (1): 57–73.

Harvey, David. 2005. *A brief history of neoliberalism*. New York: Oxford University Press.

Hawthorne, Amy. 2003. The middle east partnership initiative: Questions abound. *Arab Reform Journal* 1(3).

Huntington, Samuel. 1993. The clash of civilizations? *Foreign Affairs* 72 (3): 22–49.

Jaggar, M. Alison. 2005. Arenas of citizenship. *International Feminist Journal of Politics* 7 (1): 3–25.

Kamali, Masoud. 2001. Civil society and Islam: A sociological perspective. *European Journal of Sociology* 42 (3): 457–82.

Kamat, Sangeeta. 2004. The privatization of public interest: Theorizing NGO discourse in a neoliberal era. *Review of International Political Economy* 11 (1): 155–76.

Karam, Azza. 1998. *Women, Islamisms and the state in Egypt*. New York: Palgrave Mc-Millan.

Kean, Joan. 1998. *Civil society, new images, old visions*. Palo Alto, Calif.: Stanford University Press.

Kriemild, Saunders. 2002. *Feminist post-development thought: Rethinking modernity, postcolonialism and representation*. New York: Zed Books.

LeVine, Mark. 2002. The UN Arab Human Development Report: A critique. *Middle East Report*. http://www.merip.org/mero/mero072602.html.

Lewis, Bernard. 1990. The roots of Muslim rage. *Atlantic Monthly*. September.

Lewis, David. 2004. On the difficulty of studying "civil society": Reflections on NGOs, state and civil society in Bangladesh. *Contributions to Indian Sociology* 83 (3): 289–322.

Mamdani, Mahmood. 1995. A critique of the state and civil society paradigm in Africanist studies. In *African studies in social movements and democracy*, ed. Mahmood Mamdani and Ernest Wamba-dia-Wamba, 602–16. Dakar: CODESRIA.

———. 2004. *Good Muslim, bad Muslim: America, the cold war and the roots of terror*. New York: Pantheon.

Mbembe, Achille. 2003. Necropolitics. *Public Culture* 15 (1): 11–40.

Mendoza, Breny. 2002. Transnational feminisms in question. *Feminist Theory* 3 (3): 295–314.

Mercer, Claire. 2002. NGOs, civil society and democratization: A critical review of the literature. *Progress in Development Studies* 2 (1): 5–22.

———. 2003. Performing partnership: Civil society and the illusions of good governance in Tanzania. *Political Geography* 22:741–63.

McInerney, Stephen. 2009. The federal budget and appropriations for Fiscal Year 2010: Democracy, governance, and human rights in the Middle East. Project on Middle East Democracy. http://pomed.org.

Middle East Media Research Institute (MEMRI). 2004. Arab NGOs: Arab League Summit declaration are not for reform, but for deceiving Arab public opinion and the international community. In *Special Dispatch Series: The Middle East Media Research Institute*. http://www.memri.org/.

Moghadam, Valentine. 2000. Gender, national identity and citizenship: Reflection on the Middle East and North Africa. *Hagar International Social Science Review* 1: 41–70.

———. 2002. Islamic feminism and its discontents: Toward a resolution of the debate. *Signs: Journal of Women in Culture and Society* 27 (4): 1135–71.

———. 2005. *Globalizing women: Transnational feminist networks*. Baltimore, Md.: Johns Hopkins University Press.

Molyneux, Maxime. 1985. Mobilization without emancipation? Women's interests and revolution in Nicaragua. *Feminist Studies* 11 (2): 227–54.

Mouad, Randi. 2004. Le Grand Moyen Orient se construira t-il au Maroc? *Le Journal-Hebdo*.com. Retrieved October 19, 2004. http://LeJournal-hebdo.com/article_print .php3?id_article=2028.

Nordland, Rod. 2009. Forceful words and faithful realities. *New York Times*. June 6. http://www.nytimes.com/2009/06/07/weekinreview/07nordland.html.

Ong, Aiwa. 1999. *Flexible citizenship: The cultural logics of transnationality*. Durham, N.C.: Duke University Press.

Poster, Winnifred, and Zakia Salime. 2002. The limits of micro-credit: Transnational feminism and USAID activities in the United States and Morocco. In *Women's activism and globalization: Linking local struggles and transnational politics*, ed. Nancy A. Naples and Manisha Desai, 191–219. New York: Routledge.

Pratt, Nicola. 2004. Bringing politics back in: Examining the link between globalization and democratization. *Review of International Political Economy* 11 (2): 311–36.

Saban Center for Middle Eastern Policy. 2009. Lessons from the Middle East partnership initiative. *The Brookings Institute, memo no. 13*. http://www.brookings.edu/ papers/2009/05_democracy_promotion_wittes.aspx.

Salime, Zakia. 1997. L'entreprise feminine a Fes, une tradition. The business tradition in Fes, a tradition. In *Initiatives feminines*, ed. Aisha Belarbi, 31–46. Casablanca: Lefenec.

———. 2007. The "war on terrorism:" Appropriation and subversion by Moroccan women. *Signs: Journal of Women in Culture and Society* 33 (1): 1–4.

———. 2010 Securing the market, pacifying civil society, empowering women: The Middle East partnership initiative. *Sociological Forum* 25 (4): 725–45.

———. Forthcoming. Between feminism and Islam: Human rights and sharia law in Morocco. Minneapolis: University of Minnesota Press.

Sassen, Saskia. 1999. Embedding the global in the national: Implications for the role of the state. In *States and sovereignty in the global economy*, ed. Dorothy J. Solinger and Steven C. Topik, 158–71. New York: Routledge.

———. 2002. Governance hotspots: Challenges we must confront in the post-September 11 world. In *Understanding September 11*, ed. Craig Calhoun, Paul Price, and Ashley Timmer, 106–21. New York: New Press.

Satlof, Robert. 2002. Powell on democracy in the Middle East: Assessing the latest exposition of U.S. policy. The Washington Institute for Near East Study, Policy Watch. https://www.washingtoninstitute.org/templateC05.php?CID=1570.

Schild, Veronica. 2002. Engendering the new social citizenship in Chile: NGOs and social provisioning under neo-liberalism. In *Gender, justice, development and rights*, ed. M. Molyneux and S. Razavi, 170–203. Oxford: Oxford University Press.

Sharp, Jeremy M. 2006. U.S. democracy promotion policy in the Middle East: The Islamist dilemma. In *CRS Report for Congress: Congressional Research Service*. http://www.fas.org/sgp/crs/mideast/RL33486.pdf. Retrieved October 8, 2010.

Sivanandan, A. 2004. The global context. A keynote speech at the conference, "Racism, Liberty and the War on Terror." *Race and Class* 48 (4): 46–50.

U.S. Department of Homeland Security. 2007. Basic education in Muslim countries. Country Reports on Terrorism. Office of the Coordinator for Counterterrorism. Released on April 30, 2008. Accessed December 17, 2010. http://www.globalsecurity.org/security/library/report/2008/c-rprt-terrorism_2007-05-7.htm.

United States. Department of State. 2002. MEPI: the Middle East Partnership Initiative. http://www.wupy.org/en/whos-doing-what/funders/96-mepi-the-middle-east-partnership-initiative.html.

———. 2005. U.S. commitment to women in the Middle East fact sheet. September 6. August 9, 2007. http://www.state.gov/g/wi/rls/52487.htm.

———. 2009. Bureau of Public Affairs. "Supporting greater opportunities throughout the Middle East and North Africa fact sheet, 15 April 2009. Accessed December 17, 2010. http://www.medregion.mepi.state.gov/.../Updated_MEPI_Factsheet_-_April_2009.pdf.

———. 2010. MEPI mission and goals. Archives, information released from January 20, 2001 to January 20. Accessed December 17, 2010. http://2002-2009-mepi.state.gov/c10120.htm.

University of Maryland. 2007. Muslim public opinion on U.S. policy, attacks on civilians and al Qaeda. In *World Public Opinion.Org: The Program on International Policy Attitudes at the University of Maryland*. http://worldpublicopinion.org/pipa/pdf/apr07/START_Apr07_rpt.pdf.

Vogel, Ann. 2006. Who's making global civil society: Philanthropy and U.S. empire in world society. *The British Journal of Sociology* 57 (4): 636–55.

Wayne, E. Anthony. 2003. Creating free and dynamic economies in the Arab world, remarks to International Arab Banking Summit. Montreal, Canada. June 25. http://www.america.gov/st/washfile-english/2003/June/20030626161520tiwomods0.6242945.html.

White House Office of the Press Secretary. 2003. President Bush presses for Middle East democracy, 9 May. Accessed December 16, 2010. http://www.state.gov/p/nea.rls/rm/20497.htm/.

Windsor, Jennifer L. 2003. Promoting democratization can combat terrorism. *Washington Quarterly* 26 (3): 43–58.

Yacoubian, Mona. 2005. Promoting Middle East Democracy II: Arab initiatives. In *Special report*, 1–16. Washington, D.C: United States Institute of Peace.

Zayani, Mohamed. 2008. Courting and containing the Arab street: Arab public opinion, the Middle East and U.S. public diplomacy. *Arab Studies Quarterly (ASQ)* Spring: 207–22.

CHAPTER TEN

Accumulating Insecurity Among Illegal Immigrants

CHARLES GEISLER

Early in 2008 a small Iowa farming community found itself on the front page of the nation's media. The town, Postville, was home to the largest Kosher meat-packing plant in the country, the employees of which were immigrants from Mexico and Central America. On May 12, it was also the locus of the Bush administration's largest single-site raid of undocumented workers (*Des Moines Register* 2008). Over 10 percent of the community's population of 2,300 was incarcerated from one day to the next. As one resident stated, it was "like a natural disaster, only manmade" (Hsu 2008). The lead agency, Immigration and Customs Enforcement (ICE), detained 389 of the workers, all Latino. Of those detained, 270 went to jail, accused of being in the United States illegally and of aggravated identity theft (using stolen Social Security numbers). The latter crime is now a felony carrying a mandatory two-year prison sentence unless detainees waive their rights to a Grand Jury hearing. All the Postville detainees did this and accepted the alternative—deportation from the country.

How was national security improved by the reduction of undocumented worker security in Postville? Fact checking ICE work site arrests indicates that the 2008 raids were the culmination of a trend. Work site arrests by ICE numbered 510 in 2002, doubled by 2005, and grew ten times by 2007 for the nation as a whole (ICE 2009). By 2007, 285,000 illegal aliens were deported and nearly 100 employers faced jail sentences and fines for hiring such workers (Chaddock 2008). The last ICE raid occurred February 2009 in Washington State due to Obama administration policy shifts to employer compliance (Chaudry et al. 2010). On the other hand, fact checking U.S. immigration history for the past century suggests that ICE's predecessor, the Immigration and Naturalization Service (INS), time and again rounded up immigrants by the thousands for reasons of racism and xenophobia ("yellow peril"), political threat (anarchists and communists), and labor fears (immigrant scabs). So a twofold reality hits home. Postville descends from a long lineage of policies and politics reacting to "newcomers" and unwashed "others" that remain unresolved. Yet the Postville incident and the run-up to it may well be *sui generis* in ways that matter centrally to the social insecurities of today.

In this chapter I excavate both parts of this twofold reality and their lessons with respect to a subject not often contemplated in discussions on immigrants, migrants, and the dispossessed: property. Just as labor is increasingly disposable and insecure in the global economy, property is showing frailty as the hub of the American dream. One must ask if the alienation of labor is part and parcel of the alienation of property and of the separation of political subjects from security. We may be surprised to find the ways in which property suppression contributes to the wreckage of immigrant lives and communities.[1] But what distinguishes Postville from immigrant property experiences of the past, and were immigrants always accorded such treatment? Are race- and labor-based hysterias still drivers in disabling the property rights of aliens, especially the undocumented among them? Is property insecurity accumulating in new ways in recent decades and why?

I begin by dwelling on the connections between property and social reproduction, a narrative essential to grasping how disposability of the one jeopardizes the other. After a summary of relevant immigrant demographics and property profiles, I turn attention to the ways their property can be and has been diminished according to two different strategies, one being property obstruction and the other its seizure. But that begs the question: what is unique about the property dispossessions of today, playing out in the Postvilles of America? In a society that constitutionally embraces property as its security bulwark, even for illegal aliens, what has changed?[2]

SOCIAL REPRODUCTION AND PROPERTY

When working people become disposable, so does their property, often as a precondition. In fact, property insecurity among workers is often behind breakdowns in social reproduction. By social reproduction, I am referring to the aggregate ways in which the members of society work to meet and replenish their corporeal needs with sufficient surplus to recover from emergencies and attain socially agreed-upon levels of health, safety, and welfare specific to an era.[3] Employment is essential to this security fabric; but so too are the social conventions and relations referred to as property.[4] The absence of formal and informal property contracts protecting ownership in its many forms would more than unsettle social reproduction; it would prevent it as a social achievement and stricken the diverse claims of labor and its dependents to perpetual dispute and uncertainty.

To appreciate this in greater detail, it helps to break social reproduction into its constituent parts reliant on property. Self-ownership is the seminal principle. Locke and Hobbes, among others, wrote at length about the right of humans to own their bodies (MacPherson 1985; Olsaretti 2004). It is paramount in the labor theory of value connecting personhood (sovereign individuals engaged in work) and their possessions (Shapiro 2001); it also explains the time-honored notion of "pursuit of happiness" which, again and again in liberal proclamations, connects happiness (welfare and the collateral benefits derived from work) with possessions.[5]

But just as labor can be interrupted for a host of reasons, property can be violated and even extinguished, rendering social reproduction precarious. What is widely meant by "secure" property is property certification—that is, property accompanied with legal title, enforced by police, and protected by custom or insurance—once secured, title leverages credit for other undertakings presumed to enhance security still further. Even where title exists "free and clear," however, the value of property may be diminished by the liability claims of others or by predatory lending practices of many kinds. It can be stolen and depleted in value if poorly managed. It can be legally confiscated by governments, regulated to the point of being valueless, or lost in war to enemies. Governments can pass marital and inheritance laws that interrupt retention or flow of property within/between families and social groupings. So social reproduction can be jeopardized in many ways by paper cuts or full amputations to property.

To summarize, self-ownership and its bedrock role in the labor theory of value precondition social reproduction. Labor and property are inseparable, and the fusion between the pursuit of happiness and property is but a generalized expression of this labor-property double helix. The right to work, avail oneself of welfare, and enjoy a modicum of ordinary security rests on property relations. It follows that for governments seeking to exclude or make certain social/ethnic groups insecure—those whom Arendt (1951) once called the scum of the earth—disabling or usurping property is a strategic intervention. The American case is of interest because its highest courts have defended the right of immigrants and even illegal aliens to own property. So exactly how does the dispossession of property, the alienation of the supposedly inalienable, occur?

DISPOSSESSION

Dispossession assumes many forms, as David Harvey (2003) and others have argued. But, as suggested in the introduction to this volume, Harvey's theoretical work on dispossession fails to reveal in detail how marginalized populations experience material dispossession. In particular, how do immigrants, especially the indigent among them, undergo dispossession of their meager possessions? It is too obvious to say that would-be immigrants barred from entry to the United States, or allowed to enter but not work, are denied direct rewards of the labor theory of value. But even if permitted to work, they are dispossessed or deprived of full wages, benefits, and job security. At best they struggle to meet bare corporeal needs. Even immigrants who are employed, have job security, and acquire vehicles, homes, insurance policies, and so forth may be dispossessed. Beyond the assaults on property previously cited, their legal status may change or illegal status be exposed, jeopardizing their residency rights, civil rights, or property rights. Some of the Postville deportees had lived in the community for a decade, paid taxes, raised young families, and had come to feel generally indisposable (Rubiner 2008).

At least rhetorically, the rights in property are the same for immigrants and nonimmigrants in the United States, and among the former, for illegal aliens as well. But Cox and Posner (2010) insist that the property rights of noncitizens vary according to their legal classification. Migrants with work visas may work in certain positions but often lack the right to change jobs. Foreigners who enter the country legally as spouses of certain migrants have the basic rights to life, property, and law but they lack the right to work for pay or to remain in the country indefinitely. Importantly, even illegal aliens have rights and these extend to property rights as guaranteed in the Fifth Amendment, due to the equal protection clause of the Fourteenth Amendment.[6] The Supreme Court has consistently upheld this position for over a century (Neuman 1996). The claim that immigrant property in general and illegal alien property in particular is disposable would seem to have hit a road bump.

This brings us to what is changing in Postville and throughout the country with respect to the property rights of legally vulnerable populations. Despite legal rights and rulings in the past, in recent decades federal agencies have found extenuating circumstances—a hybrid of criminality and terrorism and failed immigration reforms—that qualify the constitutional rights of immigrants. The property implications are far-reaching and allow us to cast the Postville drama in a new light, despite similarities with immigration raids and round-ups of the past century. As De Genova (2007 and chapter 6, this volume) astutely observes, the assignment of culpability and criminality to undocumented workers at a time of deep national malaise moves the legal undoing of illegal immigrants to new heights. It has allowed, even encouraged, many states and local jurisdictions to aggressively mobilize anti-immigrant property actions that skirt the Constitution and put the security of illegal aliens at its nadir.

IMMIGRANT PEOPLE AND PROPERTY

It will be helpful at this point to pause and consider immigrant demographics and assets. Conservatively, an average of one million immigrants enter the United States each year (Federation for American Immigration Reform [FAIR] 2008). The number of illegal aliens in the United States from all regions of the world is now somewhere between 11.6 million (Pew Hispanic Center 2008) and 20 million (Chaddock 2008). In the latter half of the twentieth century and at present, the largest immigrant influx, legal and illegal, has come from Latin America (Guskin and Wilson 2007). The immigrant population of the United States is changing from European to Latino (78 percent) after many years of Asian dominance and distinct racial overtones.[7] Regarding the future, projections are stunning. A recent Pew report foresees the U.S. population in 2050 approaching 438 million people, with 82 percent of the post-2005 growth due to immigration to the United States (Passel and Cohn 2008). Otherwise stated, in the absence of immigration, the U.S. population would grow very little and age in place, probably allowing for high employment among non-immigrant Americans and very different futures regarding social reproduction and security.

Evidence of property ownership among immigrants, particularly those undocumented in the United States, is difficult to attain. Immigrants in general view homeownership as a powerful path to becoming certified American citizens and are three times more likely than other Americans to list homeownership as their number one priority (Schoenholtz and Stanton 2001). According to the Pew Hispanic Center (2008), roughly thirty-five million foreign-born people lived in the United States and just below 40 percent of these were Latinos (approximately thirteen million) in 2006. Foreign-born Latino owner-occupied housing (roughly three million) rose swiftly over the two million mark set in 2000 (table 1).

We can speculate that the homeownership pattern of foreign-born illegal aliens follows a similar tenure pattern; illegal aliens view homeownership as a way of strengthening their chances for citizenship in the United States, espe-

TABLE 1. U.S. Hispanic home rental/ownership comparisons for 2000 and 2006

	OWNER-OCCUPIED	RENTER-OCCUPIED	% OWNER-OCCUPIED
Year: 2000	4,296,099	4,976,820	46.3
Native born	2,215,456	2,188,674	50.3
Foreign born	2,080,643	2,788,146	42.7
Year: 2006	5,943,432	6,120,057	49.3
Native born	2,939,196	2,623,973	52.8
Foreign born	3,004,236	3,496,084	46.2

cially should future immigration reform include amnesty provisions like those of the Legal Immigration and Family Equity Act passed in 2000.[8]

With or without such reform, foreign-born immigrants are encouraged to attain ownership by the finance industry. A recent publication by the Federal Deposit Insurance Corporation (FDIC 2004), entitled "Linking International Remittance Flows to Financial Services: Tapping the Latino Immigrant Market," tells how civic-humanitarian and financial actors cooperated in the past decade to advance immigrant homeownership. Latin American immigrants to the United States have immense purchasing power, estimated at $926 billion by 2007. The FDIC report notes as well that the remittance market, particularly to Latin America and the Caribbean, is expected to grow by billions, much of it outside the formal banking system. An increasing number of banks have tapped both revenue streams (Pasha 2005); indeed, the Community Reinvestment Act (CRA) of 2004 obliged regulated U.S. banks to offer similar services to the full spectrum of economic groups.[9]

The subprime-lending environment further enticed Latinos with little savings or equity to buy real estate.[10] Individual Taxpayer Identification Numbers (ITINs) and Mexican *Matricula Consula* cards both became acceptable client identifiers for aliens under the Patriot Act. In 2003, a New Alliance Task Force (NAFT) dedicated itself to "asset-building strategies" that would improve the lives of Mexican immigrants in the United States (FDIC 2004). Its sixty-two members included the FDIC, the Mexican Consulate of Chicago, thirty-four banks, federal bank regulators, community-based organizations, secondary market companies, and private mortgage insurance companies. So the financial sector stood to profit by combining lucrative new products with high profile "pro-poor, pro-immigrant" services (Schoenholtz 2005; Cortes et al. 2007). Because border crossings were increasingly impeded by immigration law after September 11, 2001, aliens retooled their survival strategies to include investing in the United States, where they hoped to remain (*National Voter* 2007).

Summarizing once again, the U.S. immigrant population is growing. There is indirect evidence of immigrants' homeownership despite their marginal economic condition: homeownership as a path to legitimacy, credit, and "the American Dream," and the self-interest of banks and thrifts, encouraged by the federal government and civil society groups. The work of Garling and Mehlman (2010) connects the immigration specter with urban build-out, implying a vast reservoir of Latino interest in apartments and eventual homeownership. Legal and illegal aliens, it seems, have many inducements to own property in the United States, and much to lose if barred from or forced to give up this property without compensation.

"TURNING UP THE PAIN"

Commenting on ICE work site raids of late, former Washington officials said that the Bush administration was "turning up the pain" for political ends (Hsu 2008, 1). The United States has a long history of using property restrictions to manage immigrants as it sees fit. Slaves, indentured workers, and entrants with conditional work permits and green cards all have their property stories and traumas.[11] Property rights to control labor flows and wage levels continue to operate long after the Fourteenth Amendment passed in 1886. On some occasions, federal and state governments obstructed ownership outright, and on others have seized property once acquired. Both policies pivot on an all-powerful reality: the government determines who is illegally in the country and, in emergencies, can use this power to dislodge property owners from their assets.

Property Obstruction

The obstruction of immigrant ownership has several variations. Alien land laws were the chief means to this end in the past. Such legislation first appeared in Washington Territory in 1864 to attract immigrant homesteaders, populate the Territory, and displace resident Indians (Grant 2007). These property incentives proved effective. The Territory's population more than doubled in the 1860s, but the solution yielded "a problem": the influx was heavily Asian. Chinese workers had flocked to California during the gold rush and were thereafter drawn to jobs in mining, salmon canning, agriculture, and rail work in the region. In 1886 anti-Chinese riots occurred in Seattle and were followed by an alien land law that barred aliens ineligible for citizenship from owning land (the federal Naturalization Act of 1790 welcomed only "free white persons"). Also in the 1880s, the federal government passed explicitly race-based exclusion laws aimed at Chinese laborers (Aleinikoff, Martin, and Motomura 1998). Emboldened by this, ten states followed the Washington example early in the twentieth century, despite intervening passage of the Fourteenth Amendment. These so-called alien land laws remained on the books in Florida, Wyoming, and New Mexico into the present era.

The Florida case speaks to the durability of apprehension over Asian (as opposed to Cuban or European) land ownership. The concern in Florida and elsewhere in the 1920s was the "spectre" of Chinese farmers buying up American farmland. In 2007 an amendment was proposed to delete a 1926 provision in the state's constitution that authorizes the legislature to regulate or prohibit the ownership, inheritance, disposition, and possession of real property by aliens ineligible for citizenship (that is, Asians). Though there was strong support in 2007 to put this measure on the ballot, it failed to pass in 2008. California rescinded its law in 1956, Kansas and Wyoming repealed theirs in 2001 and 2002, and New Mexico voters deleted a similar measure from their constitution in 2006. Alien land law legislation is now being mothballed perhaps because the average age of farmers is rising and farm children are showing disinterest in taking over family operations (Allen and Harris 2005).

A more subtle way of disenfranchising immigrants from property birthrights appears in inheritance laws. These and other ordinances aimed at the property rights of undocumented immigrants continue to appear at the local level. By 2007, ordinances had been proposed, debated, or adopted in 104 cities and counties in 28 states, often including prohibitions on renting to or employing undocumented immigrants (Esbenshade 2007). In 2010, Nevada debated the need for a state law enabling County Public Administrators (responsible for handling intestate property) to prevent illegal immigrants from inheriting property from other illegal immigrants. One candidate for state office pledged to introduce legislation that, if elected, would require the Public Administrator's office to change the eligibility guidelines for county-funded burial, cremation, and funeral expenses so as to exclude illegals (the average county-funded burial costs approach $1,200). The law would allow the county to instead seize all assets belonging to deceased illegal immigrants, not pass them to his or her family, and liquidate the assets at auction.

There were and are instances where federal equal protection falls apart. A suburb of Dallas with a large foreign-born Latino population recently passed an ordinance to ban illegal immigrants from rental housing and other property. It empowered building inspectors to verify the immigration status of renters with federal authorities.[12] Landlords leasing to renters living in the country illegally would have their rental license revoked; that is, put the onus of self-policing on the rental industry itself (Weber 2010). According to the same author, a federal judge ruled the ordinance unconstitutional, not because it suppressed a property right but because it sought to enforce U.S. immigration policy, which only the federal government can do. There is something ominous in the "1920s feel" of what is happening here and in the fact that nearly half of U.S. voters support sanctions for landlords who rent or sell property to illegal aliens (*Rasmussen Reports* 2009). But something quite unlike what motivated property rights obstruction a century ago, is operating today.

Property Seizure

The other means of "turning up the pain" on property is through seizure, an anathema in American law and culture, except in times of emergency (Sewell 1979; Hyde 1995). Despite claims of magisterial impartiality in the Fourteenth Amendment, the federal government has found ways to abrogate the property rights of immigrants whose social reproduction it seeks to stifle. By seizure, I refer to an array of direct and indirect confiscatory (uncompensated) measures taken by the government under the doctrine of necessity.[13] But criminality offers a unique policy space and upends the sanctity of inalienability, even more so in times of national emergency when long-standing ideological, cultural, and ethnic biases are unleashed in patriotic guises.[14] Recall, for example, that Lincoln criminalized the Confederacy for insurgency against the Union before issuing the largest property seizure in U.S. history (southern slaves and land) through the Confiscation Act of 1861. Other extraordinary property seizures occasioned by war (or war metaphors) were the Executive Order of 1942, wherein the United States interned Japanese and Native Americans from the Aleutian Islands (National Park Foundation 2002) and the cold war. The latter played on political paranoia and led to deportation and seizure of the assets of suspected communists; it also provided criminalizing precedents for today's war on terror (Farish 2007; De Genova 2007).

Criminalization has been an abiding part of deportation and expropriation in U.S. immigration policy, and has often been accompanied with reduced (or no) right to trial and legal representation due to the victim's lack of citizenship. This tenuous status enabled massive immigrant removals as recently as 1954. In that year, General Joseph Swing, Commissioner of the Immigration and Naturalization Service (INS) under President Eisenhower, conducted a military offensive ("Operation Wetback") that deported over a million Mexican migrants—five times the number deported during the Great Depression (Hing 2004).[15] Deportees routinely lost their personal property, automobiles, homes, businesses, and other investments. This same period was a watershed era for immigration law. In 1952, the Immigration and Naturalization Act (INA) set in motion a review of all prior U.S. immigration and deportation laws, establishing criteria for removing aliens and nonaliens according to criminalized conduct, and again empowered the government to seize immigrant property (Schneier 1970). Ominously, the INA was retroactive and, with few exceptions, lacked statutes of limitation with respect to a deportable act and the timing of related proceedings. Immigrant criminality again preoccupied Congress in 1986. It amended the 1952 INA and enacted the Immigration Reform and Control Act (IRCA) in that year. Arrests of aliens by the Department of Justice's Immigration and Naturalization Service increased dramatically. With the election of George Bush Sr. and passage of the Immigration Acts of 1990 and 1991, the 1952 INA law was revised and made subject to certain statutes of limitation.

Therefore, by the 1990s the combined effect of property obstruction and seizure was devastating the property chances of undocumented immigrants. Despite ever-present discourses on property and the American Dream, it was difficult for the most at-risk immigrants to set foot on the first rung of the age-old tenure ladder in pursuit of personal security. In many ways this disabling of alien property had historic precedents, "the other" merely shifting from Asians to Latinos and occasionally to immigrants untreated in the present account. Yet the abrogation of property rights for outsiders took an extraordinary turn as the hemispheric drug war tarnished Latinos of all persuasions, accelerated the use of a new form of seizure (forfeiture), and gained momentum thanks to two other emergencies—the war on terror and the "menacing" increase in U.S. population attributed to immigrants—to expand the law of necessity.

Recall that Bill Clinton was bent on reforming national health care, welfare, and immigration during his administration. The bombing of the World Trade Center in 1993 added another priority to his plate and yielded the Antiterrorism and Effective Death Penalty Act of 1996. The law substantially changed the security chances for illegal immigrants: it expanded the grounds for deportation, eliminated judicial review of certain deportation orders, and streamlined deportation for those accused of terrorist activity (Kanstrom 2007). Also in 1996, Congress received recommendations from the U.S. Commission on Immigration Reform and enacted the Illegal Immigration Reform and Immigrant Responsibility Act (IIRAIRA). This established still stronger penalties against illegal immigration, restricted their use of public welfare benefits, and sought to curb the ability of terrorists to enter and operate in the United States as immigrants. It established an "administrative removal" procedure to expedite removal of illegal aliens and restructured the entire system of judicial review of removal orders. Finally, it retroactively expanded many grounds of inadmissibility and removal, and authorized increased state and local law enforcement involvement in removal proceedings. After September 11, 2001, the range of activities deemed illegal by noncitizens, such as voting and falsely claiming citizenship, would inflate yet again.

Perhaps the most significant criminalizing body blow to aliens within or seeking entrance to the United States occurred in 2002. The INS claimed that the use of fraudulent documents—border crossing cards, alien registration cards, nonimmigrant visas, and passports—was now rampant (U.S. General Accounting Office [GAO] 2002). That same year, the Homeland Security Act of 2002 abolished the INS and transferred most of its functions to the new Department of Homeland Security (DHS), beginning in 2003. The conflation of illegal immigrant and terrorist labeling spiked and incarceration and deportation triggered by expanding definitions of felony surged. The DHS released "Endgame," its ten year strategy to "build capacity to remove all removable aliens" (USDHS 2003, ii). Thereafter, legislation proposed in 2005 (the Border Protection, Antiterrorism, and Illegal Immigration Control Act) sought to criminalize all illegal aliens by converting even their "unlawful presence" to felonies and making them subject to mandatory detention. Had that bill become law, the government would have made immigration violations of all kinds, whether by legal or illegal aliens, into felonies subject to imprisonment—essentially making legal into illegal aliens (De Genova 2007).

This brings us back, full circle, to Postville. The raids of the new millennium are both the rule and the exception. The official handling of risky immigrants follows patterns of the past but has new juggernaut qualities. The DHS, a cabinet-level department with twenty-two member agencies, has 200,000 employees and is the largest civilian agency in U.S. history. Its budget is the envy of all and its contracts to the private sector seem inexhaustible. Yet the war on terror, with which it is closely associated, has produced few captives, put fewer still on trial, and convicted only a trickle of hapless victims. In the immediate aftermath of the Postville raid, one of the appointed immigrant interpreters wrote in the *New York Times* that ICE's poor showing in terrorist arrests since September 11, 2001, was forcing a redirection of their security resources to easier prey—undocumented workers committing victimless crimes promoted to felonies (Camayd-Freixas 2008). The 2009 ICE reporting shows striking increases in the arrest of aliens on criminal charges, almost certainly a momentum riding on the coattails of alien reclassification and crime redefinition.

The dispossessing consequences of this reclassification have potent welfare effects of now-felonized immigrants. As a new brand of property seizure it has little precedent. There is no equal protection clause to stop it and, despite the downturn in work site raids by the Obama administration, there is insufficient political will to curb it at home, at work, on highways, or anywhere that racial stereotyping plays out. I am referring to seizure qua forfeiture, which under federal law and many state laws permits police to confiscate the property of criminals and suspected criminals whether or not they are convicted of a crime. Now this extends to illegal aliens whose minimal actions have been super-sized to felonies. Unlike eminent domain and commandeering prerogatives of government, both with roots in medieval England, forfeiture is relatively new and mushroomed recently as a government response to the drug wars of the 1980s. That war is an important layer of the war on terror, both globally and, to the bane of all Latino immigrants, in Colombia, Mexico, and other enclaves of Latin America and the Caribbean (Schreiber 2009; Schroeder 2009).

Briefly, forfeiture is a widely used means of confiscating property with impunity; in a single year, more than 9,000 forfeiture cases occurred in the state of Michigan alone (Kochan 1998). The American Civil Liberties Union maintains that, with the rise in racial profiling, forfeiture has a disproportional effect on minorities (ACLU 2001). Add to this the urgency and anxiety of the war on terror, the acquiescence most Americans have toward the Patriot Act (despite its startling curbs on private property), and the public opinion results that emerge when pollsters query Americans about using forfeiture to control immigration abuse. A 2003 Roper Poll queried 1,012 adult Americans in a national survey on immigration and reported as follows: "Mandatory detention and forfeiture of property, followed by deportation, for anyone here illegally" (83 percent "agree"; 56 percent "strongly agree"); and "A mandatory prison term and forfeiture of property, followed by deportation, for anyone here illegally" (70 percent "agree"; 45 percent "strongly agree") (see Negative Population Growth 2003). Immigration reformers, particularly those seeking tougher measures of control, are currently calling for wider use of forfeiture by law enforcers at all levels both against illegal immigrants and their employers. Forfeiture has generally had the support of the Supreme Court. And, as a casual inspection of the Internet reveals, it is already being used against illegal entrants into the United States and those who employ or assist them.

Several national leaders have written lengthy condemnations of forfeiture as a breach of the Bill of Rights and an incentive for law enforcers to abuse the law (Kochan 1998; Hyde 1995; Roberts and Stratton 2000). Under forfeiture law, officials may seize homes, cars, bank accounts, personal property, or other assets without evidence of criminality. Forfeiture requires no trial, can occur before guilt is established (probable cause at the discretion of police and prosecutors is sufficient), contains incentives for malpractice (proceeds go to the seizing agency), becomes a cost-recovery device (public sector accumulation), and has come to be used with little accountability. By 2000, its impetus, seizing drugs, was radically extended by Congress to 140 offenses and surely more since (Roberts and Stratton 2000). Because law enforcement officials enjoy all proceeds, the temptation to abuse forfeiture is uncontrollable—privatized, "profit-driven" law enforcement taken to new heights (Hyde 1995, 30). Kochan (1998) claims that 80 percent of the people whose property is seized under drug laws are never formally charged.

What insecurities does forfeiture visit upon undocumented workers in the United States over and above those they have faced in the past? What is different today? In a word, the pursuit of happiness is now the pursuit of unhappiness. The majority of undocumented noncitizen workers work "on the books" for employers while in the United States; that is, they must have a Social Security Number (ssn), valid or not. In either case, they and their employers pay billions of dollars into payroll taxes every year, contributing to Social Security and Medicare and thus benefiting society as a whole (Blazer and Bernstein 2007). Between 1996 and the onset of DHS in 2003, undocumented noncitizens paid almost $50 billion in federal taxes and record numbers appear to have filed tax returns since (Blazer and Bernstein 2007). Under current law, not only are these noncitizens ineligible to receive these earned entitlements but also must use wage income to fend off poverty by purchasing health and welfare services. Upon retiring or facing disability, they have neither Medicare nor Social Security. These major social reproduction costs undoubtedly divert income away from mortgage retirement and from the income tax deductions for mortgage debt, making real property more susceptible to loss.

The insecurity does not stop here. Blazer and Bernstein (2007) speak of a cascade effect as follows:

> [M]ost undocumented workers do not have a ssn validly issued for employment and therefore cannot work on the books unless they provide an invalid number. This has become a necessary reality for the millions of undocumented people who are navigating the push and pull of the economy's demand for labor and an immigration system that provides virtually no pathways to lawful status for low-skilled immigrant workers. Using an invalid ssn to work subjects workers to

potential felony prosecution under various laws . . . [despite the fact that] these laws are aimed primarily at persons who use the violations to steal or conduct other criminal enterprises. These laws carry stiff penalties of up to five years or more of imprisonment.

To work, in other words, is to risk dispossession through forfeiture. If convicted and imprisoned, one's work terminates, as do remittances, mortgage payments, interest on loans, and contribution to the welfare of others (spouses, children, dependents) with whom they are associated. Forfeiture is legally unique for yet another reason. Guilt is assigned to *the item* to be confiscated rather than its owner in the case of civil forfeiture.[16] The implications are momentous for a legal alien sharing a house or car with an illegal alien; the federal government can seize these properties without an indictment and dispense with the right to counsel, to jury trial, to the right not to be punished prior to adjudication, to punishment disproportionate to an alleged crime, and to the presumption that the state prove culpability (Kochan 1998). Forfeiture penalties have been included in proposed immigrant control legislation and apply to employers and service providers.[17] Where might this end?

This chapter offers a cautionary tale about property policies directed at the poor, especially the legally vulnerable poor that may sooner or later unsettle the property rights and relations of those who are neither illegal nor poor. Advocates of immigrant reform and citizens committed to the war on terror see forfeiture as "necessary" (e.g., Vaughan and Edwards 2009). In July of 2007, for example, the Bush administration issued an executive order freezing the assets of people who threaten Iraq's stability—an order so sweeping, according to constitutional lawyer Bruce Stein, that it could be used to seize the property of almost anyone opposing belligerent foreign policy by the United States now or in the future (Corsi 2007). And what of the American Dream of attaining property and equal protection under the law? Are we to trade these away for protection in emergencies or for the prospect of windfall gain for governments at the expense of others who have toiled in good faith in the tracks of former immigrants? The AFL-CIO's 2009 position on immigration reform warrants serious reflection. It holds that the problem of immigrants streaming north from Latin America is rooted in free but unfair trade agreements rather than a predisposition to risk their lives in the war zone of the U.S.-Mexican border or the war zone that the United States interior has become. It is important to think about the involuntary property insecurity of aliens, the ballooning use of forfeiture and other means of seizure behind that insecurity, and the selective way we defend property as a U.S. constitutional right for all.

NOTES

1. See Chaudry et al. (2010) for extensive treatment of this wreckage.

2. The Supreme Court has also held for more than a century that aliens within the United States are persons entitled to constitutional protection. That includes aliens who are unlawfully present, although recent Supreme Court dicta suggest that intensified concerns over both drugs and migrants penetrating the border may put pressure on that commitment (Neuman 1996, 118).

3. For further discussion of social reproduction, see Sampson and Sharkey (2008) and the introduction (this volume).

4. Property is a set of multidimensional relationships, legal and social, that secures things (tangible and intangible) according to law and/or custom for individuals or groups of individuals (see von Benda-Beckmann, von Benda-Beckmann, and Wiber 2009; Hahn 2007).

5. Self-ownership underlies Locke's natural law theory of how humans come to own possessions (see Locke 1690/1982). Within a century of Locke's fertile writings, the pursuit of happiness became a powerful trope in the American Declaration of Independence and elsewhere. For elaboration on Locke's self-ownership, see Dan-Cohen (2002).

6. Section 1 of the Fifth Amendment reads: "No person shall be held to answer for a capital, or otherwise infamous crime, unless on a presentment or indictment of a grand jury, except in cases arising in the land or naval forces, or in the militia, when in actual service in time of war or public danger; nor shall any person be subject for the same offense to be twice put in jeopardy of life or limb; nor shall be compelled in any criminal case to be a witness against himself, nor be deprived of life, liberty, or property, without due process of law; nor shall private property be taken for public use, without just compensation."

Section 1 of the Fourteenth Amendment to the Constitution reads: "All persons born or naturalized in the United States, and subject to the jurisdiction thereof, are citizens of the United States and of the state wherein they reside. No state shall make or enforce any law which shall abridge the privileges or immunities of citizens of the United States; nor shall any state deprive any person of life, liberty, or property, without due process of law; nor deny to any person within its jurisdiction the equal protection of the laws."

7. Ethnic prejudice toward Chinese immigrants, mentioned later in this chapter, and others (Irish, Italians, Hmong, Africans, and American Indians) is left largely untouched. For a useful overview, see Tamayo (1995).

8. According to FAIR (2008), the Obama administration is signaling an openness to move amnesty legislation forward, a commitment reinforced by the Congressional Hispanic Caucus. Accessed June 26, 2010. http://www.fairus.org/site/News2?page=News Article&id=20193.

9. Market capture initiatives by banks have been aggressive. Citigroup Inc. and Bank of America Corporation purchased two large Mexican banks, Banamex and Serfin, launched binational credit cards, and promoted a range of services targeted to Hispan-

ics outside the financial mainstream. Other banks followed suit, seeking to be conduits for remittances and to redirect savings to domestic loans and mortgages (Newberger et al. 2006).

10. "Affordable loan products overcome financial barriers to homeownership for low- and moderate-income immigrant home buyers. They help home buyers with such unique credit profiles as no established credit rating, minimal savings for down payment, and income from seasonal work or varied sources . . . Key program criteria that ensure successful products for immigrant populations include many alternatives: lower down payments; higher qualifying ratios; acceptance of nontraditional credit history; latitude in proving legal residence; no mortgage insurance requirement; assistance with down payments and closing costs; and required native-language education and counseling" (Schoenholtz and Stanton 2001, 53).

11. Slaves, often considered less than full persons, are the limiting case: they did/do not own their persons. Indentured servants, also referred to as debt slaves or unfree labor, were workers under voluntary contract for a fixed period of time in exchange for their transportation, food, clothing, lodging, and other necessities (Foner 2004). Unlike slaves, they owned themselves but "mortgaged" themselves for employment opportunities; their property rights were restricted to modest personal belongings.

12. In 2008 a program called "Secure Communities" began in Texas wherein local police used information provided by the FBI and the Immigration and Customs Enforcement (ICE) to identify illegal aliens in local jails and assist federal agents in deportation proceedings. The program now operates in twenty-one states and will be national in scope by 2013.

13. The doctrine or "law" of necessity holds that, under threat of emergency (usually a natural disaster or threat to peace), the government not only is able but must take extraordinary measures, including suspending its own laws, in the public interest. The doctrine, with its strong parallels to Agamben's (2005) state of exception theory, states that net social welfare can increase in crisis (e.g., Christie 1999). Military rule during war is a familiar example, as is commandeering in times of war or peace. Dubber (2005) offers the paradigmatic case wherein a structure is burned to limit the advance of a conflagration and harm to others without compensation to the owner.

14. Witch hunts in Puritan England and New England are of interest here. According to Federici (2004), at least some women were stigmatized and eliminated because powerful men and religious detractors sought their estates.

15. See *Para Justicia y Libertad!* Accessed July 26, 2008. http://xicanopwr.com/2006/03/americas-cruel-history-of-mass-deportation-and-the-reasons-used/. The Immigration Act of 1924 set quotas and explicitly introduced race as reason for exclusion. Such policy was legal until 1952.

16. Forfeiture laws vary by state, jurisdiction, and crime committed. Typically, criminal forfeiture is sought when property is used in the commission of a criminal offense or obtained through criminal activity. Civil forfeiture action is brought against the property itself and does not implicate its owner.

17. See Section 274 covering felonies under the Federal Immigration and Nationality Act, INA 274A(a)(1)(A): "A person (including a group of persons, business, organization, or local government) commits a federal felony when she or he: assists an alien s/he should reasonably know is illegally in the U.S. or who lacks employment authorization, by transporting, sheltering, or assisting him or her to obtain employment, or encourages that alien to remain in the U.S. by referring him or her to an employer or by acting as employer or agent for an employer in any way, or knowingly assists illegal aliens due to personal convictions. Penalties upon conviction include criminal fines, imprisonment, and forfeiture of vehicles and real property used to commit the crime" (Walker n.d.).

REFERENCES

Agamben, Giorgio. 2005. *State of exception*. Trans. Kevin Attell. London: University of Chicago Press.

Aleinikoff, Thomas A., David A. Martin, and Hiroshi Motomura. 1998. *Immigration and citizenship: Process and policy*. St. Paul, Minn.: West Group.

Allen, Rich, and Ginger Harris. 2005. *What we know about the demographics of U.S. farm operators*. Washington, D.C.: National Agricultural Statistical Service, U.S. Department of Agriculture (February 25).

American Civil Liberties Union (ACLU). 2001. Latest ACLU advertisement targets asset forfeiture laws. Accessed June 26, 2010. http://www.aclu.org/racial-justice _prisoners-rights_drug-lawreform.

American Federation of Labor and Congress of Industrial Organizations. (AFL-CIO). 2009. The labor movement's framework for comprehensive immigration reform (April). Accessed June 30, 2010. http://www.aflcio.org/issues/civilrights/immigra tion/upload/immigrationreform041409.pdf.

Arendt, Hannah. 1951. *The origins of totalitarianism*. New York: Harcourt Brace.

Blazer, Jonathan, and Josh Bernstein. 2007. Confiscating contributions. Immigrants' Rights Watch Special Report, National Immigration Law Center. Accessed June 26, 2010. http://www.nilc.org/immlawpolicy/cir/ciro21.htm.

Camayd-Freixas, Erik. 2008. The true story of Postville. *New York Times*. July 11.

Chaddock, Gail Russell. 2008. Tide of illegal immigrants now being reversed. *Christian Science Monitor*. Posted July 31. Accessed February 3, 2010. http://www.csmonitor .com/USA/Society/2008/0731/p01s03-ussc.html.

Chaudry, Ajay, Randolph Capps, Juan Pedroza, Rosa Maria Castaneda, Robert Santos, and Molly M. Scott. 2010. *Facing our future: Children in the aftermath of immigration enforcement*. Washington, D.C.: The Urban Institute.

Christie, George C. 1999. The defense of necessity considered from the legal and moral points of view. *Duke Law Journal* 48:975–1013.

Corsi, Jerome. 2007. Bush executive order threatens the 5th Amendment? *World Net Daily* Exclusive Commentary. Posted July 25. Accessed August 2, 2008. http://www .worldnetdaily.com/news/article.asp.Id=56823.

Cortes, Alvaro, Christopher E. Herbert, Erin Wilson, and Elizabeth Clay. 2007. Factors affecting Hispanic homeownership: A review of the literature. *Cityscape* 9 (2): 12–20.

Cox, Adam B., and Eric A. Posner. 2010. The rights of immigrants: An optimal contract framework. *New York University Law Review*, February 15. Accessed June 24, 2010. http://legalworkshop.org/2010/02/15/2042.

Dan-Cohen, Meir. 2002. *Harmful thoughts: Essays on law, self, and morality.* Princeton, N.J.: Princeton University Press.

De Genova, Nicholas. 2007. The production of culprits: From deportability to detainability in the aftermath of "homeland security." *Citizenship Studies* 11 (5): 421–48.

Des Moines Register. 2008. Iowa immigration raid is largest in history, May 13. Accessed July 8, 2008. http://www.azcentral.com/news/articles/2008/05/13/20080513iowaraid.html.

Dubber, Markus D. 2005. *The police power: Patriarchy and the foundations of American government.* New York: Columbia University Press.

Esbenshade, Jill. 2007. Division and dislocation: Regulating immigration through local housing ordinances. Washington, D.C.: Immigration Policy Center. Accessed July 25, 2008. http://www.ilw.com/articles/2007,1003-esbenshade.pdf.

Farish, Matthew. 2007. Targeting the inner landscape. In *Violent geographies: Fear, terror, and political violence*, ed. D. Gregory and A. Pred, 255–71. New York: Routledge.

Federal Deposit Insurance Corporation (FDIC). 2004. Linking international remittance flows to financial services: Tapping the Latino immigrant market. *Supervisory Journal.* Accessed July 29, 2008. file:///Users/ccg2/Desktop/fdic:%20Supervisory%20Insights%20-%20Linking%20International%20Remittance%20Flows%20to%20Financial%20Services:%20Tapping%20the%20Latino%20Immigrant%20Market.html.

Federation for American Immigration Reform (FAIR). 2008. Immigration 101: A primer on immigration and the need for reform. Federation for American Immigration Reform 2000. Accessed July 25, 2008. http://www.fairus.org/site/PageServer?pagename=research_researcha233#FileAttach.

Federici, Silvia. 2004. *Caliban and the witch: Women, the body, and primitive accumulation.* New York: New York Autonomedia.

Feser, Edward. 2005. Should felons vote? *City Journal.* Accessed July 27, 2008. http://www.city-journal.org/html/15_2_felons.html.

Foner, Eric. 2004. *Give me liberty.* New York: W. W. Norton & Company.

Garcia, Juan Ramon. 1980. *Operation wetback: The mass deportation of Mexican undocumented workers in 1954.* Westport, Conn.: Greenwood Publishing Group.

Garling, Scipio, and Ira Mehlman. 2010. *The environmentalist's guide to immigration reform.* Washington, D.C.: Federation for American Immigration Reform.

Grant, Nicole. 2007. White supremacy and the alien land laws of Washington State. Seattle, Wash.: Seattle Civil Rights and Labor History Project. Accessed June 25, 2010. http://depts.washington.edu/civilr/alien_land_laws.htm.

Guskin, Jane, and David L. Wilson. 2007. *The politics of immigration: Questions and answers.* New York: Monthly Review Press.

Hahn, Chris. 2007. A new double movement? Anthropological perspectives on property in the age of neoliberalism. *Socio-Economic Review* 5 (2): 78–318.

Harvey, David. 2003. *The new imperialism.* New York: Oxford University Press.

Hing, Bill Ong. 2004. *Defining America through immigration policy.* Philadelphia, Pa.: Temple University Press.

Hsu, Spencer S. 2008. Immigration raid jars a small town. *Washington Post,* May 18. Accessed on May 19, 2008. http://www.washingtonpost.com/wp-dyn/content/zttile/2008/05/17/AR2008051702474_pf.html.

Hyde, Henry. 1995 *Forfeiting our property rights.* Washington, D.C.: Cato Institute.

Kanstrom, Dan. 2007. *Deportation nation: Outsiders in American history.* Cambridge, Mass.: Harvard University Press.

Kenrick, Donald, and Gratten Puxon. 1972. *The destiny of Europe's gypsies.* New York: Basic.

Kochan, Donald J. 1998. *Reforming property forfeiture laws to protect citizen's rights.* Mackinac, Mich.: The Mackinac Center for Public Policy.

Locke, John. 1690/1982. *Second treatise of government,* ed. Richard Cox. Wheeling, Ill.: Harlan Davidson.

MacPherson, Crawford. 1985. *The rise and fall of economic justice and other papers.* Oxford: Oxford University Press.

National Park Foundation. 2002. *The Aleutian World War II National Historical Area.* Co-produced with the Ounalashka Corporation. Accessed October 2, 2010. http://www.ounalashka.com/Aleutian%20WWII%20National%20Historic%20Area.htm.

National Voter. 2007. Immigration: Impact on U.S. economy. Accessed June 30, 2010. http://findarticles.com/p/articles/mi_moMLB/is_3_56/ai_n27263019/?tag=rbxcra.2.a.11.

Negative Population Growth. 2003. *Americans talk about illegal immigration.* Final Report prepared by Roper ASW. Alexandria, Va.: Negative Population Growth.

Neuman, Gerald L. 1996. *Strangers to the Constitution: Immigrant, borders, and fundamental law.* Princeton, N.J.: Princeton University Press.

Newberger, Robin, Anna Paulson, Audrey Singer, and Jeremy Smith. 2006. Financial access for immigrants: The challenges and opportunities facing U.S. depository institutions. *Community Investments* (October): 11–26.

Olsaretti, Serena. 2004. *Liberty, desert, and the market.* New York: Cambridge University Press.

Pasha, Shaheen. 2005. Banking on illegal immigrants. CNN Money.com. Accessed June 26, 2010. http://money.cnn.com/2005/08/08/news/economy/illegal_immigrants/index.htm.

Passel, Jeffrey S., and D'Vera Cohn. 2008. U.S. population projections: 2005–2050. Washington, D.C.: Pew Research Center, February 11.

Pew Hispanic Center. 2008. Pew Hispanic Center tabulations of 2000 Census (5% IPUMS) and 2006 American Community Survey (1% IPUMS). Washington, D.C.: Pew Hispanic Center.

Rasmussen Reports. 2009. Those who employ illegal immigrants should be punished. Accessed June 14, 2010. http://www.rasmussenreports.com/public_content/politics/ general_politics/march_2009/68_say_those_who_employ_illegal_immigrants_ should_be_punished.

Roberts, Paul C., and Lawrence M. Stratton. 2000. *The tyranny of good intentions: How prosecutors and bureaucrats are trampling the Constitution in the name of justice.* Rosewood, Calif.: Forum.

Rubiner, Betsy. 2008. Postcard: Postville. *New York Times.* June 16.

Sampson, Robert J., and Patrick Sharkey. 2008. Neighborhood selection and the social reproduction of concentrated racial inequality. *Demography* 45:1–29.

Schneier, Edward. 1970. The intelligence of Congress: Information and public policy. *The ANNALS of the American Academy of Political and Social Science* 388 (1): 14–24.

Schoenholtz, Andrew. 2005. Homeownership and integration of immigrants into the United States. In *International migration and security: Opportunities and challenges,* ed. E. Guild and J. V. Selm, 208–26. New York: Routledge.

Schoenholtz, Andrew, and Kriston Stanton. 2001. *Reaching the immigrant market: Creating homeownership opportunities for new Americans.* Washington, D.C.: Georgetown University Institute for the Study of International Migration and the Fannie Mae Foundation.

Schreiber, Bradley C. 2009. Defeating the drug cartels: A broader approach. *Homeland Security Today* 6 (8): 7.

Schroeder, Jana. 2009. The war for Mexico's future. *Homeland Security Today* 6 (3): 27–33.

Sewell, William H., Jr. 1979. Property, labor, and the emergence of socialism in France, 1789–1848. In *Consciousness and class experience in democratic justice,* ed. J. M. Merriman, 45–63. New Haven, Conn.: Yale University Press.

Shapiro, Ian. 2001. *Democratic justice.* New Haven, Conn.: Yale University Press.

Tamayo, William R. 1995. When the "coloreds" are neither black nor citizens: The United States civil rights movement and global migration. *Asian Law Journal* 2 (1): 1–32.

U.S. Department of Homeland Security (DHS). 2003. *ENDGAME: Office of Detention and Removal strategic plan: 2003–2012 detention and removal strategy for a secure homeland.* Washington, D.C.: Department of Homeland Security.

U.S. General Accounting Office (GAO). 2002. Identity fraud: Prevalence and links to alien illegal activities: Statement of Richard M. Stana Director, justice issues of June 25. Washington, D.C.: United States General Accounting Office.

U.S. Immigration and Customs Enforcement (ICE), Office of Inspector General (OIG). 2006. Detention and removal of illegal aliens. Washington, D.C.: ICE, Department of Homeland Security Office of Inspector General, April 2006, OIG-06-33.

———. 2008. Annual report fiscal year 2008: Protecting national security and upholding public safety. Washington, D.C.: Immigration and Customs Enforcements, Department of Homeland Security.

————. 2009. Workforce enforcement overview dated April 30, 2009. Accessed June 26, 2010. http://www.ice.gov/pi/news/factsheets/worksite.htm.

Vaughn, Jessica, and James R. Edwards, Jr. 2009. The 287(g) Program: Protecting home towns and homeland. Washington, D.C.: Center for Immigration Studies, October. Accessed June 26, 2010. http://www.cis.org/287/greport.

von Benda-Beckmann, Franz, Keebet von Benda-Beckmann, and Melanie G. Wiber. 2009. The properties of property. In *Changing properties of property*, ed. F. von Benda-Beckmann, K. von Benda-Beckmann, and M. G. Wiber, 1–39. Oxford, UK: Berghahn Books.

Walker, John. n.d. U.S. Immigration and Nationality Act. Accessed October 2, 2010. http://www.fourmilab.ch/uscode/8usc/.

Weber, Christopher. 2010. Texas ordinance barring illegal immigrants from renting property ruled unconstitutional. *Politics Daily.* Accessed June 28, 2010. http://www.politicsdaily.com/2010/03/25/texas-ordinance-barring-illegal-immigrants-from-renting-property/.

CHAPTER ELEVEN

Protest-as-Violence in Oil Fields

The Contested Representation of Profiteering in Two Extractive Sites

ANNA ZALIK

At a 2008 conference on violence in the Nigerian oilfields a colleague referenced the final passage of Chinua Achebe's novel *Things Fall Apart* to highlight the problematic use of the term pacification as a strategy for "resolving" the Niger Deltan crisis. In that passage a colonial official reflects on the suicide of the novel's hero, Okonkwo. The colonial officer felt he had learned a number of things from his experiences: "One of them was that a District Commissioner must never attend to such undignified details as cutting a hanged man from a tree. Such attention would give the natives a poor opinion of him. . . . The story of this man who had killed a messenger and hanged himself would make interesting reading. . . . The official had already chosen the title of the book, after much thought: The Pacification of the Primitive Tribes of the Lower Niger." The term, this colleague pointed out, recalled the notion of the "peace of the graveyard," suggestive of both violent dispossession and the distinction between peace and substantive justice.

"Pacification" is central to achieving the monopoly over the means of violence that is supposed to characterize the modern state, including the state's role as arbiter of official justice—a form of authority that Charles Tilly famously referred to as the institutionalization of organized crime (Tilly 1985). Pacification was explicitly required for a successful colonial project, which employed both consent-based strategies and physical violence to achieve it (Idahosa and Shenton 2004). In boom extractive sites industrial activity is surrounded by social and ecological violence, involving blatant physical dispossession, wholesale destruction and lifting of territory, and societal upheaval. Where claims for resource sovereignty express themselves in physical protest, the state and its security forces as well as its presumed check—the judiciary, are key agents in shaping notions of "legality" and "violence." In this chapter social consent to, or rejection of, legal norms shaping resource claims on oil fields in the Niger Delta and Canadian Tar Sands express varying degrees of internalization of particular mechanisms of authority.

In the oil fields of these two regions the notion of the "peace of the grave-yard," suggestive of violent repression, may be counterposed to the internal-ization of legal norms. To use another historically inflected use of the term, "social peace," citing Sorel's critique of bourgeois accommodation, refers to a political context in which significant demands against capitalist relations be-come muted, in part through reformism (Finlay 2006; Beetham 1969). At a meeting between Canadian First Nation and oil industry representatives in 2008, where industry sought community consent for a project, a local resident considered this problem, stating: "we know what has happened to indigenous people's due to the oil industry worldwide. I won't stand for that, I won't al-low that to happen to me, to my kids, to my grand-kids. I have two hands: One hand can sign a Memorandum of Understanding on a piece of paper, the second can motion to another 1000 people behind me saying: We won't al-low that to happen here. We're not going to give you that land." Indeed, the Southern Nigerian and Northwestern Canada context suggest how formal-ized state and industrial-corporate approaches to "pacification," whether via the means of force/state violence or its official legal counterpart, inform and shape protest in the spatial setting of the oil field. In the Nigerian context, where the United States and the United Kingdom have actively established and supported deepening foreign militarization in the Delta region, an armed insurgency challenges the state and the oil industry's monopoly on extracted resources. In parallel, the marking of insurgent participation in the contraband oil trade as "illegal," promoted through the industry endorsed Web site legaloil .com, discredits the insurgent call for "resource control" that claims sovereignty over the region's resources. In Canada, the mandating of consultation with ab-original communities via the fiduciary "duty to consult" discursively implies a recognition of aboriginal territorial rights, even as Canadian laws deem block-ades of access roads on their lands "illegal." As expressed in the Niger Deltan insurgency and facility occupations, then, alongside a burgeoning set of chal-lenges to provincial and federal jurisdiction in Canada (from indigenous and eco-justice groups), dispossessed residents contest both the categories of "legal/ licit" protest and "formally permitted" claims on strategic, heavily policed, petroleum assets. In so doing, following Dietz, these movements "reformulate citizenship rights in substantive (historically concrete) terms that challenge the abstract formal rights of the liberal subject, and politicize the meaning of sovereignty" (Dietz 2010, 196).

But whereas local residents make claims to resource sovereignty through nonviolent means, industry and government construe popular facility shutdowns as criminal acts. This criminalization contributes to the radicalization of resistance; it is also overdetermined by a security apparatus revolving around the physical embeddedness of oil and gas. In the face of the "economy of flows" said to typify contemporary globalization, oil and gas remains a critical input to "fossil capitalism" (Altvater 2006). The mining of hydrocarbon-derived energy is surrounded by a technology-intensive industrial enclave—a costly physical plant that is stuck in place. This material embeddedness and the capital value of its operating machinery offer a physical space for protest among challengers of extractive capitalism. In Nigeria this has meant that, in the context of poorly maintained facilities, disaffected residents and insurgent groups may damage the facilities themselves. Concurrently, insurgents participate alongside state and industry operatives in a contraband trade in oil. It is through these dynamics that a sort of protection racket has held in the Nigerian oil fields, wherein Niger Delta militants have acted as both security and threat to installations. In Canada, sporadic sabotage against oil installations since at least the late 1990s indicates simmering discontent with the presence of extractive capitalism and its ecological impacts. Recently this has resulted in invasive surveillance in a region where an unidentified pipeline bomber apparently surfaced in 2008. This has been used to justify a security discourse that in particular targets Canadian indigenous populations as "eco-terrorists" (Flanagan 2009; Mercredi 2009). Yet from both these sites, the destruction of infrastructure invokes histories of the destruction of machines, a tactic employed by agrarian populations dispossessed from their means of livelihood as well as colonized populations seeking autonomy (Hobsbawm and Rude 1993).

To proceed, this chapter considers these oil field protests, and the harnessing of "legality" to suppress popular resistance against oil industry expansion, on two pivots. The first centers on the juridical and discursive means that seek to control legal/illegal claims on extractive industry, the examples of legaloil.com, and the *duty to consult* as referenced previously. These aim to shape discursive boundaries around licit/illicit extraction as well as defining what constitutes sufficient consultation and redress to affected populations, thus explicitly or implicitly outlawing claims that exceed these boundaries.[1] The second concerns the possibility of the radicalization of resistance, including the use of civil disobedience. The latter is oft collapsed in representations by security analysts with the rather separate phenomenon of sabotage. While the latter cannot be understood apart from the socioecological violence brought about by oil mining, its relationship to organized popular resistance remains hazy and has been demonstrated, on occasion, to be deliberately feigned by industry and security institutions. Through this discussion, the chapter underlines how a form of biopower partially facilitates contemporary "accumulation by dispossession" (as processes of contemporary physical removal and denial of resource claims have been recently retheorized by David Harvey) via the social construction of boundaries between legal/illegal protest and licit/illicit forms of extraction. In so doing, the chapter calls attention to how the relationship between nonviolent protest and protest defined as violent requires further consideration in contemporary critical academic and policy debates: the radicalization of resistance, in a form that involves physical destruction and/or so-called criminality, emerges from a heavily securitized response to social claims on capital extraction that has repressed and constrained popular protest.

CONTENTION IN OIL FIELDS

In recent years, Canada has ranked among the top three suppliers of oil to the United States (now the top in terms of unconventional reserves) and Nigeria is the largest supplier in sub-Saharan Africa. As regions of key significance to U.S. petroleum security outside the Persian Gulf, the Niger Delta and Northern Alberta serve as significant global models for the social stabilization of hydrocarbon production in strategic regions. When viewed comparatively, conventional definitions of industrial development place the two economies on a continuum: Nigeria, through the Deltan lens, represents the ravages of the "resource curse" (RC), where dependence on extractive revenues and accompanying ecological degradation erodes social cohesion and impedes national industrial development.[2] Canada, via the Albertan case, offers an example of an industrialized economy in which the oil industry plays a proportionally less significant role in national accounts, but where regional cleavages over the allocation of oil industry revenues and royalties are increasingly manifest, and community protest against the deterioration of human and environmental health mounts. Yet despite sociopolitical and economic divergence in the two sites, resident populations face the aforementioned conditions of socioecological violence common to regions of petroleum extraction (Peluso and Watts 2001). Consent strategies to achieve the industrial "social license to operate" are shaped by an interrelated set of consultants and security institutions that constitute the oil industry as a networked sector (Bridge and Wood 2005).

Over the past decade, tensions arising from popular discontent with oil extraction have resulted in popular struggles in both regions with international resonance. Major global boycotts against specific companies have met private industry response in new public affairs strategies. The Niger Delta became a key target for global critics of corporate practice, and a central pivot in the adoption of the stakeholder accountability agenda since the Ogoni uprising and the execution of the Ogoni nine. The trend toward "corporate social responsibility" was in fact heavily influenced by Shell's experiences in Nigeria and the North Sea. In this same period, aboriginal populations in Canada have increasingly challenged the state for territorial sovereignty, while there has been a plodding but persistent critique of both provincial and federal government regulators and the complicity of private operators in environmental deterioration. These trends have deepened with the increasing significance of "unconventional" tar sands fossil fuel, critiques of its climactic impacts, and the role of redubbed "oil sands" (as opposed to the dirtier sounding "tar") for U.S. energy security.[3] They have also been accompanied with a rise of sabotage and violence against installations.

Recent turns in the political economy of resistance and pacification in these two sites express shifting concerns of government, industry, and residents in the wake of the 2008 financial crisis and concerns over climate change. While oil and gas prices decreased after the crash, this may distract from the rising comparative salience of commodities and oil and gas capital, as compared with banking, for investors.[4] In May 2009 the Nigerian military launched a full-scale offensive against portions of the Western Delta in an effort to root out militia groups.[5] These militia groups, rising in prominence since 2003, were in large part represented since 2006 through the umbrella organization MEND (Movement for the Emancipation of the Niger Delta)—described by Ike Okonta as "more of an idea than an organization" (Okonta 2006). In claiming responsibility for facility bombings MEND made demands for reparations to local communities for long-term industry/state profits and for ecological damages entailed by years of facility neglect. MEND's rise coincided with increased numbers of commercially motivated kidnappings, initially targeting foreigners but also Nigerians.

Following the May 2009 Nigerian military assault on the western Delta, MEND declared their own renewed attack on pipeline facilities. This MEND is referred to as Hurricane Piper Alpha—Piper Alpha being the Scottish oil platform at which the world's deadliest offshore oil disaster occurred in 1988, twenty years earlier (Amanze-Nwachuku, Alike, and Ogbu 2009). Reflecting the essentially transnational nature of labor safety concerning oil production, MEND's choice of name underlines the mutual constitution of local and global violence/security. That is, the dangers associated with hazardous industry shape the claims of workers/residents at extractive sites.

Also in 2008–2009, a series of bombings on pipelines belonging to the Encana corporation along the borders of provinces British Columbia and Alberta expressed rising frustrations with unbridled development of the Alberta Tar Sands, now marked as the largest energy project in the world and home to some of the world's largest open pit mines. Accompanying these attacks were a number of letters to local media, by an author alleging to be the bomber. Encana offered a $500,000 cash reward in January 2009 for information leading to arrests, which they doubled to $1 million some six months later. As discussed in more detail below, in the spring and summer of 2009, invasive surveillance of these communities received media attention, and a lawyer with the BC Civil Liberties Association stated that the RCMP (Royal Canadian Mounted Police) were acting "like state or secret police and [had] fomented a climate of paranoia and suspicion . . . by applying a level of social pressure that amounts to harassment and intimidation"(Hume 2009). Wiebo Ludgwig, an organic farmer and Christian preacher known for his disputes with the oil and gas industry, issued a plea for the bomber to desist in September 2009. Yet in January 2010 he was arrested, although released without charges after ten days of scoping his farm unsuccessfully for evidence. This move was seen by some local residents as an attempt to create the impression of having identified a culprit without evidence, and, even following his release, additional threatening letters were received by the purported Encana bomber (Venis 2010). While the Canadian media attended to the bombings, a serious leak in an Encana facility in the same area on November 22, 2009 went largely unnoticed by the national press. Field research in the summer of 2010 indicated considerable doubt among some fenceline residents as to whether the pipeline bomber had been a local at all. A commonly held view among those critical of the industry and/or the pace of development was that the reports of the bombings had mostly served to instill fear of protest among local residents—farmers and First Nations—who had been organizing for greater safety measures by industry, a number of whom were particularly targeted for police harassment in 2009.

These Canadian incidents prompt a renewed discussion on eco-terrorism. Ten years earlier, an environmental think tank in Alberta published a report entitled Beyond Eco Terrorism pointing out that "growing and legitimate concerns" about the oil industry's environmental impacts in the provincial "Oil Patch" (as it is known) had been largely ignored in the controversy over sabotage (Marr-Laing and Severson-Baker 1999). These cases of sabotage overlapped with the 1990s upswing of oil industry protest globally, from Nigeria to Burma. An investigation into the 1998 Alberta cases ultimately indicated that members of the RCMP, alongside staff of Alberta Energy Corporation, were collaborators in blowing up an oil well to facilitate investigation of Wiebo Ludwig, who was eventually charged in the case (Marr-Laing and Severson-Baker 1999).

The cases also contribute to the broader rupture of an apparent "social peace" in the province of Alberta, a peace achieved in part through political apathy facilitated by an erratic socioeconomic boom. Recent legal cases mounted against the provincial government by aboriginal communities and facility sit-ins organized by Greenpeace have also prompted considerations of their movements in light of the historical employ of civil disobedience (Adkin 2009). But quite apart, the harnessing of sabotage—physical violence—by actors operating through notes and messages in both Nigeria and Canada, evokes the Captain Swing riots of nineteenth-century Britain. These actions prompt consideration of theories of the relationship between crisis and radical event—the possibility of which has been stressed in the wake of financial meltdown (Cazdyn 2007). And as we will discuss at the conclusion of this chapter, they advise reflection on debates regarding violent resistance and its justification (Finlay 2006; Brie 2008; Amin 2008).

LEGALOIL.COM AND THE RADICALIZATION OF RESISTANCE IN THE NIGER DELTA

Over the past three years armed militias in the Niger Delta have commanded global headlines. The harsh repression of the Ogoni movement, and of the mobilizations of other Niger Delta oil minorities that followed upon it in the 1990s served as one form of pacification of such protest. The renewed possibility of sustained nonviolent protest, in the form of women who, when in 2002 occupying a Chevron platform in the western Delta and threatening to disrobe presented a possible public relations disaster for Chevron and other multinationals. A key response to these occupations came in the form of corporate-community agreements with the women, who in large part demanded employment for area youth. The terms of these agreements, including for the provision of community infrastructure, became largely moot following election-related violence in 2003 that left many of the riverine villages of the region abandoned.[6]

This 2003 violence was shaped by culturally-inflected, political competition for areas on which oil installations are sited—a problem that dates back to at least the late colonial period (Willink et al. 1958). The move to electoral democracy under Obasanjo (following the death of dictator Sani Abacha), intensified the political-economic stakes among neighboring ethnic groups seeking control of Local Government Areas on which important oil fields and installations are sited. In 2003 this political violence was largely intercommunal and resulted in residents fleeing their homes, some in fact evacuated by Chevron itself (Zalik 2004, 2009). Such dispersal only facilitated that these areas, now less densely populated, would serve as havens for the high-level prosecution of a contraband trade in oil, as well as for the militia groups that serve as both security to installations and executors of the contraband trade. Their ability to destroy these installations is also key to a local protection racket around these installations, in which armed insurgents familiar with the maze-like Delta had largely outsmarted the Nigerian forces less familiar with the region. Following the 2007 elections, the new Yar Adua government sought to deal with this problem, a project clearly supported by the U.S. Africa Command, and explicitly encouraged by Gordon Brown. Thus in a move to root out the militant groups, the Nigerian military launched a full scale attack against this region of the Western Delta, primarily as a means to show force. But following this aerial bombardment and the further depopulation of the region, Nigerian militant leaders were offered amnesty by the federal government, which various accepted. With the amnesty as backdrop, in the fall of 2009 the mainstream international press suggested that the militants had been partially successful in their aims, with the *Financial Times* employing the headline: "Nigeria to use oil revenue to end revolt" (Burgis 2009).

Mainstream media and policy analyst representation of the Delta crisis has played a role in the criminalization of protest, through the employ of terms like terrorism, state failure, and so on to describe the deepening ungovernability of the region. Yet oddly enough, the armed resisters just described seemed to have asserted their positions, whereas civil disobedience has been effectively thwarted by repression and subjective means. In the struggle to define "licit" extraction and "peaceful" protest in the Delta, are the consent mechanisms employed by the transnational oil companies and their interlocutors in private international security firms and attempts to label oil "legal" or illegal. These mechanisms have helped pathologize Deltan unarmed protest not only externally and internationally, but also in the minds of those most subject to the ravages of oil extraction. Indeed, in 2003 and into the present, many residents of the Delta's riverine region would refer to any facility takeover or shutdown as violence, a view promoted by the industry in its emphasis on avoiding work stoppages and outlawing demonstrations.[7] Ultimately, if a key tactic of un-armed resistance movements—like blockades—became equated with violent protest, few options for demonstrating aggravation with industrial impacts remain: the radicalization of protest was thus an unsurprising outcome—an outcome whose implications for industry may be no more threatening than the reputational threat posed by unarmed protest.

LEGALOIL.COM

The Web site legaloil.com promotes the discursive and material criminalization of the oil bunkering trade in the Nigerian context—equating it with conflict diamonds. The Legal Oil Web site was established in 2002–2003 when control of the contraband trade was said to have slipped increasingly out of the hands of the military and oil industry staff that previously directed it, into those of the armed youth that formerly served as their henchmen. Legaloil.com functions as a directly "global" intervention that presents data concerning bunkered shipments (the source of which is hard to verify or monitor, but becomes reified once presented as graphs and tables), tracks threats and attacks on installations, and endorses chemical fingerprinting as a means to distinguish between licit and illicit oil. The site also seeks to present its data, and its proposals, as legitimated by Nigerian sources. Indeed, to be successful internationally, the "legal oil" label requires reshaping the way exploitation in the Niger Delta is understood locally and globally so that "abusive" relations of extraction come to be associated with bunkering activities, rather than the (state-sanctioned) operations of multinational oil companies so criticized in the 1990s.

The Legaloil.com Web site states: "Tackling oil theft requires action on both the demand and supply side. It also requires attention to the root causes of the problem." As it explains: "Following the success of the 'conflict diamonds' campaign and work on disarmament, there is a clear opportunity to address oil theft by including a focus on the market for the stolen oil in a comprehensive strategy that would include measures of supply and demand." On the "supply" side, legaloil.com calls for:

> Law enforcement activities (e.g. monitoring "oil theft hot-spots" and navy checks); Initiatives on corruption and transparency; Providing sustainable developmental alternatives to communities at the source of the theft (e.g. micro-credit schemes, community development projects); Tracking funds from oil theft and stopping associated revenue flows through banks.

On the "demand" side the Web site endorses:

> "Fingerprinting" oil at source, during transport and at refineries; Auditing refineries for processing illegal oil; Establishing common industry-wide positions and action; Pressuring markets to only accept "legal" oil.

Of course the supply and demand sides of the oil bunkering equation require making links between production and consumption—that is, between Nigeria as the exporting source and various Northern/Western importers, including major strategic destinations like the United States and the United Kingdom. In general, the promotion of relinking between production and consumption in global commodity chains is a strategy endorsed by critics of economic globalization. From the perspective of these critics, local consumption is a means to promote more than just socioeconomies, since consumers are confronted directly with the source of what they eat and are able to more directly monitor the socioenvironmental conditions surrounding these sources. To promote more equitable global trade relations, these advocates of "local consumption" and fair trade often reveal the exploitative working and environmental conditions, deepened via neoliberal economic policies, that are common to many "developing" country industrial sites. It is these exploitative relations, following the now well-known theories of regional developmental gaps between global North and South, that allow for the accumulation of surplus capital in Northern, industrialized countries while surplus is extracted from the southern post-colonies.

As referenced at the outset, this view has been recently reinvigorated among academics through critical geographer David Harvey's theorization of "accumulation by dispossession," which he applied particularly to the U.S.'s appropriation of strategic oil reserves in his 2003 book *The New Imperialism*. In the Deltan context, Harvey's view may be complemented by considering how the Nigerian state is consistently reconfigured as a "joint venture" partner in the accumulation strategy common to transnational operators and some national oil companies. Similarly, Charles Tilly's insight on the aforementioned historical sociology of the state (1985) bears repeating: in the case of contemporary globalization the state serves as a facilitator of multinational corporate windfalls. Applying this perspective, what may be labeled "legally regulated oil" serves merely as a veneer for ongoing extractive relations.

Legaloil.com is, accordingly, an especially salient intervention in that it counters this view that recent capitalist expansion at the (so-called) global level, amounts to ongoing "accumulation by dispossession." In the local Deltan context, it also counters the insurgency's use of the language of "resource sovereignty"/control to frame bunkering as a rightful claim on locally extracted resources. That said, a closer examination of bunkering beyond the scope of this chapter may suggest its role as a form of localized accumulation, to which some regional and federal politicians have been closely connected. As such, its link to more oppositional local struggles for resource control against the state may be attenuated; but these relations may indeed express cleavages between federal and state-level political officeholders.

Central to understanding the discursive reordering implied in the "Legal Oil" label is the recognition that contraband oil bunkering is not the cause of socioeconomic breakdown but its consequence. Legaloil.com's concept of oil certification suggests instead that bunkered oil is the culprit in socioeconomic breakdown by "aim[ing] to hit the well-organized theft of oil by choking off the market for the stolen oil and interrupting the supply chain." Instead of the Shell boycott of the Ogoni/Abacha period, what they promote is a bunkering boycott, using the conflict diamond campaign as a model. But while the turf wars and proliferation of small arms around the oil bunkering industry may be comparable to some warlordism around conflict diamonds, oil and diamonds differ in a crucial respect from one another: energy is required for contemporary global reproduction, and the global diamond trade is based largely in a market of symbolic value and luxury goods. Whereas the conflict diamond trade was associated with classic "predatory" states (although that may be an oversimplification as the transnational diamond companies also benefit), the proliferation of arms in the Niger Delta is directly associated with the oil industry's security practices—including the much critiqued (but still common) "standby-style" payments offered to youths in areas of operations. It is clearly also linked to local competitive dynamics for control over the contraband trade. Indeed, despite the de jure outlawing of standby payments, in form they remain commonplace but with the added caveat that your firepower determines the payment's size. As one key informant put it to me in a 2006 interview in Port Harcourt: "If you negotiate with an AK47 they will pay you a price for that, with a pistol, a bazooka, a gunboat . . . they will pay you based on your coercive power."

Here it is also worth noting that Yar Adua's position concerning the Nigerian oil industry has recently been harnessed and "re-represented" by legaloil. com. Deceased as of May 2010 and replaced by Vice President Goodluck Jonathan, in the year following his election in 2007, Yar Adua had taken various positions critical of MNOCs. Indeed, he was identified by the *Financial Times* as having adopted a "firm-line" regarding the profits the multinationals have made off of Nigerian production due to high oil prices (Green 2008). But both the mark of electoral "illegitimacy" and dropping prices also pressures him to adopt pro–market-oriented policies on oil rents and foreign investment. Thus, it is interesting that Legaloil.com cited the source ISN (International Relations and Security Network) Security Watch, touting Yar Adua as an originator of the proposal to fingerprint oil (Mbachu 2008). A brief Internet search tied ISN security watch to the Hudson Institute, an arch-conservative U.S. security and economic policy think tank.

While it is certainly the case that the trade in bunkered oil has assisted the proliferation of arms in the region, this proliferation was closely tied to a protection racket fostered by industry—well-documented in the late 1990s and early 2000s by groups like Human Rights Watch. This racket is in fact implicitly approved by foreign governments and industry in some clauses of the "Voluntary Principles on Security and Human Rights," which sanctions the contracting of local residents as security providers.

This subtle reframing of exploitation endorsed via Legaloil.com is salient to current debates concerning the securing of Nigerian oil and the Gulf of Guinea region more generally. In contrast to 2004, when Governor Alamseiyeigha of the central Deltan state of Bayelsa asserted that "no Ijaw man is lifting oil," today the region's militia leaders serve as spokespeople on bunkering as resource control. And despite the relatively unsympathetic global imagery provided of the Delta's insurgent groups, their spokespeople nevertheless do manage to make their interpretation heard internationally. Indeed, the controversy surrounding Gordon Brown's 2008 announcement of military aid to the Niger Delta underscores this point. An article in *The Independent* described a MEND spokesperson's reaction to the UK proposal:

> The Prime Minister's offer to help "tackle lawlessness" in the world's eighth largest oil producer was immediately condemned by the main militant group in the Delta, which abandoned a two-week-old ceasefire and accused Britain of backing what it calls Nigeria's "illegal government." The group issued a "stern warning" to Mr. Brown in an emailed statement: "Should Gordon Brown make good his threat to support this criminality for the sake of oil, UK citizens and interests in Nigeria will suffer the consequence." (Howden et al. 2008)

The description of this act as a "blunder" in global reporting reflects the growing ability of insurgent groups to assert their view, even if those voices do not elicit broad outpourings of sympathy along the lines of the Ogoni uprising. Today, with an Ijaw man as president of the Nigerian federation, the discourse of marginality is less successful. But as demonstrated before, MEND and fellow travelers explicitly challenge the notion of "legal" extraction and profiteering by government and multinationals. When President Bush committed $4 million in military aid to Nigeria in 2002, prior to the rise in the violence surrounding oil facilities, it received relatively minimal attention. In the midst of an apparently thriving contraband market—suggesting the failure of this approach—the 2009 military assault aimed to root out insurgents from the Delta's creeks, yet the global media seeks to portray the outcome as a victory for the militants. This suggests that in the quest to establish *legitimate* oil extraction, mechanisms must be established that break social relations between insurgent groups and communities, creating shared identification—as stakeholders—between communities affected by extraction and the oil companies themselves.

SOCIAL PEACE AND ITS DISCONTENTS IN THE CANADIAN EXTRACTIVE ECONOMY

While a violent insurgency in the Niger Delta has entered the global imagination, the dynamics of extractive conflicts in the Canadian North has become increasingly subject to the fiduciary "duty to consult" with aboriginal communities (Natcher 2001; Treacy, Campbell, and Dixon 2007; Fogarassy and Litton 2004). Informed by a number of legal cases in western Canada, this "duty" is now understood as the state requirement—often devolved to the corporation holding a leasing permit—to confer with First Nations and Metis groups concerning activities that will affect their historic lands: the legislation may offer some token recognition of the significance of *traditional ecological knowledge* (often referred to as TEK). Yet corporate activity to demonstrate its fulfillment of "consultation" becomes an instrument to achieve what corporate public affairs practice refers to as the *license to operate*: Mandated consultation, without tangible community consent, is sufficient to meet its requirements.

As a consequence of the implementation of the "duty to consult," a number of somewhat contradictory tendencies have arisen in regulation of land conflicts in the strategic regions of Northern Alberta and British Columbia, the Athabasca and MacKenzie river basins, and particularly the Tar Sands. These tendencies involve, first, industrial self-regulation with minimal government oversight. Second, with respect to communities affected by extraction, the duty has been accompanied, on the one hand, by the commodification of the claims industry—with a range of lawyers seeking to represent aboriginal groups in their demands for resources from the provincial authorities that, in many cases, guide oil and gas mining. On the other hand, the requirement to consult may serve as a tool to contest the practice of provincial authorities that approve mining projects, and an instrument to critique the public hearing and impact assessment practices employed by state- and industry-funded regulatory institutions. But despite the strategic uses of the "duty," problematic legislation at both federal and state level has facilitated the direct incarceration of aboriginal leaders who dispute extraction, with recent cases in the province of Ontario serving as a stark example. In contesting the meaning of the duty to consult through the courts, and through withdrawal from state- and industry-backed institutions that provide legitimacy to this process, First Nation residents of these regions seek to contest and redefine its substantive implications. The formal, legal weight of the "duty to consult" is thus far from established and—as all legal doctrine—subject to sociohistorical reinterpretation that will shape its application.

Literature on the duty to consult, incorporating a duty to accommodate, suggests that its implementation is highly bureaucratized without substantive means for aboriginal communities to challenge development (Natcher 2001; O'Faircheallaigh 2007). The Industrial Relations Corporations that constituted in part to fulfill this duty in the Alberta Tar Sands are in various cases minimally funded and staffed, yet are expected to offer input on numerous projects. This in a context where not a single Tar Sands project has been denied, demonstrating that the duty is not complemented by a meaningful "right to say no" (Kuyek 2008; Adkin 2009). Similar problems are evident in Northern British Columbia, where aboriginal and environmental organizations have argued that the formal government review process, and industry-sponsored advisory process, for the Enbridge Gateway pipeline project is inadequate (First Nations Summit, World Wildlife Fund, Pembina Institute).[8] They hold that neither process offers opportunity to contest or change the terms of the pipeline project: Their refusal to participate thus aims to counter the possibility of future government and industry claims to "due consultation," and their withholding of participation thus demonstrates one potential strategic use of the duty by those opposing industrial expansion.

Mounting social protest in Alberta and British Columbia also reflects increased public attention to the EIA process in Canada since 2003 and particularly in the last two years. The lack of environmental regulatory oversight has manifested in socioecological and environmental impunity in cases like the dismissal of a doctor who alerted the community of Fort Chipewyan to alarming rates of bile duct cancers, and the "ducks scandal" of 2008 in which hundreds (and more recently disclosed, thousands) of birds were found dead in an oil industry tailings pond. Given rising activism among affected groups, operating companies sought greater developmental "certainty" (interview with industry representative 2008) via collaboration among industrial firms so as "to avoid (any one) company setting an unrealistic precedent for social benefits in the community." Industry representatives describe aboriginal Band Councils as hostile and/or "insufficiently representative"—the latter discursive move a strategy common to industrial divide and rule tactics globally.[9] Accordingly, public affairs branches of companies held separate meetings with youth and elders groups, which in one case I observed were intended to break the Council's consensus position against a particular industry project.

Such a model seeking "social peace" through the buy-in of subsectors of fenceline communities is central to a new model agreement proposed by industry to Northern Alberta, which promoted direct contracting to aboriginal businesses as industrial service providers. It is also apparent in the process promoted through Enbridge Northern Gateway Pipeline Advisory Boards in British Columbia.[10] Critique of industry processes has only mounted in this context as global attention has led to both Canadian and U.S. activist activity regarding the cumulative climate impacts of Tar Sands development and calling for an outright boycott of tourism in Alberta. Greenpeace has recently occupied a series of facilities in Alberta (Iltan 2009). This resurgence has led to rising attempts to criminalize the region—recent controversies reported by a Calgary-based academic, Thomas Flanagan, described indigenous communities as potential eco-terrorists (Flanagan 2009, 9).

The Encana case, in particular, has prompted this attention—with various alleged letters from the bomber released to the media. A July letter stated: "Encana. You simply can't win this fight because you are on the wrong side of the argument. So stop pushing people around here. Cease all your activities and remove all your installations. Return the land to what it was before you came" (Boutet 2009). Investigations into bombings in the BC community of Dawson Creek also placed considerable emphasis on the Cree community of Kelly Lake (Kleiss 2009); in one case the RCMP apparently targeted a Cree woman in her seventies for some hours of interrogation (Arsenault 2009). Interestingly, while much attention has been given to this case, researcher Chris Arsenault—via freedom of information requests—uncovered that state security have recorded numerous cases of pipeline sabotage. The press indicated that the RCMP had no prime suspect in the bombings, but reported aggressive interrogation of various local critics of the oil industry in Tomslake, British Columbia (Drake 2009). A BC-based environmental NGO (nongovernmental organization) indicated that the climate of fear and suspicion made it next to impossible to conduct community meetings and organizing in the area.

As reported in January 2009:

> The bombings have cast a pall over the small, tight-knit community of several
> hundred who live around Tomslake. Residents want desperately for the culprit
> to be caught—not only because of fears that an explosion could trigger a fatal

gas leak, but also to lift the cloud of suspicion that has fallen over them and their neighbors. The cabin made of thick, knotted logs where Lisa and Willy Webster have lived for 20 years is only a few meters back from a rural road. "Now security will drive by and stop and look in the windows and it's like, what do you think we're doing, building bombs at the kitchen table?" Mr. Hebert said. "They think we're all criminals," Mr. Webster added. Mr. Hebert said a close friend, who was part of a small sit-in to protest the oil and gas presence in the spring, was one of the first to face harsh scrutiny from authorities. "He finally just gave them DNA samples because he had enough." (Drake 2009)

Ultimately, one resident is quoted stating that while they would rather the bomber stop, "he's the reason people are finally paying attention." As a punctuated moment of fear, the disruptive nature of a pipeline explosion and the spill in its aftermath ruptures any banal acceptance of capital extraction in the Canadian context. A range of civil disobedience and court cases occur concurrently, which are the main target of industrial concern. While not akin to a revolutionary "event," the moment certainly shakes the sense of security of those directly *opposing* further oil industry expansion alongside its proponents.

This essay departs from a notion of profiteering-as-violence (literally, exploitative extraction). Industrial extraction entails at once sociocultural and environmental violence—referring not only to the crassest form of physical destruction and the employ of state and nonstate violence against residents, but also the securing of industrial installations through the means of force, whether encompassing oil fields in their broad extension or located in enclaves bordering particular installations (flow stations, well heads); this task may be assumed by state security and privatized forces. From this point of departure the chapter considers, as the discursive counterpart of the "violent environment" wreaked by oil extraction (Watts 2004; Peluso and Watts 2001), how the relations of power that shape monopolistic control over subsurface petroleum in turn limit popular claims against extractive industry. Whether through juridical options, or through their discursive counterpart—the marking of contraband oil as "illegal"—this chapter examines how the term violence is deployed as a label on physical blockades. Put next to destructive acts, a hegemonic "fossil capitalism" is in itself violence, just as the term is deployed to restrict resistance against it.

These Nigerian and Canadian contexts are clearly interconnected through the range of corporate consultants who shape both oil industry social practice and industrial security policy, but they are also globally constituted through the media's attention to "supply threats" to future energy sources (Zalik 2010). At the same time, and expressing the broader focus of the environmental justice movement, the distribution of harms is spatially mediated, with the bearing of negative health and social impacts visibly, and increasingly, racialized and eth-nicized in both sites. In the Niger Delta the violence surrounding the oil indus-try is commodified via a local protection racket, contributing to the deepening commodification of oil as a financial derivative in futures exchanges. Concur-rently the quagmire of sabotage confronts the observer in Canada, where the physical destruction of oil industry installations—from the perspective of the security apparatus—is collapsed into the alternative of nonviolent civil disobe-dience. Thus, the "terror" of destruction of oil installations with or without direct impact on neighboring populations is portrayed as a threat of greater consequence than the ecological damage of the industry itself.

Thus, in analyzing various forms of pacification, the attempt to ensure social peace by industry and the state, this chapter confronts what the bourgeois state may react to more repressively: industrial sabotage. This poses an analytical obstacle in the context of academic debate largely dominated by acceptance of liberal social peace through reformism. In this picture—and in the context of legal repression of peaceful protest against installations—political violence (or terrorism against industry) is commonplace in the Nigerian oil fields, and clearly of concern for corporate security in the Canadian oil fields. The ques-tion then presents itself: must normative questions of productive violence be put on the table, or does the discursive analysis of il/legal protest and its crimi-nalization provide sufficient grounds for critique?

The answer, I believe, is no. The move from analytically considering the hegemonic representation of legally mandated capital extraction as juridically regulated and politically commendable, to the designation of peaceful obstruc-tion of such extraction as illegal, requires grappling with the radicalization of resistance that arises from the criminalization of nonviolent protest—namely, sabotage against installations. Questions then arise that trouble the academic's position as a beneficiary of social peace: is the employ of such means an expres-sion of a forced radicalization of resistance, or does it represent simply a more profound challenge to the status quo that expresses what were once described as "objective" historical forces? Does the rupture represented by this most re-cent financial crisis offer space for a consideration of "revolution" or has, as Adorno implied, contemporary bourgeois democracy placed such alternatives external to theorization in the West? Is the reading of Fanon in critical devel-opmental studies and post-colonial theory classes a mere historical exercise, or does it prompt more serious contemplation?

Under analysis, then, is how the term "violence" and the formal and discur-

sive employ of "legality" are harnessed in struggles over the definition of acceptable social protest in extractive sites and as a means of criminalizing dissent.
The chapter has thus explored how state and capital mandated distinctions between legal/illegal extraction, and how violent/peaceful protest become juridically and socially established, and how they remain contested. Concurrently, it
considers the micro politics of the attempt to distinguish between these terms
via their (partial) influence on subject formation. In both sites, the law itself,
the internalization of its norms by those spatially subject to physical extraction,
and the employ of increasingly militarized and armed tactics to enforce it, serve
to dispossess residents of those rights supposedly enshrined under the modern state. But although corporate-sponsored and state-sanctioned discursive
and/or legal mechanisms partially accomplish a capital-endorsed hegemonic
view of licit extraction, this category remains contested and hegemony thus
incomplete.

NOTES

1. See, for instance, British climate change activists in 2008 planning facility shutdowns of coal plants and arrests of Greenpeace activists who took various public actions
in the Tar Sands and Calgary.

2. While easily critiqued from a (post) Marxist perspective for reifying the state as a
container of the economy, and neglecting dimensions of ownership and control over the
means of production in the oil and mining sector, the resource curse thesis does assist in
explaining how manufacturing may deteriorate under conditions of reliance on a single
high-value extractive resource.

3. These two regions are of particular strategic significance for key operators. On the
two regions, Royal Dutch Shell's *2007 Annual Report* states, "As easy-to-access oil gets
rarer, unconventional resources such as Canada's oil sands will become increasingly important sources of energy. The move will help the Oil Sands business to better integrate
bitumen upgrading with our manufacturing operations across North America. In Nigeria, bright spots were the performance of our offshore operations and the completion of
a sixth liquefied natural gas (LNG) train. In the Delta region onshore, however, much of
our production again remained shut in because of the security situation (Shell 2007, 3).

4. See, for instance, Masters (2008).

5. Notably, in less than a year of the conference on the Niger Delta where my colleague raised the problematic nature of the term "pacification."

6. The agreements, made with women representing three different ethnic groups,

were themselves subject to "renegotiation" as Chevron sought to replace its community-by-community negotiation process with a "global one" from 2006 onward (Zalik 2008).

7. At the 2003 Small Petroleum Development Company of Nigeria (SPDC) Women's Peacebuilding Forum in Yenagoa this connection was made explicit, with women-as-mothers criticized for neglecting their "duty" to foster good behavior amongst their sons.

8. See position, historic and current, of the Carrier Sekani Tribal Council on the web site at http://www.cstc.bc.ca/cstc as well as the West Coast Environmental Law comment on Enbridge Pipeline Community Advisory Boards. In 2009 the British Columbia First National Summit rejected the joint review panel process for the Enbridge Gateway Pipeline and the World Wildlife Fund decided not to participate in Enbridge's Community Advisory Board process.

9. Author's interviews with community and industry representatives, Alberta 2008.

10. See West Coast Environmental Law Backgrounders regarding the Enbridge Gateway Pipeline. For example, their December 2009 press release: "Review process for Enbridge Northern Gateway Project subject to ongoing opposition and controversy."

REFERENCES

Achebe, Chinua. 1958/2007. *Things fall apart*. New York: Everyman's Library.

Adkin, Laurie. 1998. *The politics of sustainable development: Citizens, unions and the corporations*. Montreal: Black Rose Books.

———. 2009. Non-violent civil disobedience is a far cry from terrorism. *Edmonton Journal*. October 8.

Allub, Leopoldo. 1983. Heterogeneidad Estructural, Desigualdad Social y Privación Relativa En Regiones Petroleras ("Structural Heterogeneity, Social Inequality and Relative Deprivation in Petroleum Regions") *Revista Mexicana de Sociología* 45 (1): 169–90.

Altvater, Elmar. 2006. The social and natural environment of fossil capitalism. In *Coming to terms with nature: Socialist Register 2007*, ed. Leo Panitch and Colin Leys, 37–59. New York: Monthly Review Press.

Amanze-Nwachuku, C., E. Alike, and A. Ogbu. 2009. Militants hurt oil exports, hit more pipelines. *This Day*. June 22.

Amin, Ash. 2004. Regulating economic globalization. *Transactions of the Institute of British Geographers* 29:217–33.

Amin, Samir. 2008. The defense of humanity requires the radicalization of popular struggles. In *Violence today: Actually existing barbarism, socialist register 2009*, ed. Leo Panitch and Colin Leys, 260–72. New York: Monthly Review Press.

Arsenault, Chris. 2009. Sabotage in Peace River: Bombings in northern BC/Alberta put spotlight on controversial pipelines. *The Dominion*. September 28. http://www.dominionpaper.ca/articles/2914.

Auty, Richard. 1993. *Sustaining development in mineral economies: The Resource curse thesis.* London: Routledge.

Barker, Alex. 2008. UK offers Nigeria help to train security forces. *Financial Times.* July 16.

Beetham, David. 1969. Sorel and the Left. *Government and Opposition* 4 (3): 308–23.

Bernstein, Steven. 2001. *The compromise of liberal environmentalism.* New York: Columbia University Press.

Blitz, James. 2008. Nigeria to tap UK security aid. *Financial Times.* July 10.

Bond, Patrick. 2006. Resource extraction and African underdevelopment. *Capitalism Nature Socialism* 17 (2): 5–25.

Boutet, Chris. 2009. Letter from alleged B.C. pipeline bomber demands EnCana leave Dawson Creek. *National Post.* July 16.

Bridge, Gavin. 2008. Global production networks and the extractive sector: Governing resource-based development. *Journal of Economic Geography* 8:389–419.

Bridge, Gavin, and Andre Wood. 2005. Geographies of knowledge, practices of globalization: Learning from the oil exploration and production industry. *Area* 32 (2): 199–208.

Brie, Michael. 2008. Emancipation and the Left: The issue of violence. In *Violence today: Actually existing barbarism, socialist register 2009,* ed. Leo Panitch and Colin Leys, 239–59. New York: Monthly Review Press.

Burgis, Tom. 2009. Nigeria to use oil to end revolt. *Financial Times.* October 18.

Carrier Sekani Tribal Council. 2010. Hundreds march to oppose Enbridge Northern Gateway Pipeline. September 8. http://www.este.bc.ca/news/text/670/12/hundreds+march+to+oppose+enbridge+northern+gateway+pipeline?id=1095lvsyof=53ust=2.

Castree, Noel. 2004. Differential geographies: Place, indigenous rights and "local" resources. *Political Geography* 23 (2): 133–67.

Cazdyn, Eric. 2007. Disaster, crisis, revolution. *South Atlantic Quarterly* 4:647–62.

Chastko, Paul A. 2004. *Developing Alberta's oil sands: From Karl Clark to Kyoto.* Calgary: University of Calgary Press.

Davidson, Debra J., and Norah A. MacKendrick. 2004. All dressed up with nowhere to go: The discourse of ecological modernization in Alberta, Canada. *Canadian Review of Sociology and Anthropology* 41 (1): 47–65.

Dietz, Kelly. 2010. Demilitarizing sovereignty: Self-determination and anti-military base activism in Okinawa, Japan. In *Contesting development,* ed. Philip McMichael, 182–98. New York: Routledge.

Drake, Laura. 2009. Neighbours frantic to catch pipeline bomber. *Canwest News.* January 11, reprinted in *Globe and Mail* July 12. http://www.globalnational.com/Neighbours+frantic+catch+pipeline+bomber/1167129/story.html.

Dyer, Simon, Jeremy Moorhouse, Katie Laufenberg, and Rob Powell. 2008. *Undermining the environment: The oil sands report card.* Drayton Valley: Pembina Institute, WWF.

Finlay, Christopher J. 2006. Violence and revolutionary subjectivity: Marx to Zizek. *European Journal of Political Theory* 8:373–97.

Flanagan, Thomas. 2009. *Resource industries and security issues in Northern Alberta.* Ottawa: Canadian Defense and Foreign Affairs Institute.

Fogarassy, T., and K. Litton. 2004. Consultation with Aboriginal peoples: Impacts on the petroleum industry. *Alberta Law Review* 42 (1): 41–74.

Foucault, Michel. 1976. *Power/knowledge: Selected interviews and other writings.* New York: Pantheon.

Frynas, George, Matthias Beck, and Kamel Mellahi. 2000. Maintaining corporate dominance after decolonization: The "First Mover" advantage of Shell in Nigeria. *Review of African Political Economy* 27 (85): 407–25.

Gibson, Diana. 2007. *The spoils of the boom: Incomes, profits and poverty in Alberta.* Edmonton: Parkland Institute.

Green, Matthew. 2008. Nigerian demands $2bn taxes from Oil Majors. *Financial Times.* May 22.

Harrison, Trevor. 2005. *The return of the trojan horse: Alberta and the new world (dis)order.* Montreal: Black Rose Books.

Harvey, David. 2003. *The new imperialism.* London: Oxford University Press.

Hobsbawm, Eric, and George Rude. 1993. *Captain swing.* London: Pimlico.

Howden, Daniel, Kim Sengupta, Colin Brown, and Claire Soares. 2008. Brown blunders in pledge to secure Nigeria's "black gold." *The Independent.* July 11:1.

Hume, Mark. 2009. RCMP's aggressive hunt for bomber criticized. *Globe and Mail.* July 10:A46.

Idahosa, Pablo, and Robert Shenton. 2004. The Africanist's "new" clothes. *Historical Materialism* 12 (4): 67–113.

Iltan, C. 2009. Greenpeace protest over Alberta oilsands ends with more arrests. *Edmonton Journal.* October 4.

Kleiss, Karen. 2009. New RCMP detachment in works to foil bomber. *Edmonton Journal.* July 18.

Kuyek, Joan. 2008. The Ontario Mining Act, political prisoners and the right to say NO. *The Bullet* 98 (April 16). http://www.socialistproject.ca/bullet/bullet098.html.

Lapin, Deirdre. 2000. *The leveraged buy-in: Creating an enabling environment for business through strategic social investments.* Richardson, Tex.: Society for Petroleum Engineers.

Lipschutz, Ronnie D. 2005. Power, politics and global civil society. *Millennium* 33 (3): 747–69.

MacKendrick, Norah, and Debra Davidson. 2007. State-capital relations in voluntary environmental improvement. *Current Sociology* 55 (5): 674–95.

Marr-Laing, Tom, and Chris Severson-Baker. 1999. Beyond eco-terrorism: The deeper issues affecting Alberta's oil patch. Drayton Valley, AB: Pembina Institute.

Masters, B. 2008. Oil set to replace banks as top dividend payer. *Financial Times.* October 28.

Mbachu, Dulue. 2008. Nigerian "blood oil." ISN *Security Watch*. http://www.isn.ethz.ch/isn/Current-Affairs/Security-Watch/Detail/?ots591=4888caa0-b3db-1461-98b9e20e7b9c13d4&lng=en&id=88671.

McCarthy, James, and Scott Prudham. 2004. Neoliberal nature and the nature of neoliberalism. *Geoforum* 35:275–83.

McCullum, Hugh. 2005. *Fuelling fortress America: A report on the Athabasca tar sands and U.S. demands for Canada's energy*. Edmunton: Parkland Institute, Polaris Institute.

McKillop, Jennifer. 2002. *Toward culturally appropriate consultation: An approach for Fort McKay First Nation*. Masters Thesis. Faculty of Environmental Design. University of Calgary.

McMichael, Philip. 1990. Incorporated comparison in a world historical perspective: An alternative comparative method. *American Sociological Review* 55 (3): 385–97.

Mercredi, Mike. 2009. Athabasca Chipewyan First Nation leadership appalled and shocked by the Canadian Defense and Foreign Affairs Institute. *Tar Sands Watch*. July 29.

Nader, Laura. 1972. Up the anthropologist: Perspectives gained from studying up. In *Reinventing anthropology*, ed. D. Hymes, 284–311. New York: Pantheon Books.

Nader, Laura, and Elisabetta Grande. 2002. From the trenches and the towers: Current illusions and delusions about conflict management—in Africa and elsewhere. *Law and Social Inquiry* 27:573–75.

Natcher, David. 2001. Land use research and the duty to consult: A misrepresentation of the aboriginal landscape. *Land Use Policy* 18:113–22.

Obi, Cyril. 2008. Enter the dragon? Chinese oil companies and resistance in the Niger Delta. *Review of African Political Economy* 117:414–34.

O'Faircheallaigh, Ciaran. 2007. Environmental agreements, EIA follow-up and aboriginal participation in environmental management: The Canadian experience. *Environmental Impact Assessment Review* 27:319–42.

Okonta, Ike. 2006. Behind the mask. *Pambazuka News*. October 12. http://www.pambazuka.org/en/category/features/38005.

———. 2008. *When citizens revolt: Nigerian elites, big oil and the Ogoni struggle for self determination*. Trenton: Africa World Press.

Okonta, Ike, and Oronto Douglas. 2001. *Where vultures feast: Shell, human rights and oil in the Niger Delta*. San Francisco: Sierra Club Books.

Omeje, Kenneth. 2006. *High stakes and stakeholders: Oil conflict and security in Nigeria*. Burlington, Vt.: Ashgate.

O'Rourke, Dara, and Sarah Connolly. 2003. Just oil? The distribution of environmental and social impacts of oil production and consumption. *Annual Review of Environmental Resources* 28:587–616.

Osaghae, Eghosa. 1995. The Ogoni uprising: Oil politics, minority agitation and the future of the Nigerian state. *African Affairs* 94 (375): 325–44.

Peluso, Nancy, and Michael Watts. 2001. *Violent environments*. Ithaca, N.Y.: Cornell University Press.

Peterside, Sofiri, and Anna Zalik. 2008. The commodification of violence in the Niger Delta. In *Violence today: Actually existing barbarism, socialist register* 2009, ed. Leo Panitch and Colin Leys, 199–219. New York: Monthly Review Press.

Podur, Justin. 2008. Canada's latest political prisoners. *The Bullet, no 95.* March 31.

Schnarch, Brian. 2004. "Ownership, control, access, possession" or self determination applied to research. *Journal of Aboriginal Health* 1 (1): 33–45.

Shell, Royal Dutch. 2007. Annual Review and Summary Financial Statements. http://www-static.shell.com/static/investor/downloads/financial_information/reports/2007/2007_annual_review.pdf.

Soederberg, Susanne. 2003. The promotion of "Anglo-American" corporate governance in the South: Who benefits from the new international standard? *Third World Quarterly* 24 (1): 7–27.

Tilly, Charles. 1985. War making and state making as organized crime. In *Bringing the state back in*, ed. P. Evans, D. Reuschemeyer, and T. Skocpol, 167–91. New York: Cambridge University Press.

Treacy, Heather, Campbell Tara, and Jamie Dickson. 2007. The current state of law in Canada on Crown obligations to consult and accommodate aboriginal interests in resource development. *Alberta Law Review* 44 (3): 571–618.

Ukiwo, Ukoha. 2007. From "pirates" to "militants": A historical perspective on anti-state and anti-oil company mobilization among the Ijaw of Warri, Western Niger Delta. *African Affairs* 106 (425): 587–610.

Venis, Rodney. 2010. Letter from suspected Dawson Creek bomber promises hot summer. *Prince George Daily News.* April 15.

Vitalis, Robert. 2002. Black gold, white crude: An essay in American exceptionalism, hierarchy and hegemony in the Gulf. *Diplomatic History*: 185–213.

Vlavianos, Nickie. 2003. *Health, human rights and resource development in Alberta: Current and emerging law* (Paper no. 1). Calgary: Canadian Institute of Resources Law and the Alberta Civil Liberties Research Centre.

———. 2006. *Albertans' concerns about health impacts and oil and gas development: A summary.* Human Rights and Resource Development (Paper no. 3). Calgary: Canadian Institute of Resources Law and the Alberta Civil Liberties Research Centre.

———. 2007. Public participation and the disposition of oil and gas rights in Alberta. *Journal of Environmental Law and Practice* 17 (3): 205.

Watts, Michael. 2004. Resource curse? Governmentality, oil and power in the Niger Delta, Nigeria. *Geopolitics* 9 (1): 50–80.

West Coast Environmental Law. 2009. Review process for Enbridge Northern Gateway project subject to ongoing opposition and controversy. December 4. http://wcel.org/media-centre/media-releases/review-process-enbridge-northern-gateway-project-subject-ongoing-opposit.

Wheeler, David, Heike Fabig, and Richard Boehle. 2002. Paradoxes and dilemmas for stakeholder responsive firms in the extractive sector: Lessons from the case of Shell and the Ogoni. *Journal of Business Ethics* 39:297–318.

Willink, Henry, Gordon Hadow, Philip Mason, and J. B. Shearer. 1958. The Report of the commission appointed to enquire into the fears of minorities and the means of allaying them. London: Colonial Office Nigeria. July 30.

Woynillowicz, Dan, and Marlo Raynolds. 2005. *Oil sands fever: The environmental implications of Canada's oil sands rush. Drayton Valley.* Calgary: Pembina Institute.

Woynillowicz, Dan, and Chris Severson-Baker. 2006. Down to the last drop: The Athabasca River and oil sands. *Oil Sands Issue Paper 1.* Calgary: Pembina Institute.

Yergin, Daniel. 1992. *The prize: The epic quest for oil, money and power.* New York: Free Press Mexico.

Zalik, Anna. 2004. The peace of the graveyard: The voluntary principles on security and human rights in the Niger Delta. In *Global regulation: Managing crises after the Imperial turn,* ed. L. Assisi, K. Vanderpijl, and D. Wigan, 111–27. London: Palgrave.

———. 2008. Liquefied natural gas and fossil capitalism. *Monthly Review* (November): 41–52.

———. 2009. Zones of exclusion: Offshore extraction, the contestation of space, and physical displacement in the Nigerian Delta and the Mexican Gulf. *Antipode* 41 (3): 557–82.

———. 2010. Oil "futures": Shell's scenarios and the social constitution of the global oil market. *Geoforum* 41 (4): 553–64.

CHAPTER TWELVE

National Security versus Public Safety

Femicide, Drug Wars, and the Mexican State

MELISSA W. WRIGHT

In 1994, a handful of women and their corresponding civic organizations spear-headed a political movement against violence in northern Mexico. Their initial protests sought to call attention to the violence that stalked women in Ciudad Juárez, Chihuahua, the border city famous for its export-processing maquila-doras, young female workers, and nightclubs. The protestors came to call this violence "femicide" (*feminicidio*) to refer not only to the crimes but also to the impunity provided by the state and enjoyed by the criminals. Over the next ten years, the antifemicide protestors generated criticism of the Mexican govern-ment, at all levels, for its failure to provide public safety to the country's work-ing poor and their families along the border.

By the mid-2000s, this criticism had intensified along with the violence that now terrorizes much of the Mexican border and especially Ciudad Juárez. As the Chihuahua legislator Victor Quintana has recently written, Ciudad Juárez is experiencing a "violence and social deterioration . . . in its maximum intensity" (2010). Linked to what the government broadly calls "drug violence," more than 6,000 people have died violently in the city since 2008, and the reputation of "*feminicidio*" is now giving way to the infamy of "*juvenicidio*" (youth-killing), as young men kill young women and men at alarming rates on an almost daily basis.

This violence has spiraled in direct response to the federal government's declaration in 2006 of "war" against the cartels—the organizations that control the smuggling of drugs and people through the country and across its northern border. One year later, the government deployed several thousand troops to Ciudad Juárez and other cities as part of this war—a move that has only seen a rapid increase in the murder rate across the city, where violence in 2009 broke all records since the revolution decade over a century ago. Yet as the well-known Mexican historian, Victor Orozco (2009) declares, for some the violence indicates a failure of the state to provide for public safety, while the federal Mexican government points to this same violence as actual proof of its own success in winning the war and securing the nation against threat.[1] The meaning of this violence, in other words, has become a battleground for determining whether the Mexican state is failing or is excelling in its duties to protect Mexico and its people.

In this chapter, I examine how the social movement against femicide provides a lens for understanding what is at stake for Mexican democracy in the battle over the meaning of violence. Toward this end, I juxtapose the Mexican government's militarized reaction to the drug violence to its response to the violence against women that was publicized by the antifemicide activists. To do so, I employ a post-structuralist and feminist analysis of the biopolitical strategies deployed by the governing elites of Ciudad Juárez to hew the concepts of national security from public safety as they respond both to the femicide and to the drug violence. Central to this effort has been an attempt by governing officials to portray the antifemicide activists and their allies as dangerous *public women* who, along with their demands for public safety, represent threats to the state, to the economy, and to Mexican families. In other words, I argue that the government's discourse of public women has functioned as a biopolitical tactic for marginalizing the activists and their claims that the crisis of public safety exposes a crisis of the state. I then use this discourse analysis of "public women" and the meaning of violence as a frame for examining how governing officials seek to marginalize the victims of drug violence in a way that substantiates their claims that an increase in violence (and the correlated deterioration of public safety) indicates a strong state.

This battle over the interpretation of violence and its meaning for the Mexican state and its citizens demonstrates the importance of examining the significance of fear for the relationship linking governance and subjectivity (see Foucault 2009; Mbembe 2003). For, on the one hand, the Mexican government contends that a fear wrought by uncontrolled violence in a climate of impunity is actually indicative of a secure state that is committed to the modern and liberal principles of civilian rule, while, on the other, many activists and scholars who are concerned about civil and human rights argue that the Mexican state is failing in its obligations to protect public safety. In short, they reject the government's attempts to cleave public safety from national security, and they want a public outcry against such governance. This outcry is not new with the drug violence, and as I aim to show it has some roots in the antifemicide activism that made—in a previous decade—the public safety of women a pressing concern for national security.

FEMICIDE AND SAFETY

After a handful of women occupied the Ciudad Juárez mayor's office to protest violence against women, some dozen organizations from across the city formed the city's first women-run civic coalition, La Coordinadora de Organizaciones pro de la Mujer (the Coalition of Non-Profit Organizations for Women), henceforth referred to as "the Coalition." The Coalition leaders all had experience working with the city's working poor in a city that lacked adequate housing, education, health care, day care, domestic violence prevention, and public utilities. Through a series of press conferences and public protests, the Coalition articulated three clear demands: (1) that the municipal, state, and business leaders implement procedures for preventing further deaths and kidnappings; (2) that the state conduct competent investigations into the crimes already committed; and (3) that measures be taken to address the misogyny that justified violence against women and created impunity for criminals. In short, the Coalition turned the insecurity of women into a political problem for the first time in the city's history.

These demands proved to be quite radical for the Mexican state. For one thing, they demanded that the Mexican state value the safety of poor women in a country where women in poverty experience high rates of violence and insecurity. For another, they demanded that the state end the impunity for which it had always been famous as a place where wealth and political connection provided immunity from the law. In short, their demands for an end to the violence and for competent policing were demands for a state that would make the public safety of its poorest and most vulnerable citizens a priority for governance. And to make these demands they attracted domestic and international attention to the failed promises of the political and economic development of northern Mexico, where export-processing companies (called "*maquiladoras*") paid poverty wages to a migrant population that lived in areas with inadequate urban services. Throughout the 1980s and 1990s, as the North American Free Trade Agreement (NAFTA) was being negotiated, these neighborhoods emerged as zones of tremendous insecurity, rife with violence, drug use, and desperation. By the end of the 1990s, the antifemicide campaign brought these issues to an international arena and exposed the poverty wages of the *maquiladoras*, the failed promises of NAFTA, the injustices of neoliberalism, and the privatization schemes that led to the fabulous enriching of a few at the expense of most of the country. And domestic and international political and consumer organizations pressured the political leaders of Mexico as well as the leaders of international corporations doing business in the country to improve public safety.

Unsurprisingly, political and corporate elites responded by regarding the Coalition as a threat to their base of power, and they attacked the movement's credibility by claiming that the victims of this violence were not worth protecting. They made this argument by associating the victims with "public women" (*mujeres públicas*) as a way to diminish the idea of the victims' innocence. In Mexico, the term "public woman" suggests the negative interpretation of a prostitute (*la puta*) who represents the "fallen woman" whose internal contamination threatens her country and community (see Castillo 1999). Such women, according to this widespread and familiar discourse, create the very trouble that they experience; they are, in brief, responsible for the violence that they suffer even if it results in their death. As I have argued elsewhere, the political and corporate elites have used this argument as a way to say that the victims, as public women, are therefore responsible for the violence afflicting Ciudad Juárez (see Wright 2006).

The political and corporate elites used this discourse as a way to weaken public sympathy for the victims of violence and thereby dilute the public pressure on them to prioritize women's safety. In claiming that the victims were public women who actually caused the violence that ended their lives, they refer to a line of argument that in its extreme actually justifies the violence against women as a way to rid society of trouble (*Ibid.*). If public women are the source of the violence, then the fact that they are being killed by this violence is therefore a means for ending its root causes. Therefore, the insecurity experienced by the city was a direct product of these women who actually threatened their communities and their nation with their public presence. Hence, we find seeds of a logic that cleaves national security from the safety of public women.

With this discourse of the public woman, the elites attempted to use a biopolitical strategy for creating a marginal population of public women who did not represent the larger public. Such women, they contended, did not represent normal women and their normal families and therefore their insecurity did not indicate an insecurity on the part of "normal" Mexicans. Moreover, the meaning of "public woman" in Mexico's version of democracy is apparent when contrasted to the concept of "public man" ("*el hombre público*"), which is one way of saying "citizen."[2] And, as I have discussed elsewhere, this discourse of the public woman has indeed been a powerful tool used by the governing elite to disparage women who work outside the home, as well as women who try to participate in democratic process (Wright 2006). Such descriptions of women workers are not unique to this border city, as they have been repeated through industrial cities since at least the nineteenth century, and they have extended to encompass women who participate in the public sector more broadly. For while Ciudad Juárez is globally renowned for its feminization of the international division of labor and for the sex workers who have long offered services for men from both sides of the border, the city is also well-known within Mexico for women's galvanization of the democratization movement in the 1980s that eventually brought an end to the PRI's (Institutional Revolutionary Party) monopoly over the country's governance (Hernández Hernández 2002). As a result, in a city of women workers and women activists, the discourse that associates women with "social trouble" takes direct aim at women who participate in the city's politics and in its economy. Consequently, as the Coalition protested the rights of women to be safe in the city, they had also to contend with the public discourse and its meaning for public safety and poor women. Also, the Coalition was quick to fight back against this discourse and its implications for women's participation in politics and economy.

They did so by portraying the victims as daughters (*hijas*) and argued that a state that did not protect its own daughters, and provide for their safety, was failing in its obligations to provide national security. In this way, the activists portrayed the victims as daughters who were in public space for private reasons: they were supporting their families and fulfilling their familial obligations. Therefore, violence against these "daughters" was directed at the core of Mexican society: the patriarchal family and its obedient daughters. In this way, the activists fought against the biopolitics for marginalizing the victims through the discourse of their being public women, a strategy that left the discourse intact but that deflected its deployment against the murdered women and girls of Ciudad Juárez. A key part of this strategy was the activists' emphasis on the problem of impunity. For not only was the government not providing protection for the Mexican family as innocent daughters were being murdered, the government *was* providing protection for the criminals—for the very forces that threatened this family. Thus, in focusing on impunity, the activists effectively created a link between the lack of public safety and the failure of the state—the violence against women indicated a failure of state and its basic obligations to the Mexican people.

With this approach, the Coalition and other antifemicide activists made notable progress in forcing a recalcitrant political and corporate establishment to act on the idea that women's safety in the city was reflective of national security (see Pérez García 1999). The creation of federal and state agencies to investigate the crimes and to provide services for the victims' families was a first in the country. In addition, politicians running for statewide and federal office had to answer questions regarding their approach to the violence against women in northern Mexico, and corporate officials were under heightened international scrutiny as activists beyond Mexico pressured them to take action against the insecurity of the *maquiladora* labor force.

Faced with these setbacks, the elites changed their focus on the victims and turned their attack on the activists, and they did so by using the versatile discourse of "public women" as a weapon that can take aim at any woman who is active politically or economically in the public sphere (see, for instance, Guerrero and Minjares 2004). With this shift in strategy, the elites accused the activists of selling out the families and their victims to an international public that is always eager to hear stories of violence and sex along the border. In this way, according to the elites, the activists were damaging the reputation of Ciudad Juárez, of its families, and of the country for their own personal gain. This shift from the victims to the activists reinvigorated the application of the old public woman discourse and turned it into a powerful weapon in this battle over the meaning of violence for the Mexican state and its citizens. By the late 1990s, public sympathy for the antifemicide activists began to weaken, as headlines proliferated in the local newspapers regarding the activists and their opportunistic politics (see Piñon Balderrama 2003, A1). Under increased public scrutiny, the Coalition dissolved by 2000, and the governing elites appeared to be making strides once again toward cleaving the idea of women's safety from national security as they argued that the activists, rather than the violence, represented the real threats to society.

In response to the power of the public woman discourse to disparage the antifemicide movement, some of the activists retooled their strategies and created organizations around the idea of "mother activism." This move allowed the activists to present themselves, as they had the victims, as "private women" who were in the public sphere for private reasons (see Wright 2006). Again, while not confronting the binary within the public woman discourse directly, the mother-activist organizations attempted to deflect the application of the public woman discourse to their political movement. And, at the time of this writing, their efforts, along with the other antifemicide activists, align the idea of public safety to national security as they continue to battle the biopolitical weapon of the public woman discourse. Their challenges have only increased with the 2007 deployment of troops to Ciudad Juárez and the escalation of violence along with the government's claims that public safety and national security are inversely related.

IMPUNITY AND THE NARCO-STATE

The upsurge in violence and the intensification of its public viciousness is tied, according to numerous sources, to a restructuring of the country's lucrative drug trade. Currently, six cartels control the country's production, distribution, and smuggling of drugs throughout Mexico and across its international borders: The Sinaloa Cartel, the Beltran Leyva Cartel, *La Familia* (Michoacan Cartel), the Gulf Cartel with *Los Zetas* (former military personnel), the Juárez Cartel, and the Tijuana Cartel. Some cartels have formed arrangements to create larger organizational structures, such as the "Federation" along the Pacific coast, which then create blocs against the competitors. All together, the six cartels are estimated to monopolize more than 80 percent of the cocaine shipped into the United States, along with significant percentages of the trade in methamphetamine, heroin, and marijuana, among other illicit goods (such as gun running from the United States into Mexico). The cartels are large employers throughout the country with an estimated several hundred thousand in their employment, in addition to thousands more outside of the country, and their business generates billions in annual revenue for their organizations. The cartels have succeeded not only in turning Mexico into the main avenue for the supply of drugs to the world's largest consumer market for them in the United States, but they have also succeeded in turning Mexico into a significant consumer of illegal drugs, something that before the 1990s was not characteristic of the country. Such developments, as many scholars have shown, could not have been possible without the guarantee of impunity by the Mexican state (see Serrano and Toro 2002).

Impunity, as political theorist Monica Serrano has written, is a commodity provided by the state that produces and distributes it as a valuable good that circulates throughout the country's political economy. A key requirement for the production of impunity for the drug cartels is the zone of illegality that the state constructs around the production and consumption of drugs. By declaring specific drugs to be illegal substances, those substances are then located beyond the purview of the state and its regulatory mechanisms for overseeing production, distribution, employment, and environmental standards, as well as the taxation of revenues associated with the illegal drug trade. This zone of illegality is, in other words, essential to the creation of the arena in which the cartels operate beyond the reach of the state.

A second and related requirement of impunity then is the state's promise not to meddle in this arena and not impose the sanction of illegality on the activities and people who inhabit this arena. This requirement of impunity is directly tied to the idea of "corruption," since it entails agreements with state officials who, in exchange for some kind of bribe, do not treat the drug trade as an illegal activity within the state but instead as something that exists beyond the state (Serrano and Toro 2002; Andreas 2009). And for this reason, many scholars within and beyond Mexico have referred to its governing apparatus as a narco-state in recognition of its role in providing the necessary commodity of impunity within the political economy of the country's illegal drug trade.[3]

Many of these studies indicate how impunity is directly tied to the cycles of violence directly associated with this political economy. For as the state forfeits its role in regulating the economy and the politics of the drug trade's expansive activities and social networks, it forfeits also its role for regulating the terms of trade and means for mediating disputes that emerge throughout the business. Many of these disputes derive from the tensions of competition, such as over market share and access to resources, which are common features of capitalism. However, since the cartels are unregulated by the state, they create their own rules for dealing with these tensions, and the use of violence appears to be a preferred means of operation. As a result, the violent eruptions that have historically accompanied the restructuring of drug markets, including of internal production and distribution networks, also occur beyond the purview of the state when the state has created a context of impunity. In other words, not only will the state not meddle in the business of drug production, except to help it exist, it will also not meddle in the internal affairs of the drug business, including the use of violence to regulate its social networks and business agreements. This violence, like the drugs themselves, exists beyond the state.

The scholarship into such dynamics then lays the groundwork for understanding how the government's "blame the victim" strategy for dismissing the violence associated with the drug trade is, therefore, central to its ability to provide the coveted commodity of impunity. As the government, and those backing it, assert that the drug violence is directed internally within the drug trade, it not only ropes off the violence as beyond its domain but also those directly affected by it. Neither the violence nor the victims, according to such logic, are the responsibility of the state. For this reason, the state must continually claim that the victims are part of the drug trade, since other victims might reflect on the state's inability to protect its subjects. And this claim is what the government provides in its blaming of the victims.

However, as the numbers increase and clearly include people, such as young children, who are not involved in the drug trade, the government has had to nuance its approach to blaming the victims by shifting away from the victims themselves to focusing on the interpretation of the violence and what it means for the state. This approach is one that seeks to portray the escalating violence across the country as a positive development, reflective of the government's impact on the drug trade, as opposed to a negative indication of its ability to secure the state against cartel activities. Toward this end, political elites point to the violence as indicative of a desperation on the part of the cartels who are killing each other off in response to the disruptions created by the government's military initiative (see British Broadcasting Corporation [BBC] 2008; Wilkinson 2008).

As the federal Attorney General, Eduardo Medina, told the BBC in 2008, the violence was indicative of the success that the military presence had in various Mexican cities. "We still haven't reached the peak of violence," he said, when asked to explain why the violence had worsened during the army presence in key cities (British Broadcasting Corporation 2008). Repeating the president's position that the hair-raising numbers of violence were evidence of the success of the military approach, Medina, once again, returns to the blame-the-victim strategy since those who are killed within the violence are assumed to be engaged with the drug trade. By referring to the numbers rather than to the people who are killed, the government is able to lump all victims into a catchall category that, as it grows with every murder, reflects positively on its military strategy. As the Mayor of Ciudad Juárez explained to a *Los Angeles Times* journalist: "The drug war . . . will end only when both sides have ended up killing each other" (in Wilkinson 2008).

So, according to such logic, the higher the death rate, the more successful is the government's approach to securing the state. More death means more security. Hence, public safety is not only segregated from national security, it is inversely related as a dualistic binary. The government is now pitting national security against public safety. If we stick to its logic, and there was to be no violence right now in Ciudad Juárez—or in the rest of Mexico—in relation to the drug trade, then this would indicate a failure of the Mexican state to secure its territory.

This logic has also proven popular in the United States under the Obama administration, which has enthusiastically endorsed the Calderon approach to the violence as well as its interpretation of its significance. For instance, in a Voice of America report, the Director of National Intelligence, Dennis Blair, declares: "Mexico is in no danger of becoming a failed state. [Let me] repeat that. Mexico is in no danger of becoming a failed state. The violence we see now is the result of Mexico taking action against the drug cartels. So it is in fact the result of positive moves, which the Mexican government has taken to break the baneful influence that many of these cartels have had on many aspects of Mexican government and Mexican life" (Homeland Security Newswire 2009).

Within this echo of the Mexican government's own spin on the violence, the U.S. government is providing key backing for the Calderon administration against criticism that the violence indicates its failure to secure Mexico and its people. And this echo also includes the implied blame that is placed on the victims of this violence. For example, as David Johnson, the Deputy Assistant Secretary for Narcotics explained: "We firmly believe the Mexican government is taking the steps that it needs to take and is being quite courageous as it confronts a significant problem," and, "The Mexican people are paying a very high price because drug-fueled organized crime groups are killing each other," he said. "But I believe, and I think the Mexican government believes, that only through this sort of very effective, systematic work can they retake the streets" (Whitesides 2009). So without actually claiming that all of the victims of the violence are involved in the drug trade, the U.S. government is effectively backing up the Mexican government's claim that the victims of the violence are the result of internecine violence, of criminals killing criminals. Consequently, the high numbers, as the Ciudad Juárez mayor put it, indicate that there are fewer criminals on the street. This logic therefore endorses the ongoing impunity. As long as the victims are guilty of their own murders, the Mexican state is secured through the violence as its territory becomes cleansed, through the bloodshed, of criminal elements. When it's all said and done, only the good guys will be standing.

SOME PRELIMINARY REFLECTIONS

The public protests over the drug violence and the government's military strategy has not reached the proportions of the antifemicide protests in previous years. According to my conversations with activists and scholars who have been active in both struggles, the level of fear is so high right now in Ciudad Juárez that public events are hard to coordinate because people do not want to venture into the street for fear of being shot. These conversations find corroboration with news agencies that report people in Mexico are afraid. They are afraid of the cartels, and they are afraid of the soldiers. As one woman said to a reporter for National Public Radio when a group of soldiers pulled over her family car:

"These guys make your heart stop." The reporter describes her as watching the soldiers frisk her sons in "shock and disbelief" (NPR 2009).

What is the purpose of this fear? What does it indicate about the relationship of the state to its subjects in Mexico today? Does it, as the historian, Victor Orozco, has written, show that the state has failed? Does the state, as he puts it, have an obligation to protect public safety, such that if it fails to protect the public it fails to govern? Or, as other political theorists have argued, does the failure to protect public safety actually represent an attack on civilians that is central to contemporary strategies of modern governance? Is public fear and insecurity, therefore and in contrast to Orozco's assertions, consistent with the consolidation of national security? (Orozco 2009).

These issues and the tensions they describe are on the minds of many within Ciudad Juárez, where the ongoing femicides and the drug violence continue to afflict the city's population and to call into question the meaning and character of its government. That the protests against femicide have ebbed and that they have not led to further protests against the drug violence should not be taken as an indicator of apathy or of an acceptance of the government's contention that the increased violence, and its concomitant fear, signifies a stronger state. Rather, the lack of public action is indicative of a fear that many in Mexico are trying to understand and to manage as they negotiate their relationship to their government, to their economy, and to civil society. Unraveling this fear and what it means for Mexican democracy, citizenship, and governance is a pressing political challenge for anyone concerned about public safety and national security within the country and along its borders. Moreover, as Mexico's powerful northern neighbor is now building walls along the border and deploying its own troops to secure it against the mayhem that is plaguing Mexican border cities, the meaning of this violence, the role of the military in securing the state, and the significance for democracy across North America are all called into question.

NOTES

1. Orozco puts it bluntly in *La Jornada de Morelos* on June 21, 2009, "In any case, it appears that the Mexican State is failing, failing in its battle against crime and violence. It is failing in one of its principal duties, to safeguard the public peace and the security of its people. It is, well, a failed state." The original text by Orozco in Spanish is: "*En cualquier caso, todo hace aparecer que el estado mexicano está fracasando, fallando en la lucha*

contra el crimen y la violencia. Falta a uno de sus principales deberes, el de salvaguardar la paz pública y la seguridad de las personas. Es pues, un estado fallido." This English translation is mine.

2. I would like to thank Soccoro Tabuenca for pointing out this linguistic contrast to me.

3. References to a narco-state in Mexico abound in current media reports and in interviews with analysts of the drug violence. See, for example, *The Economist*, August 1, 2010.

REFERENCES

Andreas, P. 2009. *Border games: Policing the U.S.-Mexico divide.* Ithaca, N.Y.: Cornell University Press.

Andreas, P., and H. R. Friman, eds. 1999. *The illicit global economy and state power.* New York: Rowman and Littlefield.

British Broadcasting Corporation (BBC). 2008. Mexico drug gang killings surge, December 9. Accessed October 5, 2010. http://news.bbc.co.uk/2/hi/americas/7772771.stm.

Castillo, D. 1999. Border lives: Prostitute women in Tijuana. *Signs* 24 (2): 387–433.

Foucault, M. 2009. *Security, territory, population: Lectures at the Collège de France.* New York: Picador.

Guerrero, C., and G. Minjares. 2004. *Hacen Mito y Lucro de Los Femincidios, El Diario de Ciudad Juárez,* July 22. [Making myth and profit with the feminicides].

Hernández Hernández, E. P. 2002. *La participación política de las mujeres en el gobierno local: El caso de las regidoras de Juárez, 1980–2001.* [The political participation of women in local government: The case of the councilwomen of Ciudad Juárez, 1980–2001]. Tesis de Maestría en Ciencias Sociales. La Universidad Autónoma de Ciudad Juárez.

Homeland Security Newswire. 2009. U.S. intelligence chief: Mexico not on brink of collapse. March 27. Accessed October 5, 2010. http://homelandsecuritynewswire.com/us-intelligence-chief-mexico-not-brink-collapse.

Luhnow, David, and José de Cordoba. 2009. The perilous state of Mexico. *The Wall Street Journal.* February 21. Accessed October 5, 2010. http://online.wsj.com/article/SB123518102536038463.html.

Mbembe, Achille. 2003. Necropolitics. *Public Culture* 15:11–40. Trans. Libby Meintjes.

Nathan, Debbie. 2002. The missing elements. *Texas Observer.* August 30. www.womenontheborder.org/Articles/Senorita.

National Public Radio. 2009. No end in sight for Mexico's deadly drug war. *All Things Considered,* June 17. Accessed July 20, 2009. http://www.npr.org/templates/story/story.php?storyId=105515781.

Orozco, Víctor. 2009. *¿Un estado fallido, incautado?* [A failed state, captive state?] *La Jornada de Morelos,* June 10. http://www.lajornadamorelos.com/suplementos/correo-del-sur/76399?task=view.

Pérez García, Marta Estela. 1999. *La coordinadora en Pro de los Derechos de la Mujer. Política y procesos de cambio en el Municipio de Juárez* [The coalition for women's rights: Politics and processes of change in the municipality of Ciudad Juárez, 1994–1998] *(1994–1998)*. Unpublished Master's Thesis, La Universidad Autónoma de Ciudad Juárez.

Piñon Balderrama, David. 2003. *Lucran ONGs con muertas* [NGOs profiting with dead girls]. *El heraldo de Chihuahua*. February 23.

Quintana, Victor. 2010. *El Calentamiento Social* [Social warming]. *La Jornada*. May 14. Accessed August 5, 2010. http://www.jornada.unam.mx/2010/05/14/index.php?section=opinion&article=023a2pol.

Serrano, M., and M. C. Toro. 2002. From drug trafficking to transnational organized crime in Latin America. In *Transnational organized crime and international security*, ed. M. Berdal and M. Serrano, 155–82. New York: Lynne Rienner.

The Economist. 2009. Briefing: On the trail of the traffickers. August 1, 2010. http://www.economist.com/displaystory.cfm?story_id=E1_TPNPQTVS.

Whitesides, J. 2009. U.S. says Mexico makes progress against drug cartels. February 27. http://www.reuters.com/article/worldNews/idUSTRE51Q5FM20090227.

Wilkinson, T. 2008. Mexico under siege. *Los Angeles Times*. July 16. Accessed July 10, 2010. http://www.latimes.com/news/local/crime/la-fg-innocents16–2008jul16,0,7697776.story.

Wright, M. W. 2006. *Disposable women and other myths of global capitalism*. New York: Routledge.

CHAPTER THIRTEEN

Capitalizing Humanity

The Global Disposition of People and Things

PHENG CHEAH

In the wake of September 11, 2001, and the U.S. invasion of Iraq, there has been a spate of books by theory scholars in the humanities on pressingly "real" geopolitical issues of violence, terror, and war that seem to suggest a turn in theory today away from the so-called linguistic or representational turn begun by the reception of so-called French poststructuralism in the English-speaking world. Such a conclusion is misleading because these geopolitical phenomena are analyzed in exactly the same theoretical manner as before: they are acts, processes or institutionalized structures of repression or oppression that function by means of the discursive or representational construction of a hegemonic subject and its demonized or excluded other. One key reason for this insistence on the importance of representation in all spheres of human existence was the desire to escape the economic reductionism of Marxist theory, even that of Althusserian Marxism, which spoke of "the determination in the last instance by the economic" even if "the lonely hour of the 'last instance' never comes" (Althusser 1990, 113). Today, however, the shortcomings of this linguistic turn are becoming increasingly apparent in the general reluctance and abject inability of theory to engage with the complexity of economic processes that make up our contemporary era of globalization.

This inability surfaces most clearly in the dubious attempt to extend the analytical framework of exclusion through discursive construction to all spheres of human existence. But can we adequately understand contemporary capitalist accumulation in terms of processes of violent exclusion dressed up with the vocabulary of biopolitics? It is certainly an increasingly common view that there is a fundamental continuity between extreme forms of military violence in warfare and quotidian forms of exclusion and degradation in political, economic, and social life within the borders of nation-states. This continuity, it is suggested, renders indistinguishable two spheres that are conventionally regarded as analytically distinct because they function according to different principles—the sphere of domestic order that is governed by right and law, and the sphere of defensive or aggressive relations between sovereign states and relations between a sovereign state and dangerous flows across territorial borders that require emergency measures. In the latter, legality is merely a catachresis because sovereign states have absolute power and the ability to make the exceptional decision to decide on the exception and to suspend the law. But this power of the exceptional decision, it is implied, is now increasingly employed within domestic order itself and this is best seen in the militarization of many processes in daily life.

This argument, of course, alludes to Marx's account of primitive accumulation (*die ursprüngliche Akkumulation*, literally, original accumulation). "Normal" capitalist accumulation, Marx contended, is premised on the violent expropriation of the means of production from the worker so that he is forced to consent "freely" to sell his labor as a commodity.

> The capital-relation presupposes a complete separation between the workers and the ownership of the conditions for the actualization of their labour [*Verwirklichungsbedingungen der Arbeit*]. As soon as capitalist production stands on its own feet, it not only maintains this separation, but reproduces it on a constantly extending scale. The process, therefore, which creates the capital-relation can be nothing other than the process which divorces the worker from the ownership of the conditions of his own labour; it is a process which operates two transformations, whereby the social means of subsistence and production are turned into capital, and the immediate producers are turned into wage-labourers. So-called primitive accumulation, therefore, is nothing else than the historical process of divorcing the producer from the means of production. It appears as "primitive" because it forms the pre-history of capital, and of the mode of production that corresponds to capital. . . . To become a free seller of labour-power, who carries his commodity wherever he can find a market for it, he must further have escaped from the regime of the guilds, their rules of apprentices and journeymen, and their restrictive labour regulations. Hence the historical movement which changes the producers into wage-labourers appears, on the one hand, as their emancipation from serfdom and from the fetters of the guilds, and it is this aspect of the movement which alone exists for our bourgeois historians. But on the other hand, these newly freed men became sellers of themselves only after they

had been robbed of all their own means of production, and all the guarantees of existence afforded by the old feudal arrangements. And this history, the history of their expropriation, is written in the annals of mankind in letters of blood and fire. (Marx 1990, 874–75, translation modified; Marx 1962, 742–43)

The lawful ownership of property and the lawful process of accumulation that is recorded in bourgeois historical archives are therefore based on an unwritten history, a foundational violence. This violence is moreover continuously repeated ("reproduced") and extended to secure the infinite expansion of capital. Our contemporary bellicose condition, as exemplified by the war in Iraq and all its global effects, can be understood as a confirmation of this congenital link between "normal" accumulation and violence.[1] But this link is arguably most visible in the pervasive forms of violence and exclusion that occur in zones of capitalist accumulation located in the peripheries of the international division of labor. This argument can be easily given a discursive-constructionist spin via the suggestion that these exclusions are based on the construction of certain groups or peoples by means of representational norms as unworthy, wretched, and therefore eminently exploitable, dispensable, and sacrificeable.

Human rights have an important place in this understanding of the violence of accumulation. Insofar as the suspension of the law is seen as the perversion of a desired state of lawfulness, what is presupposed is a juridical subject, a subject of right that has been wrongfully dispossessed. Human rights are therefore a limit to these violent processes. Indeed, even Marxist discourse, which views legal rights as inherently alienating because they presuppose the property form and are generated under conditions of alienation, still presupposes a subject of right in the broader sense insofar as it points to a human being with fundamental needs and capacities that cannot be fulfilled because of the expropriation of the conditions of production.

Prima facie, Foucault's account of biopower can augment our understanding of the violence of accumulation by giving more thickness or specificity to our analysis of concrete cases of accumulation. In the first place, his analysis of carcereal society frequently relied on metaphors of military training and regimentation to characterize the operations of disciplinary power on individual bodies. But more importantly, he also repeatedly characterized the government of the population in terms of the deployment of apparatuses of security. Hence, in contemporary theoretical discourse, biopolitics is generally associated with repression and exclusion. This association finds its most forceful statement in Giorgio Agamben's influential *Homo Sacer*, where Foucault's concept of biopolitics is dehistoricized and elaborated in terms of a foundational exclusion of bare life (*zoe*) by Western politics.

> What is the relation between politics and life, if life presents itself as what is included by means of an exclusion? . . . [There is] an inclusive exclusion (an *exceptio*) of *zoe* in the *polis*, almost as if politics were the place in which life had to transform itself into good life and in which what had to be politicized were always already bare life. In Western politics, bare life has the peculiar privilege of being that whose exclusion founds the city of men. (Agamben 1998, 7)

The attraction of such schemas of exclusion for understanding the plight of displaced and trafficked workers of various kinds in the contemporary global capitalist system of accumulation lies in the fact that they appear to fall readily into the category of not-quite human or mere life, either as brute quantifiable labor power to be exploited and/or as valueless and meaningless beings that are the targets of various quotidian forms of victimization in the social reproductive process because they do not count as human. Their exclusion from their host societies inevitably involves the dispossession of their very humanity and the inalienable rights that express it. Consequently, these modes of exclusion are commonly regarded as a form of neo-slavery.

The putative opposition between human rights and biopolitics is pervasive in contemporary theory.[2] Generally speaking, the discourse of human rights includes every person as a member of humanity, whereas biopolitics is viewed as repressive and exclusionary even if it is seen as inclusionary in a highly qualified sense because it constitutes human subjects through subjectification. This common misreading of Foucault's account of biopower, which focuses solely on its disciplinary aspects, has been widely popularized by Judith Butler in her account of the prohibitive law of heteronormativity, which she has recently extended into an argument about which lives count as worthy of being mourned and which do not in current wars involving the secular West, the Middle East, and the Islamic world. The antithesis between human rights and biopolitics is, however, fundamentally foreign to Foucault's more concrete and even physicalist understanding of biopower, which emphasizes the inclusionary character of its fabrication of human life at the individual and collective level. For Foucault, the human being—something that is not just an ethical or philosophical ideal (humanity), but a concrete material being with determinate physical and intellectual capabilities—is precisely what biopower produces. Hence, in the first volume of *The History of Sexuality*, he noted the irony that the struggle against power in the nineteenth century took the form of an affirmation of the rights of man as a concrete living being.

[A]gainst this power that was still new in the nineteenth century, the forces that resisted relied for support on the very thing it invested, that is, on life and man as a living being . . . . [W]hat was demanded and what served as an objective was life, understood as the basic needs, man's concrete essence, the realization of his potential, a plenitude of the possible. . . . [W]hat we have seen has been a very real process of struggle; life as a political object was in a sense taken at face value and turned back against the system that was bent on controlling it. It was life more than the law that became the issue of political struggles, even if the latter were formulated through affirmations concerning rights. The "right" to life, to one's body, to health, to happiness, to the satisfaction of needs, and beyond all the oppressions or "alienations," the "right" to rediscover what one is and all that one can be, this "right"—which the classical juridical system was utterly incapable of comprehending—was the political response to all these new procedures of power which did not derive, either, from the traditional right of sovereignty. (Foucault 1980, 144–45)

The related passage from the last lecture of Society Must Be Defended (delivered March 17, 1976) distinguishes between the negative power of the sovereign to take life or to let live versus the positive power to make live or let die. "Sovereignty took life and let live. And now we have the emergence of a power that I would call the power of regularization, and it, in contrast, consists in making live and letting die" (Foucault 2003, 247). What is crucial about the power to make live and let die is the positive ability to further a second power, that of life. This is a concrete power that invests compared to which its converse, letting die, is merely a withholding of a prior ability of investment. This power to make live is fundamentally inclusionary. The political concern for the general well-being of the population arises from it and this welfare is the basis of many of the formalized rights of human individuals, especially those that are based on needs; that is, socioeconomic rights as opposed to civil and political liberties.

What are the key features of this power to make live in contemporary global capitalist practices of accumulation? Focusing on two different modalities of female labor, that of foreign domestic workers and sex workers, I argue that these practices of accumulation should not be understood in terms of exclusionary forms of power that lead to slavery but in terms of the inclusionary processes of modern governmentality and the concept of human capital that underwrites these processes. Put another way, if one accepts Marx's premise that workers are made by being dispossessed of the means of production, these workers are also made in the first instance by positive processes that shape a milieu that improve their status as resources, enhance their capacities, and form their will and interests, rather than by ideological will-formation that mystifies the conditions of their exploitation. I then suggest that the sacrificial/exclusionary effects of these governmental practices that are in principle aimed at incorporation and inclusion occur as a result of conflicts between different regimes of governmentality in a transnational setting. How are we then to reconceptualize human rights as something that is generated by biopolitical processes rather than being a limit to them?

HUMAN CAPITAL AND THE BIOPOLITICS OF GLOBAL ECONOMIC GROWTH

The governmental tactics behind the exportation of foreign domestic workers is more obvious than those shaping the disposition of women for sex work. Since the last three decades of the twentieth century, international bodies concerned with global economic development and developing nation-states in the South have promoted labor migration as an indispensable component of economic growth and the reduction of income disparity on a global scale. Two main reasons are given: providing fruitful employment where none is to be had in a home country or positions where higher wages can be earned, and the enhancement of the skills and capabilities of the migrant worker by on-the-job training in these overseas positions or other vocational training. These two phenomena are seen to increase the resources of the home country through the encouragement of savings and foreign exchange remittances and their conversion into fixed capital and the enhancement of the worker's abilities so that she can gain better employment or initiate small business enterprises on her repatriation. These themes were prevalent in fieldwork that I conducted with various embassies of labor-exporting countries in Singapore.

The labor attaché at the Philippine Embassy emphasized the importance of saving money:

> She has to save her money. You come here to earn money and to learn new experiences. You should appreciate the experience. I always tell the worker: you came here to earn and to save money. A poor person has to work doubly hard. If you see a rich person working hard, you have to work twice as hard because you are poor. I don't want people to be wasting their resources.[3]

Her counterpart in the Sri Lankan High Commission emphasized the importance of educational training:

> The training program aims at co-ordinating skills training, religious, cultural and social activities with NGOs and religious organizations, who are involved. They

organize skills and development training programs, English language both basic and advanced, and computer skills, hairdressing, dressmaking, cookery, etc. These are six-month courses and award certificates. Some girls have completed English and are now enrolled in computing. Once they get back to their country, they can start something on their own. They make use of their leave time in this respect.[4]

He added that cultivating the good habits of saving money in foreign domestic workers was a crucial part of this education and figured this training as a form of inoculation or cure of various kinds of "diseases" that are apparently congenital to the occupation of being a foreign domestic worker.

> The maids get three diseases. First, they forget the objective of coming here, that they are here to earn money for the betterment of their lives. Second, they get a telephone disease. In Sri Lanka, there are very few telephone facilities in the villages. The maids make local calls here to their friends and boyfriends and also international calls back to Sri Lanka. They get caught by their employer and are asked to pay for these phone calls. Third, they catch the boyfriend disease. In my counseling, I tell them to set apart $100 a month to send back home. This is the targeted amount that they should save. It is equivalent to 100,000 rupees. This should be put in a fixed deposit and be viewed as a pension. You can get a 12 percent interest on this investment. You can also get an overdraft of 90,000 rupees for which you are charged 15 percent interest. I advise them to use this 190,000 rupees to invest in a house or other property.[5]

Labor exportation is therefore deemed to have a fundamental and even irreducible pedagogical function. It leads, in the best of situations, to the remaking of the individual minds of the domestic workers that will lead in turn to the remaking of their bodily habits. At the collective or aggregative level, it brings about the gradual enhancement of the forces of the population. Immediately, these new habits will lead to an increase in the remittance of savings and this capital will later be augmented by the new skills that are acquired by the maid while abroad and her new will to start a small business or form of self-employment.

This justification of labor exportation as a means of augmenting national resources and a nation's ability to tend to the welfare of its population is inconceivable without the neoliberal Chicago School economists' concept of human capital. The concept was already articulated by Adam Smith, who described the acquired skills and abilities of a member of society as a form of fixed capital of society that is actualized or embodied in a person. The acquisition of such skills requires time and expense but these costs are repaid with greater profit; that is, higher income and greater productivity:

> Fourthly, of the acquired and useful abilities of all the inhabitants or members of the society. The acquisition of such talents, by the maintenance of the acquirer during his education, study, or apprenticeship, always costs a real expence, which is a capital fixed and realized, as it were, in his person. Those talents, as they make a part of his fortune, so do they likewise of that of the society to which he belongs. (Smith 1976, Book 2, 298)

But Smith risked dehumanizing the worker because he compared the benefits of such skills to the greater efficiency that technology and machines bring to productivity: "The improved dexterity of a workman may be considered in the same light as a machine or instrument of trade which facilitates and abridges labour, and which, though it costs a certain expence, repays that expence with a profit" (Smith 1976, Book 2, 298). The neoliberal concept of human capital goes a step further. Drawing on the humanist idea of *Bildung* or self-formation/self-cultivation, it defines the human being as the being capable of the self-reflexive activity of investing in himself in order to productively enhance himself as a means of production for his own benefit. Indeed, this ability of self-investment is a crucial condition for the optimal utilization of technology and machines.

The concept of human capital is marked by three important motifs. First, although its economic capabilities are "a produced means of production" it is emphatically not a mere machine since it is capable of epigenesis or self-production with regard to these capabilities. Second, this kind of self-investment transcends mere labor. Because it leads to greater profit and accumulation, it is akin to the investment in other forms of capital. Hence, it turns every worker into an entrepreneur or capitalist who capitalizes on his own abilities. In Theodore Schultz's words, "laborers have become capitalists not from a diffusion of the ownership of corporation stocks . . . but from the acquisition of knowledge and skill that have economic value. This knowledge and skill are in great part the product of investment and, combined with other human investment, predominantly account for the productive superiority of the technically advanced countries" (Schultz 1961, 3). Third, this kind of value-adding is in principle almost limitless because it is a form of self-capitalization that every person is capable of performing. At the level of the population, it can also have cumulative effects across generations. Hence, in terms of society as a whole, it is the highest form of value-adding and the key to exponential economic growth. Indeed, the abundance of human capital in the West is taken as the main explanation of the productive superiority of technologically advanced Western countries and the backwardness of less developed countries, which lack the human capital to absorb and utilize the stock of nonhuman capital. As Schultz puts it:

> The knowledge and skills required to take on and use efficiently the superior techniques of production, the most valuable resource that we could make available to them, is in very short supply in these underdeveloped countries.... It simply is not possible to have the fruits of a modern agriculture and the abundance of modern industry without making large investments in human beings. Truly, the most distinctive feature of our economic system is the growth in human capital. Without it there would be only hard, manual work and poverty except for those who have income from property. (Schultz 1961, 16)

Given the common association of neoliberalism with hyper-exploitation, what is especially striking about the concept of human capital is the principle of universal inclusiveness that guides its themes. For in principle, every human being is capable of self-investment and self-capitalization and this ability enables us to transcend our limitations through self-uplifting and self-improvement. Hence, notwithstanding its emphasis on utility, the concept of human capital exhibits a peculiar continuity with Kantian ethics. It is important to remember here that the Kantian proscription of instrumentalizing human beings is not an outright or complete prohibition. Instead, Kant uses the fact that human beings are ends in themselves because they are rational beings that can set their own ends as a principle to check or contain the rampant pragmatic treatment of fellow human beings as means. Hence, the categorical imperative is expressed as a double qualification to the inevitability of using people:

> Now I say that the human being and in general every rational being *exists* as an end in itself, *not merely as a means* to be used by this or that will at its discretion [*als Zweck an sich selbst, nicht bloß als Mittel zum beliebigen Gebrauche für diesen oder jenen Willen*]; instead he must in all his actions, whether directed to himself or also to other rational beings, always be regarded *at the same time as an end* [*jederzeit zugleich als Zweck betrachtet werden*]. (Kant 1996a, 79; Kant 1996b, 59–60)

> So act that you use humanity, whether in your own person or in the person of any other, always at the same time as an end, never merely as a means. [*Handle so, daß du die Menschheit, sowohl in deiner Person, als in der Person eines jeden andern, jederzeit zugleich als Zweck, niemals bloß als Mittel brauchest*]. (Kant 1996a, 80; Kant 1996b, 61)

You can use humanity or treat a human being as a means. But if you treat a human being at the very same time as an end and not only as a means, then the excesses of using people can be limited. Now, you ought to treat human beings in this way because you are yourself a human being and view yourself as an end. As an objective principle or law, this imperative, injunction, or "ought" leads to the establishment of a reciprocal system of means and ends (what Kant called a kingdom of ends) such that each member of this system is at the same time a means and an end. Only within such a reciprocal system can the instrumentalization of human beings be contained (Kant 1996a, 83; Kant 1996b, 66).

The concept of human capital likewise limits instrumentality through a similar principle of the autotelic nature of human beings. The activity of investing in oneself is not a form of instrumentalization but precisely an expression of freedom and self-making, of humanity's essence as an end in itself (where one exists only for the sake of oneself) because it is a way of enhancing one's welfare by increasing one's capabilities. As Schultz puts it, "no less a person than J. S. Mill at one time insisted that the people of a country should not be looked upon as wealth because wealth existed only for the sake of people. But Mill surely was wrong; there is nothing in the concept of human wealth contrary to his idea that it exists only for the advantage of people. By investing in themselves, people can enlarge the range of choice available to them. It is one way free men can enhance their welfare" (Schultz 1961, 2).

The emphasis of neoliberal economics undoubtedly remains too much on individual choice instead of the establishment of a systematic unity of means and ends. But we can clearly see that the formation of a concrete instead of a merely ideal system of means and ends is the central aim of what Foucault called government.

> Government is defined . . . as a right way of arranging (*disposer*) things in order to lead (*conduire*) them . . . to a "suitable end," an end suitable for each of the things to be governed. This implies, first of all, a plurality of specific ends. For example, the government will have to ensure that the greatest possible amount of wealth is produced, that the people are provided with sufficient means of subsistence, and that the population can increase. So, the objective of government will be a series of specific finalities. And one will arrange (*disposer*) things to achieve these different ends. . . . [I]t is not a matter of imposing a law on men, but of the disposition of things . . . [of] arranging things so that this or that end may be achieved through a certain number of means. . . . Whereas the end of sovereignty is internal to itself and gets its instruments from itself in the form of law, the end of government is internal to the things it directs (*diriger*); it is to be sought in the

perfection, maximization, or intensification of the processes it directs, and the instruments of government will become diverse tactics rather than laws. (Foucault 2007, 99)

Indeed, we can say that the human being as an end in itself in reciprocal relations with other human beings within an ideal system of ends (Kant's formulation) is a product-effect of concrete practices of government insofar as these practices create the concrete setting that endow the human being with its capacity for autonomy. Government, in Foucault's view, is precisely the establishment and care of a "complex of men and things," the disposition or arrangement of "men in their relationships, bonds, and complex involvements with things like wealth, resources, means of subsistence" in order to achieve specific ends that are suitable to what is governed (Foucault 2007, 96). Kant's definition of humanity, which is the tacit conceptual basis of much human rights discourse, would then be a product or reflection at the level of intellectual figuration of these concrete practices of government. Or as Foucault puts it, "man, as he is thought and defined by the so-called human sciences of the nineteenth century, and as he is reflected in nineteenth century humanism, is nothing other than a figure of population. . . . Man is to population what the subject of right was to the sovereign" (Foucault 2007, 79).

The concept of human capital underwriting the deployment of various forms of female labor in contemporary globalization is an elaboration of these practices of government. This means that biopolitics is not in the first instance repressive. It does not consist of a set of artificial laws that are imposed on various types of workers from the outside but tactics that tap into and are continuous with the ends of each person, ends that these tactics seek to fulfill. The common understanding of biopower, which is based on discipline, views the functioning of disciplinary norms as micro-laws that are internalized and incorporated through processes of repetition. The isomorphism between disciplinary processes and militarization lies in the fact that the former can be described as a process of regimentation that individualizes. It breaks up an otherwise unmanageable mass or multiplicity into individuals that can be monitored and policed. In contradistinction, Foucault emphasizes that mechanisms of security (the objective of governmentality) are fundamentally different from disciplinary mechanisms in various respects.

First, whereas discipline is exercised over the bodies of individuals, security is exercised over an entire population as a collective being. Second, whereas discipline takes as its premise an ideal or imaginary space—one that is empty or to be emptied and artificial and that will be completely constructed according to a perfect model, security is concerned with a milieu—a space containing material or natural givens that is structurally uncertain because it is open to a series of possible events. Its aim is to maximize the positive elements and to minimize risk and inconvenience in this space, to control or manage an open series through an estimate of probabilities (Foucault 2007, 19–20).

Third, whereas discipline is a radical process of artificial construction, security involves a form of structural causality that works with nature and, hence, is targeted at something that is both natural or biological and artificial, namely, the population. The milieu that security tries to organize or plan is not a pre-formed ideational construction but a set of natural and artificial givens, as these give rise in their combination to effects that have an impact on all who live in this milieu. "The milieu is a set of natural givens—rivers, marshes, hills—and a set of artificial givens—an agglomeration of individuals, of houses, etc. The milieu is a certain number of combined, overall effects bearing on all who live in it. It is an element in which a circular link is produced between effects and causes, since an effect from one point of view will be a cause from another" (Foucault 2007, 21). Hence, apparatuses of security do not affect individuals as juridical subjects capable of voluntary actions (sovereignty), nor as bodies capable of required performances (discipline). Its target is the population: "a multiplicity of individuals who are and fundamentally and essentially only exist biologically bound to the materiality within which they live" (Foucault 2007, 21). Security is therefore concerned with biological lives that are fundamentally artificial because they are natural beings that can only live in an artificial environment. It is this environment or milieu that is the target of political intervention and the course of things have been altered to a point that nature itself has been made into another milieu for human existence. We can understand this as a radically materialist account of second nature, not in the conventional sense of second nature as a spiritual or cultural world generated through spiritual or moral action, but a material remaking of nature at the point where it intersects with the human species since human existence is necessarily physical as well as moral. It is in this sense that biopolitics also shapes the material conditions for the exercise of moral action.

Fourth, while both discipline and security involve norms, there is a fundamental difference in how norms operate. Discipline begins with a model of what is normal and seeks to bring about conformity. "Disciplinary normalization consists first of all in positing a model, an optimal model that is constructed in terms of a certain result, and the operation of disciplinary normalization consists in trying to get people, movements, and actions to conform to this model, the normal being precisely that which can conform to this norm, and the abnormal that which is incapable of conforming to the norm" (Foucault 2007, 57). It is more precisely a process of normation. Security, on the other hand, begins with a distinction between what is normal and what is abnormal in a concrete field, plots different curves of normality, and establishes an interplay between these different distributions of normality so as to generate a norm through this interplay of the distributions by bringing what is unfavorable in line with the favorable (Foucault 2007, 63). The norm is therefore an effect of these mechanisms instead of their intentional starting point.

We can see from this that apparatuses of security in the Foucauldian sense are quite different from the more conventional understanding of security as that which is concerned with the protection of the state or the safety and lives of its members from a host of external or internal threats or risks. The conventional understanding of security would be part of what Foucault calls sovereignty and discipline. For him, security is about the productive making of the population through the shaping of a milieu within which the very physical or biological well-being of the population and, therefore, their material needs and interests, can be formed and altered. What is important for present purposes is that unlike disciplinary power, which involves a direct causality or transitive action on bodies, governmentality involves acting on a range of factors and elements that are remote from the population itself and its immediate behavior but that have a fundamental impact on shaping the population: for instance, currency flows, imports and exports, and so forth. More importantly, governmental action works not by repressing, mystifying, or manipulating what is spontaneous or natural in individual members of the population—namely, desire—but by encouraging through regulation the play of these desires, the free pursuit of individual interests, in order to achieve the general interest of the population. As Foucault puts it:

> In his desire the individual may well be deceived regarding his personal interest, but there is something that does not deceive, which is that the spontaneous, or at any rate both spontaneous and regulated play of desire will in fact allow the production of an interest, of something favorable for the population. The production of the collective interest through the play of desire is what distinguishes both the naturalness of population and the possible artificiality of the means one adopts to manage it. (Foucault 2007, 73)

Governmental technologies are therefore a form of artifice that manages or regulates natural processes by being conjoined to them or articulated together with them instead of negating or constraining them. They shape the population's interest not by mystification or deception but by positive investment in the creation of a milieu and the encouragement of individual interests. Under liberal governmentality as distinguished from reason of state, this encouragement of interests is even a complete letting-be of the free play of interests. Government must encourage different interests and work with their interplay because "it is through interests that government can get a hold on everything that exists for it in the form of individuals, actions, words, wealth, resources, property, rights, and so forth" (Foucault 2008, 45). This means that freedom becomes an indispensable component to governmentality and its aim of increasing the forces of the state. Freedom here does not merely refer to the spontaneity of the autonomous moral will, to concrete moral action within the substrate of ethical life, or to the right of individuals in legitimate opposition to power. It is the spontaneity of the internal mechanics of economic processes as they bear on and shape individual and collective interests. This spontaneity has become a principle of good government because it is only by allowing the free play of interests that government can exert its hold over and regulate the desires of people and optimize their forces. In Foucault's view, liberalism's primary significance is that it is a technology for producing and organizing the capacity for free behavior by establishing an equilibrium between the natural pursuit of individual interests and the collective interest instead of a political ideology that promotes the juridical freedom of the individual and his basic natural rights as teleological goods (Foucault 2008, 63–64). Government and its objectives of security are therefore clearly distinct from disciplinary power.

I have dwelled at some length on Foucault's account of security and the encouragement of individual interests under it and the clear distinction of security from the kind of biopower that characterizes the police state or carcereal disciplinary society (Foucault 2007, 353–54) because in my view, these are the kinds of mechanisms that are operative in the forming of female subjects of transnational labor in the current conjuncture of global capitalist accumulation. Foucault's account of interest is uncannily close to how Pasuk Phongpaichit has characterized the place of sex work in the Thai economy in her seminal study of young rural women who migrate to Bangkok as sex-workers. The expansion of prostitution in Thailand is closely tied to the growth of international tourism as a major source of foreign exchange. As is well-known, sex tourism in the region has its historical roots in the influx of foreign military personnel participating in the wars in Asia (Korea and Vietnam). Its contemporary manifestation is part of the biopolitics of Thai economic development. The rapid industrialization of Bangkok at the expense of rural regions such as North Thailand leads to the migration of young girls to the city in search of work for the alleviation of rural poverty. This increases the supply of potential sex workers since failure to find adequate income from non-sex work such as factory or service work can lead girls to enter into sex work.[6] The confluence of this with the promotion of Thailand as a destination for international (sex) tourism opens up avenues for transnational migration for sex work, trafficked or consensual.[7] But as Phong-paichit has argued, these women are not hapless victims who are blind to their true interests and needs. They see themselves as full earning members of the household and are considered so by others because their remittances help to bolster the family's agrarian economy. They do not seek to escape family life but are helping to support the family and to improve its position in village society. "It is not some sort of helpless dependent status which ends them up in the business of selling their bodies. Rather it is the responsibilities which they themselves feel" (Phongpaichit 1982, 68).

Indeed, family members often serve as agents for recruitment and some families and villages have developed a vested interest in the business. But unknown to them, the material interests and needs of these various actors are shaped by governmental manipulation. "The migration is an intrinsic part of Thailand's economic orientation. Thailand's strategy depends internationally on accepting a dependent and vulnerable role in the world economy. . . . A business which sets girls out of the poorer parts of the countryside and sells their services to the urban earner and to the foreign visitor is merely the mirror image of this hierarchy of dependence" (Phongpaichit 1982, 74–75). At the same time, however, some kinds of transnational sex workers fit perfectly into the vocabulary of human capital. They ironically embody many of the traits and characteristics of the savvy and flexible migrant entrepreneur in their brave self-determination to migrate and capitalize on their bodies to make money so that they can have a better future.

Similarly, in the case of foreign domestic workers, it can be argued that what drives their temporary emigration is not only their ideological constitution as good wives, daughters, mothers, or sisters by patriarchal ideology, but more crucially, the crafting of their interests as subjects of needs by biopower, just as the ground for the importation of foreign workers is prepared by the crafting of their employers by similar governmental technologies. Their oppression/subjectification occurs not by silencing them, but by incorporating their very needs and interests into the fabric of global capitalism. Ideology undoubtedly plays a role in making the wills of these women migrants. But they also go with the firm desire to improve their lives because this is how their needs and interests have been shaped by governmental technologies.

This biopolitical shaping of needs and interests applies not only to low value-adding occupations but to the high value-adding ones of the global financial and new information economy. The best example of the latter is the argument about the urgency of attracting desirable foreign workers to develop a creative class in the race to ascend the hierarchy of global cities. These types of transnational labor represent the two poles of the spectrum of the global biopolitical field of human capital. Global cities can only be sustained by importing lower-end migrant labor to service those at the higher end. The coordination of these two poles of migrant labor clearly indicates that biopolitics works by productive incorporation rather than prohibition, exclusion, and repression through force or ideology even if the forms of incorporation can be coercive. We have to understand incorporation in two senses: first, the bodily aptitudes and needs and interests of these workers are crafted by biopolitical technologies. Second, they are crafted in such a way that they belong to the global capitalist system of means and ends in their very constitution as subjects.

What is crucial for present purposes is that human rights are not the ethical-juridical limit to biopolitics but part of its field. For despite their exploitative and oppressive effects, these biopolitical tactics are continuous with the understanding of humanity as an end-in-itself since biopolitics is precisely the development of concrete capacities and abilities; this time not through the training or dressage of individual bodies but by affecting the physical environment that bears directly on the needs and interests of the population. The biopolitical regulation of various forms of migrant female labor by their countries of origin and sometimes their host countries involves the enhancement of their capabilities and their subjective cultivation or humanization through religious or cultural practices. The idea of human rights is an idealization of this dynamic of investing in and augmenting of the concrete abilities of human beings. It is the thematic codification of the concrete reality produced by these processes of investment. A claim to have a human right respected or to stop a human right from being violated is essentially a demand to be invested more and not less by technologies of power. Such subjects want more and not less governmentality in their lives.

This point was made patently clear to me in a comment by the labor attaché of the Philippine embassy in Singapore. Filipino foreign domestic workers can escape state monitoring if they do not go through an accredited recruitment agency and sign the contract approved by the Philippines state. It leaves them without protection, but they have fewer hurdles to clear in obtaining employment overseas. But when they encounter problems with their employers, what they seek is precisely more government. "In Manila, they avoided the government, they didn't mind their government," the labor attaché said. "Sometimes, it is too late for the worker to realize that they made the wrong decision. Sometimes, they would disregard their government, but when they have problems, they come to the government. They say they don't need the government, but when they have problems, they will come. Our position is that the government will help you in the best way it can."[8] Indeed, one might even say that power is a silently affirmative process of physical investment that forms these human subjects as beings with needs that they then regard as being worthy of recognition. In the reflective gesture of demanding recognition, the subject willingly says "yes" to and affirms this initial investment. It asks to be invested with more power because this can improve its life. The difference between political liberalism and strong government is only a difference of degree, a difference in terms of how best to enhance capability, which is the task of governmentality. This is why Foucault views civil society, the spontaneity of which has conventionally been understood in terms of a sphere that has autonomy from government or state imperatives, as the correlate of the political technology of liberalism by which governmentality limits itself in order to respect the specificity of economic processes (Foucault 2007, 248, 349–50, 355; and Foucault 2008, 295–308). What is important for present purposes is that human rights, which are concretely generated by these biopolitical technologies, engulf us within governmentality in a way that contradicts their purported basis in natural law.

DEGREES OF INCLUSION, EFFECTS OF EXCLUSION

I am not, of course, suggesting that female migrant workers such as foreign domestic workers and sex workers are not subjected to repressive and oppressive forms of power and policing in their countries of destination or at the hands of parties within their countries of origin that participate in their commodification and export. My point, however, is that these forms of power are only applied subsequently, after they have been formed as consensual subjects of migrant labor by technologies of government. Although the essential biopolitical dynamic is one of inclusion and incorporation, biopolitics nevertheless has exclusionary effects when we are dealing with the deployment of migrant workers in contemporary globalization. Here, one touches upon a limitation of Foucault's formulation of biopower. His use of the concept to explain the rise of industrial capitalism in Europe rightly emphasized the inclusionary and productive character of the constitution of individual bodies and the care of the population. But the exercise of biopolitics tacitly remained within the framework of the nation-state even though its technologies and tactics did not necessarily emanate from the state and were not tethered to it (the thesis of the governmentalization of the state). In contemporary global capitalism, however, where we are concerned with transitory migrant workers who are not part of the permanent populations of host countries, and where the tension between the biopolitical projects of different countries attempting to climb up the economic hierarchy of the global capitalist system becomes full blown, the exclusionary effects of biopower are thrown into sharp relief.

With the deindustrialization of capital accumulation, there arises a new international division of labor where decomposed industrial production processes that are labor intensive are outsourced to knowledge- and resource-poor developing countries with lower labor costs through foreign direct investment and international subcontracting while research and development and technical and managerial control remain in the knowledge- and resource-rich North. Consequently, whereas the biopolitical project of developing human capital is accompanied by the demand for less government and the rise of neoliberalism in the North, it becomes aporetic for poorer postcolonial states desperately trying to climb up the new international division of labor. In principle, they wish to cultivate their populations and enhance their bodily aptitudes. But since attracting foreign capital is the best way to increase a country's forces, they also have to suspend care for some parts of their population and, indeed, have to sacrifice their welfare. In the name of development, there is greater governmental control where states acquiesce to harsh labor conditions for local factory workers and actively promote the exportation of migrant workers who are vulnerable to abuse in host countries because they are not part of the population there.

Practices of exclusion such as the exploitation of foreign workers and their disciplinary policing and the violation of basic rights of foreign workers—legal and clandestine, consensual and trafficked—should be understood as the consequence of the blockage of a thorough globalization of liberal governmentality by the international division of labor. Yet even here, it might be more appropriate to speak of different degrees of inclusion rather than outright exclusion given the importance of these migrant workers to the reproduction of social life in their host countries. At the very least, there must be sufficient governmentality so as not to deter migrant workers from coming even if this governmentality has to be limited since they cannot become a permanent part of the population. Hence, in Singapore, the Ministry of Manpower has stressed the importance of recognizing the positive contributions of foreign workers to Singapore society. As an official observed in an interview:

These people—foreign domestic workers—have actually given our females the opportunity to go out and work, and contribute to the economy. They have helped out in childcare and care of the elderly, especially we are also an aging population. We recognize that contribution, so we have every year, the best domestic worker competition, the best employer. And there are days we show appreciation to foreign workers. There is a day called "Make a difference" day to recognize the positive contribution.

Some of them end up teaching the children. Quite a lot of our domestic workers are fairly well educated, so they end up also playing tutor to the young kids. Quite a lot of them are also active in voluntary work, church activities. So in that sense, it has made us more cosmopolitan. The direct thing is that we learn to appreciate the culture and values of our neighbors better. It is sad that they have to send their domestic workers out to work for us. . . . The direct contact with us helps us become more regional in our thinking. At least we understand why Filipinos behave a certain way—they are more open. When an Indonesian says "yes," what it actually implies and so on—the cultural differences between the different nationalities. I think that it opens our eyes a bit more to them. In that regard, it has helped us be more understanding to our neighbors, socially and culturally.[9]

Such statements may indeed be a form of cosmetic cover-up of the exploitation of foreign labor. But it may also be the case that the very presence of foreign domestic workers is turned into a quasi-physical factor, a milieu or environment for the shaping of the Singaporean population so that they will be more sensitive and cosmopolitan in relations with other cultures and this greater sensitivity will have some impact on foreign relations in the long run.

The protection of the rights of migrant workers should likewise be understood as a successful exercise of biopolitics by labor-sending countries, sometimes with the hard-won cooperation of labor-receiving countries who have built in various concessions to migrant workers' rights as part of their own governmentality. The labor attaché of the Philippine embassy in Singapore mentions examples of such success:

In the two years that I have been here, I have seen Singaporeans express their appreciation. They have organized concerts for the workers, and they have been accommodating towards our requests. The Bayanihan Center is proof of the cooperation between the Philippines and Singapore governments. Because they realize that the objective of our government is that when the time comes, the maids need to return to the Philippines and need to be integrated into society there, so we want to prepare them for that.[10]

Here, we see cooperation between states that comes about because of overlapping interests at the state level. They in turn shape the interests of individual employers in such a way that they will overlap with the interests of the foreign domestic workers so that the latter's hard work will be reciprocated by greater recognition.

However, these forms of inclusion are at best partial since in the Singapore case, foreign domestic workers cannot become a permanent part of the population of the labor-receiving country. There is also a limit to the governmental tactics of labor-sending countries since they are afraid of losing their market share in labor exportation. The persistence of exclusion effects caused by the international division of labor raises a larger philosophical question concerning the nature of instrumentality itself and whether we can ever successfully control it. The containment of the instrumentalization of human beings by human rights discourse and, more generally, by biopolitics, is essentially based on a principle of reciprocity—the establishment of a system of means and ends where each member is both a means and an end. This principle is implied not only in the concept of human capital but also in the more progressive idea of human development most famously articulated by Amartya Sen. Both approaches involve critiques of utilitarianism and stress the importance of enhancing capabilities. The difference between them lies only in the fact that whereas the idea of human capital focuses only on economic capabilities, the theory of human development emphasizes the importance of *human* capabilities that are not only economic. The containment of instrumentality is necessarily partial in both cases. Self-development (development for one's own sake or the sake of humanity and not for the sake of something else) and the human autonomy it implies does not prohibit instrumentality completely since it gives free rein to humans to instrumentalize everything else that is not "a person."

Nevertheless, at least with respect to humanity, we can say that the biopolitical or governmental shaping of the needs and interests of the population has made it possible for us to specify more concrete rights beyond civil and political liberties such as socioeconomic rights and the right to development. This seems to me to be the philosophical work done by the transnational traffic in women's labor: the intersection of human rights claims with the discourse of global development in the economic South that makes certain uses of people acceptable generates irresolvable aporias. What is at stake here is not human rights as a limit to biopolitical oppression but the endless circumscription of the limits of human rights as the optimal solution to the problems of global capitalist accumulation. Even as we acknowledge their necessity at the level of tactics, it is important to analyze human rights as part of the same field of biopolitical technologies that make, in the most material and physical sense of the word, various subjects of transnational labor.

NOTES

1. For an interesting argument that the current war against Iraq is the Bush administration's failed attempt at reasserting U.S. hegemony by a show of military might in a period of its economic decline vis-à-vis China, see Arrighi (2007).

2. Whatever the failings of his interpretation of Foucault, Agamben does not himself subscribe to an antithesis between biopolitics and human rights. Instead, he regards the protection of human rights and formal liberties as the culmination of the long process of the conversion of bare life into a way of life, of zoe into bios. Accordingly, for Agamben, the danger of humanitarianism is precisely that it only understands human life as bare life or sacred life and therefore is complicit with the exclusion of bare life by politics.

3. Merriam Cuasay, interview, January 10, 2002.

4. Mr. Srisena, interview, January 8, 2002.

5. Ibid.

6. For a fuller discussion of the economic conditions that stimulate the supply and demand for internal migration of women for sex work and the link between sex work and the economic rationality of development in Thailand, see Phongpaichit (1982) and Bales (2004).

7. For a discussion of the transnational traffic of migrant sex-workers from and to Thailand, see Phongpaichit, Phiriyarangsan, and Treerat (1998, chapters 8–9).

8. Merriam Cuasay, interview, January 10, 2002.

9. Interview with Ministry of Manpower official, January 9, 2002.

10. Merriam Cuasay, interview, January 10, 2002.

REFERENCES

Agamben, Giorgio. 1998. *Homo Sacer: Sovereign power and bare life.* Trans. Daniel Heller-Roazen. Palo Alto, Calif.: Stanford University Press.

Althusser, Louis. 1990. *For Marx.* Trans. Ben Brewster. London: Verso.

Arrighi, Giovanni. 2007. *Adam Smith in Beijing: Lineages of the twenty-first century.* London: Verso.

Bales, Kevin. 2004. Because she looks like a child. In *Global woman: Nannies, maids, and sex workers in the new economy,* ed. Barbara Ehrenreich and Arlie Russell Hochschild, 207–29. New York: Owl.

Butler, Judith. 2004. *Precarious life: the powers of mourning and violence.* London: Verso.

Foucault, Michel. 1980. *The history of sexuality, volume 1: An introduction*. Trans. Robert Hurley. New York: Vintage.

———. 2003. *"Society must be defended": Lectures at the College de France 1975–1976*. Trans. David Macey. New York: Picador.

———. 2007. *Security, territory, population: Lectures at the College de France, 1977–78*. Trans. Graham Burchell. New York: Palgrave Macmillan.

———. 2008. *The birth of biopolitics: Lectures at the College de France, 1978–79*. Trans. Graham Burchell. New York: Palgrave Macmillan.

Kant, Immanuel. 1996a. *Groundwork of the metaphysics of morals*. In *Practical philosophy*, Trans. and ed. Mary J. Gregor, 43–108. Cambridge, U.K.: Cambridge University Press.

———. 1996b. *Grundlegung zur Metaphysik der Sitten*. In *Werkausgabe*, VII, ed. Wilhelm Weischedel, 10–102. Frankfurt am Main: Suhrkamp.

Marx, Karl. 1962. *Das Kapital: Kritik der politischen Ökonomie. Erster Band*. Berlin: Dietz.

———. 1990. *Capital: A critique of political economy, volume 1*. Trans. Ben Fowkes. Harmondsworth: Penguin.

Phongpaichit, Pasuk. 1982. *From peasant girls to Bangkok masseuses*. Women, Work, and Development no. 2. Geneva: International Labour Office.

Phongpaichit, Pasuk, Sangsit Phiriyarangsan, and Nualnoi Treerat. 1998. *Guns, girls, gambling, ganja: Thailand's illegal economy and public policy*. Chiang Mai: Silkworm Books.

Schultz, Theodore W. 1961. Investment in human capital. *American Economic Review* 51 (1): 1–17.

Smith, Adam. 1976. *An inquiry into the nature and causes of the wealth of nations* (1776). Chicago: University of Chicago Press.

CONTRIBUTORS

CLAUDIA ARADAU is Lecturer in International Studies in the Department of Politics and International Studies at The Open University (UK) and Research Director of the Securities Programme in the Centre for Citizenship, Identities and Governance (CCIG). Her research interrogates the political effects of security, risk, and catastrophe. She has worked on the securitization of human trafficking and migration, and governing terrorism and exceptionalism in the "war on terror." She is the author of *Rethinking Trafficking in Women: Politics out of Security* (Palgrave, 2008) and is currently writing a book on *Politics of Catastrophe: Genealogies of the Unknown* (Routledge, 2011) together with Rens van Munster.

PHENG CHEAH is Professor of Rhetoric at the University of California at Berkeley. He is the author of *Inhuman Conditions: On Cosmopolitanism and Human Rights* (Harvard University Press, 2006) and *Spectral Nationality: Passages of Freedom from Kant to Postcolonial Literatures of Liberation* (Columbia University Press, 2003). He has coedited *Cosmopolitics—Thinking and Feeling Beyond the Nation* (University of Minnesota Press, 1998); *Grounds of Comparison: Around the Work of Benedict Anderson* (Routledge, 2003); and *Derrida and the Time of the Political* (Duke University Press, 2009). He is currently working on a book on world literature in an age of financial globalization and another book on instrumentality.

DEBORAH COWEN is Assistant Professor at the University of Toronto in the Department of Geography and Programme in Planning. Her work investigates the role of organized violence in shaping intimacy, space, and citizenship. Deborah is the author of *Military Workfare: The Soldier and Social Citizenship in Canada* (UTP, 2008); coeditor with Emily Gilbert of *War, Citizenship, Territory* (Routledge, 2008); and coeditor of *Environment and Planning D: Society and Space.*

NICHOLAS DE GENOVA Nicholas De Genova is currently a Visiting Scholar in the Center for the Study of Race, Politics, and Culture at the University of Chicago. He was a visiting research professor in 2010 in the Institute for Migration and Ethnic Studies and the Urban Studies Program at the University of

Amsterdam. He was previously a visiting professor at the University of Bern (in Switzerland), taught anthropology at Columbia and Stanford Universities, and was an international research fellow at the University of Warwick (UK). He did ethnographic research in Chicago on the politics of immigration and citizenship in the United States. He is the author of *Working the Boundaries: Race, Space, and "Illegality" in Mexican Chicago* (Duke University Press 2005); coauthor of *Latino Crossings: Mexicans, Puerto Ricans, and the Politics of Race and Citizenship* (Routledge 2003); editor of *Racial Transformations: Latinos and Asians Remaking the United States* (Duke University Press 2006); and coeditor of *The Deportation Regime: Sovereignty, Space, and the Freedom of Movement* (Duke University Press 2010). He is completing a new book, entitled *The Spectacle of Terror: Immigration, Race, and the Homeland Security State*.

SHELLEY FELDMAN is currently International Professor of Development Sociology and Director of the Feminist, Gender, and Sexuality Studies Program at Cornell University, and Visiting Professor of Sociology at Binghamton University. She is the President of the American Institute of Bangladesh Studies. Her research explores issues in Bangladesh and the United States that include agrarian change, gender relations, moral regulation and state formation, genocide, and war museums. She is currently completing a volume on comparative state formation practices and moral regulation.

CHARLES GEISLER is an International Professor in Development Sociology at Cornell University and specializes in topics of possession and dispossession, war and environment, constructions of property in strong and weak states, development-induced displacement, and environmental justice in and around parks and protected areas. He has a sustained interest in land reform, old and new, and is currently carrying out research on the transformation of property relations in the Homeland Security State and the future of land governance under emergency conditions. His edited books include *Biological Diversity: Balancing Interests through Adaptive Collaborative Management* (CRC Press, 2001) and *Property and Values* (Island Press, 2000).

TYRELL HABERKORN is a Research Fellow in Political and Social Change in the School of International, Political, and Strategic Studies at the Australian National University. Her first book, *Revolution Interrupted: Farmers, Students, Law, and Violence in Northern Thailand*, is forthcoming from the University of Wisconsin Press in 2011.

PAULA C. JOHNSON is professor of law at Syracuse University College of Law. She was the Sparks Chair at the University of Alabama School of Law in 2008, and the Syracuse University College of Law Bond, Schoeneck and King Distinguished Professorship from 2004–2006. Professor Johnson and Professor Janis McDonald codirect the Cold Case Justice Initiative (CCJI) at Syracuse University College of Law. Professor Johnson is also codirector of the Sierra Leone UN War Crimes Tribunal Project, and founding director of the Law in Zimbabwe Summer Internship Program. Her writings also include the book, *Inner Lives: Voices of African American Women in Prison* (NYU Press, 2003). She is coeditor of *Interrupted Life: Experiences of Incarcerated Women in the United States* (forthcoming from the University of California Press).

MARTHA T. MCCLUSKEY is Professor of Law and William J. Magavern Fellow at the State University of New York at Buffalo. Her scholarship focuses on economic policy, critical legal theory, and legal feminism, and she has written articles about workers' compensation, insurance, welfare reform, family caretaking work, and the politics of economic analysis in law. She is working on a book project titled *A Field Guide to Law, Economics, and Justice.*

GAYATRI A. MENON is Visiting Assistant Professor of Sociology at Franklin and Marshall College. Her research focuses on the politics of citizenship, nation-building, and everyday forms of violence in urban India. She is currently working on a book manuscript entitled *Living Conditions: Citizens, "Squatters," and the Politics of Accommodation in Mumbai.*

JULIE A. NICE holds the Herbst Foundation Chair at the University of San Francisco School of Law. She previously held the Delaney Chair at the University of Denver College of Law. Her scholarly expertise is in constitutional law, with particular emphasis on poverty, sexuality, and the relationship between individual rights and social movements. She is lead author of *Poverty Law: Theory and Practice* (West Publishing Co. 1997).

ZAKIA SALIME is assistant professor in the Department of Sociology and Women and Gender Studies at Rutgers University. Her interests include gender, globalization, transnational feminism(s), war, political economy, and social movements. She is currently working on a book project on the dialectics of women's Islamist and feminist movements in contemporary Morocco, looking at these interactions in the context of economic and political changes as they have been shaped by neoliberal policies and discourses, as well as the global "war on terrorism."

AMY SICILIANO is a Postdoctoral Fellow at the City Institute of York University in Toronto. Her PhD research explored the racialization of suburban space and criminalization of poverty within the context of a recent crisis of gun violence in Toronto. She is currently researching the social and political dimensions of urban renewal strategies targeting poor neighborhoods in Toronto's suburbs.

MELISSA W. WRIGHT is Associate Professor of the Departments of Geography and Women's Studies at Pennsylvania State University. She is the author of *Disposable Women and Other Myths of Global Capitalism* (Routledge, 2006), as well as many articles on capitalism, gender, power, and nationality in Mexico and China. She is currently writing a book on the politics of witnessing in relation to an antiviolence movement in northern Mexico, and has started a new research project on the militarization of the Mexico-U.S. border and its impact on border communities.

ANNA ZALIK is Assistant Professor in the Faculty of Environmental Studies at York University. Her research examines the merging of industrial security and community development policy in extractive sites. Recent publications include "Zones of Exclusion: Offshore Extraction, the Contestation of Space and Physical Displacement in the Nigerian Delta and the Mexican Gulf" (*Antipode*, 2009), and "Oil Sovereignties: Ecology and Nationality in the Nigerian Delta and the Mexican Gulf" in *Extractive Economies in the Global South* (Ashgate, 2008). Prior to joining York, she was a Ciriacy-Wantrup Postdoctoral Fellow in Natural Resources and Political Economy at the University of California at Berkeley.

INDEX

GEOGRAPHIES OF JUSTICE AND SOCIAL TRANSFORMATION

www.ingramcontent.com/pod-product-compliance
Lightning Source LLC
Chambersburg PA
CBHW030637270326
41929CB00007B/110